Family Law Handbook

Family Law Handbook

JANE SENDALL

OXFORD
UNIVERSITY PRESS

Great Clarendon Street, Oxford, OX2 6DP,
United Kingdom

Oxford University Press is a department of the University of Oxford.
It furthers the University's objective of excellence in research, scholarship,
and education by publishing worldwide. Oxford is a registered trade mark of
Oxford University Press in the UK and in certain other countries

First edition 2010
Second edition 2011
Third edition 2012

Impression: 1

British Library Cataloguing in Publication Data
Data available

ISBN 978–0–19–967078–9

Printed in Great Britain by
Ashford Colour Press Ltd, Gosport, Hampshire

For my parents

ACKNOWLEDGEMENTS

The author and publisher would like to thank David Hodson for his kind permission for the use of his article on the case of *Charman*, which illuminates an area in which the decisions of the higher court become progressively more difficult to explain to students. Further information by David about English financial provision law on divorce including in the international context is available at www.davidhodson.com and www.iflg.uk.com.

OUTLINE CONTENTS

DETAILED CONTENTS

PREFACE

Working with families, children, parents, spouses, civil partners, and cohabitants in family law is a demanding job. It is also enjoyable, exhausting, stimulating, and full of variety. Learning family law means grasping a great deal of statute, case-law, and skills quite quickly over a range of topics and this book is written to assist those learning family law. Family law is in a state of flux as sweeping changes are being made to funding and the courts are extending the enforceability of pre-nuptial agreements. Keeping up to date is important and the online resources are updated with changes to law and procedure.

I would like to extend my love and thanks to my family for their support, also to my much neglected friends for their encouragement and my students, past and present, for inspiration, honesty, and stimulation. Particular thanks go to Katrina Pescott, my friend and dedicated family solicitor, who advises me on matters of practice with patience and good humour. Her advice was essential in the writing of this book. As I work largely from home, I greatly enjoyed the friendship of my neighbours in Waterhouses and their company and sociability.

I would also like to acknowledge my colleagues on the LPC and BVC family teams at BPP for their advice and assistance over a number of years, particularly Claire Illingworth, Claire Hickman, Deborah Grove, Alison Wells, Claire Dilks, Karen Haskey, Lisa Bates, and Maggie Putland, my colleagues at York University for their inspiration, and good humour.

Family law is a big subject and I would like to acknowledge the assistance of Andrew Hayward of Durham University and Emma Duff of Northumbria University for their helpful comments on Chapter 22, the former Deputy Manager of Derwentside Citizen's Advice Bureau (or 'Mum') for her assistance with Chapter 21, David Hodson for his kind permission for the use of his article on the case of *Charman,* which illuminates an area in which the decisions of the higher court become progressively more difficult to explain to students. Further information by David about English financial provision law on divorce including in the international context is available at www.davidhodson.com and www.iflg.uk.com. Invaluable information on collaborative law came from Helen Robson of Caris Robson LLP and Norman Taylor of Zermanskys & Partners.

I would like to acknowledge the advice, encouragement, and enthusiasm of Abbey Nelms, in the completion of this edition and Lucy Read throughout the start of this project and the excellent help from Fiona Tatham, Julie Stone, Moira Greenhalgh, and Kate Gilks.

All errors are entirely my own.

Jane Sendall
September 2012

NEW TO THIS EDITION

- Updates on Public Funding
- Updates on the CSA
- Case-Law after *Radmacher v Granatino*

GUIDED TOUR OF THE BOOK

Sendall's *Family Law Handbook* contains numerous features that have been specifically designed to facilitate your learning and understanding of family law and practice. To help you get the most from your text, this 'Guided Tour of the Book' highlights the features used by the author to explain the law and its application in practical situations.

WITHIN EACH CHAPTER

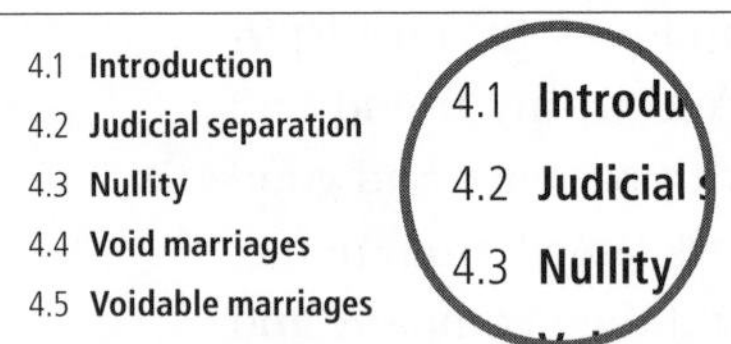

CHAPTER CONTENTS

Use the detailed contents list featured at the beginning of each chapter to identify quickly and clearly the key topics to be covered and to locate where each topic appears in the wider subject area.

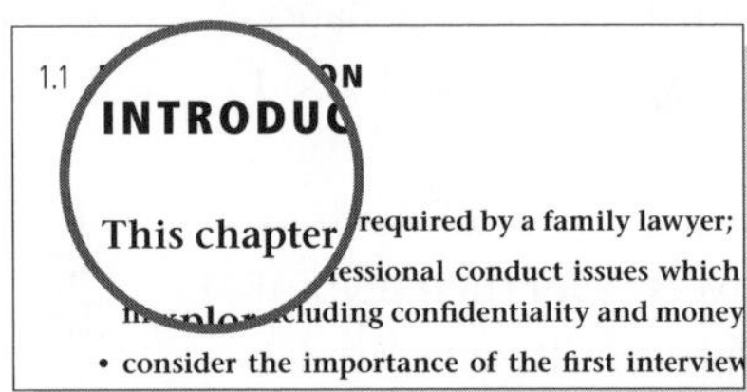

CHAPTER AIMS

Use the brief chapter aims at the start of each chapter to help you focus your reading and learning.

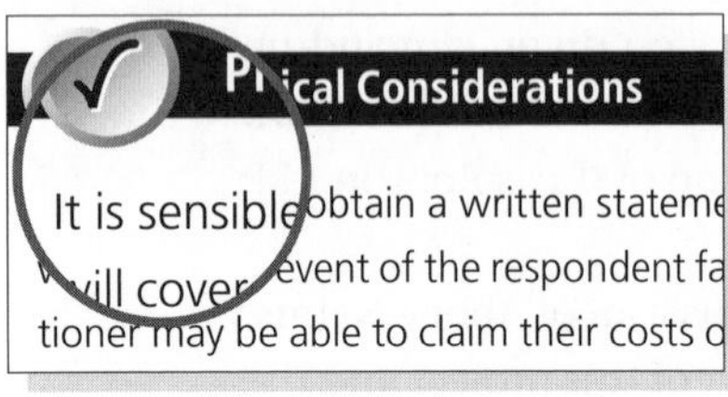

PRACTICAL CONSIDERATIONS

Use these sections to gain a practical understanding of how a solicitor may use the rules and procedures available. This is an opportunity to prepare on a practical level for your training contract.

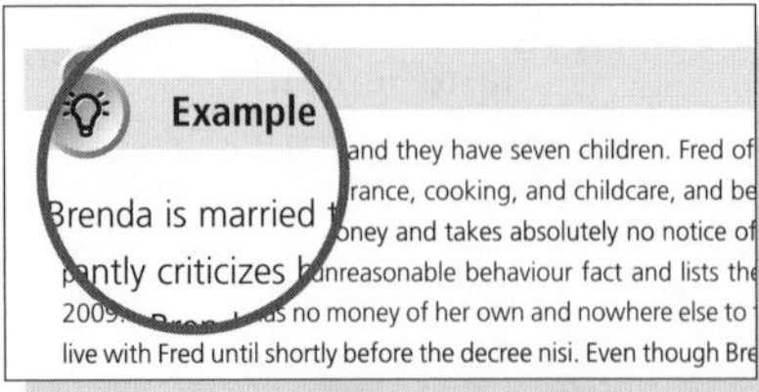

EXAMPLES

Look for the example icon to find practical scenario-based examples of how the law is applied in a realistic practice situation. These will provide you with a valuable insight into what might happen day-to-day in a solicitor's practice.

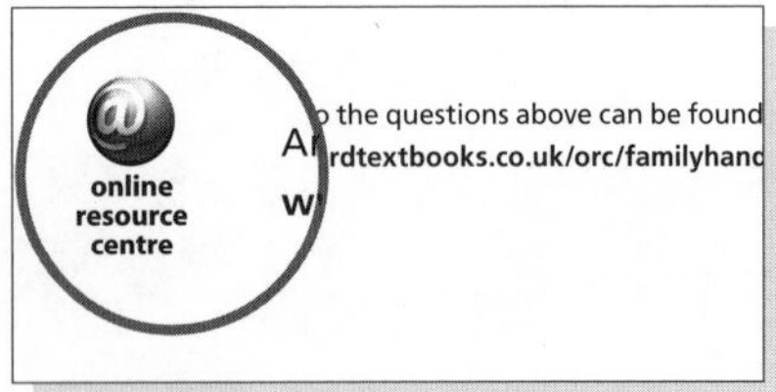

ONLINE RESOURCE CENTRE ICON

Look out for this icon, used to highlight where further information is available on the Online Resource Centre accompanying this handbook. Visit **www.oxfordtextbooks.co.uk/orc/familyhandbook13/** to see the full range of supporting resources accompanying this book. Also see page xxvi overleaf for an introduction to these online resources.

END OF CHAPTER FEATURES

SUMMARY POINTS

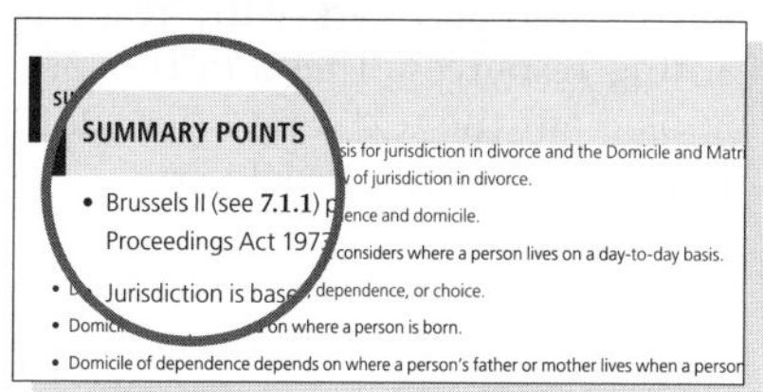

The key points covered are summarized in a user-friendly list at the end of each chapter. Look at these summaries to help you consolidate your learning or to check your knowledge at revision time.

SELF-TEST QUESTIONS

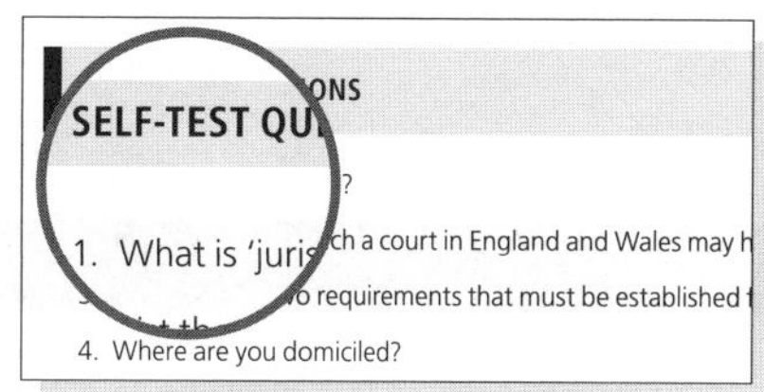

These questions allow you to test yourself on particular areas of the law in preparation for exams or to assess your learning throughout the duration of the course. Use these questions to uncover areas where you might need to improve your understanding by re-reading the text or asking your lecturer.

CASE STUDIES

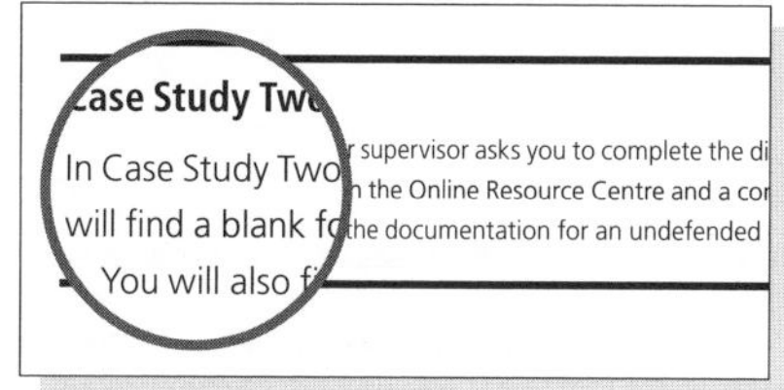

Throughout the book, the author refers to two fictional case studies, which provide a practical focus to the law and procedures described in the text. The case studies also show you how the law would be applied in an on-going scenario, allowing you to see procedures in context from the start of a case through to its conclusion. Example documents available on the Online Resource Centre ensure that these case studies remain realistic. See the 'Guided Tour of the Website' at page xxvi for more information.

GUIDED TOUR OF THE WEBSITE

Online Resource Centres have been developed to provide students and lecturers with ready-to-use teaching and learning resources. They are free of charge, designed to complement the text, and offer additional materials that are suited to electronic delivery.

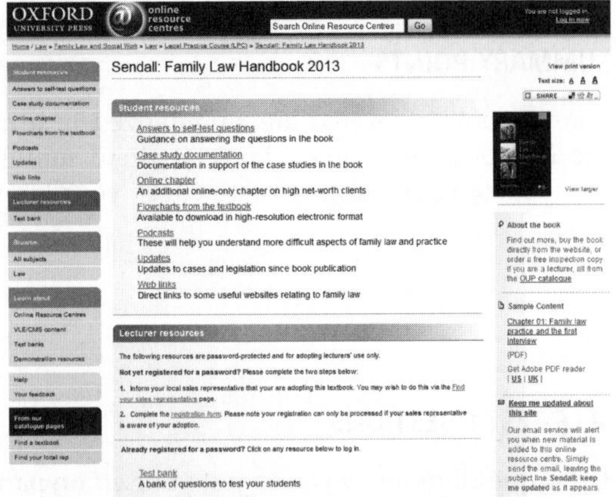

STUDENT RESOURCES

All the resources in this area of the site are freely accessible to all, with no password required. Simply visit the site at **www.oxfordtextbooks.co.uk/orc/familyhandbook13/**

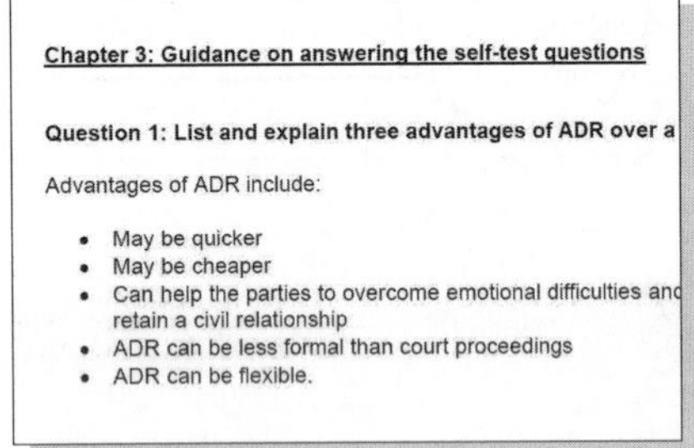

Chapter 3: Guidance on answering the self-test questions

Question 1: List and explain three advantages of ADR over a

Advantages of ADR include:

- May be quicker
- May be cheaper
- Can help the parties to overcome emotional difficulties and retain a civil relationship
- ADR can be less formal than court proceedings
- ADR can be flexible.

ANSWERS TO SELF-TEST QUESTIONS

This section has now been given student access, following recent lecturer and student feedback. Guidance is given on appropriate answers to the self-test questions which appear in the book. This provides you with feedback on your answers.

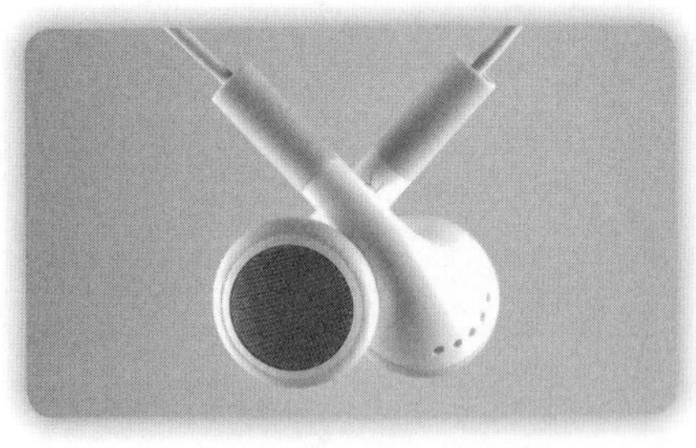

PODCASTS

Short podcasts have been created by the author to help consolidate your understanding of key aspects of family law and practice.

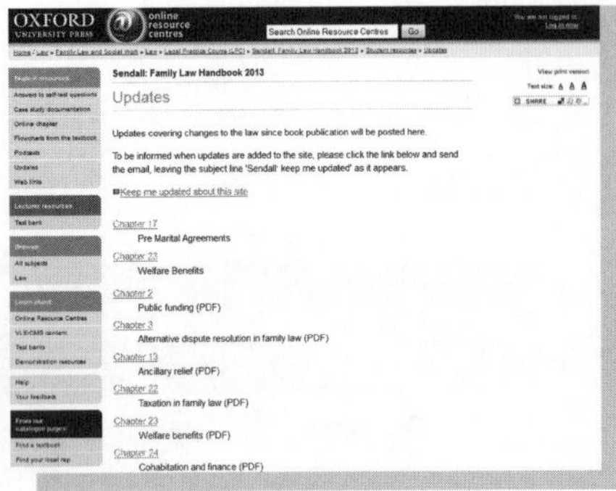

UPDATES

Updates will be posted on the website when the law changes or when significant cases pass through the courts, allowing you to keep fully informed of developments. The updates are freely accessible to all and offer an easy way to keep abreast of events in this rapidly changing subject area.

CASE STUDY DOCUMENTATION

Click on the case study section to see the questions from the book and any relevant documentation you may need to answer them. This section of the site features realistic documents that a solicitor may come into contact with at each stage of the case.

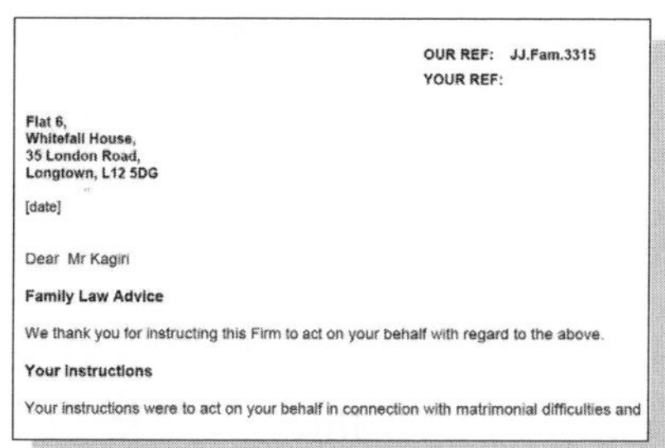
OUR REF: JJ.Fam.3315
YOUR REF:

Flat 6,
Whitefall House,
35 London Road,
Longtown, L12 5DG

[date]

Dear Mr Kagiri

Family Law Advice

We thank you for instructing this Firm to act on your behalf with regard to the above.

Your Instructions

Your instructions were to act on your behalf in connection with matrimonial difficulties and

LINKS TO USEFUL SITES

This part of the site provides links and useful information which is freely accessible elsewhere on the internet. Use this resource to find relevant guidelines, statutes, codes of practice, and other documentation quickly and easily.

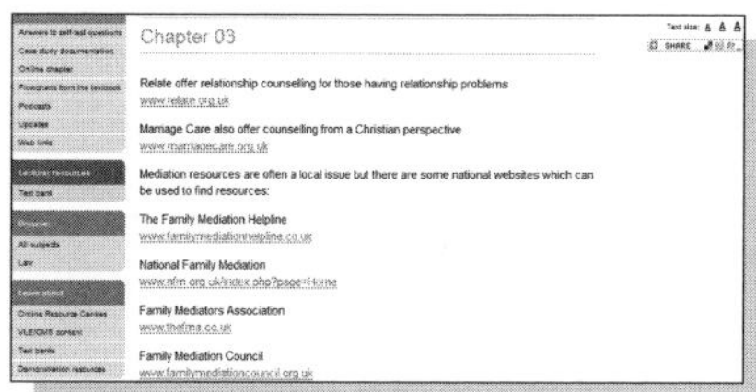

FIGURES

Flowcharts featured in the book are available online, providing you with easily accessible visuals to help you revise.

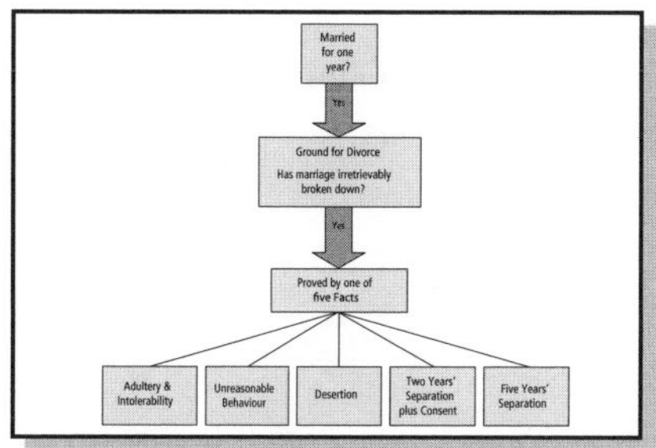

LECTURER RESOURCES

These resources are available solely to lecturers who have adopted the book as the main text on their course, and can be accessed using a free password. To obtain a password, follow the links on the main site at **www.oxfordtextbooks.co.uk/orc/familyhandbook13/**. Once you have completed the registration form, our web team will contact you with a password within three working days.

TEST BANK

A bank of questions covering all aspects of the book is available to download into your assessment software. Also available in Word format, the questions give you the ability to provide a resource that your students can use to test themselves, or that you can use to assess their learning. Once included in your assessment software, the questions are entirely customizable, enabling you to remove questions which might be less relevant to your course, or change the order of the questions to match the order in which topics are taught at your institution.

A variety of question types, from 'multiple choice' questions and 'true or false' questions through to more complex scenario-based questions ensures that your students are engaged by their learning.

Each question is accompanied by feedback which shows why the selected answer is correct or incorrect, and then points the student towards the relevant page of the text if they need to re-read.

Test bank

Test banks provide a ready-made electronic testing resource, which can be customized to meet your teaching needs. Whilst every effort has been made to ensure that this resource will be error free we suggest that you check that it meets your requirements before using it for assessment or other purposes.

This test bank contains 87 multiple choice, multiple response, fill in the blank, and true or false questions. These are organized in groups to accompany Parts One, Two, Three, Five and Six in the textbook. Part Four of the textbook does not have any accompanying questions. The number of questions varies between parts according to length and complexity of the topics.

Click on one of the options below:

Test bank in QTI XML format
Choose this option if your institution uses assessment software that conforms to the industry standard of QTI XML.

Test bank in Respondus format
Choose this option if you have Respondus at your institution and wish to download the test bank into Blackboard, WebCT or another Virtual Learning Environment/Course Management System.

Test bank in Word format
Choose this option if your institution does not have any assessment software, or you wish to view the questions available in the test bank.

For step-by-step instructions on importing and customizing test banks, please view our test bank guide.

GLOSSARY

Ancillary relief	The division of money and property following divorce or dissolution of a civil partnership
Bailiff	A person employed by the court to serve court papers and to enforce judgments
Bundle	The term given to the collation of documents to be referred to in court. A bundle will contain an index, will be paginated and organized in a useful way
CAFCASS	The Child and Family Court Advisory Support Service. CAFCASS looks after the interests of children in court proceedings and advises the court on what is in the best interests of the children
Charge	A charge is placed on a property and when the property is sold, a certain proportion of the proceeds are given to the person with the charge
Client	The most important person in a family lawyer's job
CLS	Community Legal Service administer public funding (often called legal aid) in civil matters including family law
CPS	The Crown Prosecution Service. The CPS makes decisions on the prosecution of criminal offences and prosecutes criminal cases in court
Decree	A type of court order
Deed	A written document, which must be signed
Disbursements	The name given by solicitors to the various fees which are incurred during a case, e.g. expert fees or court fees
Disclosure	The process by which one party tells the other party certain information about their case or gives information
Duress	Unlawful pressure placed on a person in order to coerce them or overcome their resistance into doing something they do not wish to do
File	To give a document to the court
Free standing	Court proceedings which are made as an application solely based on a cause of action and not within other proceedings
Guardian ad litem	Now called a Children's Guardian; they look after a children's interest in public children proceedings
Inherent jurisdiction	The ability of a superior court to hear a case unless a rule or statute restricts that jurisdiction
Injunction	A court order requiring a person to do or refrain from certain acts
Leave	The permission of the court to do a certain act
Litigant in person	A person who represents themselves at court without a lawyer—sometimes now referred to as 'Self Represented Litigants' (SRL)
LSC	Legal Services Commission who run the public funding scheme in England and Wales
Mediation	A process which aims to settle disputes between people over money and property or children
NSPCC	National Society for the Prevention of Cruelty to Children
Nullity	A decree which annuls a marriage

Privilege	A legal device which protects the disclosure (see above) of documents to the court or other party in court proceedings
Refuge	A place of safety for those fleeing domestic abuse
Return date	Following a hearing without notice to one party, a return date is the date on which the court will hear the case with all parties present
Serve	When a document is formally given to a person
Spouse	A married person
SRA	The Solicitors Regulation Authority which regulates the solicitors' profession
Undue influence	Where one person takes advantage of a position of power over another person
Usages	A firmly established practice or custom

TABLE OF CASES

References are to chapter and paragraph number

TABLE OF STATUTES

References are to chapter and paragaraph number

TABLE OF SECONDARY LEGISLATION

References are to chapter and paragraph number

EUROPEAN LEGISLATION

References are to chapter and paragraph number

INTERNATIONAL LAW

References are to chapter and paragraph number

CODES OF PRACTICE

References are to chapter and paragraph number

Part 1

INTRODUCTION

1 FAMILY LAW PRACTICE AND THE FIRST INTERVIEW

1.1 INTRODUCTION

This chapter will:

- **explore the skills required by a family lawyer;**
- **discuss the professional conduct issues which are crucial to seeing a client for the first time including confidentiality and money laundering;**
- **consider the importance of the first interview with the client and the client care letter.**

The study and practice of family law is a fascinating prospect. The sheer variety of people and problems that you will encounter enlivens an area of law that covers a variety of topics and requires the mastery of problems involving financial and property disputes, resolving where children should live and with whom they have contact, and offering assistance to those facing violence within a relationship.

Family law is in a state of flux for a number of reasons: public funding will be withdrawn from a wide variety of cases in April 2013; family courts are closing around the country; and the Family Justice Review is recommending a series of changes to the administration of family law to improve the time in which cases are heard as well as enabling parents to make their own arrangements following separation. The online resources will contain details on each of these changes and further detail on the Family Justice Review can be found in relevant chapters in this text.

Family law is practised in firms ranging from very small general practices, large commercial firms, and niche practices. It is possible to specialize within family and become an expert in a particular field, e.g. children or finances following divorce. In the early stages of a career in family law, it is common to have a mixed caseload involving divorce, property and finances, problems concerning children, and domestic abuse.

The law on family relationships comes from a wide variety of sources and includes statutes, cases, statutory instruments, European legislation and cases, and international treaties.

Example

There are many sources of family law and one of the skills of a family lawyer is to be able to find and use law. It is also important to keep up to date. Here are some examples of the sources of family law:

Statute: Matrimonial Causes Act 1973, which governs divorce.

Case-law: *White v White* [2000] 3 WLR 1571, an important case on ancillary relief.

Statutory instrument: The Domestic Violence, Crime and Victims Act 2004 (Commencement No. 9 and Transitional Provisions) Order 2007, S.I. 2007 No. 1845 introducing changes to domestic abuse legislation.

European law: Regulation (EC) No. 1347/2000 on jurisdiction and the recognition and enforcement of judgments in matrimonial matters and in matters of parental responsibility for children of both spouses.

European cases: *Glaser v UK* [2001] 1 FLR 153, which concerned the enforcement of contact orders by UK courts.

International treaties: Hague Convention on the Civil Aspects of Child Abduction governing the return of children removed by a parent to a foreign jurisdiction.

Cases handled by a family lawyer may cover the consequences of relationship breakdown including the division of money and property, disputes about children, the protection of those suffering domestic abuse, and advising clients whose children require local authority intervention.

Additionally, a family lawyer must be able to advise on how a client can fund a case and also the procedural matters involved in taking proceedings. This chapter briefly examines the issues surrounding family practice and the first interview with a client.

1.2 SKILLS

A successful family lawyer must also possess very good client care skills as family law proceedings often bring out the very worst in your client's behaviour. You may meet a client during a stressful point in their lives where their relationship, home life, and financial situation are changing rapidly. A successful family lawyer can help their client to understand the law and procedures, making this transition less bewildering and keeping costs under control. You should have excellent communication skills, be able to put yourself into the client's position to understand their point of view, but also have the strength of character to tell a client what they may not wish to hear. You will need to ensure your clients are kept up to date and all matters are explained in a clear and accessible way.

A family lawyer will act for the most vulnerable members of society, e.g. children that have been taken into the care of their local authority or a person fleeing domestic abuse. The variety of work is wide, and includes arranging personal protection for a client suffering domestic abuse (often at short notice), advising a parent who wishes to have more contact with their child, negotiating the family finances following separation, and advising on how to end a civil partnership. This challenging aspect of family practice can also be the most rewarding, as you will have a varied and interesting job. Your skills of time management, persuasion, negotiation, and diplomacy will be tested often.

Practical Considerations

What skills do you think are useful for a family lawyer?

- Advocacy: there will be a variety of hearings to attend in all types of proceedings;
- Interviewing: clients often come to meetings in a state of distress and so the solicitor should be prepared to deal with a client's emotional state. Clients are often reluctant to discuss embarrassing and sensitive issues and this requires a skilled interviewer;
- Negotiation: in family law cases it is preferable to agree a settlement rather than have an acrimonious court hearing and so a considerable proportion of a family solicitor's time is spent negotiating to reach an agreement;
- Writing: a family law client must be able to understand the advice that they receive and a family law solicitor must be able to communicate clearly;

- Drafting: a family law solicitor will be required to produce divorce petitions, client statements, and many other court documents.

As well as technical skills required by family lawyers, 'soft' skills are equally important. 'Soft' skills are the interpersonal and organizational skills that contribute to a successful practice and include:

- persuasiveness;
- tact;
- negotiation;
- diplomacy;
- time management;
- organization;
- communication.

This is not an exhaustive list!

1.3 THE FIRST INTERVIEW AND CLIENT CARE

When meeting the client for the first time, it is important to be fully prepared. The client may be nervous, apprehensive, angry, or fearful. It is important that the client is reassured and offered an appointment promptly and also that the solicitor is fully prepared for the first interview.

Before the interview, the Law Society, in a practice note, advises that when the client attends the interview the following information must be explained to them and confirmed in writing:

- name and status of the solicitor or other person conducting the interview;
- information on the costs for the interview;
- details of who to contact if they have a complaint.

This information can be prepared in a pro forma document in advance. Keep a copy on file.

Practical Considerations

What do you need to have in your office when your client comes for their first appointment?

- pens/paper;
- funding/CLS forms;
- court forms in case there is a need to make an urgent application;
- toys to distract small children;
- tissues;
- pro forma forms, e.g. file checklist;
- business card for client to keep.

1.3.1 GETTING THE BASICS RIGHT

In the first interview, you must remember to cover all of the professional conduct issues, money laundering regulations, and legal issues as well as the basic details from the client.

You must efficiently take all the client's basic details, including name, date of birth, address, and details of their family including children. Many firms have a pro forma checklist for initial interviews and there is an example of one in Case Study One.

There are times when some information must be handled with care. For instance, in cases where violence has been a feature of family life, an address must not be given to the violent partner as this will put your client in danger. You have a professional conduct duty (see **1.3.2**) to keep all client information confidential.

1.3.2 PROFESSIONAL CONDUCT

You have professional conduct rules that govern the relationship between you and your client. There are some core duties to the client found in the Solicitors Regulatory Authority's (SRA) Solicitors' Code of Conduct, which came into force in October 2011. The following principles and outcomes (O) apply to all clients and your practice in family law:

- O(1.1) you treat your clients fairly;
- O(1.2) you provide services to your clients in a manner which protects their interests in their matter, subject to the proper administration of justice;
- O(1.3) when deciding whether to act, or terminate your instructions, you comply with the law and the Code.

According to Outcome 1.4 of the Code, you are free to decide whether to take on a client but you must have the resources and skills to act in a case. This is extremely important in the early stages of a solicitor's career as it is tempting to take cases that require a very high level of expertise.

During the interview, according to the Code, a solicitor demonstrates they are achieving the principles of good client care through Indicative Behaviours (IB) and these behaviours include: agreeing an appropriate level of service and explaining your responsibilities in the case as well as the client's responsibilities. This may be the duty of full disclosure in ancillary relief. You must also inform the client, in writing, of the name and status of the person dealing with the matter as well as the person who has overall responsibility for supervision of the case.

The client should be given certain information following the first interview, including:

- the basis and terms of the firm's charges and whether they are to be increased;
- any likely payments that the client or the firm may need to make to others;
- whether the client is eligible and should apply for public funding;
- any potential liability for the other party's costs;
- details of the firm's complaints handling scheme;
- the effect of the statutory charge (if the client is a publicly funded client).

Many solicitors keep a selection of leaflets and information on local services and agencies that can help families as well as national organizations that offer advice and information. More information can be found in online resources.

Practical Considerations

There are some more family law orientated organizations that have their own codes of conduct or guides to good practice, such as Resolution.

From the Resolution website www.resolution.org.uk:

> Resolution, which was formerly known as the Solicitors Family Law Association (SFLA), is an organisation of 5000 lawyers who believe in a constructive, non-confrontational approach to family law matters. Resolution also campaigns for improvements to the family justice system.

Resolution supports the development of family lawyers through its national and regional training programmes, through publications and good practice guides and through its accreditation scheme.

Resolution's codes of conduct are excellent and very helpful for the new practitioner. It is recommended that all those practising family law learn best practice and (harder still) try to keep to best practice at all times.

1.3.2.1 Money laundering

Money laundering is the process by which criminals attempt to hide or obscure the origins of criminal proceeds in order to make it easier to spend the money. The proceeds may arise from activities as diverse as drug trafficking and selling, prostitution, people trafficking, robbery, and all other forms of illegal activity including tax avoidance, benefit fraud, or fraud.

Solicitors firms are targeted by money launderers as firms keep money within client accounts, move money from client to bank, and in property transactions. The risks to the firm include criminal and disciplinary action against the firm and individual members of staff with the attendant damage to reputation and bad publicity.

The Law Society has published a practice note which is available in the online resources. The principal statute governing money laundering is the Proceeds of Crime Act 2002 (POCA 2002) and the Money Laundering Regulations 2007.

A firm will assess the risks to it from money laundering and must have systems in place to ensure compliance with the Regulations. Customer due diligence (CDD) is the systems and processes the firm employ to verify the client's identity using documentation (e.g. a passport) and this must be done at the time of the first interview, i.e. at the time that the business relationship is established.

Each firm will have a nominated person who will be a point of contact for queries about money laundering.

There are certain warning signs that may indicate money laundering activity, e.g. disputes that settle too easily as this may indicate 'sham' litigation, or clients wishing to pay in large sums in cash.

Practical Considerations

When the client is new to a firm, their identity needs to be verified. Clients should be asked to bring some form of identification with them, e.g. a passport and verification of their address, e.g. a recent utilities bill.

Following the case of *Bowman v Fels* [2005] EWCA 226, the Law Society issued guidance on money laundering issues. The case concerned an ancillary relief case where a report to the National Criminal Intelligence Service (NCIS) had been made and an adjournment sought until the 'appropriate consent' had been obtained from NCIS to continue the case. The Court of Appeal's judgment excluded certain activities from the scope of offences under POCA 2002. These activities include litigation from issue of proceedings to its disposal by final judgment and the Law Society guidance indicates that this also includes settlements, negotiations, and alternative dispute resolution (ADR).

1.3.2.2 Conflicts of interest

There will be occasions when you find that your firm already acts for another person whose interests conflict with the new client. Chapter 3 of the Code of Conduct 2011 prevents a solicitor acting where a conflict of interest exists.

It is important to carry out a conflict check as soon as possible. Ideally, information should be obtained from the client before the interview:

- name, address, and telephone number;
- area of law on which advice is needed (e.g. matrimonial or crime);
- name and address of any potential opponent or other involved (if applicable).

If this information is not obtained in advance of the interview, a conflict check should be done when the client arrives at the office and then the interview may progress if there is no conflict of interest.

Example

There are a number of ways in which a conflict can arise. It is not uncommon for a client to seek legal advice if they are thinking about leaving a relationship, even if the other person is unaware of this. The advice sought can be general and a one-off. A conflict would arise if the other person came to the firm for advice if the relationship broke down. Another common conflict situation arises where the criminal department of a firm acts for someone accused of a criminal offence arising out of domestic abuse and then their partner/spouse/civil partner seeks advice on seeking an order preventing further harm.

1.3.3 FUNDING THE CASE

A client may come to you for a free interview, as offered by many firms, or may pay a fixed fee. You also have a duty to advise the client on whether they are eligible for public funding. Funding will be considered in detail in **Chapter 2**. Public funding is currently under review and will change enormously during 2012–13 and the online resources will contain full details.

As a matter of professional conduct, you must also give your client the best overall information about the possible cost both at the outset of the case but also as the case progresses. Outcome 1.13 of the Code of Conduct 2011 states clients should receive the best possible information, both at the time of engagement and when appropriate as their matter progresses, about the likely overall cost of their matter. The behaviour required by the Code in relation to fees includes discussing whether the potential outcomes of the client's matter are likely to justify the expense or risk involved, including any risk of having to pay someone else's legal fees, clearly explaining your fees and if and when they are likely to change, warning about any other payments for which the client may be responsible, discussing how the client will pay, including whether public funding may be available, whether the client has insurance that might cover the fees; where you are acting for a publicly-funded client, explaining how their publicly funded status affects the costs and providing the information in a clear and accessible form which is appropriate to the needs and circumstances of the client.

Any information about the cost must be clear and confirmed in writing. You must discuss with your client whether the potential outcomes of any legal case will justify the expense or risk involved including, if relevant, the risk of having to pay an opponent's costs.

1.3.4 ATTENDANCE NOTES AND FILES

A client will give you a great deal of information and it is important that you keep good records as others in your firm may assist in the case; keep a record of the time spent on the matter, and a permanent record of client instructions. Attendance notes are very important as they are a permanent record of instructions, action taken, and time recorded. Attendance notes should be sufficiently full to allow other members of the firm to use the file with ease. In case of complaint, attendance notes are a good record of the work done for a client.

It is also very important to maintain your files in an orderly and organized manner. A file should be logically organized with all documents securely stored in a way to make access to important information easy for someone not familiar with the file. The file should be reviewed regularly to avoid missing dates or allowing the case to 'drift'. As a trainee solicitor, the author was taught that files should be so well organized that if a file were dropped, it could be picked up without a single document being misplaced. Files often become very large in a complex case and so the file must be sufficiently well organized to cope with this.

Copies of documents, particularly court forms, should be kept on the file in order to keep track of the case documents. The file will be audited if it is a publicly funded case and all firms will probably have some form of file check as part of a quality control and so it is important to maintain a tidy, up-to-date, and well-organized file.

1.3.5 CLIENT CARE POST INTERVIEW

The Code of Conduct requires that certain client care and funding issues must be discussed with a client and includes:

- costs/funding;
- complaints;
- supervision of the case;
- time scales.

These are often detailed in a client care letter sent to the client following the first interview and an example can be found in Case Study One.

SUMMARY POINTS

- Family law is a fascinating and varied area in which to practise.
- The successful family lawyer will require not only an excellent grasp of the law but also good legal skills in terms of advocacy, interviewing, drafting, negotiation, and legal research.
- Family clients come to see a solicitor in often difficult circumstances and a family lawyer needs excellent interpersonal skills.
- As in all legal practice, solicitors and advisers are bound by rules of professional conduct, including rules on confidentiality, conflicts of interest, and money laundering.
- The first interview is an important meeting for both client and lawyer and it is important to get the basics right, to cover the available law and remedies fully, and to use communication skills fully.
- A conflict check should be done prior to the interview to avoid conflicts of interests between clients.
- A client needs the best possible information on costs and an estimate of the total costs likely to arise in the case.
- A client care letter should be sent to the client containing details of costs, supervision of the case, any relevant time estimates, and details of the firm's complaints procedures.

SELF-TEST QUESTIONS

1. Name two core outcomes imposed by the Code of Conduct.
2. A client asks you to accept instructions in divorce proceedings. You saw his wife this morning at an earlier appointment. Can you accept his instructions?
3. A client comes in for advice on a divorce and insists on paying 'up front' for the proceedings in cash. The client telephones later in the week to say that he and his wife have been reconciled and he wants his money back. What issues does this raise for the firm?

Case Study One

Case Study One is a stand-alone case study for Part One of the text. Read through the documents featured on the Online Resource Centre and answer the following questions:

1. Has the solicitor complied with all of their professional conduct obligations?
2. Has the client had all of their questions answered?

Answers to the questions above can be found on the Online Resource Centre: www.oxfordtextbooks.co.uk/orc/familyhandbook13/.

2 PUBLIC FUNDING

2.1 INTRODUCTION

This chapter will:

- **discuss the forthcoming changes to be made in public funding in family cases;**
- **discuss the availability of public funding for family law proceedings;**
- **examine the levels of funding available to the client;**
- **consider the tests to decide if a client is eligible for public funding;**
- **consider the recovery of public funding through the statutory charge.**

Public funding is administered by the Legal Services Commission (LSC) and it delivers two schemes of public funding, the Criminal Defence Service and the Community Legal Service (CLS) under the Access to Justice Act 1999. Family proceedings are civil proceedings and so fall within the CLS. Family law accounted for the largest proportions of all new matters funded by the Legal Services Commission in 2006–07. This chapter provides an introduction to the levels of public funding available to family law clients and the eligibility criteria. It deals with each type of funding generally; the specific considerations for each type of work will be covered separately within the relevant chapters. References are made to the LSC Manual, which contains all the guidance procedures used by the LSC, part of which is the Funding Code (which gives details of eligibility criteria).

The LSC has drastically reduced the number of firms able to offer public funding to clients in family law cases following a tendering exercise. This was challenged in a judicial review by the Law Society and the online resources contain more information.

2.1.1 CHANGES TO PUBLIC FUNDING

The Legal Aid, Sentencing and Punishment of Offenders Act 2012 has become law and enacts very wide changes to public funding of family cases. The changes will be made in April 2013. The scope of work which will be covered has been greatly reduced and will only include:

- Public family law regarding protection of children;
- Private family where there is evidence of domestic violence;
- Private law children cases where there is evidence of child abuse;
- Child abduction matters;
- Representation for child parties in private family cases;
- Legal advice in support of mediation;
- Domestic violence injunction cases;
- Forced marriage protection order cases.

This means that no client will receive public funding for divorce proceedings to resolve financial and property disputes following divorces and cohabitation disputes. Families in dispute about contact and residence of children will not receive public funding unless there is domestic violence present in the relationship. The effect of this will be immense and will mean that many clients will not be represented at hearings and will have to fund legal advice from their own pockets. The online resources contain more information on the potential impact of these changes.

There are also changes made to eligibility; capital passporting will be abolished, ensuring all applicants are subject to the same capital test regardless of benefits. Clients in the rare position of being eligible for funding will face increased monthly contributions from clients—to 30% of disposable income. There will also be a cap of £100k to apply to the Subject Matter of Dispute (e.g. the former family home) and this will be extended to apply to legal help.

The chapter retains the current scheme for public funding as it will remain in force until April 2013. Following this, the new changes will be implemented and more information will be found in the online resources.

2.1.2 PRACTICAL CONSIDERATIONS

All of the information needed to complete an application can be found on the LSC website and more details can be found in the online resources that accompany this book.

Practical Considerations

You will often hear about the 'means' and 'merits' tests in public funding. 'Means' refers to whether or not the client will qualify financially for assistance and 'merits' refers to whether or not the client's case has sufficient strength to receive funding.

2.2 DEFINITION OF FAMILY PROCEEDINGS

The Funding Code defines 'family proceedings' at section 2.2 as 'proceedings which arise out of family relationships, including proceedings in which the welfare of the children is determined (other than judicial review proceedings)'. Family proceedings include all proceedings under any one or more of the following:

- the Matrimonial Causes Act 1973;
- the Inheritance (Provision for Family and Dependants) Act 1975;
- the Adoption Act 1976 and Adoption and Children Act 2002;
- the Domestic Proceedings and Magistrates' Courts Act 1978;
- Part III of the Matrimonial and Family Proceedings Act 1984;
- Parts I, II, and IV of the Children Act 1989;

- Part IV of the Family Law Act 1996;
- the inherent jurisdiction of the High Court in relation to children;
- the Civil Partnership Act 2004.

The concept of 'family relationships' in the Code is very widely drawn and includes:

- marriage;
- heterosexual or same sex relationships between partners whether cohabiting or not;
- blood relations;
- step relations;
- adoption or long-term care of children such that they can reasonably be regarded as part of the family.

Proceedings will only come within the Code if the basis of the dispute or the jurisdiction arises out of a family relationship rather than whether the parties are family members.

 **Example**

Martin and Hannah are married. Martin drives very quickly and this is a source of dispute between them. Martin is driving them to a party one evening and drives recklessly, causing a crash, which is his fault. Hannah is injured and sues Martin for damages for personal injury. She also decides this is also the final straw and that she can't bear to be married to Martin any more.

The subsequent personal injury proceedings are not family proceedings as the dispute has not arisen in any of the statutes listed above and is not a result of the relationship between the pair. The divorce proceedings are family proceedings as they are conducted under the Matrimonial Causes Act 1973 and a result of their married status.

2.3 LEVELS OF ASSISTANCE

There are a number of levels of assistance available for family law clients. They are:

- legal help;
- family mediation;
- family help (lower);
- family help (higher);
- legal representation.

Legal help and family help (lower) are described as 'controlled work' and can only be carried out by solicitors' firms who have a specialist quality mark (SQM).

Family help (higher) and legal representation are described as 'licensed work' and an application has to be made to the LSC for a certificate to conduct the work under public funding.

Each level is suitable for different types of work or cases at different stages of proceedings. Each level is discussed separately.

2.4 LEGAL HELP

Legal help (also called level one advice) allows a client to gain advice and assistance from a solicitor on family law. Form CW1 is completed. Legal help does not cover the issue or conduct of court proceedings or any advocacy on behalf of the client. The main exception to this is undefended divorce proceedings.

The following types of work can be covered by legal help at level one:

- initial meeting with the solicitor;
- legal advice;
- letter writing;
- telephone calls;
- referrals to other organizations;
- undefended divorce proceedings (see **Chapter 5**).

The solicitor is paid a single fee for the issue dealt with under legal help. Further fees are added on for other issues (see **2.6**), e.g. a single fee is paid for advice and assistance in obtaining a divorce but a separate fee will be paid for advice on issues surrounding children or financial matters.

Legal help can also be used to complete applications for family help and legal representation.

Some work is only remunerated at legal help level, including a change of name or advice about the Child Support Agency.

2.4.1 ELIGIBILITY FOR LEGAL HELP

There are 'means' (financial eligibility) and 'merits' (whether the client's case merits the advice being given) tests in order to decide if the client is eligible for public funding. The client must provide evidence of their income.

2.4.1.1 Sufficient benefit test

The LSC will only fund a case when there will be sufficient benefit to the client, having regard to the circumstances of the matter, including the personal circumstances of the client, to justify the work being carried out. This means that cases involving no legal advice at all, e.g. simple form filling, are not eligible for legal help. The sufficient benefit test also rules out frivolous or vexatious cases.

2.4.1.2 Financial eligibility

Additionally, funding may only be provided if it is reasonable for the matter to be funded out of the Community Legal Services fund, having regard to other possible sources of funding (Part 5.2 of the Funding Code).

Some welfare benefits will mean that the client is automatically eligible.
These benefits are:

- income support;
- income-based jobseeker's allowance;
- income-based Employment and Support Allowance;
- guaranteed State Pension Credit;
- NASS support (for asylum seekers).

For those who are not on the above benefits, the gross income of the client is then worked out.

2.4.1.3 Aggregation of income

The first step is to determine whether the client has a partner whose means should be aggregated for the purposes of financial eligibility assessment. 'Partner' is defined as anyone (including a person of the same sex) with whom the applicant lives with as a couple, and includes people who are in a relationship but do not cohabit.

Practical Considerations

Volume 2F of the LSC Manual gives the following further guidance:

> . . . just because the client and their partner are physically separated, i.e. they live in separate properties, does not necessarily mean that they are living separate and apart for the purpose of the regulations. The fact that both terms are used (i.e. 'separate' and 'apart') means that more than mere physical separation is required if the partners' means are not to be aggregated. Living separate and apart is well defined in the context of matrimonial law and refers to a breakdown in the relationship. In other words, the parties must be living separate and apart because at least one of them regards the relationship as at an end and not due purely to financial or practical reasons, e.g. job location or the fact that one of the parties is in prison, hospital, residential care etc.

If the partner's income is to be aggregated, then the joint income should be calculated.

2.4.1.4 Income

The current income limit is £2,657 per month (this increases if the client has more than four children). If the gross income of the client, including that of any partner, is more than this, the client will be ineligible for funding for all levels and the process would stop there. Some forms of income are disregarded, e.g. disability living allowance and housing benefit.

If the client's income is less than £2,657, fixed allowances are made for dependants and employment expenses. Other allowances are made for tax, NI, maintenance paid, housing costs, and child minding. The table below gives the allowances:

TABLE 2.1 DEPENDANTS ALLOWANCES

Work related expenses for those receiving a wage or salary	£45
Partner	£175.76
Child aged 15 or under	£282.40
Child aged 16 or over	£282.40

If the client's gross income less allowances is less than £733 per month, the client will be financially eligible on income.

Example

Mary is a single parent with a total gross income of £1,800 per month. She pays £750 in tax, NI, and housing costs. Mary has two children aged less than 15 years old and so will have 2 × £282.40 dependants allowances.

$$£1800 - £750 - (2 \times £282.40) = £485.20 \text{ disposable income.}$$

Mary has less than £733 disposable income per month and so will be financially eligible for legal help.

Information on the income limits and a guide to assessing whether a client is eligible can be found on the CLS Keycard which is issued every April and can be accessed via the LSC website. The online resources that accompany this book contain more information.

2.4.1.5 Capital

The client's capital should be calculated. The upper limit for capital is £8,000 in family proceedings. Volume 2F of the LSC Manual, para 7 gives more detail on disregarded categories and jointly owned capital. The only items of capital that are not taken into account include the following:

- household furniture and effects (unless of exceptional value);
- clothes;
- tools and implements of trade;
- some welfare benefits or community care payments;
- capital value of the client's business in the case of the self-employed;
- cars or other vehicles in regular use (unless of exceptional value).

Under the regulations the value of the subject matter of any claim in respect of which a person is seeking funding is required to be left out of account in computing the capital of that person. This situation only applies to capital assets. It is a very important rule in the context of family/matrimonial cases as often disputed assets are the only assets that the client owns. It means that assets that are being fought over in relation to the dispute for which funding is required, where the client's interest in those assets does not exceed £100,000, must not be taken into account when assessing capital.

Where a client's main or only dwelling in which he resides is the subject matter of dispute:

1. the property should be valued at the amount for which it could be sold on the open market;
2. the amount of any mortgage or charge registered on the property must be deducted but the maximum amount that can be deducted for such a mortgage or charge is £100,000; and
3. the first £100,000 of the value of the client's interest after making the above mortgage deduction must be disregarded.

Example

The applicant has a home worth £205,000 and the mortgage is £200,000.

Value of home:	£205,000
Deduct mortgage up to maximum allowable:	£100,000
Deduct exemption allowance:	£100,000
Amount to be taken into account in assessing financial eligibility:	£5,000

In this example the client is eligible.

(Example based on the Funding Code)

The subject matter of dispute exemption (i.e. £100,000 disregard) should be applied to the main dwelling property first; the remainder (if any) should then be applied to the other assets that are in dispute. The total amount disregarded as subject matter of dispute is not to exceed £100,000.

Sometimes it will be obvious that a particular asset is in dispute between the parties, but in the family/matrimonial context the point is more difficult to determine if parties seek funding at an early stage and there are a range of assets that may or may not be at issue. The general approach should be that an asset should not be treated as the subject matter of the dispute if the other party has made no specific claim against it and if in practice it is available to the applicant to use as his or her own and could be used to fund legal costs.

2.4.1.6 Specified family proceedings

Some 'specified family proceedings' have contributions paid by the client and the amount is dependent upon the client's income. These proceedings are family proceedings before a magistrates' court other than proceedings under the Children Act 1989 or Part IV of the Family Law Act 1996, e.g. applications under the Domestic Proceedings and Magistrates' Courts Act 1978.

These contributions must be paid by the client throughout the life of the case. Clients frequently resent these contributions but it is worth reminding them that they represent a fraction of a solicitor's hourly rate.

The table below shows the levels of contributions that clients can expect to pay:

TABLE 2.2 CONTRIBUTIONS

Band	Monthly disposable income	Monthly contribution
A	£316 to £465	¼ of income in excess of £311
B	£466 to £616	£38.50 + $^1/_3$ income in excess of £465
C	£617 to £733	£88.85 + $^1/_2$ income in excess of £616

For all applications, evidence of means is required, e.g. bank statements or payslips, and a copy of this evidence must be kept on file.

If the client's income and capital are below the limit, the client can be awarded funding.

2.4.1.7 Fees

The fee paid to the solicitor for legal help is a single fee irrespective of the number of issues presented by the client. Legal help can be used to apply for higher levels of funding. Where the work done under the legal help scheme is three times the standard fee (due to the complexity of the case) a higher fee may be paid.

2.5 FAMILY MEDIATION

This level of funding authorizes mediation of a family dispute and an assessment of whether mediation appears to be suitable for the resolution of the dispute between the parties. **Chapter 3** discusses the process of mediation in more detail. Mediation may be suitable for cases where there are issues of money and property to be divided or where parents need to agree where children are to live and with whom they shall have contact.

All family mediation requires that an assessment of whether mediation will be suitable is carried out and this is called an 'assessment meeting'. This is done by a recognized mediator and the funding will only continue where the mediator is satisfied that mediation is suitable for the dispute and the parties.

If one party fails to attend the assessment meeting, a second appointment will only be given if it is reasonable under the circumstances, especially if they fail to give a good reason for non-attendance. The mediator will also screen the parties for any domestic abuse.

The criteria for financial eligibility are as for legal help above.

2.6 FAMILY HELP

2.6.1 FAMILY HELP (LOWER)

Family help (lower) is also like legal help, a fixed fee.

It is available in both public and private law cases. Family help (lower) does not include the issue or proceedings on representation in proceedings other than help in obtaining a consent order following settlement of a family dispute. Family help (lower) allows advice, and assistance in pre-proceedings work unless and until it becomes clear that the matter cannot be resolved through negotiation without the issue of proceedings.

In order to be eligible, the sufficient benefit test (see **2.4.1.1**) must be met and also the financial eligibility must be met. The client's case must also be a 'significant family dispute'. A significant family dispute is one which, if not resolved, may lead to family proceedings and for which legal advice and assistance is necessary to enable the client to resolve the issues.

There is also a cost–benefit criterion. This is a further test where family help will be refused unless the likely benefits gained from the proceedings for the client justify the likely costs, such that a reasonable private-paying client would be prepared to pay to take or defend the proceedings in all the circumstances.

Example

Melissa has recently separated from Chris. Melissa wishes to seek a divorce. There are three children of the family, and they are currently not having contact with Chris as Melissa claims that he cannot be trusted to look after them properly. She has no evidence to support this claim and eventually agrees to allow contact. Chris wishes to have all three children live with him in his one-bedroom flat. Melissa offers contact every Tuesday and Saturday. Chris wishes to have contact on Wednesday and Sunday.

Melissa will not be granted public funding as all the dispute concerns the timing of the contact. This is something that the parties should reasonably be expected to resolve themselves.

No application to the LSC is required and the solicitor should complete Legal Help Controlled Work 1 form with confirmation that the case meets the criteria to move to family help (lower) when the criteria are met.

In private cases, family help (lower) has separate fees for both children and finance issues and the solicitor can claim a separate fee for both.

A solicitor may claim a settlement fee if a case settles under family help (lower).

These fees are built up as the case progresses.

Example

Melissa has received advice and assistance on her divorce under legal help. The dispute regarding the children required negotiation between parties under family help (lower) and settled before going to court, and this will attract a settlement fee. The fees below are those that are paid to solicitors by the LSC for the work done under public funding schemes.

FIGURE 2.1 FEES FOR PUBLIC FUNDING

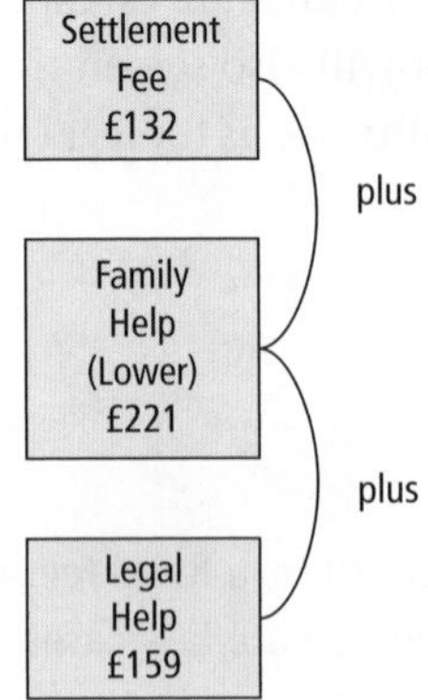

The total claimed by the solicitor would be £512 for the case.

2.6.2 FAMILY HELP (HIGHER)

This is covered by a certificate rather than being administered by the solicitor and will be paid at an hourly rate. The LSC plans to introduce fixed fees in the future but it is currently only available in private proceedings. Family help (higher) is justified only where it is necessary to issue proceedings having exhausted all other reasonable avenues to resolve the dispute or where proceedings already exist.

Family help (higher) requires an application to the LSC on a form CLS APP3 for a certificate before help can be provided. A certificate may have a limitation as to scope and costs. This means that solicitors are limited in how far proceedings can be funded unless an extension is granted. For instance, a limitation may be that an opinion from counsel is required on the likely success of the case before the proceedings will be funded to a final hearing. The standard costs limitation is £1,500.

Family help (higher) will be refused if the case is one that must be referred to a recognized mediator for a determination as to whether mediation is suitable for the resolution of the dispute, for the parties, and in all the circumstances.

The client must meet the cost–benefit criteria (see **2.6.1**), i.e. the reasonable private client approach. An element of reasonableness to the proportionality of the dispute and the benefits and costs involved is also required.

Example

Further to the example above, contact between Chris and the children has been progressing well.

He sees them every Wednesday between 4 and 7pm and Saturday between 11am and 6pm. Chris wishes to change the contact on Saturday to 10am–6pm. Melissa does not wish to change the times as it is difficult to get the children ready in time for 10am, and offers 10.30am as a compromise.

A privately paying client would probably not pay a great deal of money to argue over 30 minutes of contact nor is it proportionate to spend public money on this dispute. The costs would outweigh the benefits gained by the client.

A certificate for family help (higher) will not cover representation at a final contested hearing but it will cover the issue of proceedings where it is necessary to gain disclosure of information. In children cases, family help (higher) covers all steps short of a contested hearing.

2.6.2.1 Prospects of success

While family law is not about winning and losing, if public money is going to be used the case should have some prospect of success. The LSC Manual states that 'the aim of Family funding is to achieve results which are fair and acceptable to all parties where possible'.

The table below outlines the prospects of success:

TABLE 2.3 PROSPECTS OF SUCCESS

Case type	Successful outcome
Public law children cases	Obtaining the order sought or winning the appeal, or securing a settlement to similar effect.
Domestic violence	Obtaining the order sought or securing an undertaking or other settlement that provides the applicant and/or other person with significant protection from harm.
Private law children cases	Obtaining what the client would regard as a significant improvement in the arrangements for the children.
Financial provision and other proceedings	Obtaining what the client would regard as a significant improvement in financial or other arrangements.

2.7 LEGAL REPRESENTATION

Legal representation covers preparation for, and advocacy at, a final hearing in contested proceedings.

While it is to be hoped that a case will settle either by negotiation or in the early stages, some cases do progress as far as a final hearing. A case may have very complex legal or evidential issues. At a final hearing the court may wish to hear from witnesses and for these witnesses to be cross-examined. The court may also wish to hear legal argument and proceedings may require a solicitor or barrister who has very good advocacy skills. Legal representation allows the client to be fully represented at a final hearing and can be used to instruct a barrister, should this be necessary.

There are a range of different criteria applied to the granting of legal representation in different types of case and these will be covered within the requisite chapter. There generally is a requirement for the client's case to meet cost–benefit criteria and also have good prospects of success. Also, there should have been reasonable attempts to settle the dispute without recourse to contested proceedings. However, if the matter is urgent or there is a risk of a significant miscarriage of justice, legal representation can be granted on an emergency basis.

2.8 EMERGENCY FUNDING

There are occasions where the nature of a client's case means that public funding is required urgently, e.g. in domestic abuse or in child abduction cases. The funding can be authorized by the LSC and an application can be made by post, fax, email, or telephone if the urgency of the case dictates.

Emergency funding will only be granted if it is in the interests of justice to do so and the client must pass all of the tests required for the level of service applied for. The test for interest of justice is found in Chapter 12 of the Funding Code:

- representation (or other urgent work for which legal representation would be needed) is justified in injunction or emergency proceedings;
- representation (or other urgent work for which legal representation would be needed) is justified in relation to an imminent hearing in existing proceedings; or
- a limitation period is about to expire.

The client must be financially eligible and if it is found that he is subsequently financially ineligible, the certificate will be revoked. The client may then be liable to repay the LSC. If an emergency certificate is granted, an application must be made as soon as possible for a substantive certificate.

If the solicitor's firm has an SQM (Specialist Quality Mark) in family law, then they will have 'devolved powers' to grant emergency funding. The LSC devolves decision making powers to the solicitor to make decisions on emergency funding.

The solicitor can use their devolved powers for either family help (higher) or legal representation depending on the stage of proceedings.

2.9 STATUTORY CHARGE

'Costs' is the term commonly used to describe a party's legal expenses, including solicitor's fees, barrister's fees, court fees, payments to experts, and other expenses.

Many clients assume that when they are granted a public funding certificate the LSC will pay for their case fully and do not consider that their funding comes from public money.

The statutory charge is generally explained to clients in terms of a loan. The money is 'loaned' to the client by the LSC to pursue their case.

The LSC has a statutory duty to recoup money wherever possible and this can come from an order by the court for the publicly funded person's costs to be paid by the other party. If that is not sufficient, or a costs order is not made by the court, then the LSC will look to any money or property recovered or preserved by the client during the proceedings, in order to make up the shortfall. This is known as the statutory charge. The LSC will use the money recovered to fund other cases.

The Access to Justice Act, s10(7) allows the LSC a first charge on any property recovered or preserved by the client (whether for himself or any other person) in any proceedings or in any compliance or settlement of any dispute in connection with which the services were provided. Property includes money, e.g. a lump sum.

2.9.1 RECOVERED OR PRESERVED

Whether property has been recovered or preserved is a complex issue. The House of Lords considered the issue in *Hanlon v Law Society* [1981] AC 124 where their Lordships held that property is recovered or preserved if it was 'in issue' in proceedings and the funded party either made a successful claim in relation to it or successfully defended a claim in respect of it.

 **Example**

Melissa and Chris have begun divorce proceedings. Through mediation they agree a settlement for all their assets apart from a holiday home in the Cotswolds valued at £250,000.

Proceedings are issued for financial orders and the court awards 50% of the value to each party. Melissa was publicly funded. Chris is ordered to pay £5,000 towards Melissa's legal costs but there is a shortfall of £1,500. Melissa will pay this £1,500 out of the proceeds of the court award as the property was recovered as a result of the proceedings.

In *Curling v Law Society* [1985] 1 All ER 707, the family home was in joint names. The publicly funded wife sought an order that the house be sold. Her husband did not dispute that one half of the house belonged to the wife and eventually an agreement was reached whereby the husband bought out the wife's interest in the house. The wife argued that as the title of the property was not in dispute, the sum she had received for her share was not recovered or preserved in the proceedings. The Court of Appeal held that the ownership of the property could not be looked at in isolation and the fact that a party had recovered something to which she was already entitled did not of itself prevent the statutory charge.

Exemptions from the statutory charge include:

- periodical payments of maintenance for a spouse, former spouse, civil partner, or former civil partner;
- pension-sharing orders;
- where the family home is recovered or preserved and the only funding received by the client has been legal help;
- a lump sum received by way of a petition attachment order or attachment of death-in-service benefits under ss25B and 25C of the Matrimonial Causes Act 1973.

2.9.2 MEDIATION AND THE STATUTORY CHARGE

If a settlement has been reached by mediation and funded by a certificate for family mediation, the costs are exempt from the statutory charge.

2.9.3 MINIMIZING THE STATUTORY CHARGE

In **2.9.2** above, settling through mediation is one way to avoid the charge completely. If the issues are narrowed down as far as possible at the beginning of the case this will reduce the property 'at issue' in the proceedings.

 **Example**

In the example above, Melissa and Chris agreed all issues surrounding money, property, and maintenance at mediation. No statutory charge will be recovered.

2.9.4 RECOVERY OF THE STATUTORY CHARGE

The relevant legislation that governs the enforcement of the statutory charge is the Community Legal Service (Financial) Regulations 2000. If both cash and a dwelling house are preserved, the charge will be enforced against the cash first and then the dwelling house. The LSC has the discretion to postpone the charge, particularly if the charge relates to the family home. The LSC will register a charge over the property, payable when the property is sold unless the LSC agrees to transfer the charge to another property. Interest will accrue at a simple rate until the charge is redeemed, currently 8%. The client can pay off the statutory charge at any time.

2.9.5 IMPORTANCE OF MAKING THE CLIENT AWARE OF THE POTENTIAL IMPACT OF THE STATUTORY CHARGE

Clients will often claim that they did not know about the effect of the statutory charge. This selective memory is often despite several letters containing the advice and explanations from their solicitor. This demonstrates the importance of giving full advice at initial meetings, in client care letters, and regular updates as well as keeping detailed attendance notes.

2.10 IF THE CLIENT IS INELIGIBLE FOR PUBLIC FUNDING

Many clients will be ineligible for public funding, even clients of fairly moderate means. Conditional fees are not permitted in family law but there are other methods of funding a case:

- the client pays for the case privately and takes a loan from a bank or credit card;
- the client may be loaned money by family or friends;
- the client may be able to gain some limited assistance from voluntary agencies, e.g. a Citizen's Advice Bureau. This may be general advice only and will not cover advocacy at court;
- a 'Sears Tooth' agreement (see **Chapter 14**);
- an application for maintenance pending suit in proceedings for a financial order (see **Chapter 12**).

SUMMARY POINTS

- Public Funding will undergo radical reform in April 2013 and the scope of public funding in family law cases will be greatly reduced.
- Legal proceedings can be funded privately or through public funding. Public funding is administered by the Legal Services Commission through the Community Legal Service.

- There are a number of levels of assistance available according to the type of advice or representation required including legal help, family mediation, family help, and legal representation. Funding can be applied for in an emergency.
- In order to receive public funding, a client must be eligible financially and there must be merit in funding the case through public money.
- Public funding is recouped by the Legal Services Commission through the statutory charge. This can be mitigated by the parties agreeing as many issues as possible.

SELF-TEST QUESTIONS

1. Which type of funding is most commonly used for undefended divorce?
2. Which welfare benefits make a client automatically financially eligible for public funding?
3. Explain the statutory charge in a way that a client will understand it.

Answers to the questions above can be found on the Online Resource Centre: **www.oxfordtextbooks.co.uk/orc/familyhandbook13/**.

3 ALTERNATIVE DISPUTE RESOLUTION IN FAMILY LAW

3.1 INTRODUCTION

This chapter will:

- **discuss the methods by which a family lawyer may resolve family law disputes, including Alternative Dispute Resolution (ADR);**
- **review the various forms of negotiation which a family lawyer may undertake;**
- **discuss mediation and collaborative law as different forms of ADR used in family law.**

Family law is often complex and daunting for clients, and the very nature of the substance of the dispute means that often parties bring their emotional disputes into the case. Most clients wish to resolve disputes cheaply, quickly, and without involving lawyers. Unfortunately, this is not possible in the majority of cases for a number of reasons. Many people do not have the confidence to negotiate with their ex-partners or some will have difficulty in obtaining all the information they need in order to decide whether an offer is fair and should be accepted. Clients often have unrealistic expectations about the settlement or outcome to be achieved by the courts. As the ability to gain public funding diminishes, dissatisfaction with paying for legal advice increases. Family lawyers must also be good value for money.

However unfairly, family lawyers rarely get a good press from the general public. Family lawyers are perceived to have an interest in making the dispute last as long as possible with a view to making as much money as possible. Disputes are often very polarized and campaign groups have grown up surrounding issues of contact and residence, e.g. Fathers 4 Justice. One of the most important considerations for a new family lawyer is to ensure that a case is conducted as professionally and as calmly as possible. Family lawyers are bound by their professional codes of conduct. Family lawyers may also join organizations that promote good practice in family law, such as Resolution.

As proposals for public funding include proposals to severely curtail public funding in family cases, it is anticipated that more and more families will turn to various forms of ADR to resolve disputes quickly and more cheaply than litigation.

There are a number of ways in which a dispute can be resolved without resort to litigation. This chapter will look at a number of ADR techniques. Some, possibly all, will be relevant to your clients and some will not. It is part of the skill of a family lawyer to know which type of ADR is appropriate and available and which are not. Your firm may also wish to offer ADR services as part of the firm's services, e.g. collaborative law or mediation.

3.2 RELATIONSHIP AND MARRIAGE COUNSELLING

When a client attends your firm for advice, there should not be an automatic assumption that the client has decided that the relationship is at an end nor that they wish to move straight into divorce or dissolution proceedings. If a client is having difficulties in their relationship and they wish to try to resolve these difficulties, then there are organizations that can assist the client.

Practical Considerations

Two national organizations that provide support are:

- *Relate*. Relate offers advice, relationship counselling, sex therapy, workshops, mediation, consultations, and support face-to-face, by phone and through its website: www.relate.org.uk.
- *Marriage Care*. Marriage Care offers counselling nationwide to those wishing to become married or enter a long-term relationship or for those requiring help to sustain these relationships and can be found at www.marriagecare.org.uk.

Many practitioners keep leaflets and contact details of local services to provide to clients. It is important to be aware of local services and also to provide support where possible.

3.3 RESOLVING FAMILY LAW DISPUTES

Disputes are resolved in family law either through litigation or through some form of ADR or a combination of both. When litigation is used, not all cases end up being taken to a final hearing; the parties often agree with the assistance of the court.

Although ADR is available in family law, it is important to remember that if ADR fails, litigation will be the method by which disputes are resolved.

3.3.1 COMPARING ADR AND LITIGATION

There are many advantages and disadvantages of choosing ADR over litigation. Each type of ADR is different and so this is a general comparison.

TABLE 3.1 ADR AND LITIGATION

	ADR	Litigation
Speed	May be quicker than litigation and the parties have greater control over the timetable.	Courts' timetables try to ensure that proceedings are not too lengthy. There can be difficulties in finding court time that leads to delay.
Cost	Will often be cheaper than litigation but can be costly if counsel and other professionals become involved. Mediation may be covered by LSC Funding, although this may change.	Can be funded by LSC funding if the client is eligible, although this position may change with changes to funding. Can be very costly if proceedings are lengthy and especially if the proceedings go to a final hearing. Can also be more expensive if counsel and other professionals are required.
	If collaborative law fails (see **3.6**), there may be duplication of legal costs.	
Emotional issues involved in separation	Some forms of ADR attempt to deal with the emotional fallout of separation as well as the legal issues.	Litigation is not designed to resolve emotional difficulties. Aggressive litigation will often heighten emotions.

TABLE 3.1 CONTINUED

	ADR	Litigation
Preservation of relationships between the parties	One of the aims of ADR is to preserve the good relations between the parties, especially those families with children.	Litigation will attempt to preserve good relationships but the 'court experience' may promote hostility between the parties.
Formality	Less formal than litigation but some forms of ADR are slightly more structured, e.g. collaborative law.	Court proceedings do have greater element of formality.
Finality	Most ADR will attempt to produce a final settlement that can be recorded in a final court order.	Court will give a final order.
Proportionality	ADR costs can be more proportionate to the assets or dispute between the parties.	Litigation costs are often disproportionate to the assets in dispute between the parties.
Flexibility	ADR can meet a number of needs and can choose the method of ADR to suit the party's situations.	Court proceedings are designed to allow negotiation between the parties.

3.4 NEGOTIATION

Most lawyers will commence negotiation of some kind well before litigation is commenced. Most lawyers find that client satisfaction is higher if a settlement is reached although sometimes it is difficult to persuade the client of this!

Courts will also expect the parties to have undertaken some form of negotiation prior to issuing court proceedings. Judges are often concerned that legal costs are disproportionate to the value of the assets involved and courts are hard pressed to accommodate parties' wishes for a final hearing.

3.4.1 FORMS OF NEGOTIATION

3.4.1.1 Settlement between clients

Clients may negotiate directly between themselves. An advantage is that the client retains complete control over the dispute resolution.

Problems may occur if a spouse in a weaker position has agreed without full disclosure or has been pressurized into agreement. One party may be too afraid of the other party to disagree or negotiate properly and there is always a risk that one party may be psychologically or financially in a stronger position and may be able to dictate an agreement. Some clients feel guilty about ending a relationship and may agree an unadvisedly generous settlement. Independent advice from a family lawyer is essential before the settlement has been finalized.

3.4.1.2 Negotiation through correspondence

Negotiating through correspondence is very commonly done and works well if the correspondence is drafted well, is clear, complete, and comprehensive. Correspondence is a permanent record of the negotiation and is often the opening point for negotiations. Clients retain an element of control as correspondence can be read before sending. Some lawyers do not enjoy a round table meeting or face-to-face negotiations and some may find correspondence easier when they are a less experienced practitioner.

However, correspondence is slow as lawyers will have to wait for post or DX and then seek instructions from the client. It can be less efficient than face-to-face contact. If correspondence is poorly drafted or contains material that is likely to offend parties, problems can arise as misunderstandings may follow as well as raising the 'temperature' of the dispute.

Practical Considerations

Be careful with emails and faxes. Many solicitors use faxes to put pressure on their opponents. Faxes have a legitimate place in urgent matters. When you receive a fax, you should consider whether an immediate response is required or whether it would be better to deal with the issue in ordinary correspondence, especially if the fax supersedes a letter already awaiting a response. Do not be rushed into an ill-advised course of action.

Emails are very useful but care should be taken to ensure that they are used in a constructive way. Consider your draft carefully; don't simply type and send. Once an email has been sent, it cannot be recovered, unlike a letter that has been typed and must be considered again on signing. Emails should be drafted with the same formality as letters and one should not be tempted to treat emails as a more casual form of communication.

Resolution Guide to Good Practice is an excellent guide to avoiding common pitfalls in drafting correspondence. The Guide considers issues about the reason for writing a letter, timing of letters, and ensuring correspondence is constructive, informative, and effective.

3.4.1.3 Negotiation via telephone or in person

Many lawyers will pick up the telephone to negotiate a settlement. The advantages are that it is a quick, cheap, and relatively informal way of resolving disputes and has the advantage of human contact. Using the telephone can deal with one or more issues of the ongoing case, e.g. a contact dispute over a holiday, while negotiations in the case continue.

Using the telephone has some disadvantages. A telephone negotiation should ideally be diarized between parties or your colleague may be unavailable or unprepared. Always confirm the outcome of a negotiation in writing to ensure that no misunderstandings arise.

With careful preparation, negotiations can be conducted between lawyers in person. Lawyers may need to meet more than once to resolve the dispute but it will be an efficient way of resolving a dispute. Lawyers can discuss one or more issues at a meeting and areas of dispute can be resolved. A comprehensive note of the meeting must be kept. Clients may be present but equally, the lawyers involved in the dispute can meet separately.

3.4.1.4 Meeting between counsel

Involving counsel (barristers) is sometimes necessary in complex cases and can assist less experienced lawyers. Sometimes a fresh pair of eyes is needed to clarify the issues and also counsel can provide an objective opinion for a client as it can provide a 'reality check'. Negotiations can proceed between counsel engaged in a dispute and prove to be a good way to resolve proceedings quickly. However, involving counsel can be costly and counsel can feel remote for the client who is used to more frequent contact with their solicitor.

3.4.1.5 At-court negotiation

Negotiations can continue all the way to the door of the court and frequently produce settlement even during the course of court hearings. There is no extra cost as the lawyers are present anyway and negotiations can involve counsel. In financial relief proceedings (see **Chapter 14**), the parties will get an indication from the judge about what they can reasonably expect to gain in proceedings. The client may feel under slightly more pressure to settle if they have been unwilling to do so before then.

This form of negotiation can be problematic as a client may buckle under pressure or rush to accept and settle on less favourable terms. The court experience is rarely helpful to a client if negotiations fail.

3.5 MEDIATION

The Family Mediators Association sets out the four principles of mediation:

- it is voluntary;
- the mediator is impartial;
- it is confidential;
- it is flexible.

Mediation is a voluntary process and parties attend in person with a mediator to discuss problems. It is a safe environment, which promotes long-term agreement and hopefully reduces hostility between the parties. Parties can communicate directly with each other and any issue can be raised between the parties including more formal issues of financial and property matters or children's residence or contact.

The mediator will identify and clarify issues between the parties and discuss the choices available. The children's needs will be at the forefront of the discussions. The mediator is an impartial third party who manages the process of exchanging information, ideas, and feelings constructively, although they have no power to impose a settlement and the responsibility of settling remains with the parties participating in the mediation.

The mediator will not advise on the best option for either party nor is it their role to protect an individual and the parties will probably seek independent legal advice during or after mediation.

As the parties have been completely involved in reaching agreements, it is hoped that this will make it acceptable to the parties, as an imposed order is often resented.

Once an agreement has been reached, the agreement will be recorded as a summary and this summary can be taken by the parties to their own legal advisers for advice. Any agreement reached will not be binding on the parties unless put in the form of a consent order.

A consent order is agreed by the courts and ends the parties' claims against each other. One significant advantage of mediation is that the statutory charge will not apply to property recovered or reserved (see **Chapter 2**). If the client is publicly funded, this is a major consideration.

3.5.1 COMPULSORY MEDIATION

The Family Procedure Rules 2010 (FPR 2010) introduces a scheme of compulsory mediation for clients issuing proceedings after 6 April 2011. The rationale for this is that courts are not considered the best-suited medium for resolving family law disputes. Although this is referred to as 'compulsory' mediation, in fact the requirement is for the parties to attend a 'Mediation Information and Assessment Meeting'. There are exceptions to attending the meeting and these include: where one party is unlikely to attend; where there has been an allegation of domestic abuse (which has resulted in a police investigation or issuing of civil proceedings within the preceding 12 months); or (in financial proceedings) where one party is bankrupt. All of the exceptions can be found in FPR 2010 PD 3A. Once the meeting has been attended, a Form F1 is submitted to the court.

It is not clear how many (and whether) clients will take up mediation to resolve disputes or whether this meeting will be regarded as 'lip service' by clients and will not be taken seriously. It is hoped that cases will be diverted from a damaging adversarial system and help to preserve family relationships.

3.6 COLLABORATIVE LAW

3.6.1 INTRODUCTION

Collaborative law is a process in which lawyers and clients work together to resolve disputes respectfully without going to court, and hopes to provide the parties with a 'good divorce'. This may seem like an impossible ideal. But collaborative law aims to be a forum in which the legal, financial, and practical aspects of separation or divorce are addressed as well as considering the person's future relationships with children and wider family members. It allows the client to start to deal with their emotions too. Collaborative law is currently used most commonly in proceedings for financial orders (see **Chapter 14**).

Practical Considerations

Collaborative law may be suitable if the client:

- wishes a dignified, non-aggressive resolution of the issues;
- has children and wishes to reach a resolution by agreements with their needs and interests being the foremost consideration;
- wishes to keep open, good relations with their partner in the future;
- does not wish to 'hand over' decision making to the litigation process;
- does not want to 'seek revenge'.

Clearly, not every client will be able to meet these requirements and may not wish to pursue collaborative law. Many clients simply cannot detach their emotional reaction from their divorce or separation and will not be suitable for collaborative law.

3.6.2 WHAT IS THE DIFFERENCE BETWEEN COLLABORATIVE LAW AND MEDIATION?

In mediation, the mediator will not give legal advice and is neutral. In the collaborative law process, lawyers are present at the meetings to advise the client and negotiate. Lawyers are not generally present at mediation.

3.6.3 HOW DOES COLLABORATIVE LAW WORK?

3.6.3.1 Initial meeting with the client

The first meeting aims to establish rapport and explain the process to the client and the options available to them, to identify what the client wants, their main priorities, and consider their suitability for collaborative practice. The lawyer should discuss with the client what they would like to achieve and any issues that would make them walk away from the negotiations.

The client should be screened for suitability. A client must be able to participate in good faith, have an ability to see perspectives beyond their own, have a belief in the future, and a determination to resolve issues via collaborative law, and to acknowledge the views and needs of others. Not all clients will exhibit all of these virtues but will still be able to make the collaborative process work. One of the skills of a collaborative lawyer is to listen carefully to a client to understand their fears, concerns, and ability to participate.

3.6.3.2 Agreements between client and lawyer in collaborative law

Collaborative law is different to a situation where a lawyer is acting in litigation, where the lawyer represents the client until a final written agreement is reached.

If the collaborative process ends (either by client or the other spouse ending the process) the lawyer will no longer be able to act and the client will have to get a new lawyer. The lawyer cannot guarantee that the other side will make full disclosure nor that the other side will act in good faith but should advise the client if they have any suspicion of bad faith on the other side. Nor can a lawyer guarantee that collaborative law will definitely work!

3.6.3.3 Preparation meeting with the client

The lawyer and client will discuss goals and objectives of the client in their choice of collaborative law and lay the foundations for good faith, interest-based bargaining. There may be a number of issues to be discussed including children or finances. The process of collaborative law should be explained and the client will try to identify any anxieties or vulnerabilities before the first meeting. The lawyer should prepare the client for the meeting ahead.

3.6.3.4 Four-way meetings

Four-way meetings occur when both clients and their lawyers meet to discuss settlement.

Before the first four-way meeting, the lawyers will meet without clients to build rapport with each other and will consider the agenda, the ground rules, and work out practicalities for the first four-way meeting.

For the first four-way meeting, both clients and their lawyers will attend. The parties will reiterate the foundation and understanding of the collaborative process especially:

- constructive and respectful approach;
- pacing and timing;
- full disclosure;
- team support.

The clients will be invited to share their objectives and ensure their voices are heard.

The parties will review and sign a four-way participation agreement.

The lawyers agree:

- not to go to court to resolve the clients' differences;
- to think creatively and constructively to find a fair solution to all issues;
- that the priority is the well-being of the children and, after that, the clients;
- to be courteous and cooperative, truthful, open, and honest;
- to jointly instruct all professionals.

The clients agree:

- not to discuss past events;
- to avoid threats and inflammatory language;
- not to denigrate or criticize the other in front of the children and not to involve the children in disputes;
- to promote and support a loving and caring and involved relationship between the children and the other parent;
- to supply promptly all documentation and disclosure required;
- only to discuss the settlement at face-to-face meetings;
- to pay their lawyer.

If the collaborative process breaks down, the clients can withdraw at any time but a 'cooling off' period of 21 days is agreed to before court proceedings can start to allow the lawyers to attempt to rescue the negotiations. If there is an emergency or either client has broken the agreement, this will not apply.

If a court is involved in the family break up, then the client's instruction of the lawyers will immediately lapse and the clients must place themselves on the court record. The lawyers involved in the collaborative process *will not* then be involved in the court proceedings. The clients cannot use as evidence any of the lawyer's notes to the extent that financial information is recorded, nor any evidence given by the joint expert's reports, nor refer a judge to the negotiations conducted under collaborative law.

3.6.3.5 Intermediate four-way meetings

There may be a number of four-way meetings before all issues are resolved.

Each four-way meeting will have an agenda and will discuss the parties' priorities and concerns and deal with any pressing or short-term issues. Each meeting will review progress and revise key issues.

Part of the function of these meetings will be for information gathering and exchange and clients are encouraged to take the lead in sharing documentation.

There may be involvement from other professionals. A separation can produce a number of issues that need to be resolved. For instance, advice may be required on inheritance tax planning, financial planning, and parenting plans. Clients and lawyers may call upon a number of professionals to assist with the collaborative process, including independent financial advisers, child specialists, accountants, and pension experts. Any professional involved in the collaborative process must share a commitment to the principles of collaborative law.

The lawyers will assist the clients in brainstorming options, identifying preferred solutions, and preparing final documents.

The collaborative lawyer's role within these meetings involves:

- conflict management and resolution;
- dealing with full disclosure and organizing assets and preparing schedules of agreed assets and liabilities;
- using and instructing 'joint' experts or professionals;
- advising the client;
- keeping track of progress and moving the process forward;
- preparing court documentation to record agreement;
- planning ahead.

3.6.3.6 Final four-way meeting

Once agreement is reached, the final meeting will deal with the formalities of signing documentation and discuss how the parties will handle possible future difficulties. The lawyers will explain legal processes of divorce and consent orders (proceedings will have to be issued in order to obtain divorce and also to make a final order).

SUMMARY POINTS

- There are a number of ways in which a lawyer can negotiate a settlement in family law proceedings.
- Each form of negotiation has advantages and disadvantages and these must be carefully weighed when choosing how to negotiate.
- Negotiation can take the form of client settlement, by telephone, correspondence, meetings, through counsel, and at court.
- Mediation is a form of ADR.
- A mediator is a neutral third party who assists clients to come to a fair settlement.
- Mediation is unsuitable for some clients. Some parties may not be cooperative or there may be a power imbalance.

- Collaborative law is a process in which clients choose not to involve the court in settling family law cases.
- Collaborative law involves a negotiation in a four-way meeting with lawyers and clients present.
- Agreements between the parties and lawyers include that if collaborative law fails the lawyers will no longer be able to act for the clients.

SELF-TEST QUESTIONS

1. List and explain three advantages of ADR over a litigated settlement.
2. Explain the difference between mediation and collaborative law.
3. A client chooses collaborative law as a way of resolving their case. Explain to the client how the collaborative process works. If collaborative law doesn't work, can the client keep their lawyer?

Answers to the questions above can be found on the Online Resource Centre: www.oxfordtextbooks.co.uk/orc/familyhandbook13/.

Part 2

RELATIONSHIP BREAKDOWN

4 JUDICIAL SEPARATION AND NULLITY

4.1 INTRODUCTION

In Part 2 of this text we will be considering the law and procedure following the breakdown of a relationship. We will consider divorce, and civil partnerships, as all are likely to form part of a solicitor's caseload. The financial consequences of relationship breakdown for spouses and civil partners are considered in Part 3. This chapter focuses on alternatives to divorce, whilst subsequent chapters will cover divorce, defences to divorce, jurisdiction, and divorce procedure fully. Part 4 will consider cohabitants.

This chapter will:

- **discuss the remedy of judicial separation as an alternative to divorce proceedings;**
- **discuss nullity as a remedy including void and voidable marriages;**
- **discuss nullity as a remedy for those escaping a forced marriage.**

The number of marriages that end in judicial separation or nullity is relatively small. In 2006, there were just over 600 applications for judicial separation. Most clients will seek divorce at the end of the marriage rather than the expensive step of judicial separation that does not dissolve the marriage. Nullity is an unusual remedy in modern family law practice but remains important to a small number of clients. In 2006, there were 400 applications for nullity. Nullity remains a relevant remedy for clients escaping a forced marriage.

4.2 JUDICIAL SEPARATION

As with divorce, the principal statute concerned with judicial separation is the Matrimonial Causes Act 1973 (MCA 1973).

The petition is based upon one of the five facts listed at s1(2) MCA 1973 (see **Chapter 5**), but the court does not enquire whether the marriage has irretrievably broken down (s17(2) MCA 1973). The marriage is not dissolved by a judicial separation, but the parties do not have to live with one another and the parties can apply to the court to resolve disputes about finances (see **Chapter 11** onwards).

The family lawyer will see few applications for judicial separation and so the procedural aspects of the application are not detailed here. Most clients seeking a judicial separation do so for religious or ethical reasons.

4.3 NULLITY

A petition for nullity is based on there being a problem with marriage formalities or capacity. The marriage will be treated as if it never existed. A void marriage (see **4.4 below**) has never existed whereas a voidable marriage (see **4.5 below**) will be treated as being in existence until it is annulled.

The effect of a decree of nullity for void marriages will mean that although the marriage has never existed, financial, pension, and property orders are available under MCA 1973, children will be legitimate, and parties can still claim under the Inheritance (Provision for Family and Dependants) Act 1975. A voidable marriage will be held to exist until the date of the decree of nullity and parties can claim as above.

4.4 VOID MARRIAGES

S11 MCA 1973 lists the grounds for finding a marriage to be void, namely:

(a) that it is not a valid marriage under the provisions of the Marriage Acts 1949 to 1986 (that is to say where—
   (i) the parties are within the prohibited degree of relationship;
   (ii) either party is under the age of sixteen; or
   (iii) the parties have intermarried in disregard of certain requirements as to the formation of marriage);

(b) that at the time of the marriage either party was already lawfully married or a civil partner;

(c) that the parties are not respectively male and female;

(d) in the case of a polygamous marriage entered into outside England and Wales, that either party was at the time of the marriage domiciled in England and Wales.

4.4.1 PROHIBITED DEGREES OF RELATIONSHIP

The Marriage (Prohibited Degrees of Relationship) Act 1986 lists family relationships that are too close for marriage, e.g. mother and son. The prohibited degrees are consanguinity (e.g. mother/son, father/daughter, sister/brother, aunt/nephew etc.) and affinity. There are two classes of affinity. The first class prevents stepfather/stepdaughter, stepmother/stepson and stepgrandparent/stepgrandchild from marrying unless both parties are over 21 and the child was not at any time a child of the family in relation to the other whilst under 18 years.

The second class of affinity was changed on 1 March 2007 by the Marriage Act 1949 (Remedial) Order 2007 following a judgment in the European Court of Human Rights (ECtHR). Formerly, a person could not marry his child's former spouse or his parent's former spouse unless certain conditions were met. This was held to be incompatible with Art. 12 of the European Convention on Human Rights (ECHR).

Consanguinity prohibitions arose from genetic consideration to prevent marriage between people related by blood where the shared proportion of genes is one-quarter or more. The rules on affinity are based on social policy considerations.

4.4.2 AGE

Both parties to the marriage must be aged over 16 at the time of the ceremony. If a person is aged under the age of 18, they must have parental consent.

4.4.3 ALREADY MARRIED

Parties must not be already married or in a civil partnership when they marry or enter a civil partnership. A criminal charge of bigamy may ensue. Clients must be advised firmly that they must have a decree absolute (see **Chapter 8**) before they are free to remarry.

4.4.4 NOT MALE AND FEMALE

This provision has generated a great deal of case-law concerning transsexuals who wish to marry in their acquired gender.

In *Corbett v Corbett* [1969] 113 SJ 982 the bride was a transsexual, April Ashley (formerly George Jamieson), who had undergone successful sex-change surgery. Ormrod J held that the marriage was invalid as a person's biological sex is determined at birth and cannot be altered by subsequent surgical intervention.

The ECHR includes a right to marry (Art. 12) and a right to private and family life (Art. 8). These articles were used to challenge the UK law though, until 2002, without success. However, in 2002, in *Goodwin v United Kingdom* [2002] FCR 577 the ECtHR held that the UK was in breach of Arts 8 and 12 by refusing to allow the applicant to change her birth certificate following gender-reassignment surgery. The applicant brought evidence that being unable to change her birth certificate had caused her humiliation and distress at discriminatory practices throughout her life. The ECtHR held that Art. 8 gave the right to establish an identity and the situation of post-operative transsexuals was no longer sustainable in the UK.

Despite this decision, the UK Government did not change the law and the courts were bound by the provisions of s11(c) MCA 1973. In *Bellinger v Bellinger* [2003] UKHL 21 the House of Lords looked again at this question. Lord Nicholls stated that the tests to be applied to determine the sex of a person in the context of validity of marriage were chromosomal, gonadal, and genital and recognition of the wife in the case would mean giving the terms 'male' and 'female' in MCA 1973 a novel, extended meaning, namely that a person might be born with one sex but later become (or be regarded as) a person of the opposite sex. Such a change was not for the courts but for Parliament. The House of Lords did go on to declare that s11(c) MCA 1973 was incompatible with Arts 8 and 12 of the ECHR.

The Gender Recognition Act 2004 (GRA 2004) came into force on 4 April 2005. The GRA 2004 provides for gender recognition certificates (GRC) to be issued by a gender recognition panel to applicants aged over 18 if the applicant has, or has had, gender dysphoria, lived in their acquired gender for two years, and intends to live in the acquired gender for the rest of his or her life. Medical evidence must be presented to the panel. Once a full GRC has been granted, the applicant will be of their acquired gender for all purposes and will be entitled to a new birth certificate and be able to marry a person of the opposite gender to their new gender.

4.4.5 POLYGAMOUS MARRIAGE

A marriage in which one party is domiciled (see **Chapter 7**) in England and Wales must not be polygamous.

4.5 VOIDABLE MARRIAGES

S12 MCA 1973 lists the grounds for finding a marriage voidable:

(a) that the marriage has not been consummated owing to the incapacity of either party to consummate it;

(b) that the marriage has not been consummated owing to the wilful refusal of the respondent to consummate it;

(c) that either party to the marriage did not validly consent to it, whether in consequence of duress, mistake, unsoundness of mind, or otherwise;

(d) that at the time of the marriage either party, though capable of giving a valid consent, was suffering (whether continuously or intermittently) from mental disorder within the meaning of the Mental Health Act 1983 of such a kind or to such an extent to be unfitted for marriage;

(e) that at the time of the marriage the respondent was suffering from venereal disease in a communicable form;

(f) that at the time of the marriage the respondent was pregnant by some person other than the petitioner;

(g) that an interim gender recognition certificate under the Gender Recognition Act 2004 has, after the time of the marriage, been issued to either party to the marriage;

(h) that the respondent is a person whose gender at the time of the marriage had become the acquired gender under the Gender Recognition Act 2004.

As mentioned above, nullity is not a common remedy. As such, some limited comments on some of the grounds are included below.

4.5.1 NON-CONSUMMATION

Consummation takes place as soon as the parties have sexual intercourse after the marriage has been solemnized. For a marriage to be voidable, the failure to consummate must result from incapacity of either party or the wilful refusal of the respondent.

4.5.2 INCAPACITY

Incapacity can be based on a physical abnormality or psychological causes. An 'invincible repugnance' may suffice (*G v G* [1924] AC 348, HL) but a rational decision not to permit intercourse will not (*Singh v Singh* [1971] P 224). The incapacity must be permanent and incurable and the petitioner must prove that the incapacity exists.

4.5.3 WILFUL REFUSAL

Wilful refusal must be a settled and definite decision come to without just excuse (*Horton v Horton* [1947] 2 All ER 871). The court will look at the history of the marriage and a petition will fail if the respondent can show a just cause or reason for his/her behaviour, e.g. in *Jodla v Jodla* [1960] 1 WLR 236 where the parties had married on the understanding that they would not live together until a religious ceremony was complete. One party's refusal to go through with or organize the second ceremony would amount to a wilful refusal.

4.5.4 LACK OF CONSENT

A lack of consent can result from duress, mistake, or as a result of being of unsound mind. Duress has been refined by the courts through a series of decisions that have not always been entirely consistent. There must be fear sufficient to vitiate consent (*Singh v Singh* [1971] P 226) and this fear must be sufficiently grave. In *Szechter v Szechter* [1971] P 286 this was defined as a 'threat of immediate danger' and in *Hirani v Hirani* [1982] 4 FLR 232, CA as undue pressure overbearing the will.

4.6 FORCED MARRIAGES

In 2007, the Forced Marriage Unit at the Foreign Office dealt with 300 cases of forced marriage, although research suggests the actual number of such cases may be higher. In these circumstances, divorce can be upsetting as it carries cultural stigma and is distressing for the survivor as it indicates that the marriage was in existence. Nullity is therefore a very useful alternative to those forced into marriage.

The cases of *P v R (Forced Marriage: Annulment: Procedure)* (2003) 1 FLR 661 and *NS v MI* (2007) 1 FLR 444 established that nullity can be used with the ground being lack of consent due to duress.

In *P v R*, the petitioner was a 21-year-old woman who was persuaded to attend her sister's funeral in Pakistan. The petitioner did not live at home and was in a relationship with a man of whom her parent did not approve. At the end of mourning, the petitioner was informed that marriage arrangements had been made for her. The petitioner's movements were restricted and she was followed and she was threatened with violence. On the day of the wedding, she was forced to put on a wedding dress; her mother held the back of her head and by pushing it made her nod to indicate consent to marriage.

Coleridge J held that the petitioner had not validly consented to the marriage and her 'consent' had been vitiated by force, both because of the threats of violence and emotional pressures brought to bear in Pakistan.

4.7 BARS TO PETITION

S13 MCA 1973 sets out some bars to petitions based on voidable marriages. These include approbation where a petitioner behaved in a way that indicated acceptance of the marriage. A decree cannot be granted on the grounds of lack of consent, mental unfitness, venereal disease, pregnancy by another, or acquired gender if three years have passed from the date of the marriage. Having knowledge of the respondent's venereal disease, pregnancy by another, or acquired gender will bar a petition on these grounds.

SUMMARY POINTS

- Judicial separation is based on the same fact as divorce but the marriage is not dissolved.
- Nullity covers void and voidable marriages.
- A void marriage is a marriage that has never validly existed due to a fault.
- A marriage can be void due to marriage within prohibited decrees of relationship, parties being under 16, certain defects within the formalities of marriage, and that the parties are not respectively male and female.
- A voidable marriage exists until a decree is granted.
- A marriage can be voidable due to non-consummation, lack of consent, mental disorder, venereal disease, pregnancy by another, or an acquired gender.
- Nullity is an alternative to divorce in cases of forced marriages.
- There are bars to petitions based on voidable marriages.
- Following a decree of nullity, orders can be obtained for property, pensions, and to declare children are legitimate.

SELF-TEST QUESTIONS

1. Explain the difference between void and voidable marriages.
2. A client was put under pressure by her family to enter into a marriage. She tells you that she was locked in her bedroom and threatened with violence if she did not go through with the ceremony. Finally, your client's family told her that if she did not go through with the marriage, she would be ostracized from the family. Advise your client.

Answers to the questions above can be found on the Online Resource Centre: www.oxfordtextbooks.co.uk/orc/familyhandbook13/.

5 DIVORCE

5.1 INTRODUCTION

This chapter will:

- **discuss the ground for divorce under the Matrimonial Causes Act 1973 (MCA 1973);**
- **explore each of the five possible facts which prove the ground for divorce;**
- **discuss the relevance of continued cohabitation between the parties.**

Divorce is synonymous with family law. Whilst not every client is married, divorce will form a major part of a family lawyer's caseload. Many clients will make contact with a family lawyer to discuss divorce, but (as in **Chapter 3**) it is not the only option for a failing marriage. It is important to remember that the parties may wish to consider relationship counselling to preserve their marriage.

In England and Wales, divorce is based upon fault; one party must blame the other for the failure of the marriage unless the parties wish to wait for two or five years. The Family Law Act 1996 attempted to introduce a system of 'no-fault' divorce with parties being encouraged to enter into mediation. For a variety of reasons, the provisions were never introduced and are now repealed. For more information, see the online resources.

Statistics show that divorces are most commonly started by women and the most common basis for divorce is unreasonable behaviour of the respondent. As such, the applicant will be referred to as 'she' and the respondent as 'he' although in many cases, it will be the other way around.

Most divorces are not defended and this chapter will deal only with the law and procedure for undefended divorces. For those cases with a defended divorce, please refer to specialist family law practitioner texts. This chapter will cover the grounds and facts of divorce.

FIGURE 5.1 AVAILABLILITY OF DIVORCE

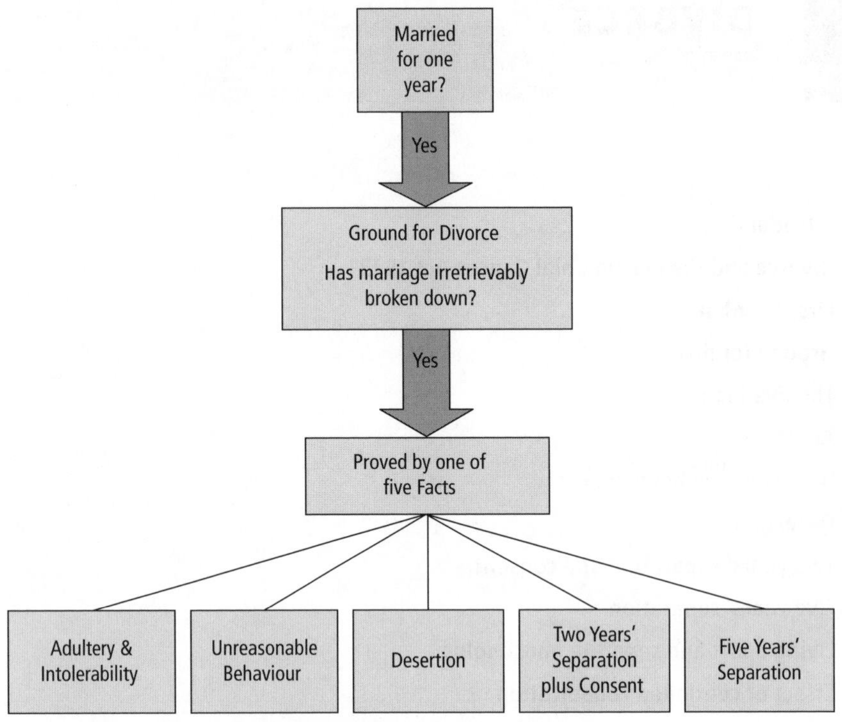

5.2 DIVORCE AND THE MATRIMONIAL CAUSES ACT 1973

The statute covering divorce proceedings is the Matrimonial Causes Act 1973 (MCA 1973). This describes the only ground for divorce and the five facts that prove the ground. The procedure for obtaining a divorce is found in the Family Procedure Rules 2010.

Figure 5.1 is a diagram showing the steps in considering the availability of divorce. Each element is covered within the chapter.

5.3 FIRST-YEAR BAR

S3 MCA 1973 places a bar on divorce within the first year of marriage. S3(1) MCA 1973 states:

> No petition for divorce shall be presented to the court before the expiration of the period of one year from the date of marriage.

Readers may not think that this is a controversial or common point raised in practice; in fact, many newly married people consult a solicitor within the first year of marriage and are often surprised at being told of this rule.

Practical Considerations

There are other options for a client within the first year of marriage:

- judicial separation (see **Chapter 4**): this does not dissolve the marriage but it does allow the courts to resolve issues of money and property;
- nullity: this applies only if the marriage is void or voidable (see **Chapter 4**) due to some fault with the parties' capacity or the formalities of marriage;

- Child Support Agency/child maintenance options (see **Chapter 18**) for maintenance for children;
- Children Act 1989 can be used to resolve disputes about children (see **Chapters 24–26**). This includes residence, contact, and issues involved in raising a child, e.g. the change of a child's name and also orders concerning money and property for the benefit of the child;
- Domestic Proceedings and Magistrates' Courts Act 1978 for maintenance payments or lump sum payments between spouses or for the benefit of a child during the marriage;
- Family Law Act 1996 provides orders for personal protection and occupation of the family home in respect of domestic abuse (see **Chapters 33–36**);

The parties can enter into mediation, negotiation, or another form of alternative dispute resolution (see **Chapter 3**). This may lead to an agreement concerning finances or children (or both) before the petition is issued. This is clearly a cheaper option which is often less fraught than legal proceedings.

The client will simply have to wait if they wish to divorce but it does not prevent the clients entering into negotiation on all issues (see **Chapter 3**). S3(2) MCA 1973 also states that this bar does not prevent the client relying on issues that occurred during the first year of marriage when a petition is presented.

5.4 GROUND FOR DIVORCE

Section 1(1) MCA 1973 states that '... a petition for divorce may be presented to the court by either party to a marriage on the ground that the marriage has broken down irretrievably'.

Practical Considerations

Clients (and some lawyers!) are often confused by the terminology of divorce.

Clients commonly refer to a divorce on the grounds of adultery. There is only one ground for divorce—irretrievable breakdown proved by one of five facts. Without wishing to be terrifyingly pedantic about such matters, the proper way of expressing this would be to say:

> I am divorcing on the ground of irretrievable breakdown, evidenced by the fact of adultery.

However, very few clients ever will!

The court must be satisfied that the marriage has irretrievably broken down. This is evidenced by proving one or more of five facts.

5.5 THE FIVE FACTS

In order to satisfy the ground of irretrievable breakdown, the petitioner must satisfy the court under s1(2) MCA 1973 of one or more of the following facts:

(a) the respondent has committed adultery and the petitioner finds it intolerable to live with the respondent;

(b) the respondent has behaved in such a way that the petitioner cannot reasonably be expected to live with the respondent;

(c) the respondent has deserted the petitioner for a continuous period of at least two years immediately preceding the presentation of the petition;

(d) the parties to the marriage have lived apart for a continuous period of at least two years immediately preceding the presentation of the petition and the respondent consents to the decree being granted;

(e) the parties to the marriage have lived apart for a continuous period of at least five years immediately preceding the presentation of the petition.

Each fact must be proved on the balance of probabilities and each fact has different considerations, which will be discussed individually.

5.6 ADULTERY

There are two limbs to the fact of adultery:

- adultery has been committed;
- the petitioner finds it intolerable to live with the respondent.

5.6.1 WHAT IS ADULTERY?

Adultery is defined as voluntary sexual intercourse between a man and a woman who are not married to each other but one of whom is a married person (*Clarkson v Clarkson* [1930] 143 LT 775).

Adultery must be proved by the applicant. There is no requirement for lurid photographs or witness statements about adultery and proof is normally based on indirect evidence.

The respondent may admit the adultery. This can be done on the acknowledgement of service (see **Chapter 8**) used in adultery cases that asks the question 'Do you admit the adultery alleged in the petition?' Alternatively, the respondent may sign a statement admitting the adultery or write or sign a confession statement of their own.

Practical Considerations

It is sensible to obtain a written statement admitting the adultery before the petition is issued as this will cover the event of the respondent failing to admit the adultery in the acknowledgement. The applicant may be able to claim their costs of issuing the petition in reliance on that confession. Proof can also come from the respondent's solicitor, e.g. an admission in previous correspondence.

If there is no admission, then indirect evidence will have to be presented to the court and adultery will be inferred:

- the respondent and another man/woman are living together. The evidence of adultery would be from the applicant's own observations or from neighbours or friends of the couple, although the court may prefer stronger evidence. In practice it may be easier to proceed under the fact of unreasonable behaviour;
- where the respondent contracts a venereal disease from a person other than the applicant;
- inclination and opportunity to commit adultery. This means that the respondent and the other party had the opportunity to commit adultery, e.g. they have been in public kissing, holding hands, or behaving as an intimate couple, emails, texts, or letters between the couple have been found, and they have spent the night together in a hotel or alone in a house, although the court may prefer stronger evidence. In practice it may be easier to proceed under the fact of unreasonable behaviour;
- the woman has given birth to a child that is not her husband's. Usually, children born during a marriage are presumed to be legitimate but there may be circumstances which give rise to suspicions, e.g. a husband absent around the time of conception (see *Preston-Jones v Preston-Jones* [1951] AC 891);
- findings in other proceedings, e.g. Child Support Agency or a rape conviction.

Please note that a person cannot rely on their own adultery for this fact.

5.6.2 INTOLERABILITY

Normally, an applicant will simply state in the petition that they find it intolerable to live with the respondent and the court will accept this as sufficient evidence of intolerability. The test is subjective: does this applicant find it intolerable to live with this respondent? There does not have to be a link between the adultery and intolerability (*Cleary v Cleary* [1974]1 All ER 498).

5.6.3 THE CO-RESPONDENT

The person with whom the respondent commits adultery can be named in the petition as a co-respondent and made a party to the suit (FPR, r2.7(1)). However, in practice this can complicate matters both procedurally as the petition has to be served on the third party but it can also raise the 'temperature' of the dispute.

The Family Law Protocol issued by the Law Society advises the practitioner that clients should be discouraged from naming co-respondents and should be advised that there is no need to do so in law.

5.7 UNREASONABLE BEHAVIOUR

'Unreasonable behaviour' is the shorthand term used to describe the fact that the respondent has behaved in such a way that the applicant cannot reasonably be expected to live with the respondent: s1(2)(b) MCA 1973.

5.7.1 WHAT IS UNREASONABLE BEHAVIOUR?

It is important to realize that there are no set precedents or list of 'usual' facts found in an unreasonable behaviour petition. Each marriage is different and so the behaviour cited in support of this fact will be different. If a client is disenchanted or bored with their marriage, this may not be sufficient to succeed on this fact. Many clients will instruct you that they simply do not love their spouse and this, again, will not be sufficient to base a petition on this fact. The court will use both a subjective and objective test—would any right-thinking person conclude that *this applicant* cannot reasonably be expected to live with *this respondent,* taking into account all the circumstances of the case and the characters and personalities of the parties?

The court will look at both parties' behaviour and will expect some disparity in conduct and what sort of people the parties are. The whole history of the marriage will be considered. Once all of this evidence has been considered, the court will objectively consider whether it is reasonable for the applicant to continue to live with the respondent.

Dunn J in *Livingstone-Stallard v Livingstone-Stallard* [1974] Fam 47 asked:

> Would any right-thinking person come to the conclusion that this husband has behaved in such a way that this wife cannot be reasonably expected to live with him, taking into account the whole of the circumstances and the character and personalities of the parties?

Practical Considerations

There is no list of behaviour to include in divorce petitions and there can be one or two very serious incidents, or more examples of continuing behaviour. From the author's practice, the following are common examples:

- domestic abuse;
- unreasonable sexual demands;
- 'improper' association with another person, e.g. spending hours in an internet chatroom with a person of the opposite sex;

- debt/financial recklessness;
- verbal abuse, shouting, belittling;
- social isolation;
- excessive/lack of socializing;
- excessive/lack of sex;
- drunkenness.

The court will look at the marriage as a whole to see if there is sufficient unreasonable behaviour to grant a divorce. The applicant's own behaviour will be examined as well as what sort of people the parties are and whether one party is unusually sensitive or vulnerable and the history of the marriage. The court then decides if it is reasonable for the applicant to go on living with the respondent.

For example in *Livingstone-Stallard*, the wife divorced the husband based on his unreasonable behaviour. The wife complained that the husband constantly criticized her dress, friends, cooking, and many other petty aspects of her life and she left after he had thrown her out of the house and locked the door. The evening was very cold and the husband threw cold water over the wife. The wife suffered bruising and required medication for nervous shock. The petition succeeded.

5.7.2 WHETHER BEHAVIOUR IS INTENTIONAL

If the respondent's behaviour is as a result of mental illness, the applicant may still obtain a divorce. The mental illness will be a factor taken into account as part of the consideration of the facts of the case: *Katz v Katz* [1972] 3 All ER 219. In *Katz*, after 13 years of marriage, the husband began to display signs of mental illness and was admitted to a mental hospital. The husband blamed the wife for sending him there and drove her to attempt suicide. When the husband received the divorce petition he read it to the children and treated it as a joke. The court granted a divorce to the wife as the husband's behaviour (for whatever reason) was such that the wife could not reasonably be expected to live with him.

In *Thurlow v Thurlow* [1976] Fam 32, as a result of severe epilepsy, the wife became progressively less able to function and threw things at her mother-in-law, burnt possessions on an electric heater, and wandered into the street. The husband was granted a decree and the court found that full account should be taken of all the obligations of marriage, including the normal burdens imposed by the wife's illness. However, the court considered the length of time the husband had to bear the stresses of the wife's illness, the effect on his health, and the husband's capacity to bear the stresses involved and decided whether he could fairly be required to live with the wife.

5.8 DESERTION

This fact is rarely used in practice. The fact of two years' separation and consent (s1(2)(d) MCA 1973) is more straightforward as, if the respondent has deserted the applicant, it is likely that he is sufficiently disenchanted with the marriage to consent to a divorce. The facts discussed below allowing divorce following separation are easier to establish.

For the fact of desertion under s1(2)(c) MCA 1973, the respondent must have deserted the applicant for a continuous period of at least two years before the presentation of the petition.

There are a number of elements to be proved:

5.8.1 SEPARATION

This can arise because of one spouse leaving the family home but there can be a separation even if the parties still remain under the same roof (see **5.11**).

5.8.2 INTENTION TO DESERT

Even if separation is established, the deserting party must intend to remain permanently separated. This intention can be inferred from words and actions and must be communicated to the other party (*Beeken v Beeken* [1948] P 302).

5.8.3 ABSENCE OF CONSENT

The applicant cannot consent to the desertion and this precludes any kind of formal and informal agreement. A separation agreement will be evidence of consent (*Crabtree v Crabtree* [1953] 1 WLR 708) but a maintenance agreement will not (*Holroyd v Holroyd* [1920] 36 TLR 479).

5.8.4 ABSENCE OF GOOD CAUSE

If the applicant behaves in such a way that the respondent would be justified in leaving her or he may have a reasonable belief that he is justified in leaving her, there will be no desertion.

The wear and tear of ordinary family life will not suffice but an example of such justification can be found in *Quoraishi v Quoraishi* [1985] FLR 780 where a husband took a second wife, even though he was legally entitled to do so.

The desertion must be for a continuous period of two years. Attempts at reconciliation may interrupt this. This is further discussed at **5.12**.

5.9 TWO YEARS' SEPARATION AND CONSENT

To rely on this fact, two matters must be proved:

- the applicant and respondent have lived apart for a continuous period of at least two years immediately preceding the presentation of the petition; and
- the respondent consents to the petition being granted.

Consent must be given by the respondent and this consent must be proved by the applicant. Generally this consent is proved by the respondent signing the acknowledgement of service in divorce proceedings (see **Chapter 8**) and s2(7) MCA 1973 requires that the respondent is given such information as necessary for him to understand the consequences of consenting to a decree being granted and the steps he must take to indicate that he consents. Consent can be withdrawn any time up to the granting of a decree nisi and a respondent may withdraw his consent if he has been misled by the applicant (see **Chapter 8**). Consent can be conditional, e.g. on the applicant paying the costs of the divorce. Should s1(2)(d) MCA 1973 be the only fact relied upon, the divorce will have to be stayed (r2.10(2) FPR).

The parties must have lived apart for a continuous period of two years. See **5.11** and **5.12** for a discussion of 'living apart' and 'continuous separation'.

5.10 FIVE YEARS' SEPARATION

The only requirement for this fact is that the parties have lived apart for five years. No consent is required from the respondent. There is a defence to divorce based on this fact and this is discussed in **Chapter 6**.

5.11 LIVING APART AND SEPARATE HOUSEHOLDS

Living apart has a physical and mental aspect and is often far from clear. S2(6) MCA 1973 states a husband and wife shall be treated as living apart unless they are living with each other in the *same household*.

There will be few problems when the parties live in different houses but problems can arise (as with desertion) when the parties remain under the same roof. The online resources contain articles about the difficulties people face when separating parties cannot afford to run two households. There may also be a dispute about the occupation of the family home and this may fail to be resolved by negotiation or by the provisions of the Family Law Act 1996 (see **Chapter 33** onwards).

In order to prove that there is a separate household, the parties must show they live completely separate lives. In *Mouncer v Mouncer* [1972] 1 All ER 289 the parties failed to show a separate household as the parties still ate together and the wife continued to do housework for both despite the fact that the parties maintained separate bedrooms.

The parties must also demonstrate a mental separation and if the parties have a reason for living apart, e.g. working away or looking after a relative, they will not be living apart. One party must decide the marriage is over, e.g. they write a letter telling their spouse not to come home (*Santos v Santos* [1972] 2 All ER 246).

5.12 EFFECT OF CONTINUED COHABITATION

It is hoped that parties will try to reconcile and to save their marriages and relationships. The MCA 1973 does allow parties to do this and s2 MCA 1973 contains provision to assist the parties.

5.12.1 ADULTERY

S2(1) MCA 1973 allows an applicant to live with the respondent for six months following the discovery of the adultery. If the parties continue to cohabit for more than six months, there will be an absolute bar to the petition based on the fact of adultery. S2(2) MCA 1973 allows the first six months of cohabitation following the discovery of adultery to be disregarded when determining if the applicant finds it intolerable to live with the respondent.

 **Example**

Jill is married to Eddie. The marriage has been under strain for a few years. When Jill starts a new job in January 2010, she meets Peter and starts a sexual relationship with him. Eddie finds out about the adultery on 1 March 2010. He and Jill agree to give the marriage another try and they start seeing a relationship counsellor. On 31 December 2010, Eddie decides the marriage is over.

Eddie cannot rely on Jill's adultery as they have cohabited for over six months since he discovered the adultery in March 2010. He will have to rely on a different fact.

5.12.2 UNREASONABLE BEHAVIOUR

S2(3) MCA 1973 allows parties to cohabit for six months from the final incident relied upon and for this to be disregarded when considering whether the applicant can reasonably be expected to live with the respondent. If the behaviour is ongoing, there is no 'final' incident and so time will not have started to have run. This provision facilitates reconciliation. The MCA 1973 gives no guidance to the courts about the approach to be taken if the cohabitation continues for more than six months after the final incident or if the behaviour and cohabitation continue for some time. The court must then consider whether the continuing cohabitation nullifies the behaviour relied upon in the petition and that the applicant can no longer live with the respondent. There is no absolute bar if the parties cohabit beyond six months but there should be good reasons why the parties continue to cohabit. An example of good reasons for a person not to move out from their partner can be found in *Bradley v Bradley* [1973] 3 All ER 750: Mrs Bradley had a number of small children, no financial resources of her own, and feared domestic violence if she moved out. The court accepted that these were good reasons and granted a divorce.

Example

Brenda is married to Fred and they have seven children. Fred often behaves violently to Brenda, constantly criticizes her appearance, cooking, and childcare, and belittles her in front of her friends. Fred leaves Brenda short of money and takes absolutely no notice of the children. Brenda issues a divorce petition based on the unreasonable behaviour fact and lists the behaviour that has occurred during 2012. As Brenda has no money of her own and nowhere else to take the children, Brenda continues to live with Fred until shortly before the decree nisi. Even though Brenda has cohabited with Fred for more than six months since the last specific incidents in 2012, this will be disregarded as the behaviour was continuing up to the date when she left and so time did not start to run.

5.12.3 CONTINUOUS SEPARATION

S2(5) MCA 1973 states that the court must disregard any period or periods not exceeding six months during which the parties resumed living together but no period during which the parties lived together shall count as part of the period of desertion or the period for which the parties to the marriage lived apart.

This has two practical effects. Any period of reconciliation exceeding six months will mean that the parties wishing to rely on the separation grounds will have to start the period of separation again. And if the parties attempt reconciliation, any period of resumed cohabitation will have to be added on to the period of living apart.

Example

Sherie and Ali have been married for eight years. After a sustained period of unhappiness, they separate and Ali moves into his own flat. After six months apart, Sherie asks Ali to move back into the house to attempt reconciliation. Things go well for a couple of weeks but after a month, Ali moves out as the marriage is clearly over.

Sherie and Ali wish to petition for divorce on the basis of two years' separation and consent. When will they be able to issue the petition?

The parties will have to be living apart for two years. As they lived together during the period of separation for one month, this will have to be added on to the two years.

Sherie and Ali will have to live apart for two years plus one month before a petition can be issued.

SUMMARY POINTS

- The principal statute involved with divorce is the Matrimonial Causes Act 1973.
- A divorce petition is issued by an applicant and the person receiving the petition is the respondent.
- A divorce petition cannot be issued within the first year of marriage.
- The sole ground for divorce is the irretrievable breakdown of marriage.
- To prove the ground for divorce, an applicant must prove one of five facts:
  - adultery and intolerability;
  - unreasonable behaviour;
  - desertion;

  - two years' separation and consent;
  - five years' separation.
- Parties 'living apart' must live separately in terms of both a physical and mental separation.
- Parties may live together to attempt a reconciliation but any period of resumed cohabitation may affect the petition.
- A period of six months of resumed cohabitation after discovery of adultery can be a bar to proceedings.
- In a petition based upon unreasonable behaviour, resumed cohabitation will be taken into account when considering whether or not the parties can reasonably be expected to remain together.
- In separation grounds, any period of cohabitation during the period of separation under six months will be added on to the time the couple have to spend apart. Any period of cohabitation over six months will result in the period of separation starting again.

SELF-TEST QUESTIONS

1. What is the ground for divorce? How is this ground proved?
2. If a client is within the first year of their marriage, advise them on their alternatives to issuing divorce proceedings.
3. Which facts require no period of separation?
4. Sunita and Ash marry in 2001. Their marriage was happy at first but the couple separated recently when Ash admitted to an affair with a work colleague. After three months apart, the couple decide to attempt reconciliation. After two weeks of living together, Sunita decides that the marriage is at an end and she moves out. Advise Sunita which fact she should rely upon and the effect of their attempted reconciliation.

Case Study Two

You are a family law solicitor in Hepple, Burrell & Young's family law department. Today's date is 3 January 2013.

You have a new client, Helena Wilson. Read the attendance note available on the Online Resource Centre and answer the following questions:

- Has the marriage irretrievably broken down?
- Which of the five facts would you choose to base a divorce petition on? Why?
- Are there any other steps which Helena could take at this stage?

online resource centre

Answers to the questions above can be found on the Online Resource Centre: www.oxfordtextbooks.co.uk/orc/familyhandbook13/.

6 DEFENCES TO DIVORCE

6.1 INTRODUCTION

This chapter will:

- **explore the limited defences available in divorce proceedings.**

Defended divorces are not common in practice. There are many reasons for this, not least that most people do not divorce lightly and divorce is a decision taken after a great deal of discussion and careful thought. Some clients are uneasy with separation grounds, as they believe that they will be divorced without having a say in proceedings. There are limited defences available for divorces that are not based on the respondent challenging the veracity of the evidence cited by the applicant. This chapter will discuss these defences although, in practice, reference should be made to practitioner texts for procedural details.

6.2 S5 MATRIMONIAL CAUSES ACT 1973

S5 Matrimonial Causes Act 1973:

(1) The respondent to a petition for divorce in which the applicant alleges five years' separation may oppose the grant of a decree on the ground that the dissolution of the marriage will result in grave financial or other hardship to him and that it would in all the circumstances be wrong to dissolve the marriage.

(2) Where the grant of a decree is opposed by virtue of this section, then—

(a) if the court finds that the applicant is entitled to rely in support of his petition on the fact of five years' separation and makes no such finding as to any other fact mentioned in section 1(2), and

(b) if apart from this section the court would grant a decree on the petition, the court shall consider all the circumstances, including the conduct of the parties to the marriage and the interests of those parties and of any children or other persons concerned, and if of opinion that the dissolution of the marriage will result in grave financial or other hardship to the respondent and that it would in all the circumstances be wrong to dissolve the marriage it shall dismiss the petition.

(3) For the purposes of this section hardship shall include the loss of the chance of acquiring any benefit which the respondent might acquire if the marriage were not dissolved.

If the applicant relies on the five years' separation in her divorce under s1(2)(e) MCA 1973 (see **Chapter 5**), the respondent can oppose the grant of a divorce on the ground that the dissolution of the marriage will result in grave financial or other hardship to him and it would in all the circumstances be wrong to dissolve the marriage. This includes the loss of a chance of acquiring any benefit that the respondent may acquire if the marriage were not dissolved. Note that the hardship must be caused by dissolution, not the breakdown of the marriage.

The court under s5(2) MCA 1973 must consider all the circumstances of the case, including the children of the family, the interests of the parties, and the conduct of the parties.

Commonly, this section was used to claim loss of a pension, especially a widow's pension. In the event of such a claim being made, proposals will have to be made for either a pension sharing order (see **Chapter 19**), a pension attachment order (see **Chapter 19**), or a lump sum order (see **Chapter 19**). Pound for pound compensation for loss of contingent widow's pension rights is not appropriate (see *Le Marchant v Le Marchant* [1966] 3 All ER 610). In *Banik v Banik* [1973] FLR Rep 65, the wife opposed the petition, claiming divorce would make her a social outcast in the society in which she lived. The court found that this could not amount to a defence and granted a decree nisi, but the wife's appeal of this decision was allowed. The Court of Appeal held that grave hardship was a matter of fact and degree, and ordered a retrial before a new judge. At the retrial, the court found as fact that if the decree was granted, the wife would remain living with her brother's family in Calcutta in an unchanged position, dressing and being regarded as still a married woman. She would not be a social outcast, and the decree should therefore be granted subject to an order for the husband to make modest periodic payments. This decision shows that a case based on this argument may be difficult to establish evidentially.

6.3 S10 MATRIMONIAL CAUSES ACT 1973

S10 Matrimonial Causes Act 1973:

(1) Where in any case the court has granted a decree of divorce on the basis of a finding that the applicant was entitled to rely in support of his petition on the fact of two years' separation coupled with the respondent's consent to a decree being granted and has made no such finding as to any other fact mentioned in section 1(2), the court may, on an application made by the respondent at any time before the decree is made absolute, rescind the decree if it is satisfied that the applicant misled the respondent (whether intentionally or unintentionally) about any matter which the respondent took into account in deciding to give his consent.

(2) The following provisions of this section apply where—

(a) the respondent to a petition for divorce in which the applicant alleged two years' or five years' separation coupled, in the former case, with the respondent's consent to a decree being granted, has applied to the court for consideration under subsection (3) below of his financial position after the divorce; and

(b) the court has granted a decree on the petition on the basis of a finding that the applicant was entitled to rely in support of his petition on the fact of two years' or five years' separation (as the case may be) and has made no such finding as to any other fact mentioned in section 1(2) above.

(3) The court hearing an application by the respondent under subsection (2) above shall consider all the circumstances, including the age, health, conduct, earning capacity, financial resources and financial obligations of each of the parties, and the financial position of the respondent, as having regard to the divorce, it is likely to be after the death of the applicant should the applicant die first; and, subject to subsection (4) below, the court shall not make the decree absolute unless it is satisfied—

(a) that the applicant should not be required to make any financial provision for the respondent, or

(b) that the financial provision made by the applicant for the respondent is reasonable and fair or the best that can be made in the circumstances.

(4) The court may if it thinks fit make the decree absolute notwithstanding the requirements of subsection (3) above if—

(a) it appears that there are circumstances making it desirable that the decree should be made absolute without delay, and

(b) the court has obtained a satisfactory undertaking from the applicant that he will make such financial provision for the respondent as the court may approve.

This section contains two distinct provisions.

Under s10(1) MCA 1973 if the petition has been based on two years' separation and consent under s1(2)(d) MCA 1973 (see **Chapter 5**) and the respondent has consented, an application may be made for rescission of a decree nisi if he can satisfy the court that the applicant misled the respondent (whether intentionally or unintentionally) about any matter that the respondent took into account in deciding to give his consent.

If an applicant relies upon either of the separation facts under s1(2)(d) and (e) MCA 1973 (see **Chapter 5**), a respondent can apply to the court for consideration of his financial position under s10(2) MCA 1973. The court considers all the circumstances of the case under s10(3) MCA 1973 and the court will not grant a decree absolute until it is satisfied that:

- the applicant should not be required to make any financial provision for the respondent;
- the financial provision made by the applicant for the respondent is reasonable and fair or the best that can be made in the circumstances.

As financial orders are available following the issue of a divorce petition, this defence is mainly used as a bargaining tool. Please note that under s10(2) MCA 1973, the decree absolute may only be delayed.

6.4 S10A MATRIMONIAL CAUSES ACT 1973

This section was passed in the wake of a number of cases of women being refused a religious divorce by their spouse.

Example

In Jewish religious law, a divorce is granted in the civil court but a divorce must also be obtained through the Beth Din, the Jewish religious courts. This is called a 'get'. It is possible for the husband or wife to withhold consent to the get. The effect of this is that the woman or man becomes agun or augunah (chained) and this has serious consequences. Remarriage without a get can be problematic and if a woman does not have a get and goes on to have another relationship with a man, she will be committing adultery. Any children born from a relationship with another man will be described as 'mamzer'. A mamzer is unable to marry any Jewish person and this status passes to all their descendants and therefore has severe repercussions for the child.

The Family Law Protocol adds guidance on ensuring that a client's religious beliefs are fully explored to ensure that a religious divorce can be obtained if necessary.

S10A will apply where a decree of divorce has been granted but not made absolute and the parties to the marriage:

(a) were married in accordance with

(i) the usages of the Jews, or

(ii) any other prescribed religious usages; and

(b) must cooperate if the marriage is to be dissolved.

Either party can apply to the court for an order that the divorce decree is not to be made absolute until a declaration by both parties that they have taken such steps as are required to dissolve the marriage in accordance with those usages is produced to the court. Such an order will be made if the court believes it is just and reasonable to do so considering all the circumstances of the case. The procedural rules are found in r2.45A Family Proceedings Rules 1991 (FPR).

This will prevent the dissolution of the marriage until the court is satisfied that all steps have been taken to secure a religious divorce. This clearly would be a bargaining point for the party wishing to obtain a religious decree of divorce. Practitioners should be aware of the religious background of their clients to ensure that this point is not missed.

The prescribed religious usages are currently Jewish law. In future, other religious marriages, e.g. under Islamic law, may come within the ambit of this section.

SUMMARY POINTS

- Under s5 MCA 1973, a divorce can be defended on the basis of hardship caused by the dissolution of the marriage.
- Under s10(1) MCA 1973, the respondent may apply to have a decree nisi rescinded if consent was obtained from the respondent after the applicant misled the respondent.
- A decree absolute may be delayed under s10(2) MCA 1973 until financial provision between the parties has been resolved.
- Under s10A MCA 1973, a decree absolute may be delayed until all steps are taken to dissolve the religious marriage.

This is a summary of the defences available to divorce. For further details and for procedural rules, refer to practitioner texts.

SELF-TEST QUESTIONS

1. Your client claims that since her husband moved out of the house six years ago, she has become very short of money. She wishes to defend the divorce on the basis of exceptional hardship. Advise your client on whether she can do this.
2. Your client is Jewish. He wishes to delay the 'get' as he believes he can use this to force his wife into agreeing to a poorer financial settlement than she is entitled to. Advise your client of the consequences of this course of action.

Answers to the questions above can be found on the Online Resource Centre: www.oxfordtextbooks.co.uk/orc/familyhandbook13/.

7 JURISDICTION

7.1 INTRODUCTION

This chapter will:

- **discuss the increasingly important question of jurisdiction in divorce proceedings;**
- **explain the concepts of 'domicile' and 'habitual residence' as they apply to divorce proceedings.**

In order to commence divorce proceedings, the parties must show a connection between themselves and the jurisdiction of the courts. In this text we refer to the jurisdiction of England and Wales. Whilst jurisdiction is not a common problem in practice, we live in an increasingly globalized world where people are more mobile and so may move from their original home to England and Wales. Complexities of jurisdiction may also arise if parties indulge in 'forum shopping'. This is not some complicated form of internet fraud but is when (usually immensely rich) parties try to find the jurisdiction where the law is more favourable to their case. Examples of this can be found in the online resources.

This chapter will discuss the European legislation that governs jurisdiction in divorce and the international law concepts that are a feature of this area of law.

7.1.1 WHY IS JURISDICTION IMPORTANT?

In order to dissolve a marriage, the court must have jurisdiction to hear the case and as a result the law requires the parties to show a connection to courts in England and Wales. The law is found in the Council Regulation (EC) No. 2201/2003, Jurisdiction and the recognition and enforcement of matrimonial matters and in matters of parental responsibility, and is sometimes referred to as 'Brussels II bis' as it replaces Regulation EC/1347/2000 of the same name. The purpose of the regulation is to bring together in one document the provisions on divorce.

The regulation states:

Article 3 General jurisdiction

1. In matters relating to divorce, legal separation or marriage annulment, jurisdiction shall lie with the courts of the Member State
   (a) in whose territory:
      - the spouses are habitually resident, or
      - the spouses were last habitually resident, insofar as one of them still resides there, or
      - the respondent is habitually resident, or

- in the event of a joint application, either of the spouses is habitually resident, or
- the applicant is habitually resident if he or she resided there for at least a year immediately before the application was made, or
- the applicant is habitually resident if he or she resided there for at least six months immediately before the application was made and is either a national of the Member State in question or, in the case of the United Kingdom and Ireland, has his or her 'domicile' there;

(b) of the nationality of both spouses or, in the case of the United Kingdom and Ireland, of the 'domicile' of both spouses.

This regulation amended s8(2) Domicile and Matrimonial Proceedings Act 1973 and this states that:

2. The court shall have jurisdiction to entertain proceedings for divorce or judicial separation if (and only if)—
   (a) the court has jurisdiction under the Council Regulation; or
   (b) no court of a Contracting State has jurisdiction under the Council Regulation and either of the parties to the marriage is domiciled in England and Wales on the date when the proceedings are begun.

A 'contracting state' means one of the original parties to the regulation, namely Belgium, Germany, Greece, Spain, France, Ireland, Italy, Luxembourg, the Netherlands, Austria, Portugal, Sweden, and the UK. Denmark is not a contracting state (see a European law text for further details).

There have been recent developments concerning couples who live in many different jurisdictions. Justice Ministers in the EU have reached agreement allowing couples of different European nationalities to choose which divorce laws will apply to them. Where the spouses are from different countries, living apart in different countries, or are from the same country but living abroad, they will be able to choose which nation's laws should apply to their divorce. The agreement will apply where one of a divorcing couple has a connection with any of the following states: Austria, Belgium, Bulgaria, France, Germany, Hungary, Italy, Latvia, Luxembourg, Malta, Portugal, Romania, Slovenia, and Spain. At the time of printing, the European Parliament has still to legislate upon the arrangement but it is thought that the momentum behind the scheme makes it likely that it will be passed.

The United Kingdom and the Republic of Ireland have not acceded to the proposed scheme.

There are some concepts contained within these rules that require some further explanation before the scope of the court's jurisdiction becomes clearer.

7.2 HABITUAL RESIDENCE

The principal definition of habitual residence is found in the case of *Mark v Mark* [2004] 1 FLR 1069, confirmed by the House of Lords at [2005] UKHL 42.

The petitioner wife had not received indefinite leave to remain in the UK at the time of divorce proceedings and was categorized as an 'overstayer'. The Court of Appeal held (and the House of Lords confirmed) that the petitioner was habitually resident and domiciled in England and Wales despite her immigration status. Thorpe LJ stated that it would be a breach of Art. 6 of the European Convention on Human Rights if the petitioner were to be denied access to the court.

In *Ikimi v Ikimi* [2001] 2 FLR 1288 the Court of Appeal considered that to be 'habitually resident' was meant to be the same as 'ordinarily resident'. In this case, the residence was 161 days in the relevant year. However, in *Armstrong v Armstrong* [2003] 2 FLR 378 the husband spent one-fifth of the year in England and Wales and the court decided this was not sufficient to show 'a sufficient degree of continuity to be properly described as settled' and so he was not habitually resident in England and Wales.

7.3 DOMICILE

This book contains only an outline of this extremely complex area of law. Domicile is a matter of private international law and reference should be made to textbooks and practitioner texts. Domicile is not the same as nationality and the two are considered separately. Again, reference should be made to specialist texts.

Domicile describes the link an individual has with a particular legal system and is used to determine which country's law should govern disputes. It is not simply a question of asking where a person lives, as domicile and residence are not synonymous.

Domicile is a link to a legal system and not to a country, e.g. I have a domicile of England and Wales, not the UK. The UK has three separate legal systems: England and Wales, Scotland, and Northern Ireland.

Every person has a domicile; in fact, a person can hold more than one domicile at one time. Domicile can change over the course of an individual's lifetime as their life changes and a person is never without a domicile.

There are three types of domicile:

- domicile of origin;
- domicile of dependence; and
- domicile of choice.

7.3.1 DOMICILE OF ORIGIN

When a baby is born, they are attributed with a domicile: their domicile of origin.

If a child has married parents, the child will take as their domicile the domicile of their father at the time of their birth. A child of unmarried parents will take the domicile of their mother. The place of the child's birth is irrelevant as the child will take the domicile of the parent. A person retains the domicile of origin throughout their life but it may be superseded by a different domicile of dependence or choice; but it will revive in the absence of another type of domicile.

7.3.2 DOMICILE OF DEPENDENCE

As above, a child will acquire their domicile from their parents. If the domicile of a parent changes, so will the child's domicile. This is the domicile of dependence. As before, the child of married parents will take the father's domicile and the child of unmarried parents will take the mother's domicile. A child acquires an independent domicile when they are 16 years old but will retain the domicile of dependence until they acquire a domicile of choice. A wife does not take the domicile of her husband (and vice versa).

7.3.3 DOMICILE OF CHOICE

For a person to acquire a domicile by choice, there are two requirements:

- residence; and
- intention.

A person must live in a country that is not the country of their domicile of origin. They must take up residence; an intention to live there is not sufficient. As well as actually taking up residence the person must also decide to live there permanently, or at least indefinitely. Intention can be inferred from all the circumstances of the person's life, e.g. what they say or do etc.

Example

Milly, Molly, and Mandy all have a domicile of origin in England and Wales. Their lives are changing and they wonder what their domicile is ...

Milly wishes to live in New Zealand. She has looked at some brochures and read some books and intends to live there at some point in the future.

Molly has been seconded by her law firm to Tokyo for six months. Molly likes the city but is homesick and wants to come back to England as soon as possible.

Mandy has moved to Edinburgh with her job. She has fallen in love with the city, bought a flat, and wishes to stay there permanently.

Answers:

Milly has insufficient intention to live in New Zealand (and hasn't actually moved there) and has not changed her domicile.

Molly does not intend to stay in Tokyo and so has not changed her domicile.

Mandy has sufficient intention to remain in Scotland and so has changed her domicile to a domicile of choice.

In *R v R (Divorce: Jurisdiction: Domicile)* [2006] 1 FLR 389, a woman claimed domicile of choice in France. The court required a fixed and settled intention to abandon her domicile of origin and to settle permanently in France, and that this must be proved beyond a mere balance of probabilities. This could not be established simply by making declarations or acquiring a home. The woman's driving licence, passport, nationality, bank accounts, credit cards, and medical insurance were all English and this undermined her claim to have acquired a domicile of choice in France.

Domicile of choice can change. If a person gives up residence in that country and decides that they intend not to live there permanently or indefinitely, domicile of choice can be lost. Both residence and intention must change. Domicile of choice may change immediately if the two elements are present in the new jurisdiction. If a person does not immediately acquire a new domicile of choice, the person's domicile will revert back to the domicile of origin, although it is not a requirement for a domicile of choice to be taken immediately.

7.4 JURISDICTION IN PRACTICE

If a client seeks a divorce, jurisdiction must be ascertained. In Case Study Two, the initial interview covers this point and it should be a point on any checklist used in practice. In practice it is usually very easy to establish jurisdiction through habitual residence or domicile. If the domicile of the client is uncertain, habitual residence is usually easier to establish.

If proceedings are issued in another contracting state before England and Wales, the court of the state in which proceedings are issued has exclusive jurisdiction. In this situation, the court has a limited scope for discretion. A practitioner text should be consulted.

The Online Resource Centre offers further reading on this topic.

SUMMARY POINTS

- Brussels II (see **7.1.1**) provides the basis for jurisdiction in divorce and the Domicile and Matrimonial Proceedings Act 1973 reflects the law of jurisdiction in divorce.
- Jurisdiction is based on habitual residence and domicile.
- Habitual residence is a concept that considers where a person lives on a day-to-day basis.
- Domicile can be based on origin, dependence, or choice.
- Domicile of origin is based on where a person is born.
- Domicile of dependence depends on where a person's father or mother lives when a person is below the age of 16 years.
- Domicile of choice is based on the intention of a person to reside somewhere permanently.

SELF-TEST QUESTIONS

1. What is 'jurisdiction'?
2. List the ways in which a court in England and Wales may have jurisdiction in a divorce case.
3. What are the two requirements that must be established for a person to have a domicile of choice?
4. Where are you domiciled?

Case Study Two

David Wilson was born in Scotland and moved to England in 1993. He set up his own business in 1995, married Helena in 1995, and bought a house for his family in Longtown, England in 1999. Since his separation from Helena, he spends a number of weekends in Scotland, with his parents.

Explain where (and if) David has his habitual residence.

Answers to the questions above can be found on the Online Resource Centre: **www.oxfordtextbooks.co.uk/orc/familyhandbook13/.**

8 PROCEDURE FOR A MATRIMONIAL ORDER

8.1 INTRODUCTION

This chapter will:

- **discuss the steps a solicitor should take before issuing divorce proceedings;**
- **explore the complete procedure for obtaining an undefended divorce.**

This chapter covers the procedure for obtaining a divorce. The procedure for obtaining civil partnership dissolution is procedurally identical to that of obtaining a divorce, although obviously the documentation differs. **Chapter 10** covers the law for obtaining a dissolution order.

The procedure for obtaining a divorce is governed by the Family Procedure Rules 2010 (FPR). These rules came into force in 2011. The rules can be a little confusing. The FPR refer to 'matrimonial orders' and this includes:

- a decree of divorce;
- a decree of nullity;
- a decree of judicial separation.

The correct term for proceedings is 'an application for a matrimonial order' rather than divorce proceedings. Confusingly, the forms for divorce have changed little in content and are still called divorce petitions. This chapter will refer to 'applications for a matrimonial order' when describing a client seeking a divorce.

As a result, the terminology used by the rules could be misleading. For the rest of this book, the person issuing the proceedings for a matrimonial order will be known as the 'applicant' and the person against whom the application is made is referred to as the 'respondent'. It is a matter of note that the Ministry of Justice chose not to dispense with the outdated divorce petition at the time of implementation of the new rules.

This chapter covers the procedure for an application for a matrimonial order, from drafting a divorce petition through to decree absolute. Other chapters deal with some procedural aspects in more detail, e.g. jurisdiction in **Chapter 7**.

8.2 FLOWCHART

FIGURE 8.1 THE MAJOR STEPS TAKEN DURING DIVORCE PROCEEDINGS

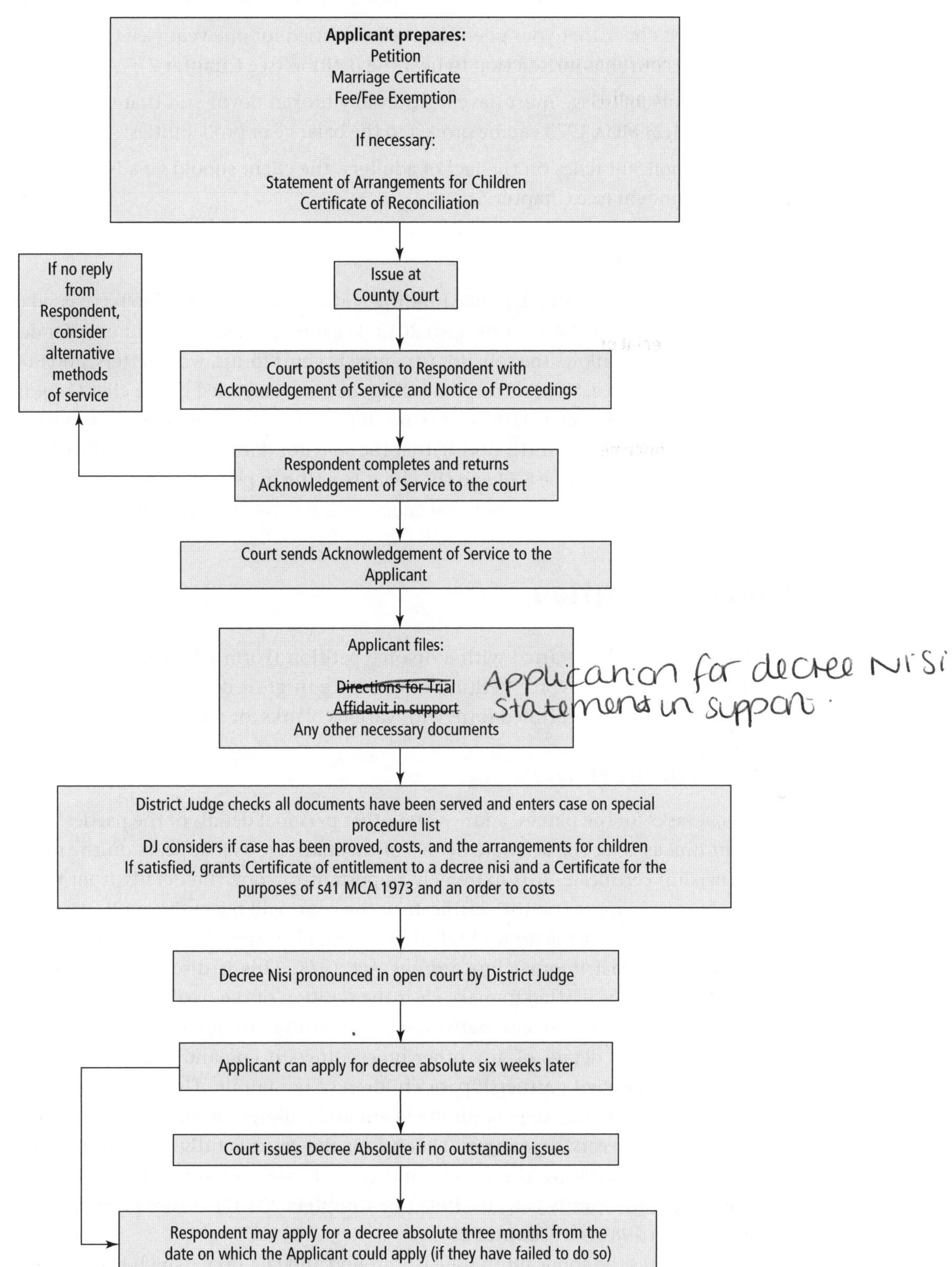

8.3 PRELIMINARY CONSIDERATIONS

There are some considerations before the issue of proceedings:

- the client is validly married (see **Chapter 4**);
- the case must be funded either privately or by public funding (see **Chapter 2**) and this must be sorted out first as the fee alone for divorce is considerable;
- the client should have been advised on the possibility of mediation or relationship counselling services, e.g. Relate, unless it is not appropriate to your client (see **Chapter 3**);
- you must check that your client has been married for one year (see **Chapter 5**) and also that the court has jurisdiction to hear the petition (see **Chapter 7**);
- the client's marriage must have irretrievably broken down and that one of the five facts under s1(2) MCA 1973 can be proved to the balance of probabilities;
- if the applicant relies on the fact of adultery, the client should be advised about citing a co-respondent (see **Chapter 5**).

8.3.1 PUBLIC FUNDING

As considered in **Chapter 2**, public funding is available to a client who has passed the merits and means test (see **2.4.1**) until April 2013. Legal help is used to fund undefended divorce proceedings and allows the solicitor to complete court forms, write letters, and take steps to finalize the divorce. Should the proceedings become defended or the client require further assistance with financial matters (see **Chapter 14**), the client will have to apply for different forms of funding. It is worth noting that the solicitor does not go on to the court record as 'acting' for the client (see **8.6**) and the client is acting in person. From April 2013, there will be no public funding for divorce and clients will have to pay privately.

8.4 DIVORCE PETITION

All divorce suits are started with a divorce petition (Form D8) and the supporting notes on completing the divorce petition offer advice in great detail on the completion of the petition. This is a pre-printed form with various blanks for completion.

8.4.1 DRAFTING THE PETITION

Part one: asks for the names, address and other personal details of the parties.

Part two: asks for the accurate details of the marriage as it appears on the marriage/civil partnership certificate. It is extremely important to copy the details from the certificate exactly as they appear on the certificate or the court will reject the application.

Part three: asks for the ground relied on to establish the court's jurisdiction under s5(2) Domicile and Matrimonial Proceedings Act 1973. This is discussed in **Chapter 7**. The petition should be drafted to make clear the position of the parties and the notes for guidance suggest a number of alternatives (see **Case Study Two** for guidance).

Part four: seeks details of any other proceedings in England and Wales with reference to the marriage, civil partnership, or children of the family. The part also seeks details of arrangements made to support the applicant and children of the family where the petition is based on five years' separation. This means the court is fully aware of past and present proceedings concerning the family and may include non-molestation and occupation orders under the Family Law Act 1996 (see **Chapters 33–37**) or care proceedings under the Children Act 1989 (see **Chapter 29**).

Part five: asks the applicant to state the ground and fact upon which the petition is based.

Part six: this is the 'Statement of Case' and seeks the particulars of fact upon which the petition is based.

Part seven: seeks details of the children of the family including gender and date of birth of all children of the family under s52 MCA 1973. The part also seeks details of children who are not children of the family.

Part eight: seeks details of any special assistance or facilities required by the applicant should attendance at court be required.

Part nine: seeks details required for the service of the petition.

Part ten is the prayer—see **8.4.3**.

8.4.2 DRAFTING PARTICULARS

The particulars give details to support the fact being used. The following is a brief and very general guide to drafting particulars. Many firms have precedent banks from old cases, practitioner's texts, and precedent texts to assist drafting.

There is no set formula for drafting the particulars of a petition but certain guidelines are offered below.

In adultery cases, a statement of when and where the adultery took place is necessary with specific dates if possible. If not known, a description of how the respondent had the opportunity and the inclination to commit adultery must be stated. The 'co-respondent' (the third party involved in the adultery) need not be named (see **5.6.3**).

Example

The respondent committed adultery on 13 May 2012 with his work colleague during a staff morale exercise at the Tenbury Hotel in Longtown. The respondent admitted the adultery to the applicant on 14 May 2012. The respondent started to cohabit with the work colleague on 15 May 2012 and the adultery continues. The applicant finds it intolerable to continue living with the respondent.

For unreasonable behaviour, the general rule (often repeated) is that the structure of an unreasonable behaviour petition is 'first, worst, last'. The idea is that generally up to 5–6 individual incidents of behaviour should be cited chronologically with the first incident with dates, the worst incidents listed, and completed by the last incident (unless the behaviour is continuing). Each new occasion of behaviour should be set out in a separate paragraph. The date should be stated. If the client cannot remember the exact date, then the month should be given. The author has resorted to stating the season on some occasions with a client with a poor memory (e.g. 'in the summer of 1999') although this is less than ideal.

Sufficient detail should be given to allow the court to assess the marriage properly and the effect of the behaviour on the applicant should be stated, even if it is obvious. Be temperate with your language as the respondent will read the petition and a balance must be struck between obtaining a decree and not unduly fanning the flames of the dispute. See **Case Study Two** for an example of such particulars. It is vital to state the effect of the behaviour on the applicant as this will help the court to understand how the particulars fulfil the subjective test required (see **Chapter 5**).

Example

Some examples of drafting particulars for unreasonable behaviour petitions featuring common types of behaviour are the following:

On the 1st day of September 2007 when the respondent was repairing the car the applicant struck him about the head and back with some force with a spanner causing bruising. The applicant sought medical treatment and was deeply shocked by the incident.

During 2007 the respondent has incurred large debts as a result of reckless and extravagant spending on clothing and the applicant is often telephoned by creditors to take proceedings to recover the debt. The applicant has often felt extremely worried about these debts. The respondent ignores the applicant's pleas to moderate her spending knowing the distress it causes him.

Since the date of the marriage the respondent has displayed an unwarranted and irrational sense of jealously where the applicant is concerned which has persisted despite the assurances of the applicant. The respondent persists in this jealously despite knowing that the applicant feels anxious and afraid.

For desertion, the date and surrounding circumstances of the respondent's desertion should be given with sufficient detail to show the respondent's intention to bring cohabitation to an end.

Separation cases should give the date and circumstances of the separation. If the parties continue to live under the same roof, sufficient information should be given to demonstrate the existence of separate households.

8.4.3 THE PRAYER

The prayer concludes the petition.

The prayer asks the court to dissolve the marriage as well as a prayer for costs and financial relief.

Costs should be given careful consideration, with a possible agreement reached before the issue of the petition. The general view is that an applicant receiving legal help should not request costs as the return for the applicant would be minimal and it may inflame the dispute if the respondent is asked to pay costs. Practice seems to vary around the country. A happy medium may be to draft a claim for costs in the terms that the applicant does not claim costs unless the petition is defended or the statutory charge (see **Chapter 2**) arises.

The prayer for financial orders should be left unamended as the full range of financial orders should be claimed, even if it is just for the claims to be dismissed.

Where the applicant is relying on desertion or separation facts the date is important, as specified periods of time, e.g. two or five years, must have elapsed before the petition is presented.

The petition is signed at the bottom by the acting solicitor or the applicant in person, if being advised under legal help. The names and addresses of the people to be served, i.e. the respondent, the co-respondent, if any, and the applicant's address for service (which is the name and address of the firm acting or usually 'care of' the firm, if the applicant is being advised as an applicant 'in person' under legal help) are inserted.

8.4.4 AMENDMENTS AND ADDITIONS TO A PETITION

A divorce petition may be amended by a party making an application for a matrimonial order if it is done before an answer is filed (r7.13 FPR 2010). When an amendment is made, it must be served correctly on the other parties according to r7.8 FPR 2010. An amendment can be made with the agreement of the parties or with permission of the court (r7.13(4) FPR 2010).

Amendments and substitutions are generally permitted if no injustice will be caused to the respondent.

Despite these provisions, it is important to get the petition right first time. Any amendments or supplemental petitions will slow down proceedings and increase costs.

8.5 STATEMENT OF ARRANGEMENTS FOR CHILDREN

If the parties have children (whether children of both parties or children of the family) a statement of arrangements for children must be completed as part of the documentation to issue proceedings. A child of the family is defined in s52 MCA 1973 in relation to married parties or to two people who are civil partners of each other:

- a child of them both; and
- any other child, other than a child placed with them as foster parents by a local authority or voluntary organization, who has been treated as a child of the family.

The statement of arrangements must be filed in addition to the petition, marriage certificate, etc. where there are children:

- under 16; or
- over 16 but under 18 if they are receiving education or are training for a trade, profession, or vocation.

The form D8A must be used in proceedings.

The statement may be agreed with the respondent prior to the issue of the proceedings. If this is the case, he will sign the form and it will be lodged on issue signed by both parties. This is the most desirable course of action. If the respondent has not signed the form before issue, it will be signed by the applicant only (in practice the respondent does not usually sign in advance). The respondent will then deal with the form when served upon him after issue. He is free to file his own statement of arrangements if the applicant's statement is not accepted (r7.12(7) FPR 2010). This may potentially result in the district judge being dissatisfied with the arrangements.

The contents of the statement of arrangements are:

- details of the children including names, dates of birth, relationship to the applicant;
- home details including address, nature of accommodation, other occupants;
- whether property rented or owned;
- education and training details;
- childcare and maintenance;
- contact arrangements in existence;
- details of the children's health.

The respondent will be required to answer additional questions on the acknowledgement of service form if children are involved to indicate whether he agrees with the proposals in the applicant's statement of arrangements. The form tells the respondent that he may file his own statement if he wishes and advises him to send it to the court office with the acknowledgement if this is what he wishes to do. A copy of a D8A can be found at the end of this chapter.

8.6 ISSUING THE DIVORCE PETITION

Practical Considerations

Civil litigation terms

Issue: to commence proceedings at court. The court will seal the application (stamp it with a court stamp), open a file, and give the proceedings a number. This number will identify the case and should be used on all court documents and correspondence with the court.

Serve: to formally give a document to a party. This can be as simple as posting documents by first class post.

File: to give a document to the court.

'Acting': a solicitor 'acts' in court proceedings when the client pays for them to do so or public funding allows a solicitor to do so.

On the court record: the solicitor is recorded on the court file as acting for the client. All correspondence will be sent to the solicitor and a client will incur the costs of this.

The marriage certificate must be filed with the petition (r2.6(2) FPR 2010). If the client does not have a copy, many practices encourage the client to obtain their own copy, particularly if publicly funded.

Divorce proceedings are issued in a divorce county court. This includes the Principal Registry (r7.5 FPR 2010).

To issue a petition, a number of documents must be taken to the court:

- petition;
- marriage certificate;
- statement of arrangements for children;
- certificate of reconciliation (D6) (see **8.7**);
- fee (or fee exemption).

The numbers of each document will depend upon the number of parties. A copy must be supplied to be kept on the court file and one for each party to be served.

Practical Considerations

Mr and Mrs Wilson are to divorce based on the fact of unreasonable behaviour. There is no co-respondent and Mrs Wilson is a litigant in person.

To issue proceedings, the documents required are:

- divorce petition and one copy;
- marriage certificate;
- statement of arrangements for children and one copy;
- fee exemption.

There is no D6 as Mrs Wilson is not legally represented.

Most solicitors also give a copy of the documentation to their client and keep a copy on the client's file.

The applicant's solicitor will ask the client to approve the issue documentation and sign where necessary. The solicitor should always obtain the client's authority to issue, since circumstances may have changed since the initial instructions. There may, for instance, have been reconciliation between the parties.

The proceedings are issued at the county court office and may be issued in person or by post. The court staff will check the documentation. If there are any obvious errors, they will return it for correction (e.g. if the original marriage certificate has not been enclosed or if the petition is not signed). If all is in order, the staff will issue the divorce proceedings by opening a court file and allocating a case number. The number must be quoted in all subsequent dealings with the court and on all documentation. The court staff will send the applicant's solicitor notification (on a standard form) of the issue date and case number.

8.7 D6: CERTIFICATE OF RECONCILIATION

Earlier it was said that this certificate is only filed when a solicitor is fully acting on behalf of the client. Legal help for divorce does not permit a solicitor to 'act' in the court proceedings for the client (the public funding only covers advice and assistance with court documents). The client is considered to be acting 'in person'.

If a person has legal help for divorce proceedings, this document is *not* required.

This certificate is a standard form that certifies whether or not the solicitor has discussed with the applicant the possibility of reconciliation and/or given the applicant the names and addresses of persons qualified to help effect reconciliation, e.g. Relate. The solicitor does not have to discuss reconciliation or give names of relevant organizations. In some cases, he may feel that it is inappropriate, e.g. because of domestic abuse. What he does need to do, however, is to state whether he has discussed the possibility.

8.8 FEE

There is a court fee for issuing a divorce petition: £340 (at the time of writing).

Some clients will qualify for a fee exemption or remission. A standard court form, an application for a fee exemption or remission, must be prepared and filed with the issue documents if an exemption or remission is claimed.

Clients who are being advised under legal help may be exempt from payment of the issue fee, but must provide details of their solicitor on the form and include evidence to show that they are receiving such help (e.g. a solicitor's letter). The court staff may contact the solicitor to verify any information given.

Clients who are in receipt of certain benefits such as income support or working families tax credit are also exempt, but they must include up-to-date evidence of receipt of such benefits (e.g. a letter from the Benefits Agency or a payment book).

Other clients may apply for fee exemption/remission (e.g. on grounds of 'hardship'), but must provide full details and evidence of their means. The court staff will then make a decision upon the fee to be paid and notify the client accordingly.

8.9 SERVICE OF THE PETITION

The normal method of service is by first class post. The court will send the respondent a sealed copy of the petition and an acknowledgement of service with detachable guidance notes.

If the petition is based on the adultery fact and has chosen to name a co-respondent, the co-respondent will also have to be served with a copy of the petition.

The respondent should complete the acknowledgement of service and return it to the court, showing that he has been properly served. If a respondent does not return the acknowledgement to the court, the applicant will have to take other steps, as she cannot proceed with the divorce until she can prove that the petition has been served.

In *Akbar v Rafiq* [2006] 1 FLR 27 the decrees nisi and absolute were held to be void as there had been no proper service of the divorce papers on the respondent wife. The court held that it was not sufficient to state after the event that, although the petition had not been duly served, the respondent wife knew of the proceedings. The FPR 2010 were designed to ensure that the respondent has direct personal knowledge of the divorce proceedings instituted by the applicant.

The applicant cannot serve the petition personally (r6.5(3) FPR 2010).

There are several options.

8.9.1 SERVICE BY COURT BAILIFF

Under r6.9 FPR 2010, service may be made by a court bailiff. Postal service is expected to have been attempted and an application must be made to the court on a standard form. It is helpful to supply a photograph or description of the respondent. Court bailiffs are very experienced at serving respondents, even in difficult circumstances where they are evading service. A bailiff will attempt to obtain the respondent's signature on an endorsement of service. This will satisfy the court that service has been effected.

8.9.2 PERSONAL SERVICE

This can be effected by a process server or enquiry agent (a person employed to serve documents) or by the applicant's solicitor himself (more unusually). Process servers will charge a fee for their services, but may be more successful in serving difficult respondents. Proof of personal service is provided by an affidavit of service, which must be sworn by the individual effecting service, indicating the date, time, and place of the service. This affidavit is then filed with the county court office as proof of service and, again, will satisfy the court that service has been effected.

8.9.3 DEEMED SERVICE

Under r6.15 and r6.16 FPR 2010, where the respondent has not returned an acknowledgement of service but the applicant can satisfy the court that he has received the petition, the court can grant an order that service be 'deemed'. This means that the court can be satisfied that the respondent has been served or had notice of the proceedings.

Under r6.16 FPR 2010, the evidence that will satisfy the court that service has occurred will differ from case to case: e.g. the respondent may have referred to having received the petition in a letter to the applicant or some third party. In all cases, however, the evidence will be indirect, e.g. a letter is received from a solicitor instructed by the respondent who is subsequently left without instructions.

Example

During the author's practice of divorce proceedings, a respondent returned the divorce petition and accompanying documents to the author torn into tiny pieces and with an abusive message written on the envelope. The respondent helpfully signed the abusive message. An application for deemed service was made with the message exhibited to the application. Deemed service was granted.

8.9.4 SUBSTITUTED SERVICE

Orders from the court for substituted service are not common. If granted, this means that service is effected in another way (e.g. by placing an advertisement of the proceedings in a place where it is likely to come to the attention of the respondent or by leaving the documents with a relative) (r6.19 FPR 2010). Before granting this type of order the district judge must be satisfied that other service methods have failed, that extensive attempts have been made to serve the respondent, and that there is a reasonable probability that the advertisement or other proposed form of substituted service will come to the respondent's attention.

8.9.5 DISPENSING WITH SERVICE

It should be noted that the court has the power to make an order that service should be dispensed with. Such an order is only granted in exceptional circumstances, where the applicant cannot trace the respondent, despite strenuous efforts.

Practical Considerations

A district judge will expect the applicant to make exhaustive enquiries of the whereabouts of the respondent. Enquiries will have been made with relatives, friends, former employers, and neighbours. Banks, accountants, former solicitors, doctors, and dentists should be asked to forward a stamped envelope to their client, which will avoid them revealing his address. The Department of Work and Pensions, if able to identify the respondent, will forward the petition to him.

Under r6.20 FPR 2010, the district judge must be satisfied that it is 'impracticable' to serve the respondent by any other means available under r6.20 FPR 2010 or it is otherwise 'necessary or expedient' to dispense with service of a copy of a petition on the respondent before an order dispensing with service will be made.

8.10 ACKNOWLEDGEMENT OF SERVICE

The acknowledgement of service contains a series of questions, which include whether the respondent has received the petition, the existence of any proceedings relating to the marriage already continuing outside England and Wales, the respondent's domicile, habitual residence and nationality, and whether the respondent intends to defend the case and details of any solicitor acting for him.

The acknowledgement of service also contains other questions, applicable only to specific divorces. In an adultery divorce, the respondent will be asked whether he admits the adultery alleged in the petition. In a two years' separation plus consent divorce, he will be asked if he consents to a divorce.

The acknowledgement must be signed by either the respondent or his solicitor, if one is acting for him. In divorce based on adultery or two years' separation plus consent, the acknowledgement must be signed by the respondent personally, as it will be used to prove not only procedural matters but also an element of the divorce fact.

The respondent must return the acknowledgement to the court within seven days of receipt. A copy will be sent to the applicant by the court.

If the respondent does not return the acknowledgement then, as explained at **8.9**, the applicant will have to take other steps to effect service or to proceed without service. Once the court is satisfied that service has been effected or dispensed with service, the applicant can proceed with the divorce.

If the respondent does return the acknowledgement, the next step of the applicant depends upon one of the respondent's responses in the acknowledgement.

If the respondent has answered 'no' to the question 'Do you intend to defend?' the applicant may proceed to the next stage of the divorce (see **8.11**) after the expiry of seven days from the service of the petition on the respondent.

If the respondent has indicated that he does intend to defend the petition, he has 25 days to file an answer. An answer is broadly equivalent to a defence in civil litigation and it must answer the allegations made in the particulars of the petition. As defended divorces are beyond the scope of this text, reference should be made to a specialist practitioner text.

A co-respondent has the same opportunity as a respondent to give notice of intention to defend and to file an answer (an even more compelling reason to persuade the client not to name a co-respondent).

If an answer is not filed within the 25-day period, the applicant can proceed with her divorce as an undefended divorce (see **8.11**).

8.11 THE SPECIAL PROCEDURE AFFIDAVIT

Evidence of the marital breakdown is supplied by the applicant for the special procedure by affidavit. An affidavit is a statement sworn (or affirmed) in accordance with the religious beliefs of the applicant and the questions will vary according to the fact relied upon. The affidavit is also an opportunity to record any changes since the issue of petition, e.g. a change of address.

The applicant will verify that she identifies the respondent's signature on the copy of the acknowledgement of service and formally requests a decree dissolving the marriage.

The affidavit must be sworn before an independent solicitor (i.e. not one in the firm advising the applicant) or a court official. It is filed with the county court.

The affidavit must be accompanied by a form of application for directions for trial. This, again, is a pre-printed form and asks the district judge for 'directions for trial' of the action by entering it into the special procedure list.

The special procedure is, in fact, the normal procedure in undefended cases and is the procedure in virtually all undefended cases. The divorce case will proceed without a hearing in court even if there are subsequent court hearings about children or financial matters.

A concern frequently expressed by clients is whether they will have to attend court during the proceedings. The vast majority of clients will not have to attend court and their divorce will not generally be publicized. On rare occasions, the parties may have to attend, for example, to discuss costs, or if the case becomes defended.

Occasionally, the applicant will file further affidavits along with these documents. These might include, for example, medical evidence where the petition was based on the unreasonable behaviour fact and the applicant received medical treatment for injuries caused by the respondent's behaviour or it might be necessary to file an affidavit from a relevant person (e.g. an enquiry agent) to substantiate the fact that adultery took place.

If there are children, the affidavit will also verify the contents of the statement of arrangements for children.

8.12 CONSIDERATION BY DISTRICT JUDGE

Once the affidavit has been filed, the file will be passed for the consideration of the district judge. The district judge will review the case to see whether it can be entered in the special procedure list. She will first check that:

- the respondent (and any co-respondent) has been properly served (or service has been dispensed with);
- no intention to defend has been filed and that the time limit for doing so has expired, or that an intention to defend was filed but no answer has been filed and the time limit for doing so has expired;
- the respondent has provided consent in respect of a petition based on two years' separation and consent;
- the adultery has been admitted or proved.

The respondent's consent/admission is proved by the applicant identifying the respondent's signature in her special procedure affidavit as corroborative evidence of the allegations made in the petition (r7.20(5) FPR 2010).

The district judge has to consider the evidence provided to decide whether the ground for divorce (the irretrievable breakdown of marriage) is proved. The district judge must be satisfied that the applicant has sufficiently proved the contents of the petition. As the wording is 'sufficiently' this is not envisaging a high standard of proof. Once the district judge is satisfied the petition has been proved, she will certify that the applicant is entitled to a decree.

This is a standard court form and not only certifies that the applicant is entitled to a decree, but also makes any orders for costs and gives notice of the place, time, and date for pronouncement of the decree nisi (see **8.14**).

If the district judge is not satisfied that the petition is proved, she may ask the applicant to file further evidence (r7.20(2(b)) FPR 2010), which would normally be filed by affidavit. Alternatively, the district judge can remove the case from the special procedure list. The parties would then seek further directions for trial.

The district judge will then carry out the duties imposed on the court by s41 Matrimonial Causes Act 1973 if the family has children.

8.13 S41 MATRIMONIAL CAUSES ACT 1973

The court will always ensure that children of a divorcing couple are fully protected in the proceedings.

Under s41 MCA 1973, before granting a decree of divorce, the court must consider:

- whether there are any relevant children; and, if there are,
- whether the court needs to exercise any of its powers in relation to them.

The district judge will check the petition for relevant children and certify the fact. 'Relevant children', for the purposes of s41, are children of the family who are under 16 and children of the family in respect of whom the court directs that s41 should apply. A 'child of the family' is defined above at **8.5**.

The district judge will consider whether the court needs to exercise its powers under the Children Act 1989 (see **Chapter 26**). He will look at the statement of arrangements filed by the applicant and check the acknowledgement of service to see the respondent's reaction to the statement. If the respondent has filed his own statement, this, too, will be considered. It is possible that a dispute has led to the issue of Children Act 1989 proceedings and this will be recorded on the petition and on the court file.

If there are relevant children, the court will go on to consider whether it should exercise its powers and s41 MCA 1973 requires that the court must consider whether it should exercise this power immediately. In the vast majority of cases there will be no need to exercise powers. The court may decide that it requires further evidence about the children and can order that:

- further evidence should be filed;
- a court welfare report should be prepared;
- one or both of the parties should attend before him on a specified time and date.

The district judge may then be satisfied that the children are adequately provided for and certify accordingly.

If the court decides it needs to act but cannot do so immediately, then the court will direct that a decree of divorce cannot be made absolute until the child's welfare has been resolved. This will have the effect of delaying a divorce. This direction will only be made where there are exceptional circumstances that make it desirable in the interests of the child to make one.

In practice, even where there is a fundamental dispute over the child's welfare (e.g. as to with which party he is to live, or indeed whether he should be taken into the care of the local authority) it is unlikely that delaying the divorce will assist the situation and directions under s41 are unusual in practice.

Careful preparation of paperwork and attention to the statement of arrangements will hopefully prevent a delay at this stage of the procedure.

8.14 PRONOUNCEMENT OF DECREE NISI

The applicant's solicitor will receive the two certificates from the court office (i.e. the certificate of entitlement to a decree and the certificate for the purposes of s41). The applicant must be advised of the date, time, and place that the decree nisi will be pronounced. The pronouncement is generally made in open court by a judge or district judge. The applicant can be reassured that this is a purely procedural matter. On the appointed date, the judge enters the courtroom and reads out a list of decree nisi appointments for the day. If there are no objections or representations, the decree nisi is formally pronounced in every case.

The decree nisi does not dissolve the marriage. It is extremely important that the client understands this and does not arrange to be married before the pronouncement of the decree absolute.

The decree nisi is the first decree in divorce proceedings and states that the marriage has broken down irretrievably and that the marriage can be dissolved unless cause be shown within six weeks from the decree why it should not be made absolute.

The form of decree stresses that it is not the final decree and that application for the final decree must be made to the court and that the parties are not free to remarry at this stage.

A copy of the decree nisi will be sent to both parties.

The applicant's solicitor will ask the client to confirm their instructions for the final step to dissolve the marriage.

8.15 MAKING DECREE NISI ABSOLUTE

Following pronouncement of the decree nisi there is a six-week waiting period before a decree absolute is pronounced. The usual practice is that the applicant will apply for a decree absolute following the lapse of six weeks from the pronouncement of decree nisi.

A decree absolute can be expedited for exceptional reasons but this is unusual. The usual practice is that the decree absolute may be applied for six weeks and one day after decree nisi is pronounced, but an applicant is not bound to so apply.

Practical Considerations

A common enquiry from students in the early stages of a family law course concerns the six-week period between decree nisi and decree absolute.

S1(5) Matrimonial Causes Act 1973 states:

> every decree of divorce shall be in the first instance a decree nisi and shall not be made absolute before the expiration of six months from its grant unless the High Court by general order from time to time fixes a shorter period...

In fact, the Matrimonial Causes (Decree Absolute) Order 1972 shortens the period of waiting from six months to six weeks.

The decree absolute is applied for on a standard application form (Form D36).

The application is posted to the court and must be accompanied by a court fee or an application for exemption.

The court staff will check that:

- no appeal has been lodged against the decree nisi;
- the correct amount of time has elapsed following the decree nisi;
- there are no children or, if there are, there is no direction holding up issue of the decree absolute under s41 MCA 1973.

If all is in order the court staff will issue the decree absolute and send a copy to both parties or their solicitors.

When the decree absolute is forwarded to the client, advice should be given on the need to keep the decree safely (in case of remarriage) and the need to consider the effect of divorce on wills and inheritance.

Although a decree absolute has been granted, the client retainer may continue with ongoing disputes about finances or children.

If the applicant fails to apply for the decree absolute, there is provision in the rules for the respondent to apply at a later date (after three months have passed from the earliest date when the applicant could have applied).

Example

P received the decree nisi on 3 June 2013. P can apply for the decree to be made absolute on the 15 July 2013 (six weeks later).

If P does not apply for the decree to be made absolute, R can apply three months after P would have been able to apply: six weeks *plus* three months. So six weeks after 3 June, 15 July, is the earliest time that P could have applied. R will wait a further three months, until 1 October, to apply for decree absolute.

A respondent must provide an affidavit to support their application and obtain an appointment before the court, at which the applicant has the opportunity to show that she will suffer prejudice if a decree absolute is granted. In *Re G (Decree Absolute: Prejudice)* [2003] EWHA 2534 (Fam), the court stated that the mere fact that the financial proceedings had yet to be heard was not a sufficient reason to refuse the decree absolute. The court did not accept the wife's allegations of substantial non-disclosure by the husband within these proceedings, nor that he was likely to frustrate her claims by moving abroad. It is suggested that the outcome may have been different if the wife could have established prejudice arising from, e.g., the loss of the possibility of a widow's pension if her status was changed from that of wife to ex-wife by the grant of a decree absolute prior to the resolution of the ancillary relief proceedings.

Following the decision in *Dennis v Dennis* [2000] Fam 163, the court will not allow an application by the respondent for the decree nisi to be made absolute before the expiry of the three months after the applicant could have applied for decree absolute.

SUMMARY POINTS

- The solicitor will take comprehensive initial instructions and advise about the appropriate divorce fact and the divorce process.
- Issue documentation will be prepared/gathered together (marriage certificate, petition, certificate regarding reconciliation (if required) and application for exemption from fee (if required)).
- The documents will be signed and copies taken. If the client so instructs, proceedings will be issued at the county court.
- The divorce process is shown at **8.2.** This diagram provides a summary of the undefended divorce procedure from issue to decree absolute and you may find it useful to turn to this diagram at this stage.

SELF-TEST QUESTIONS

1. Your client is concerned that his wife (the respondent) may not cooperate with the proceedings. Describe the different methods of service that can be used to prove service of proceedings.
2. Your client wishes to have an overview of the proceedings. Describe the procedure to him as briefly as you can. List the documents required to issue proceedings in a privately funded divorce with no children involved.
3. Will your client have to attend court at any stage?

Case Study Two

In Case Study Two, your supervisor asks you to complete the divorce petition on behalf of Helena. You will find a blank form on the Online Resource Centre and a completed form.

You will also find all the documentation for an undefended divorce in this case study.

Answers to the questions above can be found on the Online Resource Centre: www.oxfordtextbooks.co.uk/orc/familyhandbook13/.

Click here to reset form

Divorce/dissolution/ (judicial) separation petition

To be completed by the Court	
Name of court	
Case No.	
Date received by the court	
Date issued	
Time issued	

Notes to Petitioners

- This form should be used if you are making an application to the court for divorce/dissolution to end your marriage or civil partnership or (judicial) separation from your spouse or civil partner.
- Before completing this form, please read the supporting notes for guidance on completing the form.
- Please answer all questions. If you are unsure of the answer to any question, or you do not think that it applies to you, please indicate this on the form.
- If there is not enough room on the form, you may continue on a separate sheet. Please put your name, the Respondent's (your spouse/civil partner) name, and the number of the Part the information relates to, at the top of your continuation sheet.
- If completing this form by hand, please use **black ink and BLOCK CAPITAL LETTERS** and tick the boxes that apply.

See the supporting notes for guidance

I, ______________________ (please state your full name)

apply for a
- ☐ divorce
- ☐ dissolution
- ☐ (judicial) separation

in respect of my
- ☐ marriage
- ☐ civil partnership

and give the following details in support of my application.

---

continued over the page ➪

Part 1 About you (the Petitioner) and the Respondent (your spouse/civil partner)

See the supporting notes for guidance

Petitioner

My current name is
First name(s) (in full)

Last name

My address is (including postcode)

Postcode

My date of birth is
D D / M M / Y Y Y Y

My occupation is

I am
☐ male ☐ female

Respondent

The Respondent's current name is
First name(s) (in full)

Last name

The Respondent's address is (including postcode)

Postcode

The Respondent's date of birth is
D D / M M / Y Y Y Y

The Respondent's occupation is

The Respondent is
☐ male ☐ female

Part 2 Details of marriage or civil partnership

See the supporting notes for guidance

On the day of [19] [20]

(insert your name exactly as it appears on your marriage/civil partnership certificate)

☐ married ☐ formed a civil partnership with

(insert the name of the Respondent exactly as it appears on your marriage/civil partnership certificate)

at
(insert the place where the marriage/civil partnership was formed, exactly as it appears on your marriage/civil partnership certificate)

A certified copy of your marriage/civil partnership certificate must be sent to the court with this completed petition (see supporting notes for guidance).

Part 3 Jurisdiction

See the supporting notes for guidance

The Respondent and I last lived together as ☐ husband and wife ☐ civil partners at

Address

The court has jurisdiction to hear this case under

☐ Article 3(1) of the Council Regulation (EC) No 2201/2003 of 27 November 2003

or

☐ the Civil Partnership (Jurisdiction and Recognition of Judgments) Regulations 2005 on the following grounds

☐ The Petitioner and Respondent are both habitually resident in England and Wales

☐ Other (please state any other connection(s) on which you wish to rely)

or

☐ The court has jurisdiction other than under the Council Regulation on the basis that no court of a Contracting State has jurisdiction under the Council Regulation and the ☐ Petitioner ☐ Respondent is domiciled in England and Wales on the date when this application is issued

or

☐ The court has jurisdiction other than under the Civil Partnership (Jurisdiction and Recognition of Judgments) Regulations on the basis that no court has, or is recognised as having jurisdiction as set out in the Regulations, and

either:

☐ the ☐ Petitioner ☐ and/or the Respondent is domiciled in England or Wales

or

☐ the Petitioner and Respondent registered as civil partners of each other in England or Wales and it would be in the interests of justice for the court to assume jurisdiction in this case.

continued over the page ⇨

Part 4 Other proceedings or arrangements

See the supporting notes for guidance

☐ There are and/or have been

☐ proceedings in any court in England and Wales or elsewhere with reference to the

☐ marriage
☐ civil partnership
☐ or to any child of the family
☐ or between the Petitioner and Respondent with reference to any property of either or both of them

(please enter details below)

or

☐ no other proceedings in any court in England and Wales or elsewhere.

☐ This is an application based on five years' separation and

☐ agreement has been made or is proposed to be made between the parties for the support of the Petitioner (and any child of the family)

(please enter details below)

or

☐ no agreement has been made or is proposed to be made.

Part 5 The fact(s)

See the supporting notes for guidance

I apply for a

☐ divorce on the ground that the marriage has broken down irretrievably, or
☐ dissolution on the ground that the civil partnership has broken down irretrievably, or
☐ (judicial) separation

and

I rely on the following fact(s) in support of my application:

☐ The Respondent has committed adultery and the Petitioner finds it intolerable to live with the Respondent (this fact is not applicable in relation to a civil partnership)

☐ The Respondent has behaved in such a way that the Petitioner cannot reasonably be expected to live with the Respondent

☐ The Respondent has deserted the Petitioner for a continuous period of at least two years immediately preceding the presentation of this petition

☐ The parties to the marriage/civil partnership have lived apart for a continuous period of at least two years immediately preceding the presentation of the petition and the Respondent consents to a decree/order being granted

☐ The parties to the marriage/civil partnership have lived apart for a continuous period of at least five years immediately preceding the presentation of the petition.

Part 6 Statement of case

See the supporting notes for guidance

(in all cases, please state briefly any relevant details about the fact(s) on which you rely)

Part 7 Details of the children

See the supporting notes for guidance

Children of the family

Full names of the children of the family	Gender male	Gender female	Date of birth (or state if over 18)	Over 16 but under 18 and in education, training or working fulltime	(a) Child of both parties	(b) Other child of the family
	☐	☐	DD/MM/YYYY	☐	☐	☐
	☐	☐	DD/MM/YYYY	☐	☐	☐
	☐	☐	DD/MM/YYYY	☐	☐	☐
	☐	☐	DD/MM/YYYY	☐	☐	☐
	☐	☐	DD/MM/YYYY	☐	☐	☐
	☐	☐	DD/MM/YYYY	☐	☐	☐

Statement of arrangements for children

See the supporting notes for guidance

☐ I attach a completed statement of arrangements in respect of those children of the family who are either aged under 16, or aged under 18 and at school, college, or in training for a trade, profession or vocation

or

☐ No statement of arrangements is attached, because there are no children of the family, or no children of the family are either aged under 16 or aged under 18 and at school, college, or in training for a trade, profession or vocation.

Children of either party who are not children of the family

Full names of the children of either party who are not children of the family	Gender male	Gender female	Date of birth (or state if over 18)	Born to or adopted by Petitioner	Born to or adopted by Respondent
	☐	☐	DD/MM/YYYY	☐	☐
	☐	☐	DD/MM/YYYY	☐	☐
	☐	☐	DD/MM/YYYY	☐	☐
	☐	☐	DD/MM/YYYY	☐	☐
	☐	☐	DD/MM/YYYY	☐	☐
	☐	☐	DD/MM/YYYY	☐	☐

Part 8 Special assistance or facilities if you attend court

See the supporting notes for guidance

If you are required to attend court during these proceedings will you need any special assistance or facilities?

☐ Yes (please supply details below) ☐ No

continued over the page

Part 9 Service details

See the supporting notes for guidance

- ☐ I am not represented by a solicitor in these proceedings
- ☐ I am not represented by a solicitor in these proceedings but am receiving advice from a solicitor
- ☐ I am represented by a solicitor in these proceedings and all documents for my attention should be sent to my solicitor whose details are as follows:

Box 1 Solicitor's details

Name of solicitor			
Name of firm			
Address to which all documents should be sent for service		Telephone no.	
		Fax no.	
		DX no.	
Postcode		Your ref.	

E-mail	

Box 2 Petitioner's address for service

Address (including postcode)

Postcode

Box 3 Respondent's address for service

Address (including postcode)

Postcode

Box 4 Co-Respondent's details, if any

- ☐ There is no Co-Respondent
- ☐ There is a Co-Respondent whose details are as follows:

First Name	
Last Name	

Address (including postcode)

Postcode

Part 10

See the supporting notes for guidance

Prayer

The Petitioner therefore prays

(1) **The application**

☐ That the ☐ marriage ☐ civil partnership be dissolved

or

☐ That the Petitioner be (judicially) separated from the Respondent.

(2) **Costs (if you wish to claim costs from the Respondent or Co-Respondent)**

☐ That the ☐ Respondent ☐ Co-Respondent shall be ordered to pay the costs of this application

(3) **Financial Order (if you wish to make an application for a Financial Order)**

☐ (a) That the Petitioner may be granted the following Financial Order(s):

- ☐ an order for maintenance pending suit
- ☐ periodical payments order
- ☐ secured provision order
- ☐ lump sum order
- ☐ property adjustment order
- ☐ order under section 24B, 25B or 25C of the Act of 1973 (Pension Sharing/Attachment Order)

☐ (b) **For the children**

- ☐ a periodical payments order
- ☐ a secured provision order
- ☐ a lump sum order
- ☐ a property adjustment order

Signed ____________________ Dated D D / M M / Y Y Y Y

8

Click here to reset form

Statement of arrangements for children

To be completed by the parties	
Name of court	Case No. (if known)
Name of Petitioner	
Name of Respondent	

To the Petitioner

You must complete this form if you or the Respondent have any children under 16 or any children under 18 who are at school or college or are training for a trade, profession or vocation.

The Petitioner is only required to complete Parts 1, 2, 3 and the Statement of Truth. Please use **black ink and BLOCK CAPITAL LETTERS**.

Before you issue a divorce/dissolution/(judicial) separation or nullity petition try to reach an agreement with your spouse or civil partner over the proposals for the children's future. There is space for them to sign at the end of this form if agreement is reached.

If your spouse/civil partner does not agree with the proposals, they will have the opportunity at a later stage to state why they do not agree and will be able to make their own proposals.

You should take or send the completed form together with a copy to the court when you issue your divorce/dissolution/(judicial) separation or nullity petition.

To the Respondent

The Petitioner has completed Part 1, 2 and 3 of this form.

Please read all parts of the form carefully.

If you agree with the arrangements and proposals for the children you should sign Part 4 of the form. If completing this form by hand, please use **black ink and BLOCK CAPITAL LETTERS** and

If you do not agree with all or some of the proposals,**do not sign this form**. You will be given the opportunity of explaining your position when you receive the divorce/dissolution/(judicial) separation or nullity petition.

To the Petitioner and Respondent

If you wish to apply for any of the orders which may be available to you under Part I or II of the Children Act 1989 please see leaflet CB1 'Making an application - children and the family courts'. If you are unsure of which application you require, you are advised to see a solicitor or go to a Citizens Advice Bureau.

Addresses of solicitors and advice agencies can be obtained from the Yellow Pages and the Solicitors' Regional Directory which can be found at Citizens Advice Bureaux, Law Centres and any local library.

The Court will only make an order if it considers that an order will be better for the child(ren) than no order.

D8A Statement of arrangements for children (04.11)

Part 1 Details of the children

1. Are the details of the children as stated in Part 7 of the divorce/dissolution/(judicial) separation or nullity petition correct?

   ☐ Yes ☐ No

   If No, please give further information in the box below

Part 2 Arrangements for the children of the family

Please give details for each child, if arrangements are different. If necessary, continue on another sheet and attach it to this form.

Living arrangements

2. Where and with whom do the children live?

Name of child(ren)	Resides with	At address

3. Is this arrangement agreed by both the Petitioner and Respondent?

   ☐ Yes ☐ No

   If No, please give details in the box below.

4. What are the contact arrangements between the child(ren) and the non-resident parent?

5. Have you (the Petitioner) and Respondent agreed to these contact arrangements?

   ☐ Yes ☐ No

   If No, please give details in the box below.

6. Who will care for the child(ren) on a day to day basis?

7. Have you (the Petitioner) and Respondent agreed to who will care for the child(ren) on a daily basis?

☐ Yes ☐ No

If No, please give details in the box below.

Education

8. Give the name(s) of the school, college or place of training attended by the child(ren).

Name of child	Name of school, college or place of training

9. Will there be any change in these arrangements as a result of your divorce/dissolution/(judicial) separation or annulment?

☐ Yes ☐ No

If Yes, please give details in the box below (include any changes to payment of school fees).

10. Do any of the children have any special educational needs?

☐ Yes ☐ No

If Yes, please give details in the box below.

continued over the page

Details of health

11. Are the children generally in good health and do not have any special health needs?

☐ Yes ☐ No

If No, please give details of any serious disability, chronic illness, or the care needed and how it is to be provided, in the box below.

12. Do any of the children have any special health needs?

☐ Yes ☐ No

If Yes, please give details of the care needed and how it is to be provided, in the box below.

Details of care and other court proceedings

13. Are the children in the care of the local authority, or under the supervision of a social worker or probation officer?

☐ Yes ☐ No

If Yes, please give details in the box below. Please include information about any current proceedings in the youth or family courts.

14. Are any of the children the subject of a Child Protection Plan?

☐ Yes ☐ No

If Yes, please give details in the box below, including the name of the local authority and the date of registration.

15. Are there, or have there been, any proceedings in any court involving the children, for example;

a) residence or contact proceedings?
b) care or supervision?
c) adoption or wardship?

☐ Yes ☐ No

If Yes, please give details in the box below and attach a copy of any order(s) which you have.

☐ A maintenance calculation has been made under the Child Support Act 1991, or, an application has been made for a maintenance calculation, but it has not yet been determined, and the details are as follows:

☐ The following agreement has been reached in relation to child maintenance:

☐ No agreement has been reached and no application has been made for a maintenance calculation.

16. Are there, or have there been, any proceedings in any court which may impact on the children, for example non-molestation orders, or criminal proceedings relating to domestic violence?

☐ Yes ☐ No

If Yes, please give details in the box below.

Part 3 To the Petitioner

Mediation

17. If you are not agreed as to the arrangements for the children, are you intending to:

- seek to resolve matters with the Respondent directly?

  ☐ Yes ☐ No

- propose the use of Alternative Dispute Resolution such as mediation?

  ☐ Yes ☐ No

  If No, would you agree to do so?

  ☐ Yes ☐ No

- make an application to the court?

  ☐ Yes ☐ No

Statement of Truth

I believe that the facts stated in this statement of arrangements for children are true

Print full name

Signed (Petitioner) Dated D D / M M / Y Y Y Y

Proceedings for contempt of court may be brought against a person who makes or causes to be made, a false statement in a document verified by a statement of truth.

Part 4 Agreement of Respondent

☐ I agree with the arrangements and proposals contained in Part 1 and 2 of this form.

☐ I do not agree with the arrangements and proposals contained in Part 1 and 2 of this form.
If you do not agree would you be prepared to see a mediator?

☐ Yes ☐ No

Signed (Respondent) Dated D D / M M / Y Y Y Y

9 CIVIL PARTNERSHIP ACT 2004

9.1 INTRODUCTION

This chapter will:

- **discuss the Civil Partnership Act 2004;**
- **discuss the formation of a civil partnership.**

Currently, same-sex couples cannot marry. The Civil Partnership Act 2004 (CPA 2004) came into force on 5 December 2005 and, since then, there have been over 100,000 civil partnerships formed in the UK. The scope of the CPA 2004 is extremely wide and affects every area of family law. It is a lengthy piece of legislation; there are 264 sections in eight parts and also 30 schedules. Despite the size of the CPA 2004, there has been very little case-law generated by the advent of civil partnerships. The Government is currently considering the extension of the availability of marriage to same-sex couples (but not to extend civil partnerships to heterosexual couples). This is an extremely contentious issue. Scotland has signalled its intention to bring forward legislation to introduce marriage for same-sex couples. This chapter looks at the scope of the CPA 2004 and the formation of civil partnerships.

9.2 SCOPE OF THE CIVIL PARTNERSHIP ACT

The CPA 2004 enables same-sex couples to form legally recognized civil partnerships. Once a partnership has been formed, civil partners assume many legal rights and responsibilities for each other, third parties, and the State. Many of these rights and responsibilities are identical to those enjoyed by married couples.

The CPA 2004 makes many amendments to many different statutes.

The CPA 2004 amends the Children Act 1989 and the Adoption and Children Act 2002 to enable a civil partner to acquire parental responsibility (see **Chapter 25**) and the definition of a 'child of the family' includes civil partners as well as parties to a marriage. A civil partner is entitled to apply for a residence or contact order (see **Chapter 26**).

The CPA 2004 also makes wide-ranging changes to statutes as diverse as the Family Law Act 1996 to allow civil partners to apply for non-molestation orders and occupation orders (see **Chapters 33 and 34**), and the Sex Discrimination Act 1975 to allow civil partners to claim discrimination on the grounds of their civil partnership. The CPA 2004 also amends tax credits, social security, and child support legislation to ensure that civil partners are equal to married people. Wills, administration of estates, and family provision as well as intestacy are also equalized to include the same rights for civil partners.

9.3 FORMATION OF A CIVIL PARTNERSHIP

A civil partnership is a relationship between two people of the same sex and a civil partnership is formed when civil partners register their relationship (s1 CPA 2004) and a civil partnership ends only on death, dissolution, or annulment (s3 CPA 2004).

In order to register a civil partnership, notice must be given to the relevant registration authority of their intention to form the partnership. The partners must also have resided in the registration authority in England and Wales for seven days immediately before notice is given. There is a 15-day waiting period following notice (s11 CPA 2004) and then the registration authority issues a civil partnership schedule.

During a civil partnership ceremony, a civil partnership document is signed by both parties in the presence of two witnesses.

Legislative Change

Civil Partnerships now may take place in religious premises. This amendment to the Civil Partnership Act 2004 was made by the Equality Act 2010. This was a late amendment and precedes a wider consideration of marriage and civil partnership by the current Government.

As with marriage, there are some formalities and capacities that should be noted. The parties must be of the same sex, not married or already in a civil partnership, not under the age of 16 (parental consent is required for those under 18), and not within prohibited degrees of relationship.

9.4 DIFFERENCES BETWEEN CIVIL PARTNERSHIP AND MARRIAGE

There are very few differences between civil partnerships and marriage on a legal basis (although many may disagree on a political, spiritual, or religious basis).

The civil partnership is formed on the signing of the register rather than the exchange of vows.

Non-consummation and venereal disease grounds are not included in the grounds for the annulment of a civil partnership (see **Chapter 4**) as they are with marriage.

Adultery is not a fact to establish the ground for dissolution of a civil partnership as it is in marriage (see **Chapter 5**).

A civil partnership is not a marriage and this was confirmed in *Wilkinson v Kitzinger* [2006] EWHC 2022 (Fam). A female same-sex couple was married in British Colombia but under the CPA 2004, this was treated as a civil partnership in the UK. The petitioner sought a declaration of her marital status. Further she argued that the requirement for marriage that the parties must be respectively male and female under s11(c) MCA 1973 was a breach of Arts 8, 12, and 14 of the European Convention on Human Rights (see **Chapter 4**). The petitioner argued that the law should be construed so that same-sex marriages were recognized as valid in the UK. The court refused the declaration and stated that the European Court of Human Rights had interpreted Art. 12 to refer to marriage between persons of the opposite sex and found that the difference in treatment between opposite-sex and same-sex couples was reasonable and proportionate. As already stated, same-sex marriage is currently a matter of intense public debate.

SUMMARY POINTS

- This is a brief introduction to civil partnerships.
- The Civil Partnership Act 2004 introduced the concept of civil partnerships.
- Civil partnerships can be formed by same-sex couples.
- Civil partnerships confer rights and responsibilities on civil partners analogous to that of marriage.
- Civil partnerships are formed by the signing of a registration document.
- There are some differences between civil partnerships and marriage.

SELF-TEST QUESTIONS

1. List three differences between marriage and civil partnership.
2. Two elderly sisters share a house and all household management and bills. They wish to form a civil partnership to take advantage of inheritance provisions. Can two sisters form a civil partnership?

online resource centre

Answers to the questions above can be found on the Online Resource Centre: www.oxfordtextbooks.co.uk/orc/familyhandbook13/.

10 DISSOLUTION OF A CIVIL PARTNERSHIP

10.1 INTRODUCTION

This chapter will:

- **discuss the dissolution of a civil partnership.**

The Civil Partnership Act 2004 (CPA 2004) has led to the forming of over 100,000 civil partnerships since December 2005. Inevitably, there have been unsuccessful partnerships formed and by August 2008 there had been approximately 250 civil partnership dissolutions.

S37 CPA 2004 allows the court to make a number of orders, including a dissolution order which dissolves the civil partnership. As explained in **Chapter 9**, the CPA 2004 amends many statutes to make civil partnerships broadly equivalent to marriage. This chapter examines the process of dissolving a civil partnership. The process of obtaining a dissolution of a civil partnership is more or less the same as obtaining a divorce. This chapter highlights the main provisions on nullity, dissolution, and separation.

10.2 NULLITY

A civil partnership may be void or voidable (see **Chapter 4**). S37 CPA 2004 allows the court the power to issue a nullity order, annulling the civil partnership.

S49 CPA 2004 gives the grounds for a void civil partnership and mainly concerns the formalities of the civil partnership itself:

- the parties are ineligible to register as civil partners;
- the correct formalities had not been followed (e.g. lack of notice, invalid civil partnership document, registrar not present).

A civil partnership may be voidable under s50 CPA 2004 and the grounds for this are similar to those of marriage but not identical (see **Chapters 4 and 9**). The grounds include:

- lack of valid consent;
- either party suffers from a mental disorder of a kind or to such an extent to be unfit for civil partnership;
- at the time of the marriage the respondent was pregnant by some person other than the applicant.

There are bars to relief under s 51 CPA 2004 that are the same as found in the MCA 1973 (see **Chapter 4**).

10.3 SEPARATION ORDERS

As with judicial separation (see **Chapter 4**) a court can make a separation order under s56 CPA 2004 based on the facts of s44(5) CPA 2004 (see **10.4**). As with judicial separation in marriage, there is no requirement to prove that the civil partnership has broken down irretrievably.

10.4 DISSOLUTION

There exists a time bar to dissolution under s41 CPA 2004. An application for the dissolution of a civil partnership may not be made within the first year of a civil partnership. As with marriage (see **Chapter 8**) other applications may be made within this time frame, e.g. for child support under the Child Support Act 1991 or orders under the Family Law Act 1996 if there has been domestic abuse.

The sole ground for dissolution is the irretrievable breakdown of the civil partnership (s44 CPA 2004). The applicant must also satisfy one of the facts under s44(5)(a) CPA 2004, namely that:

- the respondent has behaved in such a way that the applicant cannot reasonably be expected to live with the respondent;
- the parties have lived apart for a continuous period of two years and the respondent consents to the dissolution;
- the applicant and respondent have lived apart for a continuous period of five years;
- the respondent has deserted the applicant for a continuous period of two years.

Adultery is not a separate fact and, if there is an allegation of infidelity, it should be included under the unreasonable behaviour.

 **Example**

Edwina and Margaret form a civil partnership. Edwina is a very possessive and jealous person and suspects Margaret of having an affair. Edwina begins to check Margaret's mobile telephone, emails, and Facebook entries. She finds that Margaret is indeed having an affair. Edwina confronts Margaret and a huge row ensues. Margaret accuses Edwina of being unreasonable and as the argument goes on, Margaret picks up a heavy ornament and hits Edwina very hard. Edwina suffers a broken arm.

Edwina decides to dissolve the partnership. There is no fact of adultery in CPA 2004 and so she relies on Margaret's affair and violence as evidence of unreasonable behaviour.

The rules on living apart and continuous separation are the same as relating to divorce (see **Chapter 5**) and the case-law applicable to divorce under the Matrimonial Causes Act 1973 will also be equally applicable to the dissolution of civil partnerships.

S47 CPA 2004 provides a defence to dissolution on the basis of grave hardship when the fact of five years' separation is pleaded. Under s48 CPA 2004, there is also protection for a respondent that replicates s10 MCA 1973 (see **Chapter 6**).

10.5 PROCEDURE

The procedure for obtaining a dissolution is the same as for obtaining a divorce. Further reference should be made to **Chapter 8**. The principal differences in procedure relate to the names of the documents used by the court. In civil partnership dissolution, the equivalent to a divorce petition is a dissolution petition (a copy can be seen in the online resources section).

Orders for dissolution are described firstly as conditional (the equivalent of a decree nisi) and then as final (the equivalent of a decree absolute).

10.6 MONEY AND PROPERTY

S72 CPA 2004 and Sch 5 CPA 2004 make provision for financial relief for civil partners that correspond to provision made for financial relief in connection with marriages made by Part 2 MCA 1973. This would indicate that the regime applicable to married couples under MCA 1973 extends to civil partners. See **Chapter 11** onwards for a full explanation.

SUMMARY POINTS

- If a civil partnership comes to an end, the court can make orders for nullity, separation, or dissolution.
- The ground for dissolution is the irretrievable breakdown of the civil partnership.
- There are four facts for dissolution but no fact of adultery.
- The procedure for dissolution is the same as divorce, with some differences in terminology.

SELF-TEST QUESTIONS

1. What is the ground for the dissolution of a civil partnership?
2. What is the name of the document that commences proceedings for a dissolution of a civil partnership?
3. There are four facts on which to base civil partnership dissolution. There are five in divorce. Which fact available in divorce is not available in civil partnership dissolution?
4. Look at the example given above concerning Edwina and Margaret. Would the advice given to Edwina be any different if the partnership were only five months old? What if there had been no affair or violence; which facts could Edwina rely upon?

Answers to the questions above can be found on the Online Resource Centre: www.oxfordtextbooks.co.uk/orc/familyhandbook13/.

Part 3

MONEY AND PROPERTY

11 FINANCIAL ORDERS FOLLOWING DIVORCE OR DISSOLUTION

11.1 INTRODUCTION TO MONEY AND PROPERTY

This chapter will:

- **introduce the main concepts in proceedings for financial orders under the Matrimonial Causes Act 1973;**
- **examine the factors considered by the court when deciding on financial orders;**
- **discuss the principal case-law arising from proceedings for financial orders.**

This section of the text deals with the arrangements made to divide money and property following the breakdown of a relationship. Unless a relationship has been very brief, money and property will be acquired during the relationship that must be divided. In this context, 'property' has a wide meaning and will include furniture, savings, antiques, shares (and many other types of property), as well as houses.

This section will look at the law relating to spouses and civil partners. There is also a great deal of guidance from the courts to be considered as well as statutory factors. The courts are very active in this area of family practice and online resources will contain regularly updated cases.

The case study of Helena and David Wilson will continue throughout this section of the text to demonstrate a financial order case.

This chapter will consider the factors that a court will take into account when deciding on the division of money and property following a divorce or dissolution of a civil partnership.

11.2 WHAT ARE FINANCIAL ORDERS?

Part 9 of the Family Procedure Rules 2010 (FPR 2010) refers to proceedings for a financial remedy and replaces the old terminology of 'ancillary relief'. Part 2.3 FPR 2010 defines 'financial remedy' as

(a) a financial order;
(b) an order under Schedule 1 to the Children Act 1989;
(c) an order under Part 3 of the Matrimonial and Family Proceedings Act 1984;

(d) an order under Schedule 7 to the Civil Partnership Act 2004;
(e) an order under section 27 of the Matrimonial Causes Act 1973;
(f) an order under Part 9 of Schedule 5 to the Civil Partnership Act 2004;
(g) an order under section 35 of the Matrimonial Causes Act 1973;
(h) an order under paragraph 69 of Schedule 5 to the Civil Partnership Act 2004;
(i) an order under Part 1 of the Domestic Proceedings and Magistrates' Courts Act 1978;
(j) an order under Schedule 6 to the Civil Partnership Act 2004;
(k) an order under section 10(2) of the Matrimonial Causes Act 1973;
(l) an order under section 48(2) of the Civil Partnership Act 2004.

Further the term 'financial order' means—

(a) an avoidance of disposition order;
(b) an order for maintenance pending suit;
(c) an order for maintenance pending outcome of proceedings;
(d) an order for periodical payments or lump sum provision as mentioned in section 21(1) of the Matrimonial Causes Act 1973, except an order under section 27(6) of that Act;
(e) an order for periodical payments or lump sum provision as mentioned in paragraph 2(1) of Schedule 5 to the Civil Partnership Act 2004, made under Part 1 of Schedule 5 to that Act;
(f) a property adjustment order;
(g) a variation order;
(h) a pension sharing order; or
(i) a pension compensation sharing order.

The term 'financial order' and 'proceedings for a financial order' will be used in this text to describe the process of sorting out money and property following the end of a civil partnership or marriage.

The term 'ancillary relief' will be seen in cases decided prior to the implementation of the FPR 2010 (in April 2010) and is still being used by practitioners and courts. It will be some time before the term falls out of use.

In the early stages of practice, proceedings for a financial order can appear overly complex and it can seem hard to know where to start. Most clients seek an opinion from their solicitor early on in the retainer.

This text will look at all the factors that a court considers in proceedings for financial orders. Many practitioners use different approaches to deciding what a client may obtain through proceedings and, when in practice, you will develop your own.

Clients frequently complain that proceedings for financial orders are not fair (on them). The courts have to make decisions that will affect your client's life for some years to come and, inevitably, neither party is generally satisfied with the outcome. The majority of clients do not have sufficient funds to approach the proceedings knowing there is enough money to meet all needs and desires of the parties. Clients may not appreciate that courts have guidance from statute and case-law and apply this guidance in their case. This chapter considers the guidance fully.

11.3 MATRIMONIAL CAUSES ACT 1973

The jurisdiction of the court to make financial orders is found in the Matrimonial Causes Act 1973 (MCA 1973). The orders that can be made, the scope of these orders, and the factors that the court considers when making these orders are found within MCA 1973.

The court has a duty to consider all the circumstances and so this gives the court the ability to investigate the case when making its decision. The House of Lords in *Miller v Miller; McFarlane v McFarlane* [2006] 1 FLR 1186 considered three main principles for distribution: need, compensation, and sharing with an over-arching requirement of fairness (see **11.7**). Case-law is progressing on these points and will be examined during the following chapters in Part 3.

11.4 FACTORS TO BE CONSIDERED BY THE COURT

11.4.1 ALL THE CIRCUMSTANCES OF THE CASE

S25(1) MCA 1973 states that it is the duty of the court in deciding whether to exercise its powers under s23, 24, 24A, or 24B to have regard to all the circumstances of the case, first consideration being given to the welfare while a minor of any child of the family who has not attained the age of 18.

All the circumstances of the case can include the existence of pre-marital agreements (sometimes called pre-nuptial agreements) and these are discussed further in **Chapter 13**.

11.4.2 CHILDREN

This differs from the Children Act 1989 (see **Chapter 24**) where the child's welfare is the court's *paramount* consideration. This must not be confused with the *first* consideration in proceedings for financial orders. In proceedings for financial orders the children's interests are not the overriding consideration of the court and the court has a general duty to consider all the circumstances of the case. The Court of Appeal in *Suter v Suter* [1987] 2 FLR 232 underlined this and stated that the court was to bear in mind the important first consideration of the welfare of the children and then to achieve an order that was just.

Practical Considerations

In most cases, the court will have as its priority the provision of a home for the children of the family and sufficient income to maintain the home and pay bills etc. Unless the parties have a great deal of money and property, this will account for the majority of the family's assets.

11.5 S25 MATRIMONIAL CAUSES ACT 1973

When the court is considering a financial order case, the factors to be considered are found in s25(2) MCA 1973:

> (2) As regards the exercise of the powers of the court under section 23(1)(*a*), (*b*) or (*c*), 24, 24A or 24B in relation to a party to the marriage, the court shall in particular have regard to the following matters—
>
> (a) the income, earning capacity, property and other financial resources which each of the parties to the marriage has or is likely to have in the foreseeable future, including in the case of earning capacity any increase in that capacity which it would in the opinion of the court be reasonable to expect a party to the marriage to take steps to acquire;
>
> (b) the financial needs, obligations and responsibilities which each of the parties to the marriage has or is likely to have in the foreseeable future;
>
> (c) the standard of living enjoyed by the family before the breakdown of the marriage;
>
> (d) the age of each party to the marriage and the duration of the marriage;

(e) any physical or mental disability of either of the parties to the marriage;

(f) the contributions which each of the parties has made or is likely in the foreseeable future to make to the welfare of the family, including any contribution by looking after the home or caring for the family;

(g) the conduct of each of the parties, if that conduct is such that it would in the opinion of the court be inequitable to disregard it;

(h) in the case of proceedings for divorce or nullity of marriage, the value to each of the parties to the marriage of any benefit which, by reason of the dissolution or annulment of the marriage, that party will lose the chance of acquiring.

Each of these factors has been considered by the courts. It is important to note that all factors are considered equally important by the courts. These factors are not exhaustive, and the courts must consider all the circumstances of the case.

11.5.1 INCOME AND EARNING CAPACITY, PROPERTY, AND FINANCIAL RESOURCES: S25(2)(A) MCA 1973

Practical Considerations

Many clients are tempted to dispose of assets by selling them and hiding the money, or temporarily giving them away. Clients must be told firmly at the outset that full disclosure of all property must be made and this duty to disclose continues throughout the proceedings. If a client tells you that they intend to dispose of assets and ask for your help, there will be professional conduct issues to consider.

11.5.1.1 Income and earning capacity under S25(2)(a) MCA 1973

Evidence of income and earning capacity will be found in payslips, P60, or accounts if self-employed (see **Chapter 14** and the case study for documents required to be disclosed in financial proceedings). There may also be payments in kind to be taken into account, e.g. company car, pension contributions, or free meals.

The statute states that '...in the case of earning capacity any increase in that capacity which it would in the opinion of the court be reasonable to expect a party to the marriage to take steps to acquire'.

The court may view this as being a presumption that the court can expect the parties to become financially independent following divorce. The court will look at what employment the party to the marriage could reasonably be expected to do. The court may base an order on someone making greater efforts to obtain employment, to go back into training, or to place a limit on periodical payment to encourage someone to return to work.

Example

Sarita and Anil are married and have two children. Sarita worked as an admin assistant in the civil service before her marriage. When the marriage ended, Sarita had not worked for 11 years as both had agreed that she should remain at home with the children. Sarita has no qualifications other than some GCSEs.

The court orders Anil to make periodical payments to Sarita for five years to enable her to retrain and gain further qualifications.

This could cover a wife who gave up work to look after children and the home. The court will probably not expect a spouse to go to work when children are under school age but once children are at school, the spouse will probably be expected to obtain employment or allow time to retrain. It is important to factor in the availability and cost of childcare when thinking about this aspect. The court may choose to make an open-ended periodical payment order leaving the onus on the paying spouse to make an application for a variation (see **Chapter 15**) should she or he believe that the receiving spouse is able to work.

The income available to the parties is important as both parties have to be able to support a home and be able to pay bills. An important consideration is whether the parties will be able to afford a mortgage.

Practical Considerations

When applying for a mortgage, the bank or building society will look at the income of the applicant as well as any liabilities they regularly pay. The applicant's gross salary will then be multiplied by a multiplier to produce an amount which the lender feels the applicant can afford. The multiplier is usually 3 or 3.5 times the applicant's gross income.

Before the 'credit crunch' multipliers were often far higher and could be five or more times an applicant's gross income. This led to many people taking mortgages which were very large. Lenders are now much more cautious.

11.5.1.2 Property and financial resources under S25(2)(a) MCA 1973

The court will look at all of the assets of the marriage. This will commonly include the family home, cars, savings, stocks and shares, pensions, and valuable antiques or paintings. For clients who are wealthy, this could also include holiday homes, yachts, jewellery, land, and portfolios of investments. For many clients, there are very few assets, e.g. if the parties live in rented accommodation or have little income. An increasing feature of financial order cases is the level of debt held by the parties on credit cards, secured, or unsecured loans. All of these liabilities will be taken into account by the court.

All possible assets should be considered including the family home, holiday homes, buy-to-let property, cars, antiques, jewellery, shares, endowment policies, pensions, and all other types of assets held. A good way of ensuring that you have a complete list of all assets held by your client is to have a comprehensive instructions checklist. A common practice is to give the client a list to complete or to give the client a Form E (see **Chapter 14**), which is the form that gives disclosure in proceedings for financial orders. The client completes the Form E and this begins the process of working out what assets are in the matrimonial 'pot'.

Assets are valued at the time of the court hearing (*Cowan v Cowan* [2001] 2 FLR 192). The fact that an asset is not liquid (i.e. not easily realized) does not mean that it should be disregarded, but the illiquidity should be taken into account when considering fairness.

11.5.1.3 Matrimonial v non-matrimonial assets? S25(2)(a) MCA 1973

There has been increasing discussion about whether some assets held by one spouse can be considered 'non-matrimonial' property and, as such, distributed differently to matrimonial property. For most middle and low income families, this is not a distinction that the court is able to make as all assets are required so a position is reached where all parties are adequately housed and maintained. Where there are assets in excess of basic needs, this becomes more of an issue.

Example

Anil and Sarita have few assets from their marriage. They own their own home which is worth £150,000 but they have a mortgage for £50,000 and so the 'equity' in the property is £100,000. Anil also has a pension but this is not worth very much at all. There are no other significant assets.

In this case, the court will not consider whether this is matrimonial or non-matrimonial property as the home is the only asset that the court can consider and so the need to provide a home for both parties will take priority.

In *Miller v Miller; McFarlane v McFarlane* [2006] UKHL 24 two Law Lords differed on the approach to matrimonial property. Lord Nicholls categorized non-matrimonial as property that one party brought into the marriage or acquired by inheritance or gift during the marriage, all other property being matrimonial property. Baroness Hale took a different view. She viewed non-matrimonial property not only as property brought into the marriage but also business and investment assets generated solely or mainly by the efforts during the marriage. Lords Mance and Hoffmann agreed with Baroness Hale.

The case of *Charman v Charman* [2007] EWCA Civ 503 was heard in the Court of Appeal before England's most senior family law judges outside of the House of Lords. One commentator hoped that it would iron out the contradictions between their Lordships in *Miller; McFarlane.*

The case involved colossal sums of money from the husband's outstanding business career. In a unanimous judgment, the Court of Appeal held that, subject to needs and other factors, the sharing principle applies to all property; but there are likely to be better reasons to depart from equality with non-matrimonial property, and Baroness Hale's category of 'non-business-partnership non-family asset' cases is limited to short marriage cases and possibly dual-career families.

The classification of 'non-matrimonial property' does not mean that it is left out of account altogether; rather, the importance of the distinction is in relation to equality or the sharing principle (*Norris v Norris* [2002] EWHC 2996 (Fam) and *S v S* [2007] EWHC 1975 (Fam)).

With a long marriage, the weight attached to contributions made will diminish, though sometimes it will not. In *Miller; McFarlane,* Lord Nicholls gave the examples of modest savings introduced at the beginning of a marriage that have grown (and presumably could be split) and an inherited heirloom that should be retained in its inherited form.

There will be occasions when an asset is not easily realized, e.g. a business. The courts do not generally require such an asset to be destroyed, e.g. by forcing the business to be sold or large amounts of capital to be drawn from the business. In this type of case, other assets will be used to compensate the other spouse. This may take the form of an increased share of capital assets or making larger maintenance payments to increase the spousal share without compromising the asset.

A pension is an asset that must be taken into account (see **Chapter 19**). The courts have not been entirely consistent in their approach. The courts have either used the Cash Equivalent Transfer Value (CETV) that has been added to the other assets to be taken into account (*White*) or as a whole life fixed rate interest scheme (*Cowan v Cowan*). In *Maskell v Maskell* [2001] 3 FCR 296 the approach was simply to aggregate the pension with other assets, as only part of the pension could be taken as capital and the other part was income. The court stated that like must be compared with like. In *Martin-Dye v Martin-Dye* [2006] EWCA Civ 681 Thorpe LJ stated that the pension should not be treated as capital but as another financial resource, sitting comfortably in neither the category of 'property' nor 'income'.

Some assets are created after the end of a marriage when parties have separated. The courts have taken this type of property into account, but since *Miller; MacFarlane* the approach has involved first finding whether this asset forms matrimonial or non-matrimonial property. Bonuses earned post-separation have proved a fertile ground for case-law on this point.

In *Rossi v Rossi* [2006] EWHC 1482 (Fam), Mostyn QC was of the view that the asset must have been created at least 12 months after separation for it to be classed as non-matrimonial property. In *H v H* [2007] EWHC 459 (Fam), Charles J disagreed with this approach. Charles J preferred an approach that recognized the realities and circumstances of the individual case and an arbitrary approach should be avoided.

Example

The facts of *H v H* were that the husband and wife were aged 46 and 44 respectively at the time of the trial. The parties agreed on the equal division of assets totalling £2.7 m following a 20-year marriage. The couple separated in January 2005. The issue before the court was two accrued bonuses, each of about £2.4 m and future bonuses.

Charles J held in this case that the date for the valuation of the assets was 1 January 2005, the date of the breakdown of the marriage and so the matrimonial property did not include the bonuses. Charles J said that:

> 'the concept of matrimonial property . . . is based on the concept of an equal and voluntary partnership providing mutual emotional, economic, and general support and matching contributions to it of different kinds. A point, or a line, for defining the matrimonial property is therefore a date when that mutual support ends.'

11.5.2 FINANCIAL NEEDS, OBLIGATIONS, AND RESPONSIBILITIES: S25(2)(B) MCA 1973

In the majority of cases involving middle or low income families, the primary objective of the court will be to provide a home and income for the spouse with care of the children and a home and sufficient income for the other spouse. Priority will be given to the spouse with care of the children, in line with s25 MCA 1973.

Example

Eddie and Cherry separate following a five-year marriage. They have one child, Billy aged 4. Eddie works as a civil servant and earns £19,000 per annum. Cherry is a hairdresser and earns £16,000 per annum. The pair rent a property from a private landlord and have a few hundred pounds outstanding on a credit card. There are no other assets.

The court in this situation will have a limited set of options for the parties. The court will try to ensure that both parties have sufficient income to rent a suitable property and to meet household bills. There will be little else for the court to do. This type of case is common in practice.

The regular outgoings of both spouses will have been listed in disclosure and the court will consider whether they are reasonable for a person in their financial circumstances and the standard of living enjoyed by the parties. The court will not permit a party to live beyond their means nor condemn one spouse to unused-to penury.

Practical Considerations

The court will look for parity between the parties. One party will not be expected to live in a tiny bedsit in a dubious part of town whilst their partner lives in luxurious splendour in the nicest street imaginable. In practice, it is very unusual to find one party living on benefits with little money and the other party to be wealthy.

Most clients will have some level of debt. These are responsibilities that must be met and the court does not have the power to order one party to make payments to a creditor, who is generally not a party to the proceedings. The debt must be taken into account when the court makes its decision. In the current economic climate, it may also be difficult for clients to obtain credit or a mortgage.

Many clients will have formed new relationships or even remarried. This will be taken into account as it will have an effect on the needs and obligations of the spouse. It may also have an effect on their resources. The new partner may have substantial resources that free up the resources of the spouse as well as reducing their needs. Alternatively, a new spouse or partner may increase the needs of the spouse if new children arrive or a larger home is required. The new partner or spouse does not become a party to proceedings but the court will take into account the effect of new relationships. It is important to realize that the resources of the new partner or spouse cannot be directly applied to meet the needs of the spouse bringing proceedings for financial orders.

Example

Eddie and Cherry separate following a five-year marriage. They have one child, Billy aged 4. Cherry begins a new relationship almost immediately following separation with Tom and moves into Tom's flat with Billy. Cherry and Tom now have a new baby.

Cherry now has the benefit of Tom's income and this will mean that more of her income will be available for consideration by the court. However, Cherry has both Billy and her new child to support. The court will have to consider both aspects of this new relationship carefully.

The court has the power to order a 'costs allowance' to the financially weaker party. See **Chapter 14** for further details and case-law.

In *Miller v Miller; McFarlane v McFarlane*, Lord Nicholls raised a new form of needs in the shape of 'compensation'. Compensation addresses the perceived injustice of a spouse whose earning capacity is seriously depleted by the arrangements made by the parties, e.g. a wife staying at home to care for children will be disadvantaged in the labour market. The spouse may receive a fair share of the assets but has little ability to earn the same amount in the future as the spouse with the greater earning capacity. The disparity between the parties will become more apparent as time goes on. The wife sees her capital assets diminish as well as losing the ability to share in her husband's future earnings.

Example

Katerina is a highly paid corporate lawyer when she marries Derek, a successful entrepreneur. Both agree that Katerina will stay at home with the children of the marriage until they have left home. After a 35-year marriage, Katerina and Derek separate.

The court accepts that Katerina had a very successful career when she gave it up to look after the children. Although Derek can offer Katerina sufficient money for a comfortable life, Katerina will not regain her career and Derek will continue to accrue wealth through his business. The court may decide that Katerina has a large periodical payment order to address the disparity in wealth between the parties.

In *McFarlane*, the wife was given significant periodical payments to address this issue. Since this case, in *S v S (Non-Matrimonial Property: Conduct)* [2007] EWHC 2793 Burton J stated that 'I do not believe that this head of loss can be said to arise in every circumstance.'

In *RP v RP* [2007] 1 FLR 2105, Coleridge J remarked:

> The word compensation, which has been used frequently during this hearing, does not appear in the statute. Does it, I wonder, in the end, add anything to the concept of financial . . . obligations and responsibilities which each of the parties has deriving from s25(b)?

Coleridge J seemed to suggest that the court looks to s25(2) MCA 1973 and provide for a wife in such a situation and address the problem as a 'needs' issue.

In *CR v CR* [2007] EWHC 3334 (Fam), Bodey J agreed with Coleridge J and warned that:

> these strands underlying fairness do not become elevated into separate 'heads of claim' or 'of loss' independent of the words of the statute ... It remains the statutory criteria which ultimately guide the court's overall discretion by the exercise of which fairness is sought to be achieved.

It seems that the courts remain rooted in s25 MCA 1973 and that any perceived iniquity should be remedied through the generous interpretation of s25(2) MCA 1973.

11.5.2.1 Wealthy clients: S25(2)(a) and (b) MCA 1973

When clients are very wealthy, the court may find that there is sufficient capital and income to comfortably meet all the basic needs of the clients with much to spare. The court must then decide how to divide the remainder.

In *White v White* [2000] 1 AC 596, Lord Nicholls stated that financial needs are only one of the factors to be taken into account in arriving at the amount of the award.

McCartney v Mills-McCartney [2008] EWHC 401 (Fam) is an example of an instance when the wife was confined to her reasonable needs (albeit generously interpreted) and the husband left with a much larger balance. The husband's fortune had been made before the couple had met, the marriage was short, there was no ground for including an element of compensation in the award, and the wife's contributions had not been exceptional. Bennett J said that 'In my judgment, in this case the needs of the wife (generously interpreted) are not simply one of the factors in the case but are a factor of magnetic importance.'

In *Charman v Charman* [2007] EWCA Civ 503, the Court of Appeal considered a postscript to this judgment of Coleridge J. He asked whether there might be a threshold of wealth at which the court might consider that it was appropriate to depart from equality automatically. Neither of the leading counsel in the case could agree on what this figure should be. What would be the level of wealth at which the departure from equality would occur? The figure of £40–50m was given, but the Court of Appeal found itself unable to identify any figure as a guideline threshold for special contribution and felt it would be dangerous to do so. The Court of Appeal felt that it might discourage a court from discerning special contribution at a lower level of wealth or that departure from equality was inevitable above that level of wealth. The court did not consider such an approach to be useful.

In *Charman: Sharing in the Face of the Dragon*, published by Family Law Week and available at www.davidhodson.com and www.iflg.uk.com, David Hodson summarizes the impact of the case as follows:

- equality of division is no longer just a yardstick or check; it is now a principle of financial provision law;
- since property should be shared equally unless there is good reason to depart from equality, any departure is not from the principle but takes place within the principle;
- English financial provision law is a two-stage process; first, what is the available property, income, and other resources; secondly, how should they be distributed in accordance with s25 and case-law;
- subject to needs and other factors, the sharing principle applies to all property, but there are likely to be better reasons to depart from equality with non-matrimonial property;
- this above comment differs from some recent cases in which non-matrimonial property tended towards equal sharing with longer marriages, greater contribution, mixing and mingling etc. Hereafter, all property starts with equality sharing;
- special contribution could be non-financial or financial, is not simply based on the level of wealth;
- the Court of Appeal preferred Baroness Hale and Lord Mance to Lord Nicholls on departing from equality in short marriage cases;
- it was dangerous to create a level of wealth above which there would be automatic departure from equality;

- special contribution was likely to lead to departure from equality of 5–16.6%;
- where there are unquantified debts at the final hearing, it was appropriate for these to be shared in accordance with the proportion of sharing the assets.

The problem with cases such as *Charman* is that they offer little assistance to the solicitor advising on smaller, more average cases. David Hodson commented that:

> at times higher court judges seem cocooned and exposed only to those solicitors and barristers undertaking the very big money cases. A daily diet of Charman does not give an appreciation of the bulk users of the family law finance resolution system, clients struggling to pay privately yet striving to reach a settlement, the middle-class disputes across the whole of England. These clients and their solicitors have suffered badly at the hands of the disputes, contradictions and conflicts between the senior judiciary of this country.

Example

The High Court has (rarely) recently addressed a more modest case and the case *of A v L* [2011] EWHC 3150 (Fam) (Moor J) 7 December 2011 gives a little more insight into judicial thinking in 'ordinary cases'.

In the case, the wife had primarily been a housewife and mother. At the time of the case she was unemployed but had undertaken some work after the couple separated. The husband worked as a self-employed letting agent. The husband's income was unclear but was estimated to be £28,000. Even allowing for a medical condition his earning capacity was far greater than his wife's.

The family's assets at the time of the case were:

The Former Matrimonial Home	£216,908
Egyptian properties	£45,833
Wife's accounts	£752
Husband's accounts	£5,811
Husband's debts	(£35,789)
Total	£233,515

The wife had been living in the matrimonial home since the separation in 2000 and the husband had been renting.

The judge at first instance had held that the wife needed to remain in the matrimonial home for a short period to adjust to life after separation but that it should be sold after two years. On sale, the proceeds should be divided 70:30 in the wife's favour and the husband should pay periodical payments of £500 per month for four years.

Moor J held that no sufficient justification was given for the very significant departure from equality at first instance. The judge had not adequately explained how the order would meet the needs of both parties rather than the wife's needs alone. There was also insufficient explanation of the interplay between the capital order and the periodical payments order.

Moor J concluded:

1. the disparity in earning capacity combined with the parties' needs was a good reason to depart from equality, but only on a clean break basis. The primary justification for the departure was the income disparity between the parties but other reasons, such as the wife's continuing responsibility for the two (adult) children, were given;
2. the former matrimonial home should be sold as soon as possible as the husband could not discharge his debts without this and it was doubtful whether the wife could meet the mortgage on her own;
3. the sale proceeds would be divided 70:30 in favour of the wife. It was accepted by the court that the wife would find it very difficult to buy anything other than a small flat and, once the husband had paid off his debts, he would struggle to do even that without a large mortgage.

11.5.3 STANDARD OF LIVING: S25(2)(C) MCA 1973

The courts do not have to endeavour to place the parties in the position that they would have been in had the marriage not broken down. In *Miller v Miller,* the court looked at the concept of 'legitimate expectations' and Lord Nicholls stated that 'both hopes and expectations, as such, are not an appropriate basis to assess financial needs'. The parties must be realistic about the parties' resources and both parties may have to accept a drop in the standard of living.

11.5.4 AGE OF THE PARTIES AND DURATION OF THE MARRIAGE: S25(2)(D) MCA 1973

Both the age of the parties and duration of the marriage is considered in conjunction with other s25(2) MCA 1973 factors.

If the parties are young at the time of marriage breakdown, there may be a greater argument for a clean break between the parties, especially if the marriage has produced no children. Younger parties can be expected to go back to work and become financially independent once children have gone to school. Similarly, if a party has not worked for some time, there can be an expectation with a younger person that they can retrain or re-enter work with some help. Younger parties under 50 can gain a mortgage more easily than those over 50. Younger parties have scope to increase their earning capacity more easily than those towards the end of their career.

By comparison, older parties may not be expected to find a highly paid job or any employment if they have spent the large part of their lives in the home. It may be difficult for older parties to obtain mortgages or to build up pension funds quickly.

The length of a marriage is also important. As we have seen, the longer the parties are married, the more difficult it is to untangle the finances of the parties and they will probably be more financially reliant on each other than those ending a short marriage. One must not forget that, however short the marriage, any children will be the first consideration of the court.

In a short and childless marriage, the traditional view is that the parties can expect to exit the marriage with only what they put into it in terms of money and legal rights to property may be more important than in longer marriages. In *Miller v Miller,* a very short marriage, it was held by Lord Nicholls that a short marriage was a partnership of equals but that there may be less of a claim between parties to a short marriage. Mrs Miller received less than one-sixth of the total assets.

If there are children, this will dilute the effect of the length of the marriage as the children must be cared for and be properly housed.

11.5.5 ANY PHYSICAL OR MENTAL DISABILITY OF EITHER OF THE PARTIES TO THE MARRIAGE: S25(2)(E) MCA 1973

The court will take into account any mental or physical illness of either party as this may affect the ability of that party to earn a living or they may require a greater amount of the assets and income to meet their needs. If a party has a progressive illness, the court may require a medical report giving the party's prognosis.

11.5.6 CONTRIBUTIONS TO THE MARRIAGE: S25(2)(F) MCA 1973

It may seem incredible now but before the seminal case of *White v White* [2000] 1 AC 596, the contribution of a wife (as it usually was the wife) to looking after children and the home was considered inferior to that of the husband (as it was usually the husband) to work and financial contributions to the marriage.

In *White v White*, the House of Lords found that parties would make significant and different contributions to the marriage and that it was wholly wrong to discriminate against the spouse who remained at home caring for the home and children. In different spheres of financial and family activity, both contribute equally to the family and it does not matter who built up the assets and earned the money.

S25(2)(f) MCA 1973 refers also to contributions made in the future. This encompasses the future care of children.

In cases involving great wealth, there has been a great deal of case-law on the issue of 'stellar contributions' made by one party that permits the court to move away from equality. This argument is frequently used by the husband, if he (or she) has made an unmatched contribution (whether described as 'special', 'stellar', or 'exceptional').

In *Cowan v Cowan* [2001] EWCA Civ 679, this argument succeeded. Mance LJ characterized the argument as:

> a spouse exercising special skill and care had gone beyond what was expected and beyond what the other spouse could ordinarily have hoped to do for himself or herself had the parties arranged their family lives and activities differently.

The facts of the case were that during the 35-year marriage the husband built up a fortune of £11.5 m due to his 'genius' in recognizing the potential of bin-liners in his plastics business. The court praised the husband's entrepreneurial flair, although the court acknowledged the wife's full contribution to the marriage and family life. As a result of the husband's efforts, there was a departure from equality.

However, in *Lambert v Lambert* [2002] EWCA Civ 1685, the Court of Appeal retreated from this position. After a 23-year marriage, the assets amounted to £20.2 m. At first instance the court held that the wife's full contributions were not exceptional, but the husband's contributions were really special. The Court of Appeal allowed the wife's appeal and awarded her 50% of the assets. Bodey J commented that:

> it is not possible to define once and for all, by way of some formulaic label, the precise characteristics of the fortune-maker required... However, those characteristics or circumstances clearly have to be of a wholly exceptional nature that it would be inconsistent with the objective of achieving fairness for them to be ignored.

This approach was approved in *Miller; MacFarlane*.

In *H v H* [2002] 2 FLR 1021, Peter Hughes QC rejected the argument of a highly successful city solicitor that his contribution was really special and said:

> it is not easy to define what may amount to a Stellar or really special contribution, but rather like the elephant, it is not difficult to spot one when you come across it.

The argument did succeed in *Sorrell v Sorrell* [2005] EWHC 1717 (Fam), where the assets were £75 m after a 32-year marriage with three children. The court described the husband's success resulting in the accrual of the assets as a result of his 'spark' or 'skill', and of the husband's genius. It held that it would be unfair to fail to recognize the exceptional circumstances and decided a 60/40 split in the husband's favour.

In *Charman v Charman (No. 4)* [2007] EWCA Civ 503, after a marriage of 28 years with two children, the assets amounted to £131 m. The wife conceded that some departure from equality should be made due to the husband's contribution; the wife was awarded 36.5% of the assets. The husband appealed and one of the grounds was that the court had not given sufficient recognition to the husband's contribution. The Court of Appeal rejected this argument and stated it would be hard to conceive that a percentage of division of matrimonial property should be further from equality than 66–33%.

The possible exception from this stated range is *McCartney v Mills-McCartney*, where the court rejected the arguments of the wife's 'exceptional' contributions. As stated at **11.5.2.1** the other factor of importance was the issue of non-matrimonial property.

11.5.7 CONDUCT

The courts and lawyers realistically expect that either party to a relationship breakdown will behave unpleasantly, unpredictably, or with a certain amount of negative emotion. This behaviour does not generally concern the court's consideration of the case, often to the outrage of the parties involved.

Practical Considerations

Many clients believe that the behaviour relied upon in the divorce petition should be taken into account when considering the division of money and property, e.g. adultery or domestic abuse.

The courts consider the behaviour of the parties and 'blame' (for want of a better word) within the marriage for the principal relief under the MCA 1973, i.e. divorce. The division of money and property is therefore based on the various factors of s25 MCA 1973 and not on the factors considered in divorce. Only in very narrow circumstances can conduct be considered.

The courts have consistently held that conduct is not considered by the court unless it is 'obvious and gross' (*Wachtel v Wachtel* [1973] Fam 72). In *Miller v Miller*, their Lordships were clear that adultery did not amount to such conduct and that in most cases fairness did not require the consideration of conduct.

Examples of what has amounted to obvious and gross conduct include the case of *B v B (Financial Provision: Welfare of a Child and Conduct)* [2002] 1 FLR 555 where the husband removed money from the jurisdiction to prevent the court's consideration of its disposal and the abduction of their child resulted in a conviction for child abduction. In *H v H (Financial Relief: Attempted Murder as Conduct)* [2006] 1 FLR 990 the husband was convicted of the attempted murder of his wife and refused to sell or let the family home. The wife was awarded the majority of assets and the court held that this was conduct that could not be disregarded. In fact, the husband's conduct had resulted in harm to her mental health and almost destroyed her earning capacity and, as a result, the conduct was at the top end of the scale.

11.6 CLEAN BREAK

Under s25A MCA 1973, the court has a duty to consider whether it is appropriate to impose a clean break. A 'clean break' is a settlement that finally severs the financial ties between the parties with no continuing provision between the parties for capital or income payments.

The court is not obliged to order a clean break; it is only obliged to consider the possibility of a clean break.

Further, s25A(2) MCA 1973 obliges the court to consider the terms of a periodical payments order and should consider whether it is appropriate to make an order of sufficient length to enable the spouse in whose favour the order is made to adjust without undue hardship to being financially independent of the other party. This envisages a situation where one spouse can increase their earnings and financial independence, e.g. where a spouse works part time and can increase their hours or a spouse can retrain to find work.

When there are children, it is not possible to order a complete clean break, but there is no reason why there should not be a clean break between the parties, if there are sufficient assets.

Whether or not a clean break is achievable depends entirely upon the circumstances of each individual case. There must be sufficient capital or income to enable each spouse to be financially independent of each other immediately.

Example

In *Parlour v Parlour* [2004] 2 FLR 893 the wife was awarded periodical payments at a high rate to build a capital fund. The husband was a footballer who was expected to earn very high wages but for a limited period only. As a result, the periodical payments were made for a limited term. A clean break would be achieved at the end of the term of periodical payments.

Not many clients will be footballers, but this is applicable to clients with high earnings but little capital.

11.7 *WHITE V WHITE*

The most significant decision in recent years came from the House of Lords in *White v White* [2000] (see **11.5.6**) when guidance was given on different aspects of ancillary relief (as it was called then).

The husband appealed to the House of Lords, seeking the restoration of a lump sum order for £980,000. The wife cross-appealed and sought a higher award.

The assets of the case included a dairy farm to which the parties had contributed equally, worth £3.5 m. The husband had an interest in another farm, which was not part of the partnership assets. The marriage had lasted 30 years and the parties had worked together in partnership. Both had substantial pensions.

The award to the wife was initially based on the traditional approach of allowing the wife 'reasonable requirements' to house herself and pay reasonable outgoings. The wife argued that it was appropriate for her to receive a sum roughly equivalent to half of the assets.

The leading judgment was given by Lord Nicholls. It is essential reading for all family law students and practitioners alike and a link can be found in the online resources. The main points of the case are discussed below.

The relationship between s25(2)(a) and s25(2)(b) MCA 1973 was not altogether satisfactory and the wording of the statute had led to confusion arising to 'reasonable requirements' being used as the criterion in big money cases. This was only one of many factors to which the court was to have regard and the judge should consider all the facts of the case and the overall requirement of fairness. The court in this case had fallen into error as it had confined itself to the wife's 'reasonable requirement' and ignored the fact that the husband's requirements were no greater and awarded him the majority of the assets.

The court should not make any distinction between contributions made by running the home and caring for the family on one hand and financial contributions on the other hand. Such contributions are to be considered equally.

When considering the division of assets, Lord Nicholls stated that the statute did not include a presumption of equal division but gave as a general guide that only with good reason would it be sufficient for a judge to depart from the 'yardstick of equality'. In practice, this yardstick is to be applied once the s25 MCA 1973 factors have been considered as a final check in the exercise of deciding the orders. It is not the starting point.

In fact, the wife in the case received roughly two-fifths of the assets as a whole as the House of Lords departed from equality on the basis that the husband's father had contributed money to the business and had assisted the husband to buy the second farm in the husband's sole name.

In *Parra v Parra* [2003] 1 FCR 97 the Court of Appeal allowed an appeal in favour of the husband and imposed an equal division of the assets where prior to the decision the wife had been awarded 54% of the assets. The parties had ordered their lives on the basis of equality and this ought to be recognized.

Departure from equality has been allowed on the grounds of a 12-year contribution to home and family being different in quality to a marriage of 20 years or more (*GW v RW*

(Financial Provision: Departure from Equality) [2003] 2 FLR 108) and in a short childless marriage where the court tried to give the parties the financial resources that they entered the marriage with (*Foster v Foster* [2003] 2 FLR 299).

11.8 FACTORS FOR ORDERS INVOLVING CHILDREN

As will be seen in **Chapter 12**, it is possible to apply for orders for children in proceedings for financial orders. The factors that the court will take into account are found in s25(3) MCA 1973 and include:

(a) the financial needs of the child;

(b) the income, earning capacity (if any), property, and other financial resources of the child;

(c) any physical or mental disability of the child;

(d) the manner in which he was being and in which the parties to the marriage expected him to be educated or trained.

If the child is a child of the family and not the natural child of the person against whom the order is sought, the court shall also have regard:

(a) to whether that party assumed any responsibility for the child's maintenance, and, if so, to the extent to which, and the basis upon which, that party assumed such responsibility and to the length of time for which that party discharged such responsibility;

(b) to whether in assuming and discharging such responsibility that party did so knowing that the child was not his or her own;

(c) to the liability of any other person to maintain the child.

As seen in **Chapter 18**, child support maintenance is dealt with under the Child Support Act 1995 and the Child Maintenance and Other Payments Act 2008. **Chapter 18** also contains details of applications made under Sch 1 of the Children Act 1989.

SUMMARY POINTS

- Proceedings for a financial order is the term given to the proceedings to divide money and property between divorcing spouses or civil partners dissolving a partnership.
- When the court is considering how to divide the matrimonial assets between the parties, the court must follow s25 MCA 1973 and associated decisions of the court.
- The first consideration of the court is the welfare of the children of the family and it must consider all the circumstances of the case.
- The court must consider a clean break between the parties, although this is not always possible.
- The s25 MCA 1973 factors encompass the available assets, the needs of the parties, age and duration of the marriage, standard of living, and contributions to the marriage and conduct.
- Some of these issues have generated a great deal of case-law and debate.
- *White v White* was decided by the House of Lords and affirmed that the aim of the court is to ensure fairness between the parties and for assets to be shared equally unless a departure from this is required.
- Some of the recent issues considered by the courts include how to classify property as matrimonial or non-matrimonial property, compensation for the ability to earn a future income, and whether contributions to marriage merit a departure from equality.

- No factor has any more importance than any other factor and the court must consider all the circumstances of the case.

SELF-TEST QUESTIONS

Matthew (aged 48) and Jilly (aged 49) have been married for 28 years and have three grown-up children. Matthew works as an accountant in a large firm and earns £250,000 per year. Jilly gave up work as a stockbroker when the first child of the marriage was born and has looked after the children and the home since then. The couple has a large comfortable home, which has been valued at £1,500,000 and is mortgage free. Matthew has a pension with a value of £250,000. The couple has some stocks and shares which, since the credit crunch, have decreased in value to around £18,000. There are no other significant assets as the couple admits that they have generally lived well, had many foreign holidays, and paid for their children to be educated privately.

The couple divorce following Matthew's adultery. Apply the s25 MCA 1973 factors to their case and draw some conclusions about how the court may divide the assets.

Case Study Two

Helena Wilson commenced divorce proceedings based on the fact of unreasonable behaviour. David has indicated that he will not defend the petition and has moved out of the family home into rented accommodation. He regularly has contact with his son Richard.

Helena comes to see you regarding financial relief. You take instructions and then receive a letter from David's solicitor giving some disclosure of his assets.

Your supervisor asks you to look at Helena's attendance note and the letter and to apply the s25 factors to the case. What are your conclusions about how the court will approach the case?

Answers to the questions above can be found on the Online Resource Centre: www.oxfordtextbooks.co.uk/orc/familyhandbook13/.

12 FINANCIAL ORDERS

12.1 INTRODUCTION

This chapter will:

- **discuss the principal forms of financial orders under the Matrimonial Causes Act 1973.**

As you have seen in **Chapter 11**, the courts have guidelines to assist them in deciding how much of the assets each party to the case should receive. As a family law student you should apply these factors to the case in hand to understand how the court is likely to divide assets between the parties. Once you have an understanding of the factors involved in the case, it is necessary to understand which orders to make to achieve the desired result.

To reorganize the assets of the parties involved in proceedings, the court has a number of different orders at its disposal. It is important that you understand what each order can do and, equally importantly, what they cannot. You are advised to look at **Chapter 14** for a discussion on consent orders for dealing with undertakings and drafting orders. This chapter covers the principal financial orders, their scope, and how they are used. **Chapter 19** deals separately with pensions and pension orders and you are advised to read both chapters together for a full picture.

The statute that is most important to this chapter is the Matrimonial Causes Act 1973 (MCA 1973).

12.2 AVAILABILITY OF ORDERS

The financial orders are:

- under s23 MCA 1973, financial provision orders: periodical payments order, secured periodical payments order, lump sum order (including pension sharing order under s24B MCA 1973 and pension attachment order under ss25B and 25C MCA 1973);
- under s24 MCA 1973, property adjustment orders: transfer of property, settlement of property, and variation of settlement.

S17 Married Women's Property Act 1882 (MWPA 1882) allows the court to consider disputes concerning title to or possession of a property. Applications under this section are now rare, given the more wide-ranging powers of ss23 and 24 MCA 1973. Proceedings under s17 MWPA 1882 are rare and reference should be made to a practitioner's text.

12.2.1 WHEN ORDERS ARE AVAILABLE

The court can make the orders listed at **12.2** on the granting of decree nisi of divorce or nullity or on the grant of a legal separation (see **12.2.2** for civil partnership). Orders can only take effect on the pronouncement of decree absolute in divorce and nullity.

As orders can be applied for after decree nisi, this raises the possibility of applications being made a great deal of time after divorce or of multiple applications.

In theory a spouse could make an application for financial orders and allow it to become dormant for a number of years before reviving it. This is not likely to prove successful for a number of reasons:

- if the applicant's claim for a financial remedy is not made in the divorce petition or answer, an application must be made to the court for leave before an application can be made. Any lengthy delay between petition/answer and application will militate against the court granting leave;
- if an application is made a substantial period after a divorce has been granted, the court can take this into account when considering all the circumstances of the case under s25 MCA 1973 (see **Chapter 11**).

Repeated applications for financial orders are generally not permissible. If a financial order application is heard by a court there is usually an order with dismissal of all claims (see **Chapter 14**). No further claims can be brought in this situation. As discussed at **Chapter 14**, it is imperative that all future claims are dismissed. The court's role remains only as one of variation or enforcement (see **Chapter 15**).

In the case of one spouse inheriting or gaining a sum of money in the near future, it is possible for the court to adjourn proceedings until a date when the position will become clearer. There may, of course, be an argument about whether or not the money constitutes matrimonial property (see **Chapter 11**). The issue of adjournment was considered in the case of *MT v MT (Financial Provision: Lump Sum)* [1992] 1 FLR 362. The court held, on an application for a lump sum order, that in circumstances where there was a real possibility of a source of capital becoming available in the future, a discretionary jurisdiction to adjourn would be available where it was the only way to do justice to the parties. This also fits in with the overriding objective of fairness.

A nominal periodical payments order can also preserve the entitlement of one party to periodical payments after the dismissal of financial order claims. For a fuller discussion of nominal periodical payments orders, see **Chapter 14**.

The discussion in **Chapter 14** should also be heeded for the procedural approach of preventing multiple or late applications for financial orders.

12.2.2 CIVIL PARTNERS

Civil partners are entitled to apply for financial provision on the dissolution or annulment of a civil partnership or when a separation order is made (see **Chapter 10**). Under s72(1) Civil Partnership Act 2004, Sch 5 of the CPA 2004 makes provision for financial relief that corresponds with the provision made in connection with marriages by Part 2 of the MCA 1973.

All orders available to spouses are available to civil partners with the exception of a pension attachment order. As with any proceedings for financial orders, orders will not take effect until the nullity or dissolution order has been made final or the separation order granted.

12.2.3 SPOUSES

The court can make any of the orders discussed in this chapter to the parties of a marriage.

Please note that cohabiting couples (whether same-sex or heterosexual couples) cannot apply for financial orders. For remedies available to cohabiting couples, please see **Chapters 22 and 23**.

12.2.4 CHILDREN

Under s29 MCA 1973, no provision may be made for a child of the family for financial provision or transfer of property if the child has attained the age of 18. Orders can be made for a child of the family (see **Chapter 11**) but more commonly an order will be made to one of the spouses for the benefit of the child or to achieve a situation that supports the spouse with the care of the children.

See **Chapter 18** for a discussion of Sch 1 Children Act 1989, which allows the court to make property orders for the benefit of children.

12.3 LUMP SUM ORDERS

A lump sum order, under s23(1)(c) and (f) MCA 1973, requires one party to pay a sum of money to another party (or a child of the family).

The payment can be made in one lump sum or by instalments. Instalments can be ordered to be secured to the court's satisfaction under s23(3)(c) MCA 1973. How the payments are secured will depend upon each individual case and according to the assets available to be secured. Lump sum orders are generally to be paid immediately or over a small number of instalments and so security will generally be gained by a deposit of title deeds to property, or stocks and shares, so that there is a sufficient safeguard for the recipient.

There is no power to order an interim lump sum order (*Wicks v Wicks* [1998] 1 FLR 470).

Practical Considerations

Lump sum orders are extremely useful and are used to give one party a share of a large capital asset or as compensation for their interest in the family home, pension, shares, endowment policy, or savings. They can also be used to help one party reduce a mortgage to a more affordable level.

So, if a house is transferred to one spouse, another spouse can receive a lump sum from other assets to enable them to purchase a new property.

12.4 PROPERTY ADJUSTMENT ORDERS

Under s24(1) MCA 1973, the court may make any one or more of the following orders:

(a) an order that a party to the marriage shall transfer to the other party, to any child of the family, or to such person as may be specified in the order for the benefit of such a child such property as may be so specified, being property to which the first-mentioned party is entitled, either in possession or reversion;

(b) an order that a settlement of such property as may be so specified, being property to which a party to the marriage is so entitled, be made to the satisfaction of the court for the benefit of the other party to the marriage and of the children of the family or either or any of them;

(c) an order varying for the benefit of the parties to the marriage and of the children of the family or either or any of them any ante-nuptial or post-nuptial settlement (including such a settlement made by will or codicil) made on the parties to the marriage;

(d) an order extinguishing or reducing the interest of either of the parties to the marriage under any such settlement.

A property adjustment order is one which gives the court a great deal of scope to re-order the assets of the parties.

12.4.1 TRANSFER OF PROPERTY ORDER

Under s24(1)(a) MCA 1973 the court can order that property is transferred from one party to the other party or for the benefit of the children of the family. The party must be entitled to the property, e.g. be an owner of the property. This order is most commonly associated with the transfer of the family home. However, a transfer of property order can be used to transfer any property including cars, furniture, shares, endowment policies, holiday property or investment property, antiques, or jewellery.

Rented property can be subject to a transfer of property order as tenancies are 'property'. The court can order one party to transfer a tenancy to the other party including both private sector and council tenancies, and statutory tenancies under the Rent Act 1977. It does not matter whether the tenancy is periodic (weekly) or fixed term although the landlord will need to consent.

Statutory tenancies can be transferred under Sch 7, para 2 of the Family Law Act 1996 and this is covered in **Chapter 34**.

12.4.2 SETTLEMENT OF PROPERTY

Under s24(1)(b) MCA 1973 the court can order one party to settle property to which he is entitled for the benefit of the other party or the children of the marriage. 'Settlement' does not mean that the person gives away the property completely. Generally, a settlement of property involves one party settling the property by way of a trust until a certain date is reached or a certain event occurs. For more discussion of this type of order, see **12.5.4**.

12.4.3 VARIATION OF SETTLEMENT

Under s24(1)(c) and (d) MCA 1973 the court can vary for the benefit of the parties or the children of the family any ante-nuptial or post-nuptial settlement including a settlement made by will or codicil.

An ante-nuptial settlement (an agreement made pre-marriage) could include a property bought in contemplation of marriage or during the engagement of the parties. If it is subsequently used as a family home, it can be regarded as an ante-nuptial settlement (*N v N and F Trust* [2006] 1 FLR 856).

In *C v C (Variations of Post-nuptial Settlement: Company Shares)* [2003] 2 FLR 493, a trust comprised the husband's shares in a company. The court varied the terms of the trust to give the wife 30% of the shares.

12.5 ORDERS CONCERNING THE FAMILY HOME

Whether owned by one or both parties, the family home is, for the majority of cases, the largest asset in financial order proceedings. As stated in **Chapter 11**, the priority for the court is to provide a suitable home for the children of the family and the spouse with care of the children as well as a home for the other spouse. Unless acting for wealthy clients, the central question to resolving the case is to use the family home to make an order that houses both parties adequately.

The most common orders made include the immediate sale of the property and division of proceeds, the sale of the house is postponed with the proceeds to be divided on sale, and transfer of the home into the sole name of one spouse with a charge in favour of one spouse, or immediate payment of a lump sum in compensation.

12.5.1 SALE AND DIVISION OF PROCEEDS

Under s24A MCA 1973, where the court makes an order for a lump sum, a secured periodical payments order, or a property adjustment order, on making that order or at any time afterwards, the court may make an order for sale of property specified in the order to which either or both parties have a beneficial interest. An order for sale can include an order to make a payment out of the proceeds to one of the parties. An order for sale can also be used to enforce a secured periodical payments or lump sum order.

An immediate sale may be appropriate in a number of circumstances:

- where there is sufficient equity in the family home to be divided to provide both parties with the means to purchase an adequate new home. There may not be the ability to buy a home of the same size or standard as the previous family home;
- where one party has already obtained alterative accommodation and the house proceeds are used to allow the other spouse to purchase a new property. The remainder of the proceeds can be given to the spouse with accommodation as a lump sum. This can be used as a savings 'cushion' or as a way of reducing the mortgage;
- where there is insufficient money to pay the existing mortgage and outgoings on the family home, there may be no alternative to the sale of the home if it is at risk of repossession. The proceeds of the sale can be divided between the parties, although the capital limit for certain welfare benefits must be remembered. Parties may have to seek local authority housing or housing association accommodation or private rented accommodation.

Practical Considerations

In order to calculate the equity available in a home, the following steps must be taken:

- obtain an up-to-date valuation for the property;
- obtain the balance of any outstanding mortgage(s) and secured debts;
- take into account how much it costs to sell the home (estate agent fees, conveyancing fees, etc.) for both the sale and purchase of a new property;
- take into account any stamp duty (see **Chapter 20**) payable on the new home;
- take into account any removal fees or storage fees;
- for a publicly funded client, take into account the impact of the statutory charge.

This will give a realistic picture of the equity available to the parties when dividing sale proceeds. Advice can be taken from an independent financial adviser or mortgage adviser on the availability of mortgages and loans to purchase a new property.

12.5.2 TRANSFER INTO ONE SPOUSE'S SOLE NAME

There are some situations where the court may transfer the house into one spouse's sole name. In *S v S* [1976] Fam 18, the wife cared at home for a child with a disability and could not work full time, although she paid all mortgage and other household expenses. The house was transferred to her. Most commonly, transfer of the family home is used where the family home is the only asset and the parent with care of the children requires the property as security. This is not the only situation where the court will order a transfer and the court takes into account all the circumstances of the case. For instance in *Jones v Jones* [1976] Fam 8 the husband's assault on the wife reduced her capacity to work. The husband's conduct and the wife's inability to work led the court to transfer the house to the wife.

There are a number of variations on a transfer:

- One spouse has the family home transferred to them and the other spouse has a lump sum payment as compensation for the loss of their interest in the family home. This depends on the assets and the ability of the court to find a lump sum payment from the assets.
- The property can be transferred outright to one spouse with no lump sum payable and without any charge on the home.

If the house is sold, there may be insufficient sale proceeds for one party to be compensated for the loss of the home. Instead of a lump sum, the spouse may receive a larger share of any pension provision or reduced or nil periodical payments. The mortgage will be transferred to the occupying spouse but it should not be assumed that this will happen automatically; the mortgage lender must agree to this. The transferring spouse is released from the commitment of the mortgage and is free to obtain one for a new property.

Practical Considerations

One of the problems associated with transferring the family home is whether the mortgagee will consent to the transfer of the mortgage and whether the transferee can afford to take it on. One party may be willing to transfer a property to their former spouse or civil partner but if there is a mortgage, the bank or building society must agree to the mortgage being transferred too. It may also be the case that the transferee cannot afford to pay the mortgage without the assistance of the transferor. This may leave one party in the position of not being the owner of a property but still being responsible for a mortgage. This would be a difficult position for the transferee if their former spouse defaulted on the mortgage as liability is joint and several.

This may seem a draconian measure to leave one spouse without any share of the family home but it may be necessary to house a more vulnerable party. Alternatively, one spouse may have a high wage or excellent capacity to earn enough to provide a home for them whilst paying periodical payments—it will be a question of balancing the assets available against the needs of the parties and the overall requirement of fairness. There are some options open to the court where the spouse not living in the home retains a beneficial interest.

12.5.3 CHARGE ON THE PROPERTY

A charge is where the family home is transferred to one spouse completely with the transferring spouse receiving a proportion of the sale proceeds when the house is sold or on a specified event.

This type of order is suitable for a transferring party who is able to wait for their share and the level of the charge should be carefully considered—whether or not the money is required to pay for a new home or whether it is simply a lump sum to compensate the transferring party for the loss of the asset.

Example

In *Browne (formerly Pritchard) v Pritchard* [1975] 3 All ER 721 the husband remained in the family home with his sons from a prior association. The wife left with the child of the marriage and remarried. At the time of the hearing (at the Court of Appeal) both parties were living on benefits and the wife had been deserted by her husband and was living in a council house.

The Court of Appeal ordered that a charge be placed on the house for one-third of the net sale proceeds in favour of the wife with the sale to be postponed until six months after the 18th birthday of the youngest son with liberty to apply for the charge to be realized earlier.

This type of order operates in a similar way to a Mesher order (see **12.5.4**), although the two are not identical. With a charge, one person owns the entire property with a charge against it. With Mesher orders, the ownership is held by both parties.

12.5.4 MESHER AND MARTIN ORDERS

If the court wishes to preserve both parties' interest in the family home but cannot immediately order a sale, a 'Mesher order' may be suitable. A Mesher order is named after the case of *Mesher v Mesher and Hall* [1980] 1 All ER 126, although the case was actually decided in 1973.

A Mesher order is one where the family home continues to be held by both parties as trustees of land. The type of trust that is found in most Mesher orders is:

- one party has the sole right to occupy the property until sale;
- sale is triggered upon a particular event, e.g. the occupying spouse dies, remarries, cohabits for more than six months, voluntarily sells the property, or the youngest child of the marriage attains a certain age;
- upon sale, the net proceeds of the sale (after redeeming the mortgage and paying sale costs) are divided according to proportions agreed at the time of the order.

The occupying spouse usually gives an undertaking to the court that they will maintain and repair the property and pay all outgoings.

The advantage of a Mesher order is that it allows the preservation of a family home with one party retaining an interest and gives one party a future capital interest in the property. For a while, Mesher orders became unfashionable, as the Court of Appeal found in *Martin v Martin* [1978] Fam 12 and *Hanlon v Hanlon* [1978] 2 All ER 889. Their criticism was that a Mesher order stores up trouble for the future and Mesher orders do have some disadvantages: children may require a home longer than is allowed for in the order; the home may have decreased in value over the period of the trust, leaving parties unable to buy a property; a spouse may enter the property market in their 50s without sufficient earning capacity; and an enormous gap can be left between the order and the non-occupying spouse receiving their capital interest. However, as property prices rose throughout the early part of this century, these orders have been used increasingly to achieve equality between the spouses, even if one spouse has to wait for a capital sum.

A similar type of order is the Martin order from the case of *Martin v Martin*. This order allows a spouse to occupy the family home until death or remarriage and the sale is postponed until then. It is a very unusual order that is not commonly used, but will protect an older, financially vulnerable spouse with no earning capacity.

12.6 PERIODICAL PAYMENTS ORDERS

The capital orders (12.5) will allow the courts to rearrange the assets between the parties, but both parties require an income.

Periodical payments orders under s23(1)(a) and (d) MCA 1973 are often referred to by clients as 'maintenance'. The order is for a regular payment of money by one party to another. The interval of payments can be weekly or monthly.

Under s23(1)(b) and (e) MCA 1973 the periodical payments can be secured in order to ensure payments are made without requiring enforcement.

The assets used as security will depend upon the assets in the case. In some cases, an asset will produce an income, e.g. savings or shares, and these will form the security. In other cases, an asset does not produce an income, e.g. a painting. The payments will be made from income as usual but in the case of non-payment, the asset will be charged with the amount of non-payment and the receiving spouse will be able to recover the charge. The assets cannot be disposed of during the life of the secured periodical payments order.

12.6.1 THE AMOUNT OF PERIODICAL PAYMENTS

There is no guidance in the MCA 1973 concerning the amount of periodical payments. There have been a number of different approaches by the courts, although there is no preferred method.

Considering the s25 MCA 1973 factors, the court will consider the children of the family (as their first consideration), the reasonable needs of the parties, as well as the standard of living of the parties. 'Needs' may also encompass a situation where one party can become financially independent through retraining or when the children go to school and, until then, periodical payments are needed to support that party.

The income of the parties is clearly relevant together with their future earning capacity. Clearly a balance must be struck between the ability of the payer to provide periodical payments with the need to maintain the payer's income at a reasonable level too. The availability of welfare benefits should also be considered (see **Chapter 21**).

One approach is to look at the 'net effect' of the proposed order and there is an example of this below in the case study.

As seen in the case of *Parlour v Parlour* [2004] EWCA Civ 872, periodical payments may also serve the purpose of allowing the receiving party to build up a capital sum. In *McFarlane v McFarlane* [2006] UKHL 24, Baroness Hale stated that the sharing principle applied (as well as needs and compensation). The sharing principle dictates that the receiving party will share in the future surplus and share in the fruits of the matrimonial partnership. Mrs McFarlane received a periodical payments order beyond her reasonable needs. Their Lordships were clear that capital accumulation was a permissible side-effect of periodical payments. It must be borne in mind that both cases involved very high earners and most clients will not necessarily have a surplus income.

A 'nominal' periodical payments order is one where a nominal sum of money (e.g. £1 per year) is ordered either for the joint lives of the parties or for a limited term. The purpose of such an order is to allow one party to have the security of a periodical payments order that can be varied upwards in case of illness or unemployment. The periodical payment is paid at the nominal sum unless the court decides to vary the amount upwards.

Example

In *SRJ v DWJ* [1999] 2 FLR 176, a 27-year marriage produced four children, one of whom was still dependent, with the wife unable to support herself without resort to welfare benefits. The husband was unlikely to produce sufficient income in future that would benefit the family and enable the wife to come off benefits.

The court took several factors into consideration:

- the wife still looked after a dependent child;
- the wife was unable to financially support herself but had to accept that she would have to make efforts to do so;
- this was a long marriage with four children and the wife gave up her work to look after the family.

The court made a nominal periodical payments order for £10 per annum.

12.6.2 TERM OF PERIODICAL PAYMENTS ORDERS

The term of the periodical payments orders is 'as the court thinks fit'. The term cannot begin any earlier than the making of the application for the order and cannot carry on after death or (if the order is made after the grant of a divorce, nullity, or civil partnership dissolution) the remarriage or entering into a civil partnership of the party in whose favour the order has been made (s28 MCA 1973). Commonly, orders are made to encompass the cohabitation of the receiving party as many parties would cohabit and not marry in order to allow the payments to continue.

The courts have a number of options for the making of periodical payments orders:

- adjourn the application;
- a periodical payments order for the joint lives of the parties until death, remarriage, or entering into a civil partnership. It can be subsequently varied or discharged (see **Chapter 15**). This may be suitable where one party has an illness or disability or where they are unlikely to be able to support themselves. The amount of the order can be substantive or nominal;
- a periodical payments order for a limited term under s28(1A) MCA 1973 with no extension after the limited term. An application for the variation of the amount is permitted. This type of order may be made where one party requires a period of time to become financially independent but the court finds the case unsuitable for extensions;
- a periodical payments order for a limited term but with no prohibition on extension. Prior to the expiry of the limited term, an application may be made for variation, extension, or discharge. This may be used when a party seeks to become financially independent but the court wishes to give the party the opportunity for a longer period of periodical payments;
- dismiss the application.

12.7 INTERIM ORDERS

12.7.1 MAINTENANCE PENDING SUIT

S22 MCA 1973 allows an application for maintenance pending suit. On a petition for divorce, judicial separation, nullity, or civil partnership dissolution, the court can require either party to the marriage to pay periodical payments for his or her maintenance for such term as the court thinks reasonable. The term cannot start before the date of the presentation of a petition and ends on the date of the determination of the case.

In practice, most parties agree a form of maintenance between themselves pending resolution of the case. Sometimes the parties survive financially through a combination of earnings, welfare benefits, and loans from banks or friends.

To apply for maintenance pending suit, the applicant must issue a Form A (see **Chapter 14**).

This order addresses the problem where one spouse finds themselves in need of income following the issuing of a divorce or civil partnership dissolution. Longer term issues of capital provision or the family home are left until the final hearing. The applicant must demonstrate their specific need, usually in the form of a budget. If there is not full disclosure of the payer's income and assets at this stage of proceedings, the court will err on the side of caution if the payee's need is evident to the court. In *TL v ML* [2005] EWHC 2860 (Fam) the court noted that the approach to be applied in determining the application is 'reasonableness' under s22 MCA 1973, which was described as being synonymous with fairness.

Legal costs can also be part of a claim for maintenance pending suit. The applicant must demonstrate that they are not eligible for public funding or a loan. The court in *Moses-Taiga v Taiga* [2006] 1 FLR 1074 stated that this was a discretionary remedy and does not require exceptional circumstances.

Currey v Currey (No. 2) [2007] 1 FLR 946 sets out the court's current approach. The Court of Appeal held that there must be an 'initial overarching enquiry' to demonstrate the applicant cannot procure any other means of funding and particularly that the applicant has not been able to deploy their assets directly to pay costs or to raise a loan. The applicant cannot obtain legal services through a charge upon ultimate capital recovery and there is no public funding available.

Clients of even modest means may not be able to secure public funding after April 2012. After April 2012, no public funding will be available in this area of law. See **Chapter 2** for more detail.

Lack of alternative funding is a necessary condition to an award but it may not be sufficient. The court will also look at the subject matter of the proceedings and the applicant's behaviour and position taken in the proceedings. Commonly this type of order will cease at the financial dispute resolution hearing (see **Chapter 14**) and this is regarded as a reasonable inducement to settle rather than improper pressure.

12.7.2 INTERIM PERIODICAL PAYMENTS ORDER

Under r2.64(2) FPR the court has the power to make any interim order that it sees fit. The most common such order is for periodical payments for adults. The court has limited power to make periodical payments for children.

Interim periodical payments orders for adults are generally made when proceedings for financial orders cannot be fully resolved until a substantial amount of time after decree absolute as an interim periodical payments order can only be ordered after decree nisi has been pronounced. Maintenance pending suit can be used before then.

12.8 CHILD SUPPORT

Child support is now dealt with by the Child Support Act 1991 and subsequent legislation. Please refer to **Chapter 18**.

SUMMARY POINTS

- When the courts have applied the guidance under s25 MCA 1973 to the case, a decision is made about how the assets are divided.
- There are a number of orders that allow the court to reorganize the family's money and property and they are found in ss23 and 24 MCA 1973.
- Generally orders can be made following decree nisi and come into effect on the pronouncement of decree nisi (and equivalent in civil partnerships).
- Lump sum orders can be one lump sum or by instalments and can be secured.
- Property adjustment orders are used to transfer property between parties or to vary settlements of properties.
- There are a number of orders that can be made regarding the family home, including a sale and division of proceeds, transfer to one party, a postponement with a charge, or a Mesher or Martin order attached to the home.

- Periodical payments orders provide the receiving party with an income and the orders possible vary from an order for the whole joint lives of the parties to a short, non-extendable term.
- The amount prescribed by a periodical payments order can vary from a nominal payment to a substantial sum to allow one party to build a capital sum.
- Prior to decree nisi, maintenance pending suit can be used to provide an income.

SELF-TEST QUESTIONS

1. Bilkiss and Amir divorce. Bilkiss is disabled and requires a specially adapted home and also works from home. The home has a substantial level of equity and Amir is very well paid. The couple have two children, aged 11 and 12 respectively. Bilkiss wishes to remain in the home until the children have left home and requires a large share of the equity in the house to find a suitable home. Bilkiss and Amir agree that Bilkiss can remain in the home until the youngest child is 21 years old or if Bilkiss remarries or cohabits for more than six months. Once the 'trigger' event occurs, the house will be sold and Bilkiss will receive 80% of the sale proceeds. Explain which order will be suitable to achieve this and the advantages and disadvantages of such an order.
2. Bilkiss works part time as she cares for the children. She believes that it will be very difficult for her to find full-time employment, even when the children have left home. Amir wishes to have a clean break. What income orders may be suitable for this situation? How could the court achieve a clean break?

Case Study Two

Proceedings for financial orders have been issued by Helena and the Form A can be found in the online resources. Helena wishes to know whether or not she can remain in the family home with Richard. Your supervisor asks you to look at the disclosure given on the Form E (in the online resources) and details about a Form E can be found in **Chapter 16**. What possible orders can be made concerning the family home in this case and which one would you recommend for Helena?

Answers to the questions above can be found on the Online Resource Centre: www.oxfordtextbooks.co.uk/orc/familyhandbook12/.

13 PRE-MARITAL AGREEMENTS

13.1 INTRODUCTION

This chapter will:

- **examine the nature of pre-marital agreements;**
- **discuss the enforceability of pre-marital agreements in proceedings for financial orders;**
- **discuss the potential developments in the enforceability of pre-marital agreements.**

A pre-marital agreement (PMA) is essentially a contract between the parties of a marriage that decides, in advance of a divorce, the division of money and property between the parties. There has been a great deal of discussion and case-law on whether PMAs can and should be taken into account by the courts when considering ancillary relief.

Catherine Zeta Jones reportedly receives £1 m per year of marriage to Michael Douglas under their PMA and there has been a greater public awareness of PMAs through 'celebrity' divorces. This chapter looks at features of PMAs and case-law dealing with the issue of PMAs.

13.2 WHAT ARE PRE-MARITAL AGREEMENTS?

In essence, a PMA, sometimes called an ante-nuptial agreement or a pre-nuptial agreement, is a contract made between two people before they get married. The contract generally concerns the division of money and property following divorce. There have been objections to PMAs for many years. Some of the objections made have been from a religious standpoint as it is felt that marriage is based on love and affection and should not be sullied with contracts. Others believe that PMAs discourage marriage. The courts have traditionally found that parties, as a matter of public policy, exclude the jurisdiction of the courts in deciding financial orders.

13.3 ADVANTAGES AND DISADVANTAGES OF PMAS

See **Table 13.1**.

TABLE 13.1 ADVANTAGES AND DISADVANTAGES OF PMAS

Advantages	Disadvantages
Consenting, well-advised adults can decide their own outcomes on divorce and can cut costs and acrimony on divorce.	Over time, the position of the parties can change: children may be born, one party can become ill or disabled, and the initial PMA may be unfair or inadequate to deal with such changes.
	One party can unduly influence another into an unfair PMA.
PMAs encourage openness on financial issues between the parties before marriage. Many marriages end because of disagreements over family finances.	They are 'unromantic' according to Paul McCartney (!)
PMAs may encourage marriage as certainty over proceedings for financial orders when two in five marriages fail could be a wise precaution.	They may discourage marriage for fear of losing assets.
PMAs may save costs in proceedings in financial orders.	PMAs will involve the cost of independent legal advice for both parties before the marriage.
PMAs can be used to protect wealth or family assets and to preserve property for children from earlier marriages.	

13.4 THE ENFORCEABILITY OF PMAS

The traditional position of the courts in England and Wales was that pre-nuptial agreements are not enforceable. PMAs are fully enforceable in other jurisdictions, including Sweden, Canada, certain US states, New Zealand, and marriage contracts are a feature of certain religions, e.g. Islam.

In 1998, the Government produced a White Paper called 'Supporting Families'. One of the issues that the Government raised was to make agreements concerning property legally binding, albeit with safeguards to protect a vulnerable party. The consultation revealed an equal split of opinion on the issue, with the arguments in **13.3** raised by both sides of the argument. There have been no proposals to bring forward any legislation on PMAs.

In more recent cases, PMAs have been held to be influential in courts' decisions and the Supreme Court has more recently been more positive on enforceability. The following section summarizes the main case-law on PMAs.

13.4.1 *K V K*

In *K v K (Ancillary Relief: Prenuptial Agreement)* [2003] 1 FLR 120, the husband and wife separated after 14 months of marriage and the parties had one child together. Prior to the marriage the wife discovered she was pregnant and the wife's family exerted pressure on the husband to marry her. The husband had wanted a long engagement but the couple agreed to marry and entered into a PMA, mainly at the instigation of the wife's father. The wife had assets (held in trust) of about £1 m and the husband had assets of £25 m. Both parties received independent financial advice and the solicitors were informed of the pregnancy.

The PMA was signed the day before the parties married. The terms of the PMA were that if the couple were to dissolve their marriage within five years of the date of the PMA, the wife was to receive £100,000 from the husband (to be increased by 10% pa compound) and the husband was to make reasonable financial provision for any children. There were no valuations of the husband's assets prior to the signing of the PMA and there was no reference made in the PMA to periodical payments for the wife.

The wife sought a much larger settlement from the court with sizeable periodical payments for her and the children. She also asked the court to disregard the PMA. The husband relied upon the PMA.

The judge rejected the wife's case and held that the wife understood the agreement, she was properly advised, she was under no pressure to sign, she entered the agreement in the knowledge that there would soon be a child, and that no unforeseen changes had arisen in circumstance since the PMA was made that would make it unjust to hold the parties to it. The particular features of the case that the judge took into account included: the fact that the marriage was very short, the pressure that the husband was under from the wife's family to marry, the interference of the wife's father in controlling and manipulating the wife's finances, and that the wife had been on a spending spree. The husband was substantially wealthy and could pay a settlement that prevented the disparity in the parties' financial positions having an impact on the child. The wife had contributed nothing to the husband's wealth but she would make future contributions to the upbringing of the child.

In terms of the validity of the PMA, the wife clearly understood the PMA and had received independent legal advice. The husband had not pressured her to sign.

Whilst there had not been full disclosure, the husband did not exploit his financial position. Both knew that the wife was pregnant with their child and no circumstances had changed sufficiently that would make it unjust to hold the parties to it. The husband had been heavily pressurized into the marriage by the wife's family, and had agreed to marry on the basis that the capital sum under the PMA would be a final settlement for the wife.

The judge held that the PMA should be considered by the court as one of the circumstances of the case under s25 of the Matrimonial Causes Act 1973 (MCA 1973) (see **Chapter 11**). The PMA was clear on the issue of capital provision for the wife and there were no grounds for concluding that an injustice would be done by holding the parties to its terms. Entry into the agreement constituted conduct that it would be inequitable to disregard under s25(2)(g) of the MCA 1973.

However, the PMA could not (in this case) preclude a claim for maintenance. The wife can contribute in the future by bringing up the child with an adverse effect on her earning capacity. The judge found that it would be unjust to the wife to suggest, either because of the short duration of the marriage or because of the PMA, that she should have no maintenance. The judge awarded the wife £14,000pa to enable her to bring up the child in comfortable circumstances.

13.4.2 *CROSSLEY V CROSSLEY*

In *Crossley v Crossley* [2007] EWCA Civ 1491 a PMA had been executed between the parties. Both were independently wealthy before the marriage; Mr Crossley had £45m and Mrs Crossley £18m. The PMA contained an agreement for each party to walk away with what they brought to the marriage and that neither would apply to the court. The marriage broke down after a year.

Mrs Crossley applied for ancillary relief (as it was called then). She claimed that her husband had failed to disclose assets when entering into the PMA. Mr Crossley applied to the court for a summons to show cause why Mrs Crossley's claims should not be resolved in accordance with the PMA. At the first appointment, Mr Crossley argued that the court should not simply dismiss the case and ignore the s25 MCA 1973 factors but that Mrs Crossley should be held to the PMA. Bennett J held that the exceptional facts of the case justified a departure from the usual procedure (see **Chapter 14**) and allowed a Form E, an informal questionnaire, to be completed, and set the matter down for a one-day hearing in accordance with the overriding objective found in the procedural rules.

Mrs Crossley appealed these directions to the Court of Appeal. She argued that she had been denied the right to effectively present her case and that the provisions of the procedural rules were mandatory.

The Court of Appeal dismissed the appeal. The Court of Appeal found that whilst the existence of the PMA cannot oust the court's obligation to apply the s25 MCA 1973 factors, the exceptional facts of the case gave rise to a 'very strong case that a possible result of the s25 exercise will be that the wife receives no further financial reward' and that '...if ever there is to be a paradigm case in which the court will look to the prenuptial agreement as... a factor of magnetic importance, it seems to me that this is just such a case'. Thorpe LJ also remarked that 'It does seem to me that the role of contractual dealing, the opportunity for the autonomy of the parties, is becoming increasingly important.'

Before the court could then reach a decision on what Mrs Crossley should receive, Mrs Crossley withdrew her application.

13.4.3 *MACLEOD V MACLEOD*

The Privy Council in *MacLeod v MacLeod* [2008] UKPC 64 (on appeal from the Isle of Man) was asked to rule on PMAs. The law on family finances in the Isle of Man is virtually identical to that of the MCA 1973 and so the decision can be treated as one by the House of Lords. Although there are not individual judgments given by the Privy Council, the voice of the judgment is undoubtedly Baroness Hale's.

Mr and Mrs MacLeod are both American and married in Florida in 1994. Mr MacLeod had a substantial fortune and the parties entered into a PMA on the day of the marriage. The PMA would probably have been enforceable in Florida, but would have been considered inadequate provision for the wife under English law. The parties had five children and had moved to the Isle of Man.

In July 2002, the parties entered into another PMA, which was more generous to the wife than the 1994 agreement but less generous than a court applying the MCA 1973 would have been. The court found that the wife had entered into the agreement freely, voluntarily, and with full understanding. Mrs MacLeod had taken independent legal advice, but she chose to ignore it.

The marriage broke down in 2003 and the husband complied fully with the 2002 PMA, including the transfer of a property to Mrs MacLeod. There were contested proceedings concerning the children, resulting in shared residence. The husband accepted that the property transferred to Mrs MacLeod was not suitable for times when the children lived with her.

Proceedings were issued and Mrs MacLeod sought to avoid the PMA and asked for £5 m as a lump sum. Mr MacLeod's position was that Mrs MacLeod should be held to the PMA that offered £1 m on divorce but offered a further lump sum for rehousing that would be held on trust.

At first instance the court held that Mrs MacLeod should receive £1.25 m as a housing fund in addition to the £1 m offered by the PMA (Mr MacLeod had offered £750,000) and that the housing fund should not be held in trust. At appeal the parties repeated their positions, except that the husband accepted that the additional housing fund should be £1.25 m, but his position remained that this should be held on trust. Both appeals were dismissed.

Mr MacLeod appealed to the Privy Council. The husband's appeal was allowed and a trust arrangement was substituted for the lump sum.

The Privy Council stated that 'the case is not about the validity and effect of ante-nuptial agreements as such'. It is to be regretted that the court did not take the opportunity to develop the law further on PMA. At para 31 the Privy Council stated that:

> it is not open to them to reverse the long standing rule that ante-nuptial agreements are contrary to public policy and thus not valid or binding in the contractual sense... there is an enormous difference in principle and practice between an agreement providing for a present state of affairs which has developed between a married couple and an agreement made before the parties have committed themselves to the rights and responsibilities of the married state purporting to govern what may happen in an uncertain and unhoped for future.

The Privy Council drew a distinction based on the fact that any financial agreement between the parties during the marriage would be a maintenance agreement (see **Chapter 17**) capable of being varied under s35 MCA 1973, whereas one made before a marriage probably would not. In reality, it is difficult to see the difference between an agreement made on the day before the marriage ceremony and one made after the ceremony (or indeed between one made in the throes of a disintegrating marriage).

An important point emerged from the judgment. An agreement made prior to the marriage is not valid on the basis of public policy (although the court can take it into account) whereas one made after marriage is valid subject to normal contractual considerations and the power of the court under s35 MCA 1973 to vary such an agreement. This may have the effect of making applications under s35 MCA 1973 more common than they are presently.

The Privy Council remarked in *MacLeod* that it was a matter for Parliament, to be guided by the Law Commission. The conclusion to be drawn from the case is that a PMA executed before the marriage will carry less weight and is less likely to be upheld than an agreement reached during marriage.

13.4.4 *RADMACHER V GRANATINO*

In *Radmacher v Granatino* [2009] EWCA Civ 649 the wife was a German national from a very rich family. The wife was very wealthy and her income was in the region of £2.7 m pa. The husband, a French national, who had been a City banker with earnings peaking at £300,000 gross in 2001, was by the time of the hearing studying for a doctorate at Oxford University. The parties met in 1997 in London when the wife was 28 and the husband 26 and earning £50,000 gross pa. The parties became engaged in 1998 and agreed to enter into a pre-marital agreement.

The Court of Appeal, whilst acknowledging that pre-marital agreements are, as a matter of public policy, unenforceable, held that in the right circumstances they will be given such weight in the balancing exercise so as to be the decisive factor in determining an application for ancillary relief (as it was then called). Thorpe LJ highlighted the fact that the law in this area in England and Wales is increasingly out of step with the majority of countries of the European Union and Rix and Wilson LJJ also considered the need to balance the 'public interest in a fair and just exercise of the court's discretion' and the need to ensure there are safeguards in place to protect those who may enter into an agreement without a clear understanding of the possible consequences of their doing so.

The Court considered that the judge at first instance had failed to give sufficient weight to a number of factors, including: that such agreements are standard practice in France and Germany; that the husband was very able and was well established in the financial world and had had ample opportunity to take independent legal advice (although he had chosen not to do so); that the husband knew the wife was from a very wealthy family; and that the husband had chosen not to initiate negotiations. Provision for the husband should be in accordance with that envisaged by the agreement.

The husband appealed to the Supreme Court and the decision can be found at *Radmacher v Radmacher (formerly Granatino)* [2010] UKSC 42. There was an unusually large bench hearing the matter with Lord Phillips, Lord Hope, Lord Rodger, Lady Hale, Lord Brown, Lord Mance, Lord Collins and Lord Kerr all sitting.

The judgment of the Supreme Court has given the clearest indication that there may be a significant shift in attitude by the courts towards pre-marital agreements and that there may be a change in the law. The judgment of the Supreme Court does not seek to alter the principle that it is a court, and not any prior agreement between the parties, that will determine the appropriate financial provision on divorce as this is embodied in the MCA 1973. Lord Phillips stated that 'the court should give effect to a Nuptial Agreement that is freely entered into by each party with a full appreciation of its implications unless in the circumstances prevailing it would not be fair to hold the parties to their agreement'. Applying the law to the case, Lord Phillips goes on to say in conclusion that the circumstances were such that the court felt that it 'was fair that [the husband] should be held to [the] agreement [namely not to claim anything against the wife] and that it would be unfair to depart from it'. In short, the court placed decisive weight on the terms of the agreement in determining the outcome.

It should be noted that Lady Hale handed down a dissenting judgment which powerfully explored the position of women when considering pre-nuptial agreements. The Law Commission has yet to report on the issue of pre-marital agreements and this may yet bring about a change in statute.

13.4.4.1 Case-law following *Radmacher v Granatino*

In the case of *NG v SG* [2011] EWHC 3270 (Fam), Mostyn J considered the implications of *Radmacher v Granatino.*

The parties were Italian and Swedish and entered into a pre-nuptial agreement under Swedish law at the husband's request and upon which neither took legal advice. It was a short document providing that:

1. All property owned by the husband prior to the marriage was his private property and the wife had no right to it;
2. All inherited property would remain the sole property of the recipient; and
3. All other property acquired during the marriage would be marital property.

Charles J considered that there were no vitiating factors (duress, fraud or misrepresentation) and he disagreed with arguments that the pre-nuptial agreement should be given limited weight as:

1. Whilst the parties did not receive legal advice there was nothing unfair or difficult to understand;
2. The wife was indifferent to the value of the husband's property so there was no material non-disclosure;
3. There was no finding that the wife felt under undue pressure to sign or that she was acting against her better judgement;
4. The inequality in bargaining power did not reduce the weight to be given to the agreement.

For these reasons he concluded that the agreement was a 'good and powerful' reason for departing from an equal division and it was an important factor in assessing the overall award. Mostyn J also looked at the issue of 'need' and whether a spouse left in straightened circumstances could invalidate a PMA. Mostyn J set the level of 'need' at a fairly low level, mentioning 'destitution' should be avoided. As the word 'destitution' is not mentioned in *Radmacher v Granatino*, further judicial guidance may be needed.

In *B v S (Financial Remedy: Matrimonial Property Regime)* [2012] EWHC 265 (Fam), the agreement involved was made in Catalonia. At the final hearing, there was an issue about the weight to be accorded to the 'tacit' agreement of the parties to apply the Catalonian default matrimonial property regime. Neither party was actually from Catalonia originally.

There had been no discussions between the spouses nor had either party taken independent legal advice as to the question of whether the agreement would have been influential or binding upon a court in England and Wales. Mostyn J accorded 'absolutely no weight' to the matrimonial property regime and proceeded to conduct the usual s25 MCA 1973 exercise in its absence.

13.5 NEGOTIATING AND DRAFTING A PMA

Following *Radmacher* (**13.4.4**), the Supreme Court did not discuss the circumstances in which a PMA would be considered too unfair to be upheld. The following are drawn from case-law and may assist a PMA to be considered fair:

- the parties have confirmed that they have each received independent legal (and, if possible, accountancy) advice prior to entering into the agreement. Ideally the parties should confirm in the PMA that they intend to enter into a legally binding contract. It is also best practice for the solicitor advising the client in relation to a PMA to include a certificate of competency into the agreement, in acknowledgement that they have the relevant expertise to advise on this area of the law. If such a declaration is not made in the PMA then less weight will be given to it should it be considered at a final ancillary relief hearing;
- there should be a minimum time for reflection, e.g. 21 days;
- the parties have fully and frankly disclosed to each other their means and relevant circumstances, which should be set out as an attachment to the PMA;
- clarification should be provided in relation to who would have control of assets acquired by either party prior to the marriage and furthermore how jointly acquired property should be divided;
- the parties did not enter into the agreement less than 21 days away from the date of the marriage. If the marriage does take place shortly after the parties have signed the agreement then it is less likely to be enforced (however see *K v K* at **13.4.1**);
- a recital that without the PMA there would have been no marriage;
- provision for children should be considered with a possible review of any agreement during the marriage (a post-nuptial agreement?) with generous provision for children.

From the case-law cited above, even following these steps does not guarantee that a PMA will be followed by the courts. The client must be fully advised of the enforceability of PMAs and the risk that the court will not take the PMA into account fully or at all. Negotiations should commence well before a wedding in order that the agreement is not rushed into or a party may claim that they were pressured into an agreement. Full and frank disclosure is essential.

13.6 PMAS IN THE FUTURE

The Law Commission has been looking into 'marital property agreements' since 2009 and was due to report in 2012 but the consultation has been extended. PMAs are before the courts with increasing regularity and it has been argued that as property prices have risen and people enjoy greater personal wealth or enter into second marriages wishing to protect assets, that PMAs may become more common amongst all clients and not just the very wealthy.

The online resources contain a selection of articles on PMAs and links to case-law.

SUMMARY POINTS

- Pre-marital agreements (PMAs) are contracts that allow spouses to agree how they wish their money and property to be divided after divorce.
- PMAs have traditionally been unenforceable due to public policy considerations, as they purport to oust the jurisdiction of the courts but this position has changed with recent case-law.
- Opponents of PMAs claim that they undermine marriage and could be used against a weaker party to deprive them of a proper settlement.
- Proponents of PMAs claim that they represent an expression of a spouse's autonomous wishes, and reduce costs and acrimony following divorce.
- The courts have indicated a number of factors that assist the PMA in being recognized by the courts.

- Although the Government has declined to legislate on PMAs, the Law Commission was due to report on marital arrangements in 2012. However, this has been delayed due to an extension of the consultation period.

SELF-TEST QUESTIONS

Mario is a very wealthy businessman who owns several vineyards in Italy, although he spends most of his time living and working in the UK running his wine business. He meets Cordelia, who owns a large farm in Wiltshire, which she inherited from her father. The couple wish to marry but do not want to risk the other party being awarded their farm or vineyards in financial order proceedings. Neither party has children.

Cordelia's brother, Hugo, insists that Cordelia should not get married and put the farm at risk. Mario also faces pressure from his family to protect the Italian vineyards.

1. Explain the advantages and disadvantages of PMAs.
2. What steps can be taken to assist the PMA being recognized by the courts?
3. Mario and Cordelia sign a PMA after their wedding and honeymoon. The PMA states that each party should retain their own pre-marital assets and that there will be no maintenance for either party, with property accumulated during the marriage to be shared equally. Cordelia discovers that she is pregnant with twins. Advise Cordelia on the validity of the PMA once the couple have children.

Answers to the questions above can be found on the Online Resource Centre: www.oxfordtextbooks.co.uk/orc/familyhandbook13/.

14 PROCEDURE FOR FINANCIAL ORDERS

14.1 INTRODUCTION

This chapter will:

- **discuss the funding options available to clients seeking financial orders;**
- **discuss the protection of assets forming part of proceedings for financial orders;**
- **discuss the pre-action protocol;**
- **explore the procedure for obtaining financial orders including the first appointment, financial dispute resolution hearing, and the final hearing;**
- **discuss the role of consent orders in proceedings for financial orders.**

In proceedings for financial orders, the party making the application for financial orders is called the 'applicant' and the party against whom the application is made is called the 'respondent'. Either party to the marriage can make an application for financial orders. It is not uncommon for the respondent to a divorce petition or civil partnership dissolution to be the applicant in proceedings for financial orders.

This chapter considers both pre-action considerations and the procedure for financial orders. This chapter considers funding arrangements, the pre-action protocol, as well as the drafting of consent orders and appeals. Reference should be made to the Law Society's Family Law Protocol for more details on pre-action considerations; it is also a guide to good conduct of the proceedings.

14.2 FUNDING PROCEEDINGS AND THE STATUTORY CHARGE

Proceedings for financial orders are expensive as they are time consuming for solicitors and are often very complex.

14.2.1 PUBLIC FUNDING

Until April 2013, there will still be some clients who are eligible for public funding. If a client is eligible for legal help, initial advice can be given on financial orders. It is likely that the client will be advised to enter into mediation (see **Chapter 3**) especially as this is a pre-condition for application for certain types of funding. Family help (lower) can be used to advise the client, negotiate a settlement and to obtain a consent order (see **14.12**). If it is necessary to issue proceedings, family help (higher) will be required and this will cover all proceedings up to a final hearing. If the matter proceeds to a contested final hearing, legal representation will be required.

See **Chapter 2** for eligibility on means and merits.

From April 2013, public funding for cases involving proceedings for financial orders will cease to exist. Clients will have to fund proceedings privately, leading to concerns that some clients may not seek advice over settlements and may not receive a fair settlement. Clients may have to resort to a variety of funding devices (see **14.2.3**).

14.2.2 STATUTORY CHARGE

The statutory charge arises when the client does not recover all of the public funding spent during proceedings (see **Chapter 2** for more details). As financial order cases involve money and property, the statutory charge must be raised with the client at the start of the case and during proceedings to ensure that the client understands the impact of the statutory charge on their settlement.

14.2.3 PRIVATELY FUNDED CLIENTS

For clients ineligible for public funding, there are a variety of funding options.

Practical Considerations

When a client consults a solicitor, one of the requirements of the Solicitors Code of Conduct is that the client is given an estimate of costs. The client should be given the best information possible about the likely overall cost of a matter and, when appropriate, as the matter progresses.

A solicitor must give the client a realistic estimate of costs at the outset of the case and must regularly update the client. This is particularly important before a major step is taken in the case, as costs will rise. Any step in proceedings for financial orders should be proportionate to the costs and assets involved.

A client who is paying privately can use funding arrangements provided by banks, e.g. loans or specially arranged finance deals. Alternatively, some firms offer a monthly direct debit payment. Costs are high in proceedings for financial orders and, although the procedure is designed to encourage early settlement, clients should be regularly advised about their costs.

There is also a 'Sears Tooth' agreement. This is where the client assigns in a deed the full settlement to the solicitor so at the end of a case the costs can be paid first. A client must gain independent legal advice before signing such a deed and be aware of its effects. A Sears Tooth agreement must be disclosed to the court and the other party.

A client can apply for maintenance pending suit (see **Chapter 12**) in certain circumstances for the other party to pay a contribution to costs.

In the case of *Re Z* [2009] EWHC 3621 (Fam) an application was made by a husband seeking an order preventing the wife's solicitors from acting for her on the ground that the senior partner of that firm had previously acted, while at another firm, for the husband in financial proceedings with the wife.

The husband had retained the solicitor to act in connection with a freezing order to prevent the wife from disposing of assets and had regarded the solicitor as a friend. After several separations and reconciliations, the marriage broke down in 2009 and the wife approached a firm of solicitors where the husband's solicitor was now the senior partner, although the wife was being advised by another partner.

The solicitor had left her previous firm to start the new firm in concert with several colleagues although the old firm still operated and retained the relevant files. When the husband found out, he requested through his solicitors that the firm cease to act for the wife, who at first refused to do so. After a five-week wait, the husband renewed his request for the firm to cease to act. The wife's solicitors said they were prepared to put in place undertakings that the senior partner would not discuss the case with her colleagues, attend any related meetings, and the wife would not attempt to discuss the case with the solicitor. The husband applied to the court.

Bodey J identified three principal questions for the court:

- Was there a real risk of disclosure?
- If so, have the wife's solicitors refuted the burden to show that there is no risk?
- If the order is granted, what effect should the five weeks' hiatus between raising the issue and seeking this order have?

Bodey J concluded that the wife's current solicitor possessed information which is 'confidential to the husband' and that the risk is neither 'merely fanciful nor theoretical'. The judge took account of the solicitor's 'hands on' approach as senior partner and the fact that systems to prevent disclosure did not always deal with accidental or inadvertent disclosures. Bodey J granted the husband an order but ordered that the husband contribute to the wife's costs incurred during the five-week wait between requests.

14.3 PROTECTING ASSETS

Even before proceedings are issued, assets may need to be secured. In **Chapter 16**, the issue of protecting or recovering assets is dealt with in detail. It is essential that mortgage payments or rent are paid throughout the proceedings to avoid losing the asset.

14.4 APPLICABLE RULES

The Family Procedure Rules 2010 (FPR 2010) came into force in April 2010 and apply to proceedings for a financial order. The rules made changes to existing rules but did not fundamentally alter the procedures and so cases decided prior to the change will still apply. Prior to the FPR 2010, proceedings for a financial order were called 'ancillary relief' proceedings and cases decided prior to the FPR 2010 will use this terminology.

The FPR 2010 also apply to applications under s10(2) MCA 1973 (see **Chapter 6**). Applications for financial provision made by civil partners following civil partnership dissolution under s48 Civil Partnership Act 2004 are also covered by the FPR 2010.

The FPR do not cover an application under the Trusts of Land and Appointment of Trustees Act 1996 (see **Chapter 23**).

14.5 PRE-ACTION PROTOCOL

The pre-action protocol can be found in Practice Direction 9A FPR 2010.

The protocol is designed to apply to all applications for financial remedies. The protocol encourages the parties (and their solicitors) to consider mediation at an early stage and to consider court proceedings as a method of starting the court timetables, controlling disclosure, and to endeavour to avoid a costly final hearing.

14.5.1 THE FIRST LETTER

No specimen letter of claim is given in the protocol as the circumstances of financial remedy cases are so varied. All correspondence should follow similar guidelines; consideration should be given to the impact of the correspondence on the parties and should not cause the other party to adopt an entrenched, polarized, or hostile position. The first letter and subsequent correspondence should focus on relevant issues and should ideally be approved by the client. The first letter should direct the recipient to seek legal advice, provide a second copy of the letter for this end, and allow at least 14 days for a reply.

Practical Considerations

Resolution publishes a *Guide to Good Practice* which includes a guide to correspondence. It is an excellent guide to avoiding writing letters that set an adversarial tone for proceedings and applies to all proceedings, not just proceedings for a financial order. The aim of correspondence should be to:

- address and safeguard children's needs;
- give/obtain reasonable disclosure and to identify and resolve issues;
- advance the proceedings;
- record issues of conduct and fact.

Letters must serve a constructive purpose in moving the matter forward and take into account the interests of your client and the family as a whole. Do not write a letter where the purpose is to:

- satisfy the client's feelings;
- satisfy your own feelings;
- create or perpetuate conflict between family members;
- attack the other lawyer.

14.5.2 DISCLOSURE

The protocol underlines the obligation on the parties to undertake full and frank disclosure of all material facts, documents, and other information relevant to the issues. This is regarded as essential to reduce costs and to clarify the issues between the parties at an early stage. This duty is ongoing and must be carefully explained to the client by their solicitor.

Form E (see **14.8.1**) can be used by the parties as a guide to the format of the disclosure and documents should only be disclosed as required by Form E. This helps to prevent excessive or disproportionate disclosure at excessive costs.

14.5.3 EXPERT EVIDENCE

Practical Considerations

The value of assets within proceedings for financial orders is often in dispute. It is essential that the court has a valuation to rely upon in order that it knows how much money is available to be split between the parties. Commonly assets requiring valuation include the family home, the value of a business, or a share in a business or a valuable asset, e.g. an antique or a painting.

Experts are often used to give independent, expert valuations for the court to rely upon. For the valuation of a family home, an estate agent working the relevant local area can be relied upon to give a realistic market value. For a business, a forensic accountant may be required in order to report on the accounts of a business.

Part 25 FPR 2010 covers the use of expert evidence. Expert evidence should only be required when the parties do not know or cannot agree the value of a significant asset. The cost of valuation should be proportionate to the sums in dispute. The protocol directs that a single valuer should be instructed by both parties and this was approved in *P v P (Financial Relief: Illiquid Assets)* [2005] 1 FLR 548. This method of valuation is also considerably cheaper than both parties instructing experts.

In order for parties to agree an expert, one party should give the other party a list of the names of one or more experts in the relevant specialty. Within 14 days, the other party must indicate any objection to the experts and, if so, should supply names of experts considered suitable. There should be a joint letter of instruction, which is disclosed to the court, and all meetings and conferences should be attended by both parties. If the parties cannot agree, the parties must carefully consider the cost implications of instructing their own individual expert and should consider whether to disclose the reports produced. It may be that the court has to manage the issue of disclosure of such reports.

Good practice in expert evidence can be found in a 'Best Practice Guide for Instructing a Single Joint Expert' issued by the President of the Family Division's Ancillary Relief Advisory Group and this can be found at [2003] 1 FLR 573.

14.5.4 OVERRIDING OBJECTIVE

Part 1 FPR 2010 has an overriding objective, which applies to all proceedings. The court must give effect to the overriding objective when it exercises powers given to it by financial order rules or when it interprets any rule. The parties are also required to help the court to further the overriding objective.

In so far as is practical, dealing with a case justly involves:

- ensuring the parties are on an equal footing;
- saving expense;
- dealing with the case in ways that are proportionate to the amount of money involved, the importance of the case, and the complexity of the issues;
- ensuring the case is dealt with expeditiously and fairly; and
- allotting a fair share of the court's resources.

The court is also given a duty of 'active case management'. This includes:

- encouraging the parties to cooperate and to resolve disputes through mediation where appropriate;
- identifying the issues at an early stage;
- regulating the extent of disclosure of documents and expert evidence to be proportionate to the issues in question;
- helping the parties settle part or the whole of the case;
- fixing timetables and controlling the progress of the case;
- giving directions to ensure that the trial of the case proceeds quickly.

The aim of the protocol is to ensure that pre-application disclosure and negotiation takes place in appropriate cases and that it is cost effective.

14.6 PROCEDURE

FIGURE 14.1 AN OVERVIEW OF PROCEDURE FOR FINANCIAL ORDERS

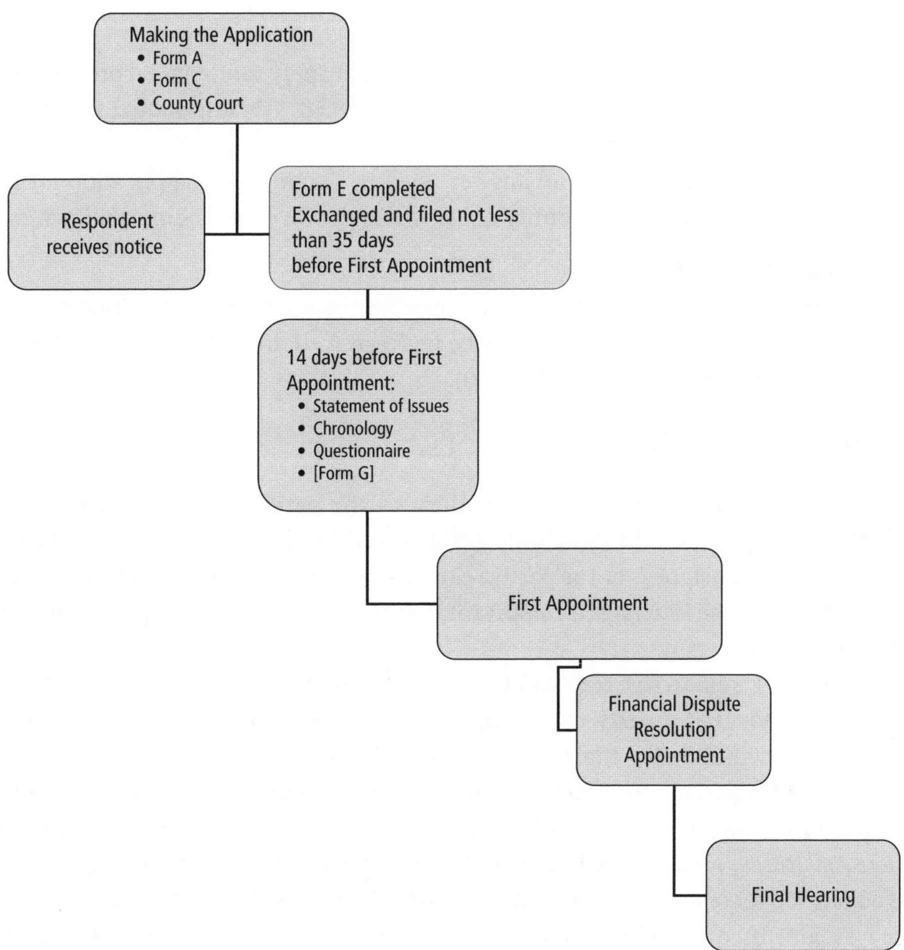

14.7 COMMENCING PROCEEDINGS

14.7.1 MAKING AN APPLICATION FOR FINANCIAL ORDERS

As seen in **Chapter 8**, the divorce petition contains a prayer, which asks for the various forms of financial orders (apart from an order for sale under s24A MCA 1973) and this is made operational by the petitioner in the divorce suit filing a Form A at court. A copy of Form A can be found in the case study. Form A should be filed at the same court that the divorce or civil partnership dissolution is being heard (r9.5 FPR 2010). In addition to the Form A, the following documents must also be filed:

- if the client is publicly funded, a copy of the funding notice;
- notice of acting if the solicitor is not already on the court record;
- a fee or fee exemption.

S26 MCA 1973 allows applications for financial remedies to be made at any time following the presentation of the petition for divorce, nullity, or judicial separation.

Applications for a pension sharing or pension attachment order must be included either in general terms or specifically if the client is in a position to do so.

The Form A is served on the respondent by the court. The acting solicitor must also serve any pension provider where there is a pension sharing or pension attachment order. If an application is made in respect of property subject to a mortgage, a copy of the Form A should be served on the mortgagees as soon as possible and in any event within 14 days.

14.7.1.1 Respondent's application

Under r9.4 FPR 2010 a respondent to a divorce suit can apply for financial orders through an answer to the petition and an answer is discussed at **8.10**. The respondent should make his financial relief claims in the answer.

If the respondent does not file an answer, then he can make an application for financial orders by filing a Form A at the county court where the divorce is being conducted.

14.7.1.2 Application with leave

If no claim has been made in the divorce petition or an answer, an application must be made with the leave of the court by notice in Form A. If an order has been agreed by the parties, no leave is required (r9.4 FPR 2010).

14.7.2 PROTECTING THE CLIENT

The full range of orders should be applied for in the petition or answer or in Form A. It may seem strange to ask for some orders, e.g. a lump sum where the spouse is on income support, but circumstances of the parties can change. The common example is usually that a spouse may win the lottery. It is important that the court can use their full powers to make a suitable set of orders.

There is also a 'remarriage trap' (and, presumably, a re-civil partnership trap too). S28(3) MCA 1973 states that a party cannot *apply* for a financial provision order or a property adjustment order following the grant of a decree of divorce or nullity or the dissolution of a civil partnership. If a client wishes to preserve their claim, they should make their claim before the marriage or civil partnership is dissolved. In *Re G (Financial Provision: Liberty to Restore Application for Lump Sum)* [2004] 1 FLR 997, the wife's application for a lump sum was adjourned for several years in anticipation of the husband's significant inheritance. The wife was permitted to claim on the basis of her reasonable need, a new car, and discharge of her debts. The exception to this is periodical payments (see **Chapter 12**), which end on marriage or civil partnership (s28 MCA 1973).

14.7.3 STEPS TAKEN BY THE COURT FOLLOWING APPLICATION FOR FINANCIAL ORDERS

Once a Form A has been filed, the court fixes a first appointment not less than 12 weeks and no more than 16 weeks from the date of filing. Notice of this date is given to the applicant and the respondent is served with a copy of that notice not less than four days from the date of filing of that notice (r9.12(1) FPR 2010). Once the first appointment date has been set by the court, it cannot be cancelled unless the court gives permission (r9.12(3) FPR 2010).

14.8 FIRST APPOINTMENT

14.8.1 FORM E

Under r 9.14 FPR 2010, both parties must, at the same time, exchange with each other, and each file with the court, a statement in Form E. This must be signed by the party who made the statement, sworn to be true, and contain and attach the information required by Form E.

The timing is important. Form E must be exchanged and filed not less than 35 days before the date of the first appointment. The Form E contains details of income and capital assets of each party as well as the outstanding liabilities and the income requirements of each party. Towards the end of the Form E, there is a section that allows each party to state which orders they are seeking and the contributions made to the marriage.

Form E is a large document and requires practice in completion. There are many IT applications available to firms to make this process more straightforward. A copy of a Form E can be found at the end of this chapter as well as in the online case study.

14.8.2 PREPARATION FOR THE FIRST APPOINTMENT

A good deal of preparation is required for the first appointment, which continues the procedural aim of identifying issues early in proceedings, thereby hopefully reducing costs.

R9.14(5) FPR 2010 requires both parties to simultaneously exchange and file at court the following documents at least 14 days before the hearing of the first appointment:

- a concise statement of issues between the parties;
- a chronology;
- a questionnaire setting out by reference to the concise statement of issues any further information and documents requested from the other party or a statement that no information and documents are required;
- a notice in Form G stating whether that party will be in a position at the first appointment to proceed on that occasion to an FDR appointment.

14.8.2.1 Statement of issues

The statement of issues is described in the FPR 2010 as 'concise' and should not be unduly long or complex. This document enables the parties and the court to define at an early point in proceedings the matters in issue between the parties.

As discussed at **14.8.1** above, the parties indicate on Form E the orders sought and this is a good place to look first when compiling the statement of issues. Other issues will become apparent when both parties' Form E and other information are examined closely.

An example of such an issue may be where one party wishes to sell the family home and the other party wishes to have it transferred to them. An example of a statement of issues can be found in Case Study One.

14.8.2.2 The chronology

The chronology sets out the personal details of the parties and any children, e.g. dates of birth, employment details, and details of ill health or disability. Important dates should be included of cohabitation prior to marriage, dates of marriage, separation, and key dates within the divorce and associated cases.

14.8.2.3 The questionnaire

The protocol included a duty of active case management by the court. The court and parties must ensure that disclosure of documents is managed properly and the amount of disclosure is sufficient to enable the court to decide the case but that it is also proportionate to the case. The parties are not permitted to ask informally for disclosure of documents once proceedings for financial orders are commenced. As a result, the questionnaire is extremely important at this early stage in proceedings.

Again, the Form E is the starting point for examination of the issues raised by the parties and the information required to resolve them. Firstly, check whether all the documentation required by Form E has in fact been disclosed. Concentrate on the relevant issues of the case rather than undertaking fishing expeditions for information that may be old or not entirely relevant.

In *K v K (Financial Relief: Management of Difficult Cases)* [2005] 2 FLR 1137 it was stated that active case management could include obliging solicitors to pursue disclosure through the questionnaire procedure. It would be permissible to wait and use lack of disclosure as an ambush at the final hearing.

14.8.2.4 Form G

There is a procedural mechanism that allows cases to skip the first appointment if the parties are in a position to proceed straight to an FDR. This, again, is a feature of active case management.

14.8.3 THE FIRST APPOINTMENT

The conduct of the first appointment is governed by r9.15 FPR 2010. The objective of the first appointment is to define issues and save costs. It is the first opportunity for a district judge to examine the case. The parties must attend the hearing personally. This hearing is a good opportunity for negotiations between the parties.

Practical Considerations

In addition to the documents considered above, many solicitors also prepare a summary of the income, assets, and liabilities of the parties and provide details of any large discrepancies in valuations between the parties. This document is helpful to the court and the Law Society Protocol recommends the preparation of such a document.

There are a number of issues to be resolved during the first appointment.

The district judge must determine the extent to which any questions seeking information must be answered and which documents requested must be produced. The district judge may also give directions for the production of further documents as may be necessary. The overriding objective seems to indicate that disclosure should only be allowed if it is relevant and proportionate to the issues between the parties. It is important to note that under r9.15 FPR 2010, after the first appointment a party is not entitled to production of any further documents except in accordance with directions given in the first appointment or with the permission of the court. If permission of the court is sought for disclosure after the first appointment, the district judge will seek to understand why permission was not requested at the first appointment. There may also be adverse costs consequences for that party.

In *Tchenguiz v Imerman; Imerman v Imerman* [2010] EWCA Civ 908 the court examined the position where one party resorts to 'self help'. This is where one party removed documents in paper or electronic form belonging to the other party without their knowledge or permission.

In a case involving large sums of money and property, the documents were removed from the husband's computer. He shared a work office and computer system with his wife's brothers. As she commenced divorce and ancillary relief proceedings against the husband, one of her brothers (possibly with others) accessed and copied information and documents of the husband's from a server in the office, and passed them to their (the brothers') solicitor. These solicitors had a barrister assess all documents for possibly privileged material, leaving seven files of documents which were then passed to the wife's matrimonial solicitors. The solicitors then disclosed the seven files to the husband's solicitors in the ancillary relief proceedings.

In the initial decision, the High Court gave judgment in the husband's favour and granted him an injunction against the brothers and their solicitor requiring them to return all copies of the documents and against disclosing anything obtained from the server to any third party including the wife or her solicitors. The Court of Appeal upheld this order.

The Court of Appeal held that there is a need to ensure that a husband does not avoid his liability on divorce by concealing assets. However, that does not entitle a wife, or some other person on her behalf, to breach the husband's rights to protect the confidentiality of his documents and information. It does not entitle her or another to breach any statutory duty or the criminal law.

It is an actionable breach of confidence for a person, without the authority of another to whom a document is confidential, to examine, or to make, retain, or supply to a third party a copy of, or to use the information contained in, such a document. Confidence in principle exists between a husband and a wife. It might be lost in relation to a bank statement left lying around open in the matrimonial home, or in relation to information shared between the particular spouses. However, if information is confidential, it is entitled to protection.

The court commented that illegal 'self-help disclosure' is not to be condoned. It is only at the point at which a party is required to file and serve Form E that his duty arises to give disclosure of his assets. At that point, indeed throughout an application for financial orders, the Family Procedure Rules 2010 and the court closely regulate the process of discovery of documents. It is a matter for the court to determine what evidence is admissible, and whether it should be admitted, balancing one spouse's rights under the European Convention on Human Rights (under Arts 6 and 10) against the other's (under Arts 6 and 8) and applying the provisions of the FPR 2010. It is not open to a wife to pre-empt consideration of a husband's Form E (or other) disclosure by self-help.

The difficulty of this decision may be felt in 'ordinary' cases where the sums of money involved are considerably smaller. In such cases, parties do not have the luxury of separate studies at home to keep documents (as the Court of Appeal discussed) and parties will often keep personal documents in easily accessible parts of the family home. The online resources will contain updates on cases arising from this judgment.

The district judge can give directions on:

- the valuation of assets (including the joint instruction of joint experts);
- obtaining and exchanging expert evidence, if required;
- evidence to be adduced by each party and, where appropriate, further chronologies or schedules.

If the parties fail to settle at the first appointment, the district judge must direct that the case should be referred to a financial dispute resolution hearing, unless it is not appropriate. There may be cases when moving to an FDR is not appropriate. In *Crossley v Crossley* [2008] FCR 323, the case required argument on the validity of pre-nuptial agreements (**Chapter 13**) and required a modified approach to the rules.

The district judge may also make a number of orders including an order for maintenance pending suit (see **Chapter 12**) for the filing of a pension inquiry form.

There may also be a decision on costs. Although costs are more fully discussed at **14.11**, the court can make a costs order. In deciding whether to do so, the court must consider the conduct of the parties including whether the parties have complied with their duty of disclosure with the Form E.

At every hearing, there is a requirement for both parties to produce an estimate of costs in Form H. Form H must contain an estimate of costs and disbursements incurred up to the date of hearing. This enables the parties to understand the level of costs incurred in proportion to the assets in question.

14.9 FINANCIAL DISPUTE RESOLUTION

The financial dispute resolution (FDR) hearing is designed as a forum for negotiation and discussion between the parties.

14.9.1 PREPARING FOR THE FDR

One week before the FDR, the applicant must file a schedule of offers and counter offers and any responses to offers between the parties (r9.17(3) FPR 2010). These are returned to the parties at the end of the FDR. This includes documents that are privileged.

Practical Considerations

'Privilege' is a legal concept that allows certain documents not to be revealed to the courts during proceedings. There are a number of forms of privilege. The form most relevant to ancillary relief proceedings is legal professional privilege. Legal professional privilege concerns communications between client and lawyer for the purposes of legal advice or for the purposes of litigation. The letters and documents produced under such privilege are protected and will generally not be shown to a court.

The court sees all offers made but, as explained below, should the matter not settle, the documents are not seen by the district judge at a final hearing.

14.9.2 FDR

The purpose of the FDR, as stated in r9.17(1) FPR 2010, is to meet to discuss and negotiate. There are important procedural devices that enable this.

Practical Considerations

The Law Society Protocol recommends that a solicitor must:

- ensure clients are aware of the need to attend the FDR hearing and that it can last all day;
- encourage clients to make and consider offers and proposals in advance of the FDR;
- if offers are made, ensure the recipients give them proper consideration and reply promptly where possible;
- be clear what the client's 'bottom line' is to aid settlement, bearing in mind delays and cost involved in prolonging the proceedings;
- explain to clients the requirement to use their best endeavours to reach agreement bearing in mind the court's sanctions if one party does not make or receive proposals;
- do not pressure clients to accept offers that they are not satisfied with.

A solicitor or fee earner attending the FDR must have full knowledge of the case and be able to conduct the case personally. An FDR may overrun and it may not be wise to attempt to attend more than one in a day.

The district judge that hears the FDR will have no further involvement in the case other than to conduct other FDR, to make consent orders, or a further directions order. The parties must attend in person and use their best endeavours to reach agreement on the matters in issue between them (r9.17(6) FPR 2010). As a result, the parties can approach the FDR openly and the court expects the parties to 'place their cards on the table'. The role of the district judge in the FDR is to hear the parties' arguments and put their respective positions. The district judge will then give what recommendations and comments are necessary to assist the parties to come to an agreement. It is the author's experience that exactly the same advice given by you (but ignored) is taken very seriously when it comes from the district judge.

In *Myerson v Myerson* [2008] EWCA Civ 1376, the case was brought before the Court of Appeal as the husband sought to exclude Baron J, from hearing the husband's application for variation of a consent order (see **14.12**). Baron J had presided over the financial dispute resolution (FDR) where the consent order was drawn up. Baron J refused to excuse herself from the husband's application and an application was made to the Court of Appeal.

Thorpe LJ considered the equivalent of r9.17(2) FPR 2010, which provides:

> The district judge or judge hearing the FDR appointment must have no further involvement with the application, other than to conduct any further FDR appointment or to make a consent order or a further directions order.

The court held that this Rule should be strictly interpreted. A judge presiding over an FDR cannot deal with any subsequent applications, since she had been privy to without prejudice material. If the agreement was incomplete or peripheral issues remained, these needed to be dealt with by a different judge.

The FDR is conducted on a privileged basis (see **14.9.1**) and the parties must be aware that anything said during the FDR will not be part of the final hearing.

If the matter settles, a consent order can be made (r9.17(8) FPR 2010). If the matter does not settle, the court can make directions for the future course of proceedings and, if appropriate, the filing of evidence and fixing of a final hearing date (r.9.17(9) FPR 2010).

14.10 FINAL HEARING

14.10.1 PREPARATION AND BUNDLES

All directions made at the FDR must be complied with or there may be cost consequences (see **14.11**). For a final hearing, bundles must be prepared.

Practical Considerations

'Bundle' is the term used for the collated documents prepared by solicitors for the court hearing. Unless the hearing is very short, some form of bundle will be required. Bundles are agreed between the parties and are indexed and numbered in order to allow all parties to find and use documents easily. Bundles and the preparation of bundles is a key job for paralegals, trainee solicitors, and junior solicitors. Ultimately, it is the responsibility of the person with conduct of the case to ensure that the bundle is correct. If a bundle is incorrect or sloppily compiled, the court will at least be very displeased and, at worst, cost consequences can follow.

Preparation of bundles is governed by Practice Direction 27A FPR 2010 which reproduces the Practice Direction (Family Proceedings: Court Bundles)(Universal Practice to be Applied in All Courts other than Family Proceedings Court) [2006] 2 FLR 199. The Practice Direction can be found in the online resources.

The Practice Direction applies to hearings in the High Court and in hearings in all family proceedings except for the Family Proceedings Court. A hearing includes all appearances before a judge or district judge whether with or without notice and whether for directions or substantive relief. It does not apply to cases under one hour or an urgent hearing where it is impossible to comply.

The main features of the Practice Direction (PD) are:

- the responsibility for preparation of the bundle lies with the applicant or the respondent if the applicant is a litigant in person;
- if possible, the content of the bundle should be agreed between the parties;
- the bundle should be paginated and indexed and the files should be clearly marked on the front and spine to identify the court case;
- the documents should be in chronological order and divided into sections as listed in the PD;
- preliminary documents (listed in the PD) should be inserted at the start of the bundle.

In the case of *Re X and Y (Bundles: Failure to Comply with Practice Direction)* [2008] EWHC 2058 (Fam), Munby J commented that:

> Too often bundles arrive late or not at all. Too often bundles are incomplete or not up to date. Too often skeleton arguments and other preliminary documents (see paragraph 4.2 of the Practice Direction) are handed in on the morning of the hearing—at 10 am, 10.15, or even later—and at a time when the judge is already sitting or is struggling to assimilate other documents which have also been handed in late. The problem, in my experience, is particularly acute when the judge is sitting as urgent applications judge and, in those circumstances, particularly serious in its consequences.

Munby J suggested that defaulters could be publicly named and shamed in particularly egregious cases.

14.10.2 THE HEARING

Following all the disclosure that the parties have given, the court will already be in possession of a great deal of information about the case. The hearing will be in private in the judge's chambers. The case can be heard by either a district judge or a district judge can refer the matter to a judge.

The district judge will decide how she wishes to conduct the hearing and may decide to outline to the parties their own view of the case and to invite comment from the parties (sometimes a district judge does this by calling the advocates for a meeting before the hearing starts and the advocates communicate these views to the parties as an attempt to settle the matter). The district judge may also decide to run the case in the normal fashion, as any other hearing.

The applicant's advocate will generally open the proceedings succinctly and guide the judge through the history of the case, although the district judge will have had the chance to read the bundle in advance. The district judge may hear evidence from the parties. Advocates may outline their own proposals for orders.

The district judge will make her decision and communicate this to the parties. A careful note of the decision should be made to explain to the client and in case of possible appeal. Your client may not have achieved the result that they wanted and you may have to explain the decision carefully.

14.11 ORDERS FOR COSTS

'Costs' refers to the legal costs of your client including solicitors' and barristers' fees, disbursements, court fees etc. Both during a case and at the end, someone has to pay these costs. An order for costs describes the decision of the court about who has to pay which costs and it is possible that one client becomes responsible for paying the other party's costs.

14.11.1 COSTS DURING THE CASE

At every hearing a Form H must be completed by both parties (r9.27 FPR 2010). Form H details the costs incurred by that party up to the date of the hearing. The parties can see how much is being spent on proceedings and this may encourage a settlement.

14.11.2 COSTS ORDERS AT THE END OF THE CASE

No fewer than 14 days before the final hearing, both parties must file and serve a Form H1 (r9.27(2) FPR 2010). Form H1 gives full particulars of all costs incurred or that are expected to be incurred during proceedings and allows the district judge to take account of the parties' liabilities when deciding what order to make.

The overall position on costs is found under r28.1 FPR 2010: the court may at any time make such an order as to costs as it thinks just. Under r28.3 FPR 2010, there is a presumption that the court will not make an order as to costs in proceedings for financial orders (with an exception for maintenance pending suit and interim periodical payments).

The court will only have the power to make a costs order when this is justified by the litigation conduct of one of the parties. R28.7 FPR 2010 allows the court to have regard to:

- any failure by a party to comply with the rules, any order of the court, or practice direction that the court considers relevant;
- any open offer to settle made by the party;
- whether it is reasonable for a party to raise, pursue, or contest a particular allegation or issue;
- the manner in which a party has pursued or responded to the application or a particular issue;
- any other aspect of a party's conduct that the court considers relevant;
- the financial effect on the parties of any costs order.

An open offer is one that is made in open correspondence between the parties and is not privileged. Most offers made in proceedings for financial relief are now open offers.

The starting point for costs orders is that parties will pay their own costs and only in the circumstances listed above will an order be made that one party pay the whole or part of the other party's costs.

Practical Considerations

A client may allege that his ex-spouse has been taking money from the joint accounts and putting it in another bank account. You check the bank statements supplied with the Form E and can find no evidence for this. Your client insists on seeking bank statements for the past ten years, despite your advice to the contrary. The court agrees on allowing disclosure of bank statements for the past three years. Following close examination, you still cannot find any evidence for your client's allegation. At the final hearing (as the parties have refused to settle), the district judge makes an order that your client pays the costs of the application for the additional disclosure as this was an unreasonable point to raise.

Another common example is wishing to spend many hours arguing over a relatively inexpensive asset. When a client wishes to argue over a dinner service or set of cutlery (both occurred in the author's practice), unless the asset has great sentimental value or is unique, it may simply be a waste of fees. In practice, the author would find out the value of the disputed item (most memorably a commonly available dinner service) and tell the client how many hours of solicitor's time was represented by the value of the asset—usually no more than one or two hours. Compared with several hours of time paid to argue about the asset, the client usually opted to spend the money on buying a new dinner service!

In *KSO v MJO* [2008] EWHC 3031 (Fam) the costs of the case amounted to £430,000 equivalent to 71% of the assets. Eventually, the husband became bankrupt.

The judgment is worth reading as a cautionary tale. Munby J commented:

> Not for the first time I have here been faced with ancillary relief litigation conducted at ruinous expense to the parties. I should like to think it will be the last time, but I doubt it. The picture is deeply dispiriting. And it is not as if it is only the adults who suffer from the consequences of such folly. The luckless children do as well. The present case is a sobering, and for me deeply saddening, example. If, instead of spending—squandering—over £430,000 in costs, the wife and the husband had been able to resolve their differences at a more modest and, dare I say it, more seemly level of costs, there might very well have been enough left in the matrimonial 'pot' to house the wife and children and to enable the children to remain at their school, whilst still leaving something more than a mere consolation prize over for the husband. As it is, it is hard to see much being left from the wreck, not least after the trustee in

bankruptcy has had his costs, expenses, and remuneration. And the wife and the husband—and for this purpose I refer to them as the mother and the father, for that is what they are—are faced now with the wretched and thankless task of trying to explain to their daughters how it has all come to this.

14.12 CONSENT ORDERS

If an application for a financial order is settled without a contested hearing, a consent order records the details of the settlement and is approved by the court.

14.12.1 PROCEDURE FOR CONSENT ORDERS

The first point to note is that the duty of full disclosure applies to consent orders (*Livesey v Jenkins* [1985] 2 WLR 47) and the procedure attempts to ensure this is achieved.

R9.26 FPR 2010 states that if the parties wish to apply for a consent order before financial order proceedings have been issued, an application can be made by either party in Form A with two copies of the draft order (one of which must be signed by the respondent giving their consent). If proceedings have been issued, two copies of the consent order should be filed together with a request for the judge to make the order as requested. The court should make the order unless they believe that circumstances exist that should be examined further, e.g. if the court feels that inadequate provision has been made for one spouse.

In addition, r9.26 FPR 2010 also requires a statement of information to be lodged with the draft orders and this should be done in Form D81. This form gives the court details about the parties, children of the marriage, a summary of the parties' capital and income resources, as well as pension provision, details of the family home, and any plans for remarriage or new civil partnership.

A copy of a Form D81 can be seen in Case Study One.

14.12.2 DRAFTING CONSENT ORDERS

Drafting a consent order is a skill required of all lawyers dealing with ancillary relief as well as being able to analyse a consent order drafted by another lawyer.

A consent order has a number of parts and each is examined below.

The preamble to the order records the parts of the agreement that the court has no power to order under the MCA 1973.

Practical Considerations

A court can make orders only where the law gives it the power to do so. A court in financial proceedings may desire an order to force one party to make mortgage payments but there is no power under the MCA 1973 to make this order. The preamble is used to record agreements that cannot be the subject of an order.

The preamble can include a record of the basis upon which the order is made, e.g. that a lump sum is made to pay off a debt.

Undertakings form part of the preamble and will generally cover aspects of an agreement that are not covered by the MCA 1973, e.g. paying a mortgage.

Practical Considerations

An undertaking is a promise to do something. An undertaking can be drafted to achieve a particular outcome, e.g. to pay off a debt. Alternatively, an undertaking can be drafted for a party to try to achieve a specific outcome using their 'best endeavours'. This form of drafting is used to avoid the situation where a promise is made that subsequently proves to be impossible, e.g. obtaining the release of one party from a mortgage. It is better to draft this as using a party's best endeavours as there is no guarantee that a mortgagee will release one party to a mortgage.

Orders are then drafted in the main body of the order. An example can be seen in the online case study.

14.12.3 SETTING ASIDE A CONSENT ORDER

Consent orders cannot be easily set aside. The court would have to be satisfied that the agreement was reached on the basis of a serious mistake by one of the parties, as a result of fraud or serious misrepresentation, or through non-disclosure of material facts that would have led the court to make a substantially different order than it would have otherwise (see *T v T (Consent Order: Procedure to Set Aside)* [1997] 1 FLR 205).

The procedure can be found in Ord 37, r1 of the County Court Rules 1981 and the dissatisfied party should apply for a rehearing.

When the appeal is out of time, it is generally only very recent events that can be relied upon to set aside a consent order. The criteria for application are found in *Barder v Barder (Caluori intervening)* [1988] AC 20:

- new events have occurred since the making of the order that invalidate the basis or fundamental assumptions upon which the order was made;
- the new events have occurred within a relatively short period of time of the order being made;
- application for permission to appeal has been made promptly in the circumstances of the case;
- the granting of permission should not prejudice third parties who have acquired in good faith, for valuable consideration, interests in a property that is the subject matter of the dispute.

In *Myerson v Myerson* [2009] EWCA Civ 282, the appellant husband was seeking to appeal an order on the grounds that the fall in value of his shares caused by the financial crisis constituted a *Barder* event that undermined the basis of the order.

Thorpe LJ dismissed the appeal and stated that the order was not imposed but was the product of the will of the parties. The husband, with all knowledge both public and private, agreed to an asset division that left him 'captain of the ship', and certain to keep for himself whatever profits or gains his enterprise and experience would achieve in the years ahead. When a businessman takes a speculative position in compromising his wife's claims, the court asked whether the court should subsequently relieve him of the consequences of his speculation by rewriting the bargain at his behest. As the payment of the lump sum was spread over five instalments there exists, and the appellant husband had invoked, the statutory power of variation. Given that the outstanding instalments amounted to £2.5 m this was much more than token relief, albeit subject to the exercise of the judicial discretion. Thorpe LJ held that:

> the appellant fails to satisfy the court that the appeal would be certain, or very likely, to succeed. Given the width of the discretion given to the judge deciding the application for variation in the exercise of statutory powers, an appeal directed to the majority of the lump sum already paid and/or the transfer of property order would seem to me to have most uncertain prospects of success.

14.13 APPEALS

R30.5(4) FPR 2010 sets out the appeal period as 14 days from the date of the district judge's order. The appeal would be heard before a judge in chambers.

A party cannot appeal simply because they disagree with the decision made. Many clients do not appreciate this. The order made should be carefully explained to the client and should directly address grounds of appeal as soon as possible in order to either settle the grounds for appeal or to implement the order. Under r30 FPR 2010, permission to appeal is required. The details of procedure can be found in Practice Direction 30A FPR 2010, which is, unfortunately, extremely complex. Permission to appeal under r30.3 FPR 2010 will only be given if there are real prospects of success or there is a compelling reason why the appeal should be heard.

The grounds for appeal can be found in r30.12 FPR 2010:

- the appeal should be limited to a review of the decision or order of the district judge unless the judge considers that in the circumstances of the case it would be in the interests of justice to have a rehearing.

Grounds for appeal are that the court was wrong on:

- the law;
- fact (to a more limited degree (see *Piglowska v Piglowska* [1999] 2 FLR 763)).

Where the order was based on judicial discretion, the decision must be shown to be 'plainly wrong'. In *V v V (Financial Relief)* [2005] 2 FLR 697, it was held that any appeal should be allowed only if it had been demonstrated that there had been some form of procedural irregularity or that, in conducting the necessary balancing exercise, the district judge had taken into account matters that were irrelevant, or ignored matters that were relevant, or had otherwise arrived at a conclusion that was plainly wrong.

SUMMARY POINTS

- Prior to commencing proceedings, clients should consider how to fund the proceedings and the impact of the statutory charge.
- Careful consideration should be given to the protection of any vulnerable assets.
- There is a pre-action protocol that should be followed, with care being given to the beginning of correspondence, disclosure, and expert evidence.
- The overriding objective of proceedings for financial orders is to be just and for the court to actively manage the case.
- Proceedings are commenced by a Form A and either party to the divorce can apply.
- Between the commencement of proceedings and the first appointment, the Form E must be filed and served.
- A statement of issues, chronology, questionnaire, and Form G must also be completed.
- The first appointment is where the court defines issues and resolves the extent to which disclosure should be ordered in an attempt to save costs.
- If settlement is not reached, the parties prepare to attend a financial dispute resolution (FDR) and negotiations must continue.
- The FDR is privileged and is heard by a judge who will have no further involvement with the case and will give the parties a realistic view of the case to assist settlement.
- If settlement is not reached at the FDR, the case will proceed to a final hearing.
- Costs orders are unusual as the starting position is that each party will pay their own costs. The court can make a costs order where a party's conduct of the proceedings requires sanction.
- Consent orders are used where the parties reach agreement to formalize orders and agreements.

SELF-TEST QUESTIONS

1. Draw a diagram to illustrate the order of proceedings for a financial order.
2. Explain the differences between the first appointment and FDR.
3. Your client, Miranda, has instructed you in proceedings for financial orders. She reluctantly disclosed assets following an order from the district judge at the first appointment. At the FDR you inadvertently discover that Miranda has concealed £300,000 in savings in a previously undiscovered bank account. Advise Miranda on the potential consequences of non-disclosure.

Case Study Two

Helena has decided that she wishes to have the house transferred to her as she does not wish to disrupt Richard's life any further. However, David does not agree and wishes to sell the family home. Using the Form E on the Online Resource Centre, find the part of the Form E dealing with this and draft that part of the Form E on behalf of Helena.

Look at the statement of issues and questionnaire in the case and Helena's instructions. Draft the reply to David's questionnaire for your supervisor and then look at the documents online.

The first appointment passes without agreement and the court sets a date for the FDR. Draft a letter to Helena explaining what will happen at the FDR. Will Helena have to attend? Look at the Online Resource Centre for a letter to Helena.

Finally at FDR, an agreement is reached. Take a look at the draft consent order online. Can you suggest any improvements?

online resource centre

Answers to the questions above can be found on the Online Resource Centre: **www.oxfordtextbooks.co.uk/orc/familyhandbook13.**

Click here to reset form

Financial statement for a financial order or for financial relief after an overseas divorce or dissolution etc

of

To be completed by the relevant party	
Name of court	Case No.
Name of Applicant	
Name of Respondent	

(please tick appropriate boxes)

☐ Husband ☐ Wife ☐ Civil partner

Dated D D / M M / Y Y Y Y

The parties are

and

Who is the	Who is the
☐ husband ☐ wife ☐ civil partner	☐ husband ☐ wife ☐ civil partner
☐ Petitioner ☐ Applicant ☐ Respondent in the	☐ Petitioner ☐ Applicant ☐ Respondent in the
☐ divorce ☐ dissolution ☐ nullity	☐ divorce ☐ dissolution ☐ nullity
☐ (judicial) separation ☐ financial relief application	☐ (judicial) separation ☐ financial relief application
Applicant in this matter	Respondent in this matter

This form should only be completed in applications for a financial order or for financial relief after an overseas divorce/dissolution etc. If the application is for any other financial remedy in the county court please complete Form E1. If the application is for a financial remedy in the magistrates court please complete Form E2.

Please fill in this form fully and accurately. Where any box is not applicable, write 'N/A'.

You have a duty to the court to give a full, frank and clear disclosure of all your financial and other relevant circumstances.

A failure to give full and accurate disclosure may result in any order the court makes being set aside.

If you are found to have been deliberately untruthful, criminal proceedings may be brought against you for fraud under the Fraud Act 2006.

The information given in this form must be confirmed by an affidavit. Proceedings for perjury may be brought against a person who makes or causes to be made, a false statement in a document confirmed by an affidavit.

You must attach documents to the form where they are specifically sought and you may attach other documents where it is necessary to explain or clarify any of the information that you give.

Essential documents that must accompany this statement are detailed in the form.

If there is not enough room on the form for any particular piece of information, you may continue on an attached sheet of paper.

If you are in doubt about how to complete any part of this form you should seek legal advice.

This statement is filed by

Name and address of solicitor

Form E Financial statement for a financial order or for financial relief after an overseas divorce or dissolution etc (04.11)

1 General Information

1.1 Full name

1.2 Date of birth

Date	Month	Year

1.3 Date of the marriage/ civil partnership

Date	Month	Year

1.4 Occupation

1.5 Date of the separation

Date	Month	Year

Tick here if not applicable ☐

1.6 Date of the

Petition for divorce/ dissolution/nullity/ (judicial) separation			Decree nisi/ conditional order/ (judicial) separation order			Decree absolute/ final order (if applicable)		
Date	Month	Year	Date	Month	Year	Date	Month	Year

1.7 If you have subsequently married or formed a civil partnership, or will do so, state the date

Date	Month	Year

1.8 Are you living with a new partner? Yes ☐ No ☐

1.9 Do you intend to live with a new partner within the next six months? Yes ☐ No ☐

1.10 Details of any children of the family

Full names	Date of birth			With whom does the child live?
	Date	Month	Year	

1.11 Details of the state of health of yourself and the children if you think this should be taken into account

Yourself	Children

1.12 Details of the present and proposed future educational arrangements for the children.

Present arrangements	Future arrangements

1.13 Details of any child support maintenance calculation or any maintenance order or agreement made in respect of any children of the family. If no calculation, order or agreement has been made, give an estimate of the liability of the non-resident parent in respect of the children of the family under the Child Support Act 1991.

1.14 If this application is to vary an order, attach a copy of the order and give details of the part that is to be varied and the changes sought. You may need to continue on a separate sheet.

1.15 Details of any other court cases between you and your spouse/civil partner, whether in relation to money, property, children or anything else.

Case No	Court	Type of proceedings

1.16 Your present residence and the occupants of it and on what terms you occupy it (e.g. tenant, owner-occupier).

Address	Occupants	Terms of occupation

2 Financial Details

Part 1 Real Property (land and buildings) and Personal Assets

2.1 Complete this section in respect of the family home (the last family home occupied by you and your spouse/civil partner) if it remains unsold.

Documentation required for attachment to this section:
a) A copy of any valuation of the property obtained within the last six months. If you cannot provide this document, please give your own realistic estimate of the current market value
b) A recent mortgage statement confirming the sum outstanding on **each** mortgage

Property name and address	
Land Registry title number	
Mortgage company name(s) and address(es) and account number(s)	
Type of mortgage	
Details of who owns the property and the extent of your legal and beneficial interest in it (i.e. state if it is owned by you solely or jointly owned with your spouse/civil partner or with others)	
If you consider that the legal ownership as recorded at the Land Registry does not reflect the true position, state why	
Current market value of the property	
Balance outstanding on any mortgage(s)	
If a sale at this stage would result in penalties payable under the mortgage, state amount	
Estimate the costs of sale of the property	
Total equity in the property (i.e. market value less outstanding mortgage(s), penalties if any and the costs of sale)	

TOTAL value of your interest in the family home: Total A £ 0.00

2.2 Details of your interest in any other property, land or buildings. Complete one page for each property you have an interest in.

Documentation required for attachment to this section:

a) A copy of any valuation of the property obtained within the last six months. If you cannot provide this document, please give your own realistic estimate of the current market value

b) A recent mortgage statement confirming the sum outstanding on **each** mortgage

Property name and address	
Land Registry title number	
Mortgage company name(s) and address(es) and account number(s)	
Type of mortgage	
Details of who owns the property and the extent of your legal and beneficial interest in it (i.e. state if it is owned by you solely or jointly owned with your spouse/civil partner or with others)	
If you consider that the legal ownership as recorded at the Land Registry does not reflect the true position, state why	
Current market value of the property	
Balance outstanding on any mortgage(s)	
If a sale at this stage would result in penalties payable under the mortgage, state amount	
Estimate the costs of sale of the property	
Total equity in the property (i.e. market value less outstanding mortgage(s), penalties if any and the costs of sale)	
Total value of your interest in this property	

TOTAL value of your interest in ALL other property: Total B	£

2.3 Details of all personal bank, building society and National Savings Accounts that you hold or have held at any time in the last twelve months and which are or were either in your own name or in which you have or have had any interest. This applies whether any such account is in credit or in debit. For joint accounts give your interest and the name of the other account holder. If the account is overdrawn, show a minus figure.

Documentation required for attachment to this section:
For each account listed, all statements covering the last 12 months.

Name of bank or building society, including branch name	Type of account (e.g. current)	Account number	Name of other account holder (if applicable)	Balance at the date of this statement	Total current value of your interest

TOTAL value of your interest in ALL accounts: (C1) £

2.4 Details of all investments, including shares, PEPs, ISAs, TESSAs, National Savings Investments (other than already shown above), bonds, stocks, unit trusts, investment trusts, gilts and other quoted securities that you hold or have an interest in. (Do not include dividend income as this will be dealt with separately later on.)

Documentation required for attachment to this section:
Latest statement or dividend counterfoil relating to each investment.

Name	Type of Investment	Size of Holding	Current value	Name of any other account holder (if applicable)	Total current value of your interest

TOTAL value of your interest in ALL holdings: (C2) £

2.5 Details of all life insurance policies including endowment policies that you hold or have an interest in. Include those that do not have a surrender value. Complete one page for each policy.

Documentation required for attachment to this section:
A surrender valuation of each policy that has a surrender value.

Name of company			
Policy type			
Policy number			
If policy is assigned, state in whose favour and amount of charge			
Name of any other owner and the extent of your interest in the policy			
Maturity date (if applicable)	Date	Month	Year
Current surrender value (if applicable)			
If policy includes life insurance, the amount of the insurance and the name of the person whose life is insured			
Total current surrender value of your interest in this policy			

TOTAL value of your interest in ALL policies: (C3) £

2.6 Details of all monies that are OWED TO YOU. Do not include sums owed in director's or partnership accounts which should be included at section 2.11.

Brief description of money owed and by whom	Balance outstanding	Total current value of your interest

TOTAL value of your interest in ALL debts owed to you: (C4) £ 0.00

2.7 Details of all cash sums held in excess of £500. You must state where it is held and the currency it is held in.

Where held	Amount	Currency	Total current value of your interest
		TOTAL value of your interest in ALL cash sums: (C5)	£

2.8 Details of personal belongings individually worth more than £500.

INCLUDE:

- Cars (gross value)
- Collections, pictures and jewellery
- Furniture and house contents

Brief description of item	Total current value of your interest
TOTAL value of your interest in ALL personal belongings: (C6)	£ 0.00
Add together all the figures in boxes C1 to C6 to give the TOTAL current value of your interest in personal assets: TOTAL C	£ 0.00

2 Financial Details Part 2 Capital: Liabilities and Capital Gains Tax

2.9 Details of any liabilities you have.

EXCLUDE liabilities already shown such as:

- Mortgages
- Any overdrawn bank, building society or National Savings accounts

INCLUDE:

- Money owed on credit cards and store cards
- Bank loans
- Hire purchase agreements

List all credit and store cards held including those with a nil or positive balance. Where the liability is not solely your own, give the name(s) of the other account holder(s) and the amount of your share of the liability.

Liability	Name(s) of other account holder(s) (if applicable)	Total liability	Total current value of your interest in the liability

TOTAL value of your interest in ALL liabilities: (D1) £ 0.00

2.10 If any Capital Gains Tax would be payable on the disposal now of any of your real property or personal assets, give your estimate of the tax liability.

Asset	Total Capital Gains Tax liability

TOTAL value of ALL your potential Capital Gains Tax liabilities: (D2) £

Add together D1 and D2 to give the TOTAL value of your liabilities: TOTAL D £ 0.00

2 Financial Details Part 3 Capital: Business assets and directorships

2.11 Details of all your business interests. Complete one page for each business you have an interest in.

Documentation required for attachment to this section:
a) Copies of the business accounts for the last two financial years
b) Any documentation, if available at this stage, upon which you have based your estimate of the current value of your interest in this business, for example a letter from an accountant or a formal valuation.
It is not essential to obtain a formal valuation at this stage

Name of the business	
Briefly describe the nature of the business	
Are you (please tick appropriate box)	☐ Sole trader ☐ Partner in a partnership with others ☐ Shareholder in a limited company
If you are a partner or a shareholder, state the extent of your interest in the business (i.e. partnership share or the extent of your shareholding compared to the overall shares issued)	
State when your next set of accounts will be available	
If any of the figures in the last accounts are not an accurate reflection of the current position, state why. For example, if there has been a material change since the last accounts, or if the valuations of the assets are not a true reflection of their value (e.g. because property or other assets have not been re-valued in recent years or because they are shown at a book value)	
Total amount of any sums owed to you by the business by way of a director's loan account, partnership capital or current accounts or the like. Identify where these appear in the business accounts	
Your estimate of the current value of your business interest. Explain briefly the basis upon which you have reached that figure	
Your estimate of any Capital Gains Tax that would be payable if you were to dispose of your business now	
Net value of your interest in this business after any Capital Gains Tax liability	

TOTAL value of ALL your interests in business assets: TOTAL E | £

2.12 List any directorships you hold or have held in the last 12 months (other than those already disclosed in Section 2.11).

2 Financial Details

Part 4 Capital: Pensions and Pension Protection Fund (PPF) Compensation

2.13 Give details of all your pension rights and all PPF compensation entitlements, including prospective entitlements. Complete a separate page for each pension or PPF compensation entitlement.

EXCLUDE:

- Basic State Pension

INCLUDE (complete a separate page for each one):

- Additional State Pension (SERPS and State Second Pension (S2P))
- Free Standing Additional Voluntary Contribution Schemes (FSAVC) separate from the scheme of your employer
- Membership of ALL pension plans or schemes
- PPF compensation entitlement for each scheme you were a member of which has transferred to PPF

Documentation required for attachment to this section:

a) A recent statement showing the cash equivalent (CE) provided by the trustees or managers of each pension arrangement; for the additional state pension, a valuation of these rights or for PPF a valuation of PPF compensation entitlement

b) If any valuation is not available, give the estimated date when it will be available and attach a copy of your letter to the pension company, administrators, or PPF Board from whom the information was sought and/or state the date on which an application for a valuation of an Additional State Pension was submitted to the Department of Work and Pensions

Name and address of pension arrangement or PPF Board			
Your National Insurance Number			
Number of pension arrangement or reference number or PPF compensation reference number			
Type of scheme e.g. occupational or personal, final salary, money purchase, additional state pension, PPF or other (if other, please give details)			
Date the CE, PPF compensation or additional state pension was calculated	Date	Month	Year
Is the pension in payment or drawdown? (please answer Yes or No)	☐ Yes ☐ No		
State the CE quotation, the additional state pension valuation or PPF valuation of those rights			
If the arrangement is an occupational pension arrangement that is paying reduced CEs, please quote what the CE would have been if not reduced. If this is not possible, please indicate if the CE quoted is a reduced CE			
Is the PPF compensation capped? (please answer Yes or No)	☐ Yes ☐ No		

TOTAL value of ALL your pension assets: TOTAL F | £

2 Financial Details Part 5 Capital: Other assets

2.14 Give details of any other assets not listed in Parts 1 to 4 above.

INCLUDE (the following list is not exhaustive):

- Any personal or business assets not yet disclosed
- Unrealisable assets
- Share option schemes, stating the estimated net sale proceeds of the shares if the options were capable of exercise now, and whether Capital Gains Tax or income tax would be payable
- Business expansion schemes
- Futures
- Commodities
- Trust interests (including interests under a discretionary trust), stating your estimate of the value of the interest and when it is likely to become realisable. If you say it will never be realisable, or has no value, give your reasons
- Any asset that is likely to be received in the foreseeable future
- Any asset held on your behalf by a third party
- Any asset not disclosed elsewhere on this form even if held outside England and Wales
  You are reminded of your obligation to disclose all your financial assets and interests of ANY nature.

Type of asset	Value	Total NET value of your interest

TOTAL value of ALL your other assets: TOTAL G £

2 Financial Details Part 6 Income: Earned income from employment

2.15 Details of earned income from employment. Complete one page for each employment.

Documentation required for attachment to this section:
a) P60 for the last financial year (you should have received this from your employer shortly after the last 5th April)
b) Your last three payslips
c) Your last Form P11D if you have been issued with one

Name and address of your employer	
Job title and brief details of the type of work you do	
Hours worked per week in this employment	
How long have you been with this employer?	
Explain the basis of your income i.e. state whether it is based on an annual salary or an hourly rate of pay and whether it includes commissions or bonuses	
Gross income for the last financial year as shown on your P60	
Net income for the last financial year i.e. gross income less income tax and national insurance	
Average net income for the last three months i.e. total income less income tax and national insurance divided by three	
Briefly explain any other entries on the attached payslips other than basic income, income tax and national insurance	
If the payslips attached for the last three months are not an accurate reflection of your normal income briefly explain why	
Details and value of any bonuses or other occasional payments that you receive from this employment not otherwise already shown, including the basis upon which they are paid	
Details and value of any benefits in kind, perks or other remuneration received from this employer in the last year (e.g. provision of a car, payment of travel, accommodation, meal expenses, etc.)	
Your estimate of your net income from this employment for the next 12 months. If this differs significantly from your current income explain why in box 4.1.2	

Estimated TOTAL of ALL net earned income from employment for the next 12 months: TOTAL H £

2 Financial Details   Part 7 Income: Income from self-employment or partnership

2.16 You will have already given details of your business and provided the last two years accounts at section 2.11. Complete this section giving details of your income from your business. Complete one page for each business.

Documentation required for attachment to this section:
a) A copy of your last tax assessment or, if that is not available, a letter from your accountant confirming your tax liability
b) If net income from the last financial year and estimated net income for the next 12 months is significantly different, a copy of management accounts for the period since your last account

Name of the business	
Date to which your last accounts were completed	
Your share of gross business profit from the last completed accounts	
Income tax and national insurance payable on your share of gross business profit above	
Net income for that year (using the two figures directly above, gross business profit less income tax and national insurance payable)	
Details and value of any benefits in kind, perks or other remuneration received from this business in the last year e.g. provision of a car, payment of travel, accommodation, meal expenses, etc.	
Amount of any regular monthly or other drawings that you take from this business	
If the estimated figure directly below is different from the net income as at the end date of the last completed accounts, briefly explain the reason(s)	
Your estimate of your net annual income for the next 12 months	

Estimated TOTAL of ALL net income from self-employment or partnership for the next 12 months: TOTAL I £

2 Financial Details

Part 8 Income: Income from investments e.g. dividends, interest or rental income

2.17 Details of income received in the last financial year (the year ended last 5th April), and your estimate of your income for the current financial year. Indicate whether the income was paid gross or net of income tax. You are not required to calculate any tax payable that may arise.

Nature of income and the asset from which it derived	Paid gross or net	Income received in the last financial year	Estimated income for the next 12 months

Estimated TOTAL investment income for the next 12 months: TOTAL J £

2 Financial Details Part 9 Income: Income from state benefits (including state pension and child benefit)

2.18 Details of all state benefits that you are currently receiving.

Name of benefit	Amount paid	Frequency of payment	Estimated income for the next 12 months
Estimated TOTAL benefit income for the next 12 months: TOTAL K			£

2 Financial Details Part 10 Income: Any other income

2.19 Details of any other income not disclosed above.

INCLUDE:

Any source including a Pension (excluding State Pension), and Pension Protection Fund (PPF) compensation

- from which income has been received during the last 12 months (even if it has now ceased)
- from which income is likely to be received during the next 12 months

You are reminded of your obligation to give full disclosure of your financial circumstances

Nature of income	Paid gross or net	Income received in the last financial year	Estimated income for the next 12 months

Estimated TOTAL other income for the next 12 months: TOTAL L £

2 Financial Details **Summaries**

2.20 Summary of your capital (Parts 1 to 5).

Description	Reference of the section on this statement	Value
Current value of your interest in the family home	A	
Current value of your interest in all other property	B	
Current value of your interest in personal assets	C	0.00
Current value of your liabilities	D	0.00
Current value of your interest in business assets	E	
Current value of your pension and PPF compensation assets	F	
Current value of all your other assets	G	
TOTAL value of your assets (Totals A to G less D):		£ 0.00

2.21 Summary of your estimated income for the next 12 months (Parts 6 to 10).

Description	Reference of the section on this statement	Value
Estimated net total of income from employment	H	
Estimated net total of income from self-employment or partnership	I	
Estimated net total of investment income	J	
Estimated state benefit receipts	K	
Estimated net total of all other income	L	
Estimated TOTAL income for the next 12 months (Totals H to L):		£ 0.00

3 Financial Requirements Part 1 Income needs

3.1 Income needs for yourself and for any children living with you or provided for by you. ALL figures should be annual, monthly or weekly (state which). You ***must not*** use a combination of these periods. State your current income needs and, if these are likely to change in the near future, explain the anticipated change and give an estimate of the future cost.

The income needs below are: (delete those not applicable)	Weekly	Monthly	Annual
I anticipate my income needs are going to change because			

3.1.1 Income needs for yourself.

INCLUDE:

- All income needs for yourself
- Income needs for any children living with you or provided for by you only if these form part of your total income needs (e.g. housing, fuel, car expenses, holidays, etc)

Item	Current cost	Estimated future cost
	SUB-TOTAL your income needs	£

3.1.2 Income needs for children living with you or provided for by you.

INCLUDE:

- Only those income needs that are different to those of your household shown above

Item	Current cost	Estimated future cost
	SUB-TOTAL children's income needs:	£
	TOTAL of ALL income needs:	£ 0.00

3 Financial Requirements Part 2 Capital needs

3.2 Set out below the reasonable future capital needs for yourself and for any children living with you or provided for by you.

3.2.1 Capital needs for yourself.

INCLUDE:

- All capital needs for yourself
- Capital needs for any children living with you or provided for by you only if these form part of your total capital needs (e.g. housing, car, etc.)

Item	Cost
SUB-TOTAL your capital needs:	£

3.2.2 Capital needs for children living with you or provided for by you.

INCLUDE:

- Only those capital needs that are different to those of your household shown above

Item	Cost
SUB-TOTAL your children's capital needs	£
TOTAL of ALL capital needs:	£ 0.00

4 Other Information

4.1 Details of any significant changes in your assets or income.

At both sections 4.1.1 and 4.1.2, INCLUDE:

- ALL assets held both within and outside England and Wales
- The disposal of any asset

4.1.1 Significant changes in assets or income during the LAST 12 months.

4.1.2 Significant changes in assets or income likely to occur during the NEXT 12 months.

4.2 Brief details of the standard of living enjoyed by you and your spouse/civil partner during the marriage/civil partnership.

4.3 Are there any particular contributions to the family property and assets or outgoings, or to family life, or the welfare of the family that have been made by you, your partner or anyone else that you think should be taken into account? If there are any such items, briefly describe the contribution and state the amount, when it was made and by whom.
INCLUDE:

- Contributions already made
- Contributions that will be made in the foreseeable future

4.4 Bad behaviour or conduct by the other party will only be taken into account in very exceptional circumstances when deciding how assets should be shared after divorce/dissolution. If you feel it should be taken into account in your case, identify the nature of the behaviour or conduct below.

4.5 Give details of any other circumstances that you consider could significantly affect the extent of the financial provision to be made by or for you or any child of the family.
INCLUDE (the following list is not exhaustive):

- Earning capacity
- Disability
- Inheritance prospects
- Redundancy
- Retirement
- Any agreement made between you and your spouse/civil partner before or after your marriage/civil partnership stating whether or not you rely upon the agreement giving your reasons
- Any plans to marry, form a civil partnership or live with a new partner
- Any contingent liabilities

4.6 If you have subsequently married or formed a civil partnership (or intend to) or are living with another person (or intend to), give brief details, so far as they are known to you, of his or her income, assets and liabilities.

Annual Income		Assets and Liabilities	
Nature of income	Value (if known, state whether gross or net)	Item	Value (if known)
Total income:	£	Total assets/liabilities:	£

5 Order Sought

5.1 If you are able at this stage, specify what kind of orders you are asking the court to make. Even if you cannot be specific at this stage, if you are able to do so, indicate:

a) If the family home is still owned, whether you are asking for it to be transferred to yourself or your spouse/civil partner or whether you are saying it should be sold

b) Whether you consider this is a case for continuing spousal maintenance/maintenance for your civil partner or whether you see the case as being appropriate for a 'clean break' *(A 'clean break' means a settlement or order which provides amongst other things, that neither you nor your spouse/civil partner will have any further claim against the income or capital of the other party. A 'clean break' does not terminate the responsibility of a parent to a child.)*

c) Whether you are seeking a
   i) pension sharing order
   ii) pension attachment order
   iii) pension compensation sharing order
   iv) pension compensation attachment order

d) If you are seeking a transfer or settlement of any property or assets, identify the property or assets in question

5.2 If you are seeking a variation of an ante-nuptial or post-nuptial settlement or a relevant settlement made during, or in anticipation of, a civil partnership, identify the settlement, by whom it was made, its trustees and beneficiaries and state why you allege it is a settlement which the court can vary.

5.3 If you are seeking an avoidance of disposition order, or if you have already applied for such an order, identify the property to which the disposition relates and the person or body in whose favour the disposition is alleged to have been made.

Sworn confirmation of the information

I, [ ] Enter your full name

of [ ] Enter your full residential address

The above named ☐ Applicant
☐ Respondent

☐ make oath
☐ affirm

and confirm that the information given above is a full, frank, clear and accurate disclosure of my financial and other relevant circumstances.

SWORN/AFFIRMED at [ ]

in the County of [ ]

on D D / M M / Y Y Y Y

[ ]

Before me, [ ]

☐ A Commissioner for Oaths
☐ Officer of the Court appointed by the Judge to take Affidavits

---

Address all communications to the Court Manager of the Court and quote the case number.
If you do not quote this number, your correspondence may be returned.

Schedule of Documents to accompany Form E

The following list shows the documents you must attach to your Form E if applicable. You may attach other documents where it is necessary to explain or clarify any of the information that you give in the Form E.

Form E paragraph	Document	Please tick		
		Attached	Not applicable	To follow
1.14	**Application to vary an order:** if applicable, attach a copy of the relevant order.	☐	☐	☐
2.1	**Matrimonial home valuation:** a copy of any valuation relating to the matrimonial home that has been obtained in the last six months.	☐	☐	☐
2.1	**Matrimonial home mortgage(s):** a recent mortgage statement in respect of each mortgage on the matrimonial home confirming the amount outstanding.	☐	☐	☐
2.2	**Any other property:** a copy of any valuation relating to each other property disclosed that has been obtained in the last six months.	☐	☐	☐
2.2	**Any other property:** a recent mortgage statement in respect of each mortgage on each other property disclosed confirming the amount outstanding.	☐	☐	☐
2.3	**Personal bank, building society and National Savings accounts:** copies of statements for the last 12 months for each account that has been held in the last twelve months, either in your own name or in which you have or have had any interest.	☐	☐	☐
2.4	**Other investments:** the latest statement or dividend counterfoil relating to each investment as disclosed in paragraph 2.4.	☐	☐	☐
2.5	**Life insurance (including endowment) policies:** a surrender valuation for each policy that has a surrender value as disclosed under paragraph 2.5.	☐	☐	☐
2.11	**Business interests:** a copy of the business accounts for the last two financial years for each business interest disclosed.	☐	☐	☐
2.11	**Business interests:** any documentation that is available to confirm the estimate of the current value of the business, for example, a letter from an accountant or formal valuation if that has been obtained.	☐	☐	☐
2.13	**Pension and PPF compensation:** a recent statement showing the cash equivalent (CE) provided by the trustees or managers of each pension arrangement or valuation of each PPF entitlement provided by the PPF Board that you have disclosed (or, in the case of the additional state pension, a valuation of these rights). If not yet available, attach a copy of the letter sent to the pension company, administrators or the PPF Board requesting the information.	☐	☐	☐

2.15	**Employment income:** your P60 for the last financial year in respect of each employment that you have.	☐	☐	☐
2.15	**Employment income:** your last three payslips in respect of each employment that you have.	☐	☐	☐
2.15	**Employment income:** your last form P11D if you have been issued with one.	☐	☐	☐
2.16	**Self-employment or partnership income:** a copy of your last tax assessment or if that is not available, a letter from your accountant confirming your tax liability.	☐	☐	☐
2.16	**Self-employment or partnership income:** if net income from the last financial year and the estimated income for the next twelve months is significantly different, a copy of the management accounts for the period since your last accounts.	☐	☐	☐
State relevant Form E paragraph	Description of other documents attached:	☐	☐	☐

Form E Financial statement for a financial order or for financial relief after an overseas divorce or dissolution etc (04.11)

15 VARIATION, COLLECTION, AND ENFORCEMENT OF FINANCIAL ORDERS

15.1 INTRODUCTION

This chapter will:

- **discuss the circumstances in which a financial order can be varied;**
- **discuss the collection of monies due under financial orders;**
- **discuss the enforcement of financial orders.**

To clients' immense frustration, gaining a financial order is not the end of proceedings. It is tempting to close a file at the end of a financial order hearing, but it is essential that compliance is carefully monitored until all orders are fully complied with by all parties. It is not uncommon for a disgruntled spouse or civil partner to refuse to comply with the terms of an order, even a consent order, and so a family law solicitor must be able to use enforcement mechanisms to enforce the court order.

Some orders made by the court may be in force for a number of years, e.g. a periodical payments order. Circumstances within clients' lives change through, e.g., remarriage or the loss of a job. There is scope within financial orders for the court to reconsider such an order and this will be discussed in this chapter. All methods of variation, collection, and enforcement apply equally to civil partners as well as spouses.

15.2 VARIATION OF FINANCIAL ORDERS

15.2.1 ORDERS SUBJECT TO VARIATION

S31 of the Matrimonial Causes Act 1973 (MCA 1973) states the orders made in financial proceedings that can be varied:

- order for maintenance pending suit or an interim maintenance order;
- any periodical payments order or secured periodical payments order;
- lump sum by instalments;
- a pension attachment order (income or lump sum from the pension) made under s25B(4) or s25C MCA 1973;
- an order for sale under s24A MCA 1973;
- a pension sharing order under s24B MCA 1973 if made before decree absolute.

Some orders cannot be varied and these include a transfer of property under s24(1)(a) MCA 1973 (although there are a limited set of circumstances where a property transfer order is made following judicial separation). There is no power to vary the amount of a lump sum order, only to adjust the arrangements if payable by instalments.

15.2.2 APPLICATIONS FOR VARIATION

When a party applies for variation of an order, the court can vary, discharge, or suspend the order. The order most commonly varied is periodical payments following a change in circumstances of either the payer or payee.

In an application for the variation of a periodical payments order, the court has the power under s31(7C) and (7D) MCA 1973 to commute the order into a lump sum, a property adjustment order, or a pension sharing order. This is often described in practice as a 'capitalization' of a periodical payments order and allows the parties to have a clean break. The court must decide how much could be paid under a periodical payments order and then balance the harm to the spouse in the termination of the payments against the desirability of a clean break (*Boylan v Boylan* [1988] 1 FLR 282). The calculation of the lump sum capitalization is complex and students are referred to practitioner texts.

The factors that the court takes into account when considering an application for variation are found in s31(7) MCA 1973 and include:

- all the circumstances of the case with first consideration to the children of the family;
- any change in any of the matters which the court was required to consider when making the order to which the application relates.

The court has the power to end the order or to limit the term of the order to enable one party to adjust to the end of payments.

In terms of a variation of the amount of the payments, it is vital to advise clients that the court can look at capital accumulated since the order was made, to look afresh at the evidence of parties' means, and to vary the order down as well as up. Clients should be aware that the court may decide to look afresh at the issue of periodical payments to the detriment of the client.

 **Example**

Millie and Lucas divorce in 2004. The court ordered that Millie pay Lucas £125 per week as she was the higher earning spouse and Lucas needed to retrain after looking after the children for a number of years. In 2012 Lucas applies for an upward variation of periodical payments following a rise in the cost of living.

However, in the intervening years, Millie has lost her highly-paid job and has taken a less well-paid job. Lucas has bought a house, inherited a large sum, and has a very well-paid job. At the hearing the district judge decides that Lucas no longer requires periodical payments and discharges the order.

15.3 COLLECTION OF FINANCIAL ORDERS

The main issue with collection of financial orders is when periodical payments are not paid. It is a source of immense frustration for clients as collection procedures are slow and complex.

15.3.1 COLLECTION OF PERIODICAL PAYMENTS

As payments are directly between parties, clients are advised to keep a record of payments made. The permission of the court is required to enforce arrears over 12 months old under s32 MCA 1973. An application can also be made for an oral examination before a district judge to find out the financial position of a non-paying spouse.

15.4 ENFORCEMENT OF FINANCIAL ORDERS

One of the major benefits of the new Family Procedure Rules 2010 (FPR 2010) has been the introduction of a harmonized enforcement procedure under Part 33. Applications are now made on one form, the D50K, for all types of enforcement. The form allows the applicant to specify the type of method of enforcement or to apply for such order as the court considers appropriate.

15.4.1 PERIODICAL PAYMENTS

For periodical payments, methods of enforcement include a judgment summons requiring the non-payer to attend court and be examined on their means. The district judge makes an order based on this information. A non-payer can be committed to prison but this is generally suspended on the basis that the payments are made. The procedure for such an order can be found in a practitioner civil procedure text.

In addition, the Maintenance Enforcement Act 1991 allows the High Court or county court to specify that periodical payments are paid by standing order or through an attachment of earnings (the employer sends the payment directly from the non-payer's wages). Payments may also be made through the court.

Periodical payments can also be registered with the family proceedings court. The payments will be collected and enforced through the court. A new EU Regulation No. 4/2009 of 18 December 2008 on jurisdiction, applicable law, recognition, and decisions, and cooperation in matters relating to maintenance obligations came into force in June 2011. The regulation covers a situation where maintenance is owed by someone living in another jurisdiction. A maintenance creditor should be able to obtain easily in a member state a decision which will be automatically enforceable in another member state without further formalities.

If the non-payer is not within the jurisdiction, there are mechanisms for recovery but this is beyond the scope of this text.

15.4.2 ENFORCEMENT OF OTHER ORDERS

 **Example**

Anoushka and Pavel agree a consent order during the financial dispute resolution. One of the orders made was for Pavel to transfer £20,000 to Anoushka within 14 days of the order. Six months after the order, Pavel has failed to make the transfer. Anoushka cannot purchase a new property as she was relying on the money as a deposit.

Anoushka will have to rely on the normal methods of civil enforcement to force Pavel to give her the money.

In some cases, the final order is not the final step of the proceedings. Some spouses fail to implement the orders of the court and the receiving spouse has to enforce the order. As the order is made in the county court, the receiving spouse will have to rely on civil procedure enforcement, e.g. judgment summons, third party debt orders, and execution against goods. A civil procedure text should be consulted.

The receiving spouse could apply to make the non-payer bankrupt. The problem with this is that the unpaid periodical payments will be only one debt amongst many others and the spouse may only receive a proportion of the actual amount owed to them.

For lump sum orders, an order for sale under s24A MCA 1973 can be made with a direction that part of the proceeds are directed to pay off arrears.

Property adjustment orders are generally concerned with the family home. Occasionally, spouses or civil partners may refuse to execute the documentation to complete the property adjustment order. The answer lies within s38 County Courts Act 1984 (for county courts) or occasionally s39 Supreme Court Act 1981 (in the High Court). Orders under these sections allow the court to require the offender to complete the act (e.g. signing the contract of sale) within a prescribed time. If the act is not done, the district judge can execute the necessary documentation to complete the transaction. This is often a surprise to recalcitrant clients! Orders can also be made to require a party to vacate a property. The author once had to use several bailiffs to complete this type of order.

There are also a range of enforcement methods used in civil litigation, including warrant of execution, attachment of earnings, charging orders, and third party debt orders. Details of these orders can be found in most good civil procedure texts.

SUMMARY POINTS

- Not all orders are complied with and it is essential that compliance with orders is carefully monitored.
- Only some orders are able to be varied by the court, including periodical payments and lump sums by instalments.
- Care must be taken when applying for variation as the court has the ability to consider matters afresh.
- Periodical payments are paid directly between the parties in most cases.
- There are a variety of methods for enforcement of periodical payments, including a judgment summons or registration at a family proceedings court.
- Property adjustment orders can be completed by a district judge if one party fails to complete the transaction.
- All methods of civil enforcement are available in family proceedings.

SELF-TEST QUESTIONS

1. Your client has not been receiving their periodical payments for the past six months. Describe one method of enforcement. Would your answer be any different if the arrears were over two years old?
2. Sam and Gene's case was heard in the county court. A property adjustment order was made about their home and Gene was ordered to transfer it to Sam. Gene is refusing to sign the contract for sale. Can you suggest the next steps to take?

online resource centre

Answers to the questions above can be found on the Online Resource Centre: www.oxfordtextbooks.co.uk/orc/familyhandbook13/.

16 PROTECTING ASSETS AND THE FAMILY HOME IN FINANCIAL ORDER PROCEEDINGS

16.1 INTRODUCTION

This chapter will:

- **examine whether a client can protect assets in financial order proceedings;**
- **examine the provisions of s37 Matrimonial Causes Act 1973;**
- **discuss the availability of 'home rights' under the Family Law Act 1996.**

Every family law solicitor will have been asked by a client about hiding or disposing of assets in financial proceedings. Apart from the professional conduct issues involved in such an issue, the courts will take such attempts to hide or dispose of assets in proceedings very seriously. It is tempting for clients to minimize the assets available to the court, but the Matrimonial Causes Act 1973 (MCA 1973) has the power to prevent and recover such disposals. This chapter will look at the scope of the court's power, as well as considering the procedural and evidential issues in making or defending such an application.

16.2 SCOPE OF THE LAW

S37 MCA 1973 gives the court the power to make orders concerning the disposal of property to prevent or reduce financial relief. 'Financial relief' means relief under any of the provisions of ss22, 23, 24, 24B, 27, 31 (except sub-s (6)), and 35 of the MCA 1973. As in **Chapter 14**, these are applications for maintenance pending suit, financial provision, property adjustment, wilful neglect to maintain, or a variation application.

Defeating a claim for financial relief is a reference to preventing financial relief from being granted to that person, or to that person for the benefit of a child of the family, or reducing the amount of any financial relief which might be so granted, or frustrating or impeding the enforcement of any order which might be or has been made at his instance under any of those provisions under s37(1) MCA 1973.

A 'disposition' is defined in s37(6) MCA 1973. It does not include any provision contained in a will or codicil but (with that exception) includes any conveyance, assurance, or gift of property of any description. The courts have defined the term widely. Lord Hoffmann described 'disposition' as a 'familiar enough word in the law of property and ordinarily means an act by which someone ceases to be the owner of that property in law or in equity'

(*Newlon Housing Trust v Alsulaimen* [1999] 1 AC 313). S37 MCA 1973 also applies to property held abroad (*Hamlin v Hamlin* [1986] Fam 11).

Example

Xavier separates from Yolande and commences proceedings for divorce and financial relief. Yolande and Xavier have considerable savings in SaverBank. Xavier checks the balance one morning and finds that the savings have gone. Yolande tells him that she gave the money to her sister, Maria, as a gift. Xavier believes that Maria will give the money back once the financial order proceedings are finished. Xavier could apply for an order under s37 MCA 1973 as Yolande has disposed of savings in an attempt to reduce the amount of money available to the court in financial relief.

In order for the court to consider an application, proceedings for financial orders must be in existence. There must be sufficient evidence for the court to believe an order is necessary to prevent a disposition or to review a disposition that has already occurred. The vague suspicion of a client is not sufficient. An application should be proportionate according to the amount of money and other disputed issues in a case.

Example

From the example above, consider instead that Xavier and Yolande have savings of just £400. Although Yolande has removed the savings in the same circumstances, it would probably not be a proportionate step to institute proceedings under s37 MCA 1973 due to the relatively small sum of money involved.

16.2.1 CIVIL PROCEEDINGS

In some circumstances, freezing orders and search orders may be available under the Civil Procedure Rules. A freezing order does what is indicated by its name and freezes assets enabling the court to prevent their dispersal. A search order allows the applicant to enter premises and search for documents. These orders are complex and draconian. Reference should be made to a specialist practitioner text.

16.3 WHAT CAN THE COURT DO?

S37 MCA 1973 has two functions. Firstly, the section allows the court to prevent a future disposal or further dealings with property. It states:

> (2) Where proceedings for financial relief are brought by one person against another, the court may, on the application of the first-mentioned person—
>
> (a) if it is satisfied that the other party to the proceedings is, with the intention of defeating the claim for financial relief, about to make any disposition or to transfer out of the jurisdiction or otherwise deal with any property, make such order as it thinks fit for restraining the other party from so doing or otherwise for protecting the claim.

Example

Martin and Becky are married and own several rental properties. Most of the properties are in Martin's sole name. Following an application for financial relief by Becky, Martin arranges to sell two properties and Becky only becomes aware of this when she comes across a letter from an estate agent.

Becky applies for an order under s37 MCA 1973 and the court makes an order forbidding Martin from selling any of the rental properties.

Secondly, s37 MCA 1973 allows the court to set aside dispositions that have already been made where, if the disposition were set aside, different financial relief would be granted to the applicant. The court may also make an order where a disposition impedes the operation of an enforcement order.

S37(2)(b) and (c) MCA 1973 state:

> (b) if it is satisfied that the other party has, with that intention, made a reviewable disposition and that if the disposition were set aside financial relief or different financial relief would be granted to the applicant, make an order setting aside the disposition;
>
> (c) if it is satisfied, in a case where an order has been obtained under any of the provisions mentioned in subsection (1) above by the applicant against the other party, that the other party has, with that intention, made a reviewable disposition, make an order setting aside the disposition;

and an application for the purposes of paragraph (b) shall be made in the proceedings for the financial relief in question.

Example

Hari and Saira are in the middle of financial order proceedings. Hari's solicitors have discovered that Saira has 'donated' her collection of rare paintings to her uncle, which were valued at £100,000 and was one of the largest assets within the proceedings.

On an application by Hari, the 'donation' is set aside by the court.

16.4 PROVING INTENTION TO DEFEAT FINANCIAL RELIEF

Any application must show that the act of the respondent was made with the intention of defeating the claim for financial relief. S37(5) MCA 1973 assists the applicant if the act in question took place less than three years ago: if the court is satisfied that the disposition would have the consequence of defeating the applicant's claim for financial relief, it shall be presumed, unless the contrary is shown, that the person who disposed of or is about to dispose of or deal with the property did so or is about to do so with the intention of defeating the applicant's claim for financial relief.

The court must have some evidence of intention; a mere suspicion will not suffice.

16.5 THIRD PARTIES

Third parties may be affected by an order either by having taken ownership of the property in question or by being served with an order to disclose documents.

In terms of third parties taking ownership of property, s37(4) MCA 1973 makes all dispositions reviewable unless made for valuable consideration (other than marriage) to a person who, at the time of the disposition, acted in relation to it in good faith and without notice of any intention on the part of the other party to defeat the applicant's claim for financial relief. Thus third parties who give valuable consideration in good faith will not be deprived of the property. The valuable consideration given to the person making the disposition may become the subject of a s37 MCA 1973 order.

Example

Miriam sells a holiday cottage she bought before her marriage to Leslie. The couple are now divorcing. The house was in her sole name but Leslie has spent a great deal of money renovating the property and it is one of the assets being considered by the court in financial order proceedings. Miriam sells the property for valuable consideration of £125,000.

The court makes an order that the third party keeps the house but the £125,000 becomes subject of an order.

An order under s37 MCA 1973 may require a third party, e.g. a bank, to disclose documents or information. This information can be given to the court in affidavits. It is a breach of Art. 6 of the European Convention on Human Rights (ECHR) to give the court information following a without notice order if that information cannot be revealed to the respondent party to the application (*C v C (Without Notice Orders)* [2006] 1 FLR 936).

In *Ansari v Ansari & Ors* [2008] EWCA Civ 1456, the husband had left the matrimonial home, which was in his sole name, and the wife registered her home rights under ss30–33 of the Family Law Act 1996. The husband then proceeded to sell the house although the wife remained in occupation. The solicitors acting for the purchasers and the mortgage bank had requested that the notice be removed but this was not completed. The wife then started proceedings to prevent the husband dealing with the sale proceeds but did not seek any relief against the bank's charge. At first instance, the district judge set aside the sale and the charge as a reviewable disposition under s37 MCA 1973. On appeal, the Circuit Judge allowed the bank's appeal against setting aside the charge so the wife appealed that decision.

In the Court of Appeal, Longmore LJ identified three questions:

(i) was the transaction a reviewable disposition under s37?
(ii) could the bank claim that it had acted in good faith and with no notice of the husband's intention to defeat the wife's claims?; and
(iii) was setting aside the charge consequential on setting aside the sale?

He found that the disposition was not reviewable as only dispositions made by the respondent to the financial order proceedings (i.e. the husband) can be reviewed. Secondly, even if it was a reviewable disposition, the bank had acted in good faith (under s37(4)) and notice of the wife's rights was not the same as notice of the husband's intention to defeat her claims. Finally, the charge could not be set aside as a consequence of setting aside the sale, again as the bank had acted in good faith.

16.6 CIVIL PARTNERS

S74 of and Sch 5 to the Civil Partnership Act 2004 (CPA 2004) gives the court analogous powers to s37 MCA 1973 to review dispositions made to prevent or reduce financial relief.

16.7 PROCEDURE FOR AN APPLICATION UNDER S37 MCA 1973

R9.6 Family Procedure Rules 2010 (FPR 2010) governs the procedure for application. Applications are made to a district judge under Part 17 FPR 2010 and proceedings for financial relief must be in existence. The application is made by filing an application notice D50G together with a draft order. The FPR 2010 do not specify whether a sworn statement should be attached. The application will most probably be made without notice in order to avoid alerting the respondent to the application.

If the application is successful and the district judge makes an order, a return date must be given and the respondent to be at liberty, on two days' notice, to make an application to discharge the order.

16.8 THE FAMILY HOME

The family home is generally the largest asset in financial proceedings. It may be held in the name of one spouse only and, as such, is vulnerable to sale without the other spouse having notice.

16.8.1 JOINT NAMES

If the house is in joint names, the property cannot be transferred or conveyed without both owners' consent.

16.8.2 HOME RIGHTS

If the home is owned in the sole name of a spouse or civil partner, they can, theoretically, sell the property without the consent of the other spouse or civil partner. However, a spouse or civil partner has 'home rights' under s30 Family Law Act 1996 (FLA 1996) (as amended by the Domestic Violence, Crime and Victims Act 2004).

Home rights under s30(1) FLA 1996 encompass one spouse or civil partner occupying a dwelling house by virtue of:

- a beneficial estate or interest or contract; or
- any enactment giving 'A' the right to remain in occupation; and where
- the other spouse or civil partner 'B' is not so entitled.

The spouse or civil partner in the position of 'B' has the right under s30(2) FLA 1996 not to be evicted or excluded from the house by 'A' except with the leave of the court. If 'B' is not in occupation, they have the right to enter and occupy the house. If the person in position of spouse 'B' pays the rent or mortgage, this will be accepted as if made by 'A' (s30(3) FLA 1996). The dwelling house must have been or must have been intended to be the matrimonial or civil partnership home (s30(7) FLA 1996). Under s63(1) FLA 1996, a dwelling house can include a caravan or a houseboat. These rights subsist as long as the marriage or civil partnership. These rights do not extend to cohabitants.

Home rights are a charge (see the **Glossary**) on the estate or interest under s31 FLA 1996. Home rights should be registered as a charge against the property and a solicitor should do this as soon as possible. In unregistered land, a Class F land charge should be registered against the spouse or civil partner's name in the register of land charges (s2 Land Charges Act 1972). In the case of registered land, a notice should be entered into the charges register under the Land Registration Act 1925. Please note, such a registration will lead to a notice being issued by the Land Registry and there is no provision for this to be withheld. If this is likely to provoke a strong reaction from the other spouse or civil partner, please consider the methods of protection available under the FLA 1996 (see **Chapter 33** onwards). The protection afforded by registration is lost once decree absolute is granted and this may be a reason to delay an application for a decree.

Spouses with only an equitable interest in the property fall under s30(9) FLA 1996. This is beyond the scope of this text and reference should be made to a specialist text.

SUMMARY POINTS

- Assets must be protected during financial proceedings in order that they are available to the court for division between the parties.
- S37 MCA 1973 assists the parties and the courts to prevent the disposition of any assets by either party to the proceedings.

- Proceedings for financial relief must be in existence before an application can be made.
- An order can be made preventing a party from making a disposition with the intention of defeating the claim for financial relief or an order reviewing a disposition that has already been made.
- Property is widely defined as is the concept of a 'disposition'.
- Third parties can be the subject of orders for information, although a bona fide purchaser for money's worth will not lose their property—the consideration for the transaction will form the subject of the order.
- The procedure for such an application is found in r9.6 and Part 17 FPR 2010.
- The family home can be protected using 'home rights' under s30 FLA 1996.
- Home rights protect the right of occupation of a spouse or civil partner in the family home and can be registered as a charge in registered land or as a Class F land charge in unregistered land.

SELF-TEST QUESTIONS

1. Martine and Malcolm are in the middle of divorce and financial order proceedings. The couple are very wealthy and each spouse owns a number of valuable assets as well as the joint family home. During the course of the proceedings, Martine finds that Malcolm has been selling his collection of valuable paintings over the past six months and putting the money into a secret bank account. The buyers of the paintings have paid the market price. Malcolm has six more paintings and she worries that he will sell these too. Martine also finds that Malcolm sold his yacht four years ago for £1 m.

   (a) Describe the concept of 'disposition' to Martine.

   (b) Advise whether Martine can recover the paintings. If not, how would you advise her to proceed?

   (c) Can Martine recover the yacht or the sale proceeds?

online resource centre

Answers to the questions above can be found on the Online Resource Centre: www.oxfordtextbooks.co.uk/orc/familyhandbook13/.

17 SEPARATION AND MAINTENANCE AGREEMENTS

17.1 INTRODUCTION

This chapter will:

- **examine the use of separation and maintenance agreements and the essential features of both types of agreements;**
- **discuss the advantages and disadvantages of separation and maintenance agreements.**

If parties wish to avoid expensive, time-consuming, and emotionally draining litigation, a separation or maintenance agreement can be drawn up. Such agreements can include a wide variety of terms and are a useful tool for family lawyers.

This chapter looks briefly at separation and maintenance agreements: their form, drafting, and enforcement.

There is a distinction between separation and maintenance agreements. Separation agreements essentially record that the parties wish to live apart and can include terms about children, property, and maintenance. Maintenance agreements deal with the payment of maintenance to or for the benefit of spouses, civil partners, or children, but do not deal with the separation of the parties; it can include other terms.

17.2 SEPARATION AGREEMENTS

There are very few limitations on the terms that the parties can agree to include in a separation agreement. The wishes of the parties should be explored fully when advising. As with any agreement concerning money and property on relationship breakdown, the agreement should be comprehensive and realistic.

Practical Considerations

The terms that are common to separation agreements include:

- arrangements for contact and where the children of the family shall live;
- the arrangements for the family home and other assets; but parties would be advised to agree only following full and frank disclosure of all assets;
- an agreement to live apart and not to molest each other;

- an agreement that one spouse or civil partner will pay maintenance for the benefit of the other spouse or civil partner or the children. As noted in Chapter 18, parties are now free to agree child support maintenance even when on benefits. The agreement would not prevent the resident parent with care from applying to the Child Maintenance and Enforcement Commission. See 17.4 for further considerations on drafting maintenance agreements.

Sections 34–36 Matrimonial Causes Act 1973 (MCA 1973) deal with maintenance agreements. S34(2) MCA 1973 defines a maintenance agreement as either an agreement containing financial arrangements or a separation agreement that contains no such financial information. S34(1) MCA 1973 states that any provision in a maintenance agreement seeking to restrict the right to apply to court is void, but other terms will remain valid. Parties can apply under ss35–36 MCA 1973 for a variation of the agreement during their joint lives or following the death of one of the parties. These provisions are very rarely used in practice.

17.3 ADVANTAGES AND DISADVANTAGES OF SEPARATION AND MAINTENANCE AGREEMENTS

Not many clients are aware of the availability of such agreements. It is worth understanding the possible advantages and disadvantages of separation and maintenance agreements in order to advise clients fully.

TABLE 17.1 ADVANTAGES AND DISADVANTAGES OF SEPARATION AND MAINTENANCE AGREEMENTS

Advantages	Disadvantages
Agreements are flexible and can address the client's need specifically.	The agreement is not final; the parties cannot exclude the court's jurisdiction and so parties may still seek an order through the courts.
The parties retain control of the process and this can help to preserve good relations. The parties do not have to adopt an adversarial stance and so can avoid becoming entrenched in a dispute.	It is a contract and so the enforcement procedures are not easy and can be costly.
As court processes are avoided, costs can be lower.	Maintenance orders can be varied in certain circumstances but if the agreement falls outside this exception, variation can only occur by consent.

17.4 DRAFTING MAINTENANCE AGREEMENTS

Great care should be taken when drafting maintenance agreements. Clients need to be advised on the issue of the termination of maintenance payments. Options include drafting an agreement that continues even following divorce, remarriage, or cohabitation of the receiving spouse or civil partner or the death of the paying spouse or civil partner. If this is not what the parties want, the agreement should be drafted to address when payments will be terminated.

 **Example**

Hari and Saira separate as they no longer love each other and do not want to remain living in the same house. They intend to wait for two years in order to use s1(2)(d) MCA 1973 (two years' separation plus consent) as the basis of their divorce.

Hari does not wish Saira to struggle with money as he has a well-paid job, whereas Saira is pursuing a full-time degree. Hari asks you to draw up a maintenance agreement for the sum of £750 per month to be paid to Saira. He is concerned that once Saira leaves university, she should get a job and he does not want to support her if she meets someone else. A maintenance agreement is drafted where maintenance will cease upon Saira finishing her undergraduate degree or if she cohabits with someone for more than three months.

17.5 FORM OF SEPARATION AND MAINTENANCE AGREEMENTS

Separation and maintenance agreements are contracts and will require an offer, acceptance, and intention to create legal relations. There may be difficulty with consideration and so the agreement is generally embodied in a deed (see the **Glossary**). Agreements can be made in writing or orally, although an oral agreement may attract evidential difficulties. As with all contracts, separation and maintenance agreements can be set aside for duress, undue influence, or misrepresentation. In order to prevent any accusations, it is desirable that both parties receive independent legal advice.

17.5.1 EXCLUDING THE MCA 1973

It is not possible for either party to exclude the other's right to apply to the courts for financial relief under s34 MCA 1973 and also *de Lasala v de Lasala* [1980] AC 546. This may appear to a client to make a maintenance or separation agreement rather pointless. A separation agreement is useful if the parties separate but do not intend to divorce immediately and such an agreement records the parties' agreement. Should the parties divorce in the future, this agreement can be formalized in a consent order. The parties would save a great deal of money in legal costs and avoid the need to take adversarial proceedings in court.

17.6 ENFORCEMENT

As stated above, separation and maintenance agreements are contracts and are enforceable as such. Civil litigation methods of enforcement are expensive and are often very frustrating. For more information consult a civil procedure text.

SUMMARY POINTS

- Separation and maintenance agreements are a commonly used device for separating parties to draw up in binding form any agreement reached between the parties.
- As long as full disclosure is given and independent legal advice is obtained, these agreements have many advantages.
- Such agreements are contracts and must have all the legal elements of a contract. They are best contained in a deed.
- The jurisdiction of the court cannot be excluded.
- Maintenance agreements can be altered under ss34–35 MCA 1973 but it is a rare application.
- Agreements are enforced by usual civil enforcement methods.

SELF-TEST QUESTIONS

1. Advise your client Hari on the following terms in a separation agreement for Saira requested by your client:
   (a) maintenance is agreed at £750 per month and child maintenance is agreed at £250 per month for their three children;
   (b) the provisions of the MCA 1973 are to be ousted by the agreement;
   (c) Hari will have contact with the children of the family from 10am Saturday until 4pm Sunday;
   (d) Saira has made full and frank disclosure of all of her assets and has sought independent legal advice before signing the agreement.

online resource centre

Answers to the questions above can be found on the Online Resource Centre: www.oxfordtextbooks.co.uk/orc/familyhandbook13/.

18 CHILD SUPPORT

18.1 INTRODUCTION

This chapter will:

- **examine the system for the payment of child support maintenance;**
- **examine the Child Support Act 1991 and subsequent legislation;**
- **examine the changes currently being made to child support maintenance.**

The Child Support Act 1991 (CSA 1991) introduced a mechanism to recover maintenance from absent parents for their children. It is a controversial area of family law that raises strong feelings in clients. The CSA 1991 created the Child Support Agency (CSA) as the organization responsible for the collection of child support maintenance. It has not been a popular organization amongst some and has been heavily criticized.

The CSA has been heavily criticized as just one in three parents with care of the child receive child support maintenance through the CSA, and although the purpose of the CSA was to save taxpayers money, the CSA actually costs £20 m net per year.

This chapter will look at the framework of child support, when a client may be required to pay child support, what a client can do if they do not receive child support, and the future of child support. The CSA 1991 has been heavily amended and there are substantial changes to come in the next few years. **Chapter 24** looks at the position where a parent can make a claim under Sch 1 Children Act 1989 and **Chapter 14** contains details of orders a court can make for children under the Matrimonial Causes Act 1973 (MCA 1973).

18.2 CHILD SUPPORT ACT 1991

The CSA 1991 was enacted to introduce a new regime for the maintenance of children, which previously had been within the purview of the courts. The CSA 1991 came into force on 5 April 1993. It introduced responsibility for parents to maintain their children, which means that there can never be a clean break between parents and children (see **Chapter 12** for clean break between parents). The CSA 1991 was amended first by the Child Support Act

1995 and then by the Child Support Pensions and Social Security Act 2000 (CSPSSA 2000). The CSPSSA 2000 simplified the system of calculating child support and made some fairly radical changes. The Child Maintenance and Other Payments Act 2008 makes even more changes, which are discussed at **18.9**.

This chapter will discuss the current child support regime but will also look at future changes and the reasons behind these changes.

18.3 THE BASIC PRINCIPLES

S1 CSA 1991 makes a natural parent of a qualifying child responsible for maintaining them. A 'qualifying child' is defined in s3 CSA 1991 as a child where one or more of his parents are 'non-resident' parents. The parent is the biological parent of the child. A non-resident parent shall be taken to have met his responsibility to maintain the qualifying child by making periodical payments of maintenance. The CSA 1991 describes these payments as 'child support maintenance'.

A 'non-resident' parent is also defined in s3 CSA 1991 where the parent is not living in the same household as the child and the child has his home with a person who is, in relation to the child, a person with care. A 'person with care' is defined by s3(3) CSA 1991 as a person with whom the child has his home, who provides day-to-day care for the child (whether exclusively or with another person), and is not within a prescribed category of persons (e.g. a foster parent or a local authority).

 **Example**

Anoushka and Pavel have three children aged between three and nine years. The couple separated two years ago and Pavel moved out of the family home. Pavel formed a new relationship with Anna and the couple have a daughter.

Pavel is a non-resident parent and has the responsibility to maintain the children that live with Anoushka. Anoushka is the parent with care as she looks after the children on a day-to-day basis.

18.3.1 NET INCOME

The calculation for child support maintenance is based on net weekly income. Net weekly income is calculated with reference to the Schedule to the Child Support (Maintenance Calculation and Special Cases) Regulations 2000.

For those who are employed, earnings include all wages, overtime, bonus, commissions, statutory sick pay, and regular payments made in addition to wages. Income tax, national insurance, and pension payments (including personal pension payments) are disregarded.

Self-employed net weekly income is based on the total taxable profits that are taken into account by HMRC with the deduction of tax and national insurance together with pension contributions.

For both categories of earners, other income can be taken into account including pensions payments (net of tax) and working tax credit.

 **Example**

Pavel earns £300 per week, net of income tax and national insurance (NI) payments. He contributes £56 to his pension but receives £80 (net of tax and NI) overtime.

Pavel's net weekly income will be as follows:

£300 (– £56 + £80) = £324.00

18.4 THE CHILD SUPPORT CALCULATION

The person with care of the child or the non-resident parent can apply for a child support maintenance calculation and this will be calculated using a set formula. The child support maintenance is currently collected and enforced by the Child Support Agency.

The CSPSSA 2000 simplified a previously very complex way of calculating child support maintenance and this came into operation in March 2003. There will, therefore, still be cases where the calculation dates back to the original calculation and reference should be made to a specialist text.

The calculation follows a number of stages. Based on the number of children and the net earned income of the non-resident parent, four rates are applicable.

18.4.1 BASIC RATE

Where the non-resident's weekly net income is £200–2,000, the child support maintenance payable is

- 15% of net income for one child;
- 20% of net income for two children;
- 25% of net income for three or more children.

Where the non-resident parent has one or more 'relevant other children', then the following percentages are applied to the non-resident parent's net weekly income before the calculation for qualifying children is performed:

- 15% of net income for one relevant other child;
- 20% of net income for two relevant other children;
- 25% of net income for three or more relevant other children.

'Relevant other children' are children other than qualifying children in respect of whom the non-resident parent or his partner receives child benefit.

 **Example**

Pavel has a daughter with his new partner and she is a relevant other child. His income will be reduced by 15% to take account of this child:

$$£324 \times 15\% = £48.60.$$

Pavel's net weekly income will be reduced by £48.60 and his net weekly income for the purposes of the basic rate calculation will be:

$$£324 - £48.60 = £275.40.$$

As Pavel has three qualifying children with Anoushka, his liability for these children will be 25% of his net income:

$$£275.40 \times 25\% = £68.85.$$

Anoushka will receive £68.85 in child support maintenance.

18.4.2 REDUCED RATE

Where weekly net income is over £100 but less than £200, the non-resident parent pays £5 on the first £100 and a percentage of the income over £100 but less than £200. This percentage is calculated using the following formula:

TABLE 18.1 REDUCED RATE

Number of qualifying children	One				Two				Three or more			
Number of relevant other children of the non-resident parent	0	1	2	3 or more	0	1	2	3 or more	0	1	2	3 or more
Percentage payable	25%	20.5%	19%	17.5%	35%	29%	27%	25%	45%	37.5%	35%	32.5%

Example

Pavel's net weekly income falls to £180 due to the economic slowdown. There is one relevant other child (Pavel's daughter with his current partner) and three qualifying children (Pavel's children living with Anoushka).

The child support maintenance payable will be calculated as follows:

£5 + (£80 × 37.5%) = £35.

18.4.3 FLAT RATE

There is a flat rate of £5 per week where weekly net income is less than £100 or if the non-resident parent is on certain benefits or is in receipt of the state pension.

18.4.4 NIL RATE

The non-resident parent will pay no child support maintenance (the nil rate) where s/he is:

- a student;
- a prisoner;
- a child (see s55 CSA 1991);
- a person who is 16 or 17 years old in receipt of income support or job seekers allowance.

A full list of those paying the nil rate can be found at reg 5 of the Child Support (Maintenance Calculation and Special Cases) Regulations 2000.

18.4.5 REDUCTION FOR SHARED CARE

If the non-resident parent shares care with the resident parent, adjustments are made. The more nights spent with the non-resident parent, the greater the reduction:

TABLE 18.2 REDUCTION FOR STAYING CONTACT

Number of nights	Fraction to subtract
52–103	1/7
104–155	2/7
156–174	3/7
175 or more	1/2

Example

From **Table 18.1**, Pavel is contributing £35 child support maintenance to Anoushka.

However, Anoushka asks Pavel to have the children to stay overnight every Thursday and Sunday so she can have a rest. This averages out over the year to 80 nights.

Pavel's child support maintenance will be reduced by 1/7 (1/7 × £35 = £5) to £30.

18.4.6 VARIATIONS

Under the Child Support (Variations) Regulations 2000, the non-resident parent may apply for a variation (often referred to as 'departure directions') according to circumstances, which have the effect of notionally increasing or decreasing the non-resident parent's weekly income for these purposes. As these are complex, reference should be made to a specialist text.

18.5 BENEFIT CASES

It used to be the case that if a parent with care was in receipt of income support, income-based jobseeker's allowance or a prescribed benefit, the CSA 1991 treated them as having applied for a maintenance calculation and the parent with care was required to supply information to allow the non-resident parent to be traced or identified (unless the parent requests otherwise).

Since 27 October 2008, changes were introduced to the child maintenance system aimed at encouraging more couples to reach voluntary agreements and to use the Child Support Agency as a last resort. Parents with care who are on benefit are no longer required by law to use the Agency to claim maintenance and can choose to leave its books.

These changes undoubtedly allow parents greater choice regarding child support maintenance, and the Child Support Agency will benefit from a reduced caseload; but advisers must be vigilant that one parent does not bully the other parent into a higher or lower payment and that vulnerable children and families do not suffer as a result. A new helpline, called Child Maintenance Options, is available to advise parents on the level of maintenance required. The online resources have further details.

Since 2010, all child support maintenance payments made to an out-of-work parent are disregarded which means that the parent with care benefits greatly from the payments.

18.6 DISPUTES ABOUT PARENTAGE

When a person is alleged to be the parent of a qualifying child and denies this, a maintenance calculation should not be made unless:

- the person was married to the mother at some time in the period beginning with conception and ending with the birth of the child;
- the person is registered as the father on the birth certificate;
- the alleged parent refuses to take a scientific test (a paternity test by DNA samples) or a test shows he is the parent;
- a parent has adopted the child;
- there has been a previous declaration of parentage;
- the parent has been adjudged to be the father in other court proceedings.

An application for a declaration of parentage can be made under s55A Family Law Act 1986 if parentage is disputed. A specialist practitioner text should be consulted.

18.7 COURT INVOLVEMENT

As a result of s8 CSA 1991, the courts lost their general jurisdiction over the issue of child support maintenance. The courts have not been completely ousted however.

S23 MCA 1973 and ss2, 6, and 7 of the Domestic Proceedings and Magistrates' Courts Act 1978 (DPMCA 1978) allow an application to be made for periodical payments for a stepchild who has been treated as a child of the family. As discussed in **Chapter 12**, a lump sum, property adjustment order, or transfer or settlement of property can be ordered for the benefit of a child under Sch 1 of the Children Act 1989, the DPMCA 1978, and MCA 1973.

A court can make a 'Segal' order where an order is made through financial proceedings for the maintenance of the payee and child with the understanding that if a child support maintenance calculation is made, the amount paid will be reduced by that amount. In *Dorney-Kingdom v Dorney-Kingdom* [2000] 2 FLR 855, the court warned that courts had no jurisdiction where the mother only had a nominal claim to financial support herself.

18.8 COLLECTION AND ENFORCEMENT

One of the most contentious areas of child support has been the enforcement of unpaid child support maintenance. There have been problems with parents with care not receiving child support with the result that the poorest of families go without much-needed income.

The methods available to the Child Support Agency for the collection and enforcement of child support maintenance include:

- deduction from earnings;
- liability orders;
- enforcement by distress;
- warrant of committal to prison for up to six weeks;
- disqualification from driving.

18.9 FUTURE CHANGES

Sir David Henshaw was asked to report on the Child Support Agency, as it has been heavily criticized. His report was unambiguous that the current system of child support maintenance was failing to deliver. Although the report was clear that the ultimate responsibility for child support remained with parents, the Child Support Agency had suffered policy and operational failures. As parents on certain benefits were required to use the Agency, this prevented private arrangements being made and created a large group who did not want to use the Agency. The reduction of benefit pound per pound for maintenance paid meant that parents with care saw little or no rise in income and non-resident parents saw their money going to the state rather than their children. The Agency had not been successful operationally, with well-documented IT failures.

The Henshaw Report made many recommendations, which the Government has addressed in the Child Maintenance and Other Payments Act 2008 (CMOPA 2008). The 'Other Payments' refers to claims made by people with mesothelioma and has nothing to do with family law.

The CMOPA 2008 contains measures to reform the policy and delivery of child maintenance and established a non-departmental public body to replace the Child Support Agency, known as the Child Maintenance and Enforcement Commission (CMEC). The CMOPA 2008 received Royal Assent on 5 June 2008 and the CMEC took over legal responsibility for the CSA's work on 1 November 2008, but (as a result of the current Government's QUANGO reorganization) it is now part of the Department of Work and Pensions (DWP). Child maintenance is still collected through the CSA.

The Welfare Reform Act 2009 (WRA 2009) has received Royal Assent. The WRA 2009 introduces legislation enabling the DWP to remove the passports and driving licences of parents who have wilfully and culpably failed to meet their child maintenance obligations. These powers are now in force and during 2010–2011, 165 suspended driving bans were implemented and more than £2m was forcibly deducted from bank accounts.

There are forthcoming changes to the calculation of child support maintenance. There are proposals for a new 'gross income' statutory maintenance scheme but it has yet to have an implementation date. The latest available tax year information from Her Majesty's Revenue and Customs would be used for child maintenance calculations, which will be based on gross rather than net income. Existing clients on both the existing statutory schemes will be actively supported either to make their own arrangements or to apply to the new 'gross income' scheme. At the time of writing, no further details are available concerning implementation. Further details will be available in the online resources when the scheme comes into operation.

18.10 FINANCIAL PROVISION FOR CHILDREN UNDER THE CHILDREN ACT 1989

S15(1), Sch 1 to the CA 1989 gives the courts the power to make orders for financial provision for children. This is considered in this chapter as most spouses or civil partners receive provision for the person caring for children of the family through the Matrimonial Causes Act 1973. The schedule states that on an application made by a parent or guardian of a child, or by any person in whose favour a residence order is in force with respect to a child, the court may make one or more of the following orders:

> (a) an order requiring either or both parents of a child to make to the applicant for the benefit of the child; or to make to the child himself, such periodical payments, for such term, as may be specified in the order;
>
> (b) an order requiring either or both parents of a child to secure to the applicant for the benefit of the child; or to secure to the child himself, such periodical payments, for such term, as may be so specified;
>
> (c) an order requiring either or both parents of a child to pay to the applicant for the benefit of the child; or to pay to the child himself, such lump sum as may be so specified;
>
> (d) an order requiring a settlement to be made for the benefit of the child, and to the satisfaction of the court, of property to which either parent is entitled (either in possession or in reversion); and which is specified in the order;
>
> (e) an order requiring either or both parents of a child to transfer to the applicant, for the benefit of the child; or to transfer to the child himself, such property to which the parent is, or the parents are, entitled (either in possession or in reversion) as may be specified in the order.

18.10.1 WHO IS A PARENT?

Parents include the child's natural mother and father and any party to a marriage or civil partnership in relation to whom the child is a child of the family. This therefore includes step-parents. A child of the family is defined in s105(1) CA 1989 as being, in regard to the parties to a marriage or a civil partnership:

- a child of both those parties;
- any other child, not being a child who is placed with those parties as foster parents by a local authority or voluntary organization, who has been treated by both of those parties as a child of a family.

In deciding whether to exercise their powers, para 4 of Sch 1 CA 1989 requires the court to have regard to all the circumstances including:

(a) the income, earning capacity, property, and other financial resources which each person mentioned in sub-paragraph (4) has or is likely to have in the foreseeable future;

(b) the financial needs, obligations, and responsibilities which each person mentioned in sub-paragraph (4) has or is likely to have in the foreseeable future;

(c) the financial needs of the child;

(d) the income, earning capacity (if any), property, and other financial resources of the child;

(e) any physical or mental disability of the child;

(f) the manner in which the child was being, or was expected to be, educated or trained.

In deciding whether to exercise its powers under paragraph 1 against a person who is not the mother or father of the child, and if so in what manner, the court shall in addition have regard to—

(a) whether that person had assumed responsibility for the maintenance of the child and, if so, the extent to which and basis on which he assumed that responsibility and the length of the period during which he met that responsibility;

(b) whether he did so knowing that the child was not his child;

(c) the liability of any other person to maintain the child.

Parent includes unmarried mothers, unmarried fathers without parental responsibility (see **Chapter 25**), guardians, or special guardians or those with a residence order (see **Chapter 26**).

18.10.2 CASE-LAW CONCERNING SCH 1 CA 1989

There has been a proliferation of applications under Sch 1 CA 1989, especially in cases involving wealthy parents.

The Court of Appeal gave a landmark decision in *Re P (Child: Financial Provision)* [2003] EWCA Civ 837. A two-year-old child had parents who had not cohabited. The husband described himself as fabulously wealthy. At first instance, the mother was awarded £450,000 for a house, £30,000 for furnishings, and periodical payments of £35,560 to be reduced to £9,333 on the child's ninth birthday. On appeal, the Court of Appeal increased the housing fund to £1 m, furnishings to £100,000, and periodical payments to £70,000. The following points arose from the judgment:

- children should not suffer just because their parents had (for whatever reason) not been married to one another;
- the child's welfare should come before that of the adults;
- no great significance should be attached to whether or not the pregnancy was planned;
- the child in question was entitled to be brought up in circumstances that bore some sort of relationship to the father's current resources and standard of living, although the court should guard against unreasonable claims;
- the child's home should be set up on the basis of a settlement of property during the child's minority.

It should be noted that once the child reaches 18 years, the home or property settled during the child's minority will revert back to the parent who owns it. The property is held on trust by the parent caring for the child. The parent caring for the child does not ultimately gain from the order.

In *F v G* [2004] EWHC 1848 (Fam), Singer J looked at the issue of standard of living and held that the court should be cognizant of the child's current standard of living if there has been a long separation from the other parent. If the mother develops a new relationship, the contribution of the new partner does not detract from the value of the mother as a primary carer. If and when any relationship of the mother has an impact on her domestic economy, that will be the time for consequential amendments to the father's contributions to be discussed.

SUMMARY POINTS

- Child support maintenance is governed by the Child Support Act 1991 and is administered by the Child Support Agency.
- Non-resident parents must pay child support maintenance for qualifying children to the parent with care from their net income.
- There are four different rates depending upon the circumstances of the non-resident parent:
  - the basic rate which is a percentage of income according to the number of qualifying children. This can also be reduced to take into account the non-resident parent's relevant other children;
  - the reduced rate for net income between £100 and 200;
  - the flat rate and nil rate for those with little or no income.
- Parents are now free to decide whether to apply to the CSA, even if the parent with care is in receipt of benefits.
- The CSA has a wide range of enforcement powers for those parents who fail to pay child support maintenance.
- The Children Act 1989 can be used to provide a range of orders for the benefit of children.

SELF-TEST QUESTIONS

Barry and Sharon have two children, Emma aged 3 and Louis aged 2. Barry had a previous marriage to Maisie and they had two children, Sam and Ellie, aged 6 and 7. The children live with their mother, Sandra. Barry has contact with Sam and Ellie two nights per week.

Barry works as a sheet metal welder and earns £299 per week after tax and national insurance and he pays £50 per week into a private pension. Barry earns a bonus monthly, which works out at around £25 per week.

1. Sandra applies to the CSA. Advise Barry on how much the CSA are likely to ask for.
2. Would your answer change if Barry became unemployed and claimed job seekers allowance?

Case Study Two

Helena wishes to know how much David should pay in child support maintenance for Richard. In the Online Resource Centre, check David's net income on the Form E and advise Helena.

Answers to the questions above can be found on the Online Resource Centre: www.oxfordtextbooks.co.uk/orc/familyhandbook13/.

19 PENSIONS IN FINANCIAL PROCEEDINGS

19.1 INTRODUCTION

This chapter will:

- **discuss pensions as a financial instrument;**
- **discuss how pensions are dealt with following divorce or dissolution.**

Pensions can seem something of a mystery to most people new to proceedings for financial orders and clients often do not understand how the courts deal with pensions. In most 'average' cases, pensions can be one of the largest assets held by the parties and can be pivotal to obtaining a settlement. There have been changes to legislation in relation to pensions and that will be covered in this chapter as well as the orders that a court can make in relation to pensions.

Pensions are an extremely complex area within proceedings for financial orders. This chapter provides a basic outline of pensions and pension orders available to the court. Practitioner texts provide greater detail and, in practice, pension specialists, such as independent financial advisers, are often instructed to provide expert advice.

This chapter *must* be read in conjunction with **Chapter 12** as pension orders are orders that are available to the court when considering financial orders, as well as **Chapter 14** for the procedural aspects involving pensions.

19.2 WHAT IS A PENSION?

One of the many skills that a solicitor dealing with finances must have is the ability to understand common financial instruments (e.g. pensions, endowment policies etc.) and to explain to a client how they work and how the court can deal with them. Pension legislation was simplified fairly recently and came into force on 6 April 2006: this is referred to as 'A' Day.

A pension provides a regular source of income when a person retires. As people are living longer, a pension provides income for a large proportion of a person's life. A pension is a long-term investment, and during their working life a person pays a proportion of their income into a pension fund. There is a state pension, where the Government takes money from wages (national insurance), and also private pension funds, e.g. occupational pensions (work or company pensions) or personal pensions. Tax relief is paid on contributions to a pension.

The fund cannot be accessed until retirement and so is not like a savings account. This fund builds over working life until retirement. How the pension fund is converted into an income depends upon the type of pension.

The online resources contain further sources of information.

19.3 HOW IS A PENSION VALUED?

It is usually the case that a pension has to be valued during the financial proceedings and the method of valuation requires further examination.

A cash equivalent transfer value (CETV) is the prescribed method of valuing a pension, irrespective of the pension order made (see **19.4**). The CETV is the capital value of the pension rights calculated by the pension scheme provider. Further details of how this is done can be found in the Pension Sharing (Valuation) Regulations 2000. The CETV relates only to pensionable service up to the date of the calculation and does not take into account future salary increases. The CETV gives an idea of how much the pension is currently worth but may be challenged if it is felt to be unfair. This is highly complex and requires specialist actuarial assistance.

S25B(1) Matrimonial Causes Act 1973 (MCA 1973) states that the matters to which the court must have regard under s25(2) include any benefit under a pension arrangement that a party has or is likely to have and any benefits under a pension arrangement which, by reason of the dissolution or annulment of the marriage, a party to the marriage will lose the chance of acquiring. The most common benefit in practice is widows' benefit or death in service benefit, which benefit spouses if the pension holder dies before retirement.

Pensions are complex and technical issues in the context of family law and it is usual to involve an independent financial adviser (IFA) to advise on the best approach.

Form P is used to acquire more information from pension providers and is a standard form. Not all information required is free and a charge may be levied.

19.4 OPTIONS FOR PENSIONS IN FINANCIAL PROCEEDINGS

19.4.1 OFFSETTING

Pension offsetting is less complex than attachment or sharing orders. The parties look at all available assets including pensions and offset one party retaining a pension by compensating the other with assets.

Example

Phil and Christine divorce. They have no children, are young, and own few assets. There is a family property, a car, and Phil has an occupational pension, which he has paid into for some years. A CETV of the pension is obtained and it is found to be roughly the same as the available equity in the family home.

Phil retains his pension and Christine retains the family home. The pension is 'offset' by the equity in the family home.

It should be noted that the pension should be correctly valued and that a pension is a long-term investment that will grow in time. Offsetting may be useful in situations where a pension is too small to be attached or shared, if the parties have equal pensions of their own, where the greatest priority is to house the children of the marriage/civil partnership, or where the parties are very young and will be able to build up their own pensions.

19.4.2 PENSION ATTACHMENT

Under s23 MCA 1973, attachment orders allow the court to order the pension provider to pay all or part of the pension scheme member's benefit to their ex-spouse on retirement or death, i.e. when the pension becomes payable. The order should be worded carefully to make clear whether the order attaches to the income of the pension, retirement lump sum, or lump sum payment on death. Any order made against income benefits will cease on remarriage as attachment orders are a form of deferred spousal maintenance (see **Chapter 12**). This order was introduced by s166 Pensions Act 1995 on 1 August 1996, amending the MCA 1973 to include ss25B, 25C, and 25D.

In *T v T* [1998] 1 FLR 1072, Singer J stated that the MCA 1973 does not compel the court to compensate for pension loss and the court's obligations are limited to considering orders for periodical payments, lump sum orders, and then to look at pension considerations. An attachment order does not transfer legal ownership of the benefits from the member to the ex-spouse.

Attachment orders may be useful to provide lump sum life cover, as maintenance in retirement, without ownership being transferred.

Practical Considerations

There have been problems with attachment orders as some people have delayed retirement to delay the payment of the pension to the other party or have stopped paying into the fund. This results in the party with the pension attachment order being in a vulnerable position if they are relying on the income. It does not achieve a clean break between the parties.

19.4.3 PENSION SHARING

A solution to the problems and unpopularity of pension attachment orders is the pension sharing order introduced by the Welfare Reform and Pensions Act 1999. This came into force on 1 December 2000. A pension sharing order divides pension benefits between the parties at the time of divorce and there is a transfer of legal ownership of benefits. This is expressed as a percentage of the CETV. There are some types of pension that cannot be shared including the state pension and any lump sum payable on death. The order takes effect on decree absolute.

Once a pension sharing order has been made, the recipient (if the pension is a private pension or a funded occupational scheme) may transfer their share into a new pension fund or remain with the present scheme, but with that share of the pension held in their own right. If the pension is an unfunded and a public service pension scheme, transfer is not possible.

Sharing orders may be useful where it is the only major asset, one party has no pension and is unlikely to be able to build one up, and the pension is very large and can withstand sharing, where there are no other assets that can be offset. Please note that it is not possible to make both a pension attachment order and a pension sharing order in respect of the same pension.

Example

Hari works for Good Company plc and has done since the start of his career. Good Company offer a very good pension scheme and Hari has contributed the maximum amount possible to his pension fund for 35 years. Unfortunately, Hari and his wife Suzi divorce when both are 59. Suzi has a very low paid job following years at home looking after the house. The court orders that the family home is sold as there is sufficient capital to house both parties in modest accommodation. The only other asset of the marriage is Hari's pension. The pension is subject to a pension sharing order where Suzi receives 50% of the pension to give her an income in retirement.

SUMMARY POINTS

- A pension is a long-term investment which provides income during retirement.
- The court must consider a pension when considering the case under s25(2) MCA 1973.
- A pension is valued using the cash equivalent transfer value (CETV).
- A pension can be offset against other assets as part of a settlement.
- A pension attachment order can be used to attach part of a pension to give the recipient a share of the pension on retirement.
- A pension sharing order allows a share of the pension to be given to the recipient to be transferred into a new scheme or retained in the same scheme and title to the share is transferred to the recipient.

SELF-TEST QUESTIONS

1. Explain what a pension is and name two different types of pension schemes.
2. There have been some problems with pension attachment orders—what are they?
3. Explain when a pension sharing order may be used within financial proceedings and its advantage over pension attachment orders.

Case Study Two

David has a pension and this has been disclosed in the proceedings. In the Online Resource Centre, find the CETV in the Form E and comment on the size of the pension fund. What pension orders are available to Helena and David? Explain to your supervisor which order David may prefer in this case.

Answers to the questions above can be found on the Online Resource Centre: www.oxfordtextbooks.co.uk/orc/familyhandbook13/.

20 TAXATION IN FAMILY LAW

20.1 INTRODUCTION

This chapter will:

- **examine the types of tax most relevant to family law including income tax, capital gains tax, inheritance tax, and stamp duty land tax.**

Family law students are often surprised to be told that tax is part of the study of family law. Tax is more often associated with business law or private client practice but it is also essential that a family law practitioner is aware of the tax implications of any financial settlement and to make it tax efficient for the client. As we have seen with pensions (see **Chapter 19**) this is an area where it may be necessary to involve other professionals, e.g. an accountant, to give expert advice.

This chapter gives a basic outline of income tax, capital gains tax, and inheritance tax as it applies to the practice of family law, rather than as a general consideration of tax rules. For further details, it is recommended that the student consult a practitioner text. Tax rates, schemes and allowances change with the Budget in April every year and updates will be available in the online resources.

20.2 INCOME TAX

Income tax is paid on taxable income. Everyone has a basic personal allowance which in the 2012–13 tax year is £8,105 and this increases when over 65. This allowance is increased if married or in a civil partnership and where either of the spouses was born before 6 April 1935.

The rates for income tax in the tax year 2012–13 are as follows:

- basic rate (20%) £0–34,370;
- higher rate (40%) on taxable income between £34,371 and £150,000;
- from April 2010, a further rate of 50% on taxable income over £150,000.

 **Example**

Jennie works in a cake shop and earns £12,250 pa. She is married to William who works as a family lawyer and earns £46,000 pa.

Jennie and William both have a personal allowance of £8,105.

Jennie has the following taxable income: £12,250 – £8,105 = £4,145. Jennie does not earn enough to pay higher rate tax and so will pay tax on £4,145 at the rate of 20%.

William has the following taxable income: £46,000 – £8,105 = £37,895.

William will pay the first £34,370 at 20% and the remaining £1,525 at 40%.

This is a simplified tax calculation for illustrative purposes.

20.2.1 MAINTENANCE AND INCOME TAX

When a person pays maintenance, there is no longer any tax relief available and maintenance is paid from the payer's net income. This is irrespective of the way that maintenance is paid, e.g. through the Child Support Agency, as a result of a court order, or by agreement. If a party pays towards household expenses directly to the suppliers, no tax relief is available.

20.3 CAPITAL GAINS TAX

Capital gains tax (CGT) arises on the disposal of an asset or the receipt of money in respect of an asset if there is a 'chargeable gain'. A chargeable gain may arise if a person:

- sells, gives away, exchanges, or transfers—disposes of—all or part of an asset;
- receives a capital sum, such as an insurance payout for a damaged asset.

Assets that commonly attract CGT include:

- land;
- buildings, for example a second home;
- personal possessions such as a painting worth more than £6,000;
- shares or securities;
- business assets, e.g. business premises or goodwill.

You work out CGT by:

- working out separately the gain or loss for each asset you sell or dispose of, taking off any allowable expenses and reliefs;
- taking away your total allowable losses from your total gains—this gives you your net gain or loss;
- taking off allowable losses brought forward from an earlier year;
- taking off the annual tax-free allowance (known as the 'annual exempt amount'). This is £10,600 for an individual for 2012–13;
- a net gain will be subject to CGT, which until June 2010 was a flat rate of 18%. From 23 June 2010 onwards, the rates of CGT are 18% and 28% depending upon the amount of total taxable income.

Example

Jennie and William own a holiday cottage in the Yorkshire Dales, which they bought five years ago for £200,000. In the time since the purchase, the BBC have filmed a popular costume drama and the village has become a major tourist attraction. The cottage is sold for £400,000. The chargeable gain is £200,000 less £10,600 = £189,400.

Tax will be paid at 18% on the £189,400 = £34,182 until 2 June 2010 and thereafter at 18% or 28% depending upon their total taxable income.

There have been recent changes in relief available on chargeable gains for disposals made before 6 April 2008. For further details, refer to a specialist practitioner text.

20.3.1 CGT AND SPOUSES/CIVIL PARTNERS

Spouses and civil partners, if living together, will generally not pay CGT on transfers between one another, as they are treated as one person. The transfer is not treated as a chargeable gain or loss (the exception is trading stock).

If the spouses or civil partners are separated, then they are not treated as one person for the purposes of CGT and so a chargeable gain may arise.

The issue of transfers of assets between separated spouses or civil partners arises when the parties agree a settlement or an order is made under s24 Matrimonial Causes Act 1973 (MCA 1973) in financial order proceedings as they may give rise to CGT liability.

20.3.2 FAMILY ASSETS AND CGT

There is no CGT liability on certain assets including premium bonds, a private car, and cash. Other assets that do not attract CGT include tangible moveable property that is a wasting asset (has less then 50 years of useful life or less). One of the most important exceptions to CGT is the family home.

However, a party may have to dispose of an asset to raise cash and so this would attract CGT.

Most disposals of the family home are covered by the private residence exception. Any gain accruing to an individual on a disposal of a dwelling house that is or has been at any time in his period of ownership the only or main residence will be wholly or partly exempt from CGT by virtue of the private residence exemption provided by ss222 and 223 of the Taxation of Chargeable Gains Act 1992 (TCGA 1992). If a person occupies the property as his home for the whole period of ownership, the whole gain will be CGT exempt otherwise the gain will be apportioned to the portion for which he was not in occupation. However, an individual will be treated as having been in residence during their final 36 months of ownership, whether he was actually there or not.

SI 2009/730, The Enactment of Extra-Statutory Concessions Order 2009, implemented a concession to spouses and civil partners under s215B TCGA 1992 and is important in a case where a party transfers his share in the family home when he has been out of occupation for more than three years.

This concession applies to a situation where a spouse transfers an interest in the family home to the other spouse as part of a financial settlement on divorce or separation, and:

- the other spouse continues to occupy the family home as her only or main residence; and
- the transferring spouse has not elected to treat any other property as his only or main residence.

The transferring spouse is deemed to continue in occupation of the home until the date of the transfer, however long it is since they left. Other assets may also attract CGT, e.g. a holiday home or company shares, and it is important to be vigilant for assets attracting a chargeable gain.

20.4 INHERITANCE TAX

Inheritance tax was introduced by the Finance Act 1975 and substantial changes have been made to the inheritance tax regime by the Finance Act 2006. The general rule is that inheritance tax may be payable on any transfer of value made by a person while that person is alive. On death, a person is deemed to make a transfer of value equal to the value of his entire estate immediately before death.

An individual is entitled to a 'nil rate band' within which transfers of value made within a seven-year period will be free of tax. The nil rate band announced for the tax year 2012–13 is £325,000.

20.4.1 INHERITANCE TAX DURING MARRIAGE/CIVIL PARTNERSHIP

During a marriage or civil partnership transfers of assets are exempt from inheritance tax (IHT) until the date of decree absolute: s18 Inheritance Tax Act 1984 (IHTA 1984).

Following divorce or dissolution, spouses or civil partners have fewer opportunities to make exempt transfers. If a transfer is made pursuant to an order of the court following a decree of divorce or nullity, it will generally be regarded as a transaction at arm's length not intended to confer gratuitous benefit (Senior Register of the Family Division statement (1975) 119 SJ 596). It would appear that this will extend to transfers made pursuant to an agreed settlement.

20.5 STAMP DUTY LAND TAX

Stamp duty is charged in respect of 'land transactions', which are broadly the transfer of interests of land. The amount of stamp duty is based on the amount of consideration provided for the land. Most commonly, this tax is encountered during house sales and purchases and should be taken into account when calculating the money available to the parties.

The rates are as follows:

Residential property—purchase price	Rate of stamp duty land tax
up to £125,000	0%
£125,001–£250,000	1%
£250,001–£500,000	3%
£500,001–£1 m	4%
£1 m–£2 m	5%
Over £2 m from March 2012	7%

The rate for first time buyers is nil if the property is sold for less than £250,000.

SUMMARY POINTS

- Tax must be taken into account when considering a settlement between the parties.
- Income tax is relevant where a party will start work and a client may need to understand the net income available.
- If the parties transfer or sell assets, there may be liability for either CGT or IHT.
- When buying and selling property, stamp duty land tax will be paid.

SELF-TEST QUESTIONS

1. Minnie and Boris divorce. Boris earns £100,000 per year and Minnie earns £150,000. As part of their financial proceedings they sell their family home, a yacht, and a very valuable painting that

Boris bought in 1999. Minnie buys a new house worth £489,000. Advise Minnie and Boris on any potential tax issues.

Case Study Two

David has a small fishing boat that he bought for £1,000 in 1980. He has restored it to bring it back to life as a fishing vessel, as it was a shell when he bought it. It has been valued as being worth £25,000. David will sell the boat as part of the financial proceedings. Advise on the tax implications of this sale.

online resource centre

Answers to the questions above can be found on the Online Resource Centre: **www.oxfordtextbooks.co.uk/orc/familyhandbook13/**.

21 WELFARE BENEFITS

21.1 INTRODUCTION

This chapter will:

- **discuss the main forms of welfare benefits available to family law clients.**

As well as being able to advise on the law and procedure involved with ancillary relief, a family lawyer must have a working knowledge of welfare benefits. In **Chapter 2**, it was seen that some welfare benefits 'passport' the client into certain forms of public funding. You are unlikely to find situations in practice where one party is on welfare benefits and another is earning a large salary. In practice, it is more likely that one party is on welfare benefits and the other party is earning a low wage. For this reason, it is very important to understand your client's potential eligibility for welfare benefits and the effect on their eligibility of any financial change in circumstances.

In this chapter we will look in outline at the main types of welfare benefit that a new family lawyer will come across in their practice. This is not a comprehensive account of all welfare benefits available but does cover most benefits commonly encountered by family lawyers. The welfare benefits system is currently undergoing a series of changes, including the imposition of a Benefits Cap from April 2013. For further assistance, see the online resources.

21.2 INCOME SUPPORT

Income support is available for those who are financially eligible and cannot be available for work full time but do not have sufficient money to live on, e.g. lone parents, registered sick or disabled, or a student who is a lone parent or disabled or caring for someone who is elderly or sick.

21.2.1 ELIGIBILITY

Clients should be habitually resident and present in the UK, be aged between 18 and 60, and not engaged in remunerative work for more than 24 hours a week (or have a partner engaged in remunerative work for more than 24 hours a week). Students in 'relevant education' will not be eligible.

The first £6,000 of capital is disregarded but clients will be ineligible if they have capital of £16,000 and must work less than 16 hours per week. If a client's partner works more than 24 hours per week, then they will be ineligible. The client's income must be below the amount necessary to live on (the 'applicable amount').

Income is calculated according to the family income and this includes spouses, civil partners, and cohabitants (including same-sex couples). The first £10 of child maintenance is disregarded, as well as lump sum orders, statutory sick pay, statutory maternity payments, part-time earnings, and child benefit as well as income from capital sums over £6,000.

21.2.2 WHAT WILL THE CLIENTS RECEIVE?

What the clients receive will depend on a number of factors including:

- age;
- whether they live alone or as a couple;
- age and income of dependants;
- disability;
- earnings.

The rate of benefit for 2012–13 is:

- single people—aged 16–24: £56.25, aged 25 or over: £71.00;
- couple—both aged 18 and over: £111.45;
- lone parents—aged 16–17: £56.25, aged 18 and over: £71.00.

Those in receipt of income support will automatically gain the following benefits:

- free dental care;
- free prescriptions;
- free school meals;
- housing benefit;
- council tax benefit.

These are described as 'passport benefits' and their value to the client should be remembered when advising on the level of maintenance. To set the level of maintenance at exactly the same monetary level as income support may mean the person is worse off as they lose entitlement to passport benefits.

Example

Helen and Seamus have one child together. Seamus leaves Helen to live with another woman. Seamus works out that Helen would be entitled to income support and other benefits. Seamus pays this amount in maintenance to Helen. Unfortunately, this means that Helen has to pay for her child's prescriptions and school meals and loses some entitlement to housing benefit. Helen is financially worse off as a result.

21.2.3 SUPPORT FOR MORTGAGE INTEREST

Support for mortgage interest (SMI) can be paid to people on income support, income-based jobseeker's allowance, income-related employment and support allowance, and pension credit, if they are experiencing problems with the interest payments on their mortgage. No payment is made towards the endowment or repayment element of a mortgage.

On 2 September 2008, the Government announced reforms to the system to more accurately reflect the value of people's property and reduce the waiting time before help from SMI becomes available.

From 5 January 2009:

- the waiting period for which homeowners have to wait before help towards their mortgage is paid was cut from 39 weeks to 13 weeks for all new working age claims;
- the capital limit on loans for which SMI can be paid was increased from £100,000 to £200,000 for new working age claims.

Pensioners getting pension credit do not have to wait to get help with their mortgage interest payments. From 5 January 2009 there was a time limit on SMI of 104 weeks for new jobseeker's allowance claims only and this has started to affect people claiming since the beginning of the scheme. Time-limiting does not apply to existing claims or to new claims for income support or pension credits.

21.3 JOBSEEKER'S ALLOWANCE

Jobseeker's allowance is the main benefit for people who are out of work. There are two types of jobseeker's allowance. The first is called 'contribution-based jobseeker's allowance'. A client may receive contribution-based jobseeker's allowance if they have paid or been credited with class 1 national insurance (NI) contributions in the relevant tax years. Self-employed contributions will not generally qualify for contribution-based jobseeker's allowance.

The other form of jobseeker's allowance is based on income and savings. This is called 'income-based jobseeker's allowance'.

21.3.1 WHAT ARE THE BENEFIT RATES (WEEKLY)?

- Contribution-based jobseeker's allowance:
  - single person:
    person aged 16–24: £56.25;
    person aged 25 or over: £71.00.
- Income-based jobseeker's allowance:
  - single person:
    person aged 16–24: £56.25;
    person aged 25 or over: £71.00.
  - couples:
    both aged 18 or over: £111.45.

21.4 TAX CREDITS

A client may be able to claim two tax credits, child tax credit and working tax credit, which have been payable since April 2003 under the Tax Credits Act 2002. The administration of tax credits has not been straightforward as the system is complex and clients must keep HMRC up to date with changes in circumstances. An outline of the system follows; for further information see the online resources.

Tax credits are based on the claimant's income (please note that income for tax credits differs from income tax calculations). The first award is based on the previous year's income, which is then revised to the current year's income (this is either when the claimant provides an estimate or when the award is finalized at the year end). The personal circumstances on which the award is based are those of the current tax year but the award can be changed during that year or the year end to reflect any change in circumstances.

The general rule is that to qualify for tax credits the applicant must be aged 16 or over and usually live in the UK. Spouses and civil partners are required to make joint claims. The amounts of credits will depend upon the income of the applicant as the tax credit operates to increase the income available. If the applicant is on certain benefits, the maximum credit will be received. The amount of credit available decreases as the applicant's income increases. This chapter will look briefly at child tax credit and working tax credit. Pension credits are also available for people of retirement age.

21.4.1 CHILD TAX CREDIT

Child tax credit is for people who are responsible for at least one child or qualifying young person. Child tax credit is paid directly to the person who is mainly responsible for caring for the child or children or directly to a lone parent. An applicant does not have to be working to claim.

The rules for entitlement to child tax credit are found in the imaginatively titled Child Tax Credit Regulations 2002. Further information can be found on the online resources.

Child tax credit is made up of the following elements:

- family element:

  this is the basic element for families responsible for one or more children. A higher rate of family element, often known as the baby element, is paid to families with one or more children under one year old. There is only one family element for each family, regardless of how many children usually live with the applicant(s);

- child element:

  is paid for each child for whom the claimant has responsibility;

- disability element:

  is paid for each child for whom the claimant has responsibility if:

  - receiving disability living allowance for the child; or
  - the child is registered blind.

21.4.2 WORKING TAX CREDIT

Working tax credit is for people who are employed or self-employed (either on their own or in a partnership), who:

- usually work 16 hours or more a week;
- are paid for that work; and
- expect to work for at least four weeks;

and who are:

- aged 16 or over and responsible for at least one child; or
- aged 16 or over and disabled; or
- aged 25 or over and usually work at least 30 hours a week.

Working tax credit is paid to the person who is working 16 hours or more a week (and responsible for at least one child), and where the applicants are a couple, if both are working 16 hours or more a week, one must choose which will receive it. Working tax credit cannot be claimed if an applicant is not working. If a person is not responsible for a child, they must be working over 30 hours per week and be over the age of 25.

As part of working tax credit, an applicant may qualify for help towards the costs of childcare. If the applicant receives the childcare element of working tax credit, this will always be paid direct to the person who is mainly responsible for caring for the child or children, alongside payments of child tax credit.

Working tax credit is made up of the following elements:

- basic element:

  this is paid to any working person who meets the conditions;

- lone parent element (if applicable);
- couples element (if applicable);
- 30-hour element:

  this is paid to people who work at least 30 hours a week. Couples with at least one child can claim the 30-hour element if they work at least 30 hours a week between them providing at least one of them works 16 hours or more a week;

- disability and severe disability element:

  for people who have a disability or severe disability;

- 50 plus element:

  paid to people aged 50 or over and who are starting work after a period on benefits.

The rules regarding working tax credit can be found in the Working Tax Credit (Entitlement and Maximum Rate) Regulations 2002. The online resources contain more information.

21.4.3 UNIVERSAL TAX CREDIT

The Government has published a timetable for the introduction of Universal Tax Credit which will replace some existing benefits. This will be phased in from October 2013 and more information will be available in the online resources.

21.5 EMPLOYMENT AND SUPPORT ALLOWANCE

Employment and Support Allowance (ESA) replaced Incapacity Benefit and provides financial help to those who cannot work due to illness or disability. The online resources has more details about this benefit.

21.6 HOUSING BENEFIT

Housing benefit helps those on a low income to pay for rental accommodation. An applicant may be entitled to housing benefit if they pay rent and their income and capital (savings and investments) are below a certain level. For all new tenancies, local housing allowance will be granted, especially for private tenancies. It is a more generous benefit than housing benefit and is paid directly to the client. Different rates are payable in different local authorities. For more information see the online resources.

The housing benefit available is the same as 'eligible' rent. This is the amount used to work out the benefit but may not be the same as the full rent. Eligible rent may be limited to an amount that is reasonable for a suitably sized property and will depend on whether in the area the applicant lives:

- the amount of rent is reasonable for the particular home;
- whether the home is a reasonable size for the applicant and their family;
- the amount of rent is reasonable for the area where the applicant lives.

Eligible rent includes:

- rent for the accommodation;
- charges for some services, such as lifts, communal laundry facilities, or play areas.

21.6.1 WHO IS ELIGIBLE?

If the client has capital between £6,000 and £16,000, a 'tariff' is applied where £1 = £250 and housing benefit will not be available if:

- there are savings of over £16,000, unless the applicant is aged 60 or over and getting the 'guarantee credit' of pension credit;
- the applicant lives in the home of a close relative;
- the applicant is a full-time student (unless disabled or has children);
- the applicant is an asylum seeker or is sponsored to be in the UK.

Further, if the applicant lives with a partner or civil partner only one can get housing benefit. If the applicant is single and aged under 25, housing benefit is only available for bed-sit accommodation or one room in shared accommodation.

21.7 COUNCIL TAX BENEFIT

Council tax benefits are available if the applicant pays council tax and their income and capital (savings and investments) are below a certain level.

Rebates are available for a second adult if the home is shared with a person who is not their partner or civil partner, is aged 18 or over, is not paying rent or council tax themselves, and is on low income. A person living alone will receive a 25% reduction.

21.7.1 WHO IS NOT ELIGIBLE?

The applicant is not eligible if they have savings of over £16,000, unless they are aged 60 or over and getting the 'guarantee credit' of pension credit.

Council tax benefit is administered by local councils and they will look at:

- income, including earnings, some benefits and tax credits, and occupational pensions;
- savings;
- family circumstances including age, the size of the family and their ages, and disability.

The most council tax benefit obtainable is 100% reduction.

21.8 CHILD BENEFIT

Child benefit is a tax-free payment that is claimed for a child. It is usually paid every four weeks but in some cases can be paid weekly, and there are separate rates for each child. The payment can be claimed by anyone who qualifies, whatever their income or savings.

A person is eligible for child benefit if any of the following apply:

- the child is under 16;
- the child is over 16 and in relevant education or training;

- the child is 16 or 17, has left relevant education or training, and is registered for work, education, or training with an approved body.

There are two separate amounts, with a higher amount for the eldest (or only) child. The rate is £20.30 a week for the oldest child and £13.40 a week for each of the other children (from 5 April 2012). The rates increase annually.

Child benefit can be paid into any bank or building society and is usually paid every four weeks, but it can be paid weekly if the claimant is in receipt of income support or income-based jobseeker's allowance.

SUMMARY POINTS

- It is important to be able to give basic advice on welfare benefits and be aware of the main types of welfare benefits to clients.
- A knowledge of welfare benefits is also essential when considering eligibility for public funding (see **Chapter 2**).
- It is also important to understand how benefits can assist those on low incomes as well as those who have lost an income and also the 'passport' benefits that some forms of welfare benefits bring and the impact that their loss has on a family's income.
- This chapter gives a brief overview of the main benefits that are encountered in practice. The online resources give more information on calculating eligibility.

SELF-TEST QUESTIONS

1. Margaret and Nick live in rented accommodation with their two children. Nick decides that he cannot live with Margaret any longer and leaves the home. Margaret works 12 hours per week as a cleaner but is worried that she may lose her job in the recession. She earns £68.76 per week and has no savings.

   (a) Advise Margaret if she may be able to claim any welfare benefits.

   (b) Would your advice change if Margaret were to lose her job?

Case Study Two

Helena is concerned that she is not claiming all the benefits that she is entitled to. Look at the case study documents and advise Helena. You will find an email in the case study materials giving you a solution.

Answers to the questions above can be found on the Online Resource Centre: www.oxfordtextbooks.co.uk/orc/familyhandbook13/.

Part 4

COHABITATION

22 COHABITATION

22.1 INTRODUCTION

This chapter will:

- **make a comparison between marriage, civil partnership, and cohabitation;**
- **examine the law on cohabitation contracts;**
- **examine future developments on cohabitation.**

Part 4 deals with the legal position of cohabitant families. Families are amazingly diverse and do not always fall within the neat categories of spouses and civil partners, and as a result, the law does not deal well with cohabitant families. This is partly as a result of social policy not recognizing families who have chosen not to enter into legally recognized relationships. It is important to consider the law that exists for cohabitants as many clients will consult a solicitor when their cohabiting relationships have broken down.

When a cohabiting relationship ends, there is not the same coherent body of law available to married couples or civil partners. Many cohabitants mistakenly believe that they acquire legal rights after a number of years of cohabiting, but this is incorrect. The myth of the 'common law wife/husband' persists, despite having no legal foundation. Many clients are shocked to find they have few legal remedies and those available are far from straightforward.

In this chapter, 'cohabitation' includes couples living together, both opposite- and same-sex couples. This chapter will compare remedies available to married couples, civil partners, and cohabitants as well as the emerging law on cohabitation contracts. The legal remedies available to cohabitants will be further considered in **Chapter 23** in much more detail.

22.2 COMPARISON OF COHABITATION, MARRIAGE, AND CIVIL PARTNERSHIPS

See **Table 22.1**.

22.3 COHABITATION CONTRACTS

Cohabitation contracts have been traditionally regarded as void on the grounds of public policy as they undermined the status of marriage and were considered sexually immoral. As the numbers of people living together outside of marriage (or civil partnerships) have increased, the courts appear to be taking a less absolute view. The courts have drawn a

TABLE 22.1 COMPARISON OF COHABITATION, MARRIAGE, AND CIVIL PARTNERSHIPS

Issue	Marriage	Civil partnerships	Cohabitants
Legal process to end relationship?	Divorce under MCA 1973	Dissolution under the CPA 2004	None required
Duty to provide financial support during relationship?	Spouses must provide financial support during the marriage	Partners must provide financial support during the civil partnership	No legal duty to provide financial support to cohabitant
Finance and property division following relationship breakdown	Financial relief under MCA 1973 or orders from the magistrates' court under the Domestic Proceedings and Magistrates' Courts Act 1978	Financial resolution under the CPA 2004 equivalent to financial relief under the MCA 1973	No specific rights or remedies. Parties may negotiate and reach an agreement. No right to maintenance for either party. Proceedings may be taken in property and trust law
Parental responsibility (PR) for children	Both parents automatically gain PR for their natural child (from 1 December 2003)	Natural mother automatically has PR. Civil partners can acquire PR by agreement or court order	Natural mother will have automatic PR but father does not acquire PR unless on the child's birth certificate, by agreement or court order
Children (disputes about contact and residence)	Proceedings can be taken under the CA 1989 and both natural parents may apply	Proceedings can be taken under the CA 1989 and the natural parent may apply for a s8 order but the civil partner may apply only if he has PR, and contact and residence if not a natural parent but child is the child of the family	Proceedings can be taken under the CA 1989 and both parents may apply for a s8 order if natural parents
Financial support for children	Spouses have a duty to maintain their children	Both partners have a duty to maintain a child of the family	Both parents have a duty to maintain their children
	May apply for child support from the Child Support Agency	May apply for child support from the Child Support Agency and under Sch 1 CA 1989	May apply for child support from the Child Support Agency and under Sch 1 CA 1989
Wills and probate	Married couples will be treated as having pre-deceased the spouse in a will when divorced and there may be a partial intestacy	Civil partners will be treated as having pre-deceased the civil partner in a will once the partnership has been dissolved and there may be a partial intestacy	Breakdown of a cohabiting relationship has no effect on existing wills

	Once divorced, the spouse will not inherit under the Intestacy Rules	Once the civil partnership has been dissolved, the spouse will not inherit under the Intestacy Rules	Cohabiting couples have no right to inherit each other's property under the Intestacy Rules
	A claim may be made under the Inheritance (Provision for Family and Dependants) Act 1975 (I(PFD)A 1975)	A claim may be made under the I(PFD)A 1975	A claim may be made under the I(PFD)A 1975 if the requirements of the Act are satisfied
Domestic violence	Proceedings under the Family Law Act 1996 (FLA 1996) as spouses are associated persons	Proceedings under the FLA 1996 as civil partners are associated persons	Proceedings under the FLA 1996 if the parties are associated persons
The family home	S33 FLA 1996 gives spouses 'home rights' that entitle the spouse to live in the family home	S33 FLA 1996 gives civil partners 'home rights' that entitle the civil partner to live in the family home	No statutory right to ocupy the family home

distinction between a 'contract for cohabitation' and a 'contract for the regulation of property and financial matters between cohabitants'.

In *Sutton v Mischon de Reya and Gawor & Co* [2004] 1 FLR 837 a cohabitation contract was drafted for a gay couple. The contract concerned a 'master and slave' relationship. The claimant was to be the 'master' and the other man to be the 'servant'. The 'servant' agreed to transfer his considerable property and wealth to the 'master'. The 'servant' changed his mind with the parties never having cohabited. The men negotiated a settlement through the defendant solicitors that was considerably less advantageous than the original cohabitation contract.

The claimant sued the solicitors for negligence in drafting. The court held that the contract was for cohabitation and therefore void.

Hart J, in his judgment, indicated that there is nothing contrary to public policy in a cohabitation agreement governing the property relationship between adults who intend to cohabit or who are cohabiting for the purposes of enjoying a sexual relationship.

The defendant solicitors had advised their client that the agreement would be unenforceable and so they were not negligent for alleged errors of drafting. The court further held that the instant cohabitation agreement could not have withstood further scrutiny of the parties' legal intention to create the agreement; particularly undue influence or misrepresentation.

Cohabitation contracts may not be void for public policy if they regulate the property and financial relationship of cohabitants but the courts will scrutinize such agreements carefully and parties should seek professional advice.

22.4 LAW COMMISSION PROPOSALS AND FUTURE DEVELOPMENTS

Many solicitors encounter cases where cohabitants are left without a home following the end of a relationship and many clients must use remedies that were not designed to resolve family relationships. The remedies available to resolve property and financial affairs between cohabitants are considered in more detail in **Chapter 23**.

The Law Commission published a report, 'Cohabitation: The Financial Consequences of Relationship Breakdown', in July 2007. The Law Commission looked at the financial consequences of the end of a cohabiting relationship by separation or death and the adequacy of existing remedies. It found that a majority of people supported the availability of legal remedies for cohabitants.

The Law Commission did not believe that cohabitants should have the same remedies as married couples or civil partners due to the lack of distinctive public and formal commitment between cohabitants. The Law Commission's proposal would be to extend financial relief to cohabitants who:

- had satisfied certain eligibility criteria;
- had not opted out of the scheme; and
- made certain financial contributions to the relationship giving rise to certain enduring consequences at the end of the relationship.

The details of the proposed scheme can be found in **Chapter 23**. There is currently no move by the Government to make legislation to enact the Law Commission proposals.

Lord Lester of Herne Hill introduced the Cohabitation Bill into the House of Lords in 2008 and the Bill has reached committee stage. The Cohabitation Bill is largely based on the Law Commission's proposals. The Cohabitation Bill has attracted some wide support from family lawyers but also has some significant opponents. The opposition to the Cohabitation Bill, combined with a reluctance from the previous Government to grant the Cohabitation Bill more time, means that the Cohabitation Bill will not become law within the foreseeable future, if ever.

SUMMARY POINTS

- Cohabitants will often seek legal advice at the end of a relationship but the legal remedies are not straightforward.
- There are differences in law between married couples, civil partners, and cohabitants, including the availability of financial support and the rules on inheritance.
- Contracts to regulate property and financial arrangements between cohabitants are beginning to receive judicial acceptance.
- The Law Commission has made proposals for the reform of the law concerning cohabitants but no legislation has been proposed by the Government.

SELF-TEST QUESTIONS

1. A client tells you that after she has lived with her partner for two years, she is a 'common law wife'. Is she correct?
2. Does a cohabitant have the right to maintenance for herself after the end of a relationship?
3. Your cohabitant client wishes to have a contract drawn up to deal with the family home following any relationship breakdown. Explain whether this is permitted.

online resource centre

Answers to the questions above can be found on the Online Resource Centre: www.oxfordtextbooks.co.uk/orc/familyhandbook13/.

23 COHABITATION AND FINANCE

23.1 INTRODUCTION

This chapter will:

- **discuss the legal position of cohabitants;**
- **discuss the legal remedies available to separating cohabitants;**
- **examine the position of cohabitants in relation to the family home.**

There is a very persistent myth that once a couple have lived together for a number of years (curiously, most clients put this at about two years) a cohabitant gains the status of a 'common law' wife/husband. Further, once a person becomes a 'common law' wife/husband, they gain a number of rights including a 'right' to part of the family home or other assets.

This is a myth and there is no such thing as a 'common law' wife/husband. Your clients will often argue with you and tell you that you are wrong. In 1753, Lord Hardwicke's Marriage Act legislated that no other marriage other than one presided over by an Anglican clergyman would be valid (although now one can marry in a register office or in a civil ceremony). The online resources give a fuller picture of the history of the law of marriage. Suffice to say that your clients must be firmly advised that no rights of 'common law marriage' exist. Clients must be married before home rights are accrued or relief can be given under the Matrimonial Causes Act 1973 (MCA 1973).

So, where does this leave cohabitants? This chapter will discuss the rights and remedies available to cohabiting couples in terms of money and property. In this chapter, the term 'cohabitant' will include both same-sex and heterosexual couples.

23.2 COHABITANTS AND FINANCIAL REMEDIES

In the introduction (**23.1**), we see that cohabitants have no rights inherent in the fact that they live together. There is no right to maintenance for cohabitants other than that of child support maintenance for the natural children of the couple. Property disputes between cohabitants are resolved using existing property and trust law and not the MCA 1973 or any other family law.

The difficulty that cohabitants face is that the law is a patchwork of remedies and lacks the cohesion of the law relating to spouses or civil partners. The law is complex, uncertain, and expensive to litigate and not designed for families. There are often very unjust conclusions to such proceedings.

Cohabitation contracts are discussed fully at **22.3**. The court may become more sympathetic to cohabitation contracts in the future.

If the cohabitants require protection from domestic abuse, the Family Law Act 1996 can be used (see **Chapter 33** onwards). If there are disputes involving children, the Children Act 1989 (CA 1989) will apply (see **Chapter 24** onwards).

This chapter will concentrate on the availability of financial remedies for cohabitants.

23.2.1 LAW COMMISSION PROPOSALS

The Law Commission considered the hardships faced by cohabitants following the breakdown in a cohabiting relationship. The Law Commission recognized that simply improving public awareness would be insufficient as many people cannot 'simply get married' as their partners might refuse to and that person is faced with remaining with the status quo or leaving the relationship. The Law Commission did not agree that cohabitants should have the same legal rights as spouses and civil partners as there are a broad range of cohabiting relationships.

The Law Commission proposed a scheme where cohabitants can gain some financial relief but remedies should only be available where:

- the couple satisfy certain eligibility requirements (having a child or living together for a specified number of years);
- the couple had agreed not to disapply the scheme; and
- the applicant had made certain qualifying financial contributions to the relationship giving rise to certain enduring consequences.

Since the publication of the report by the Law Commission in July 2007, there has been no move on the part of the Government to pass legislation enacting the recommendations. The Government's response to the report has been to await research on the Family Law (Scotland) Act 2006, which is similar to the Law Commission's proposals.

Lord Lester of Herne Hill introduced the Cohabitation Bill into the House of Lords in 2008 and the Bill has reached committee stage. The Cohabitation Bill is largely based on the Law Commission's proposals. The Cohabitation Bill has attracted some wide support from family lawyers but also has some significant opponents. There was opposition to the Bill and the previous Government did not grant it Parliamentary time. It is very unlikely to become law in the foreseeable future.

The online resources have more details.

23.3 JOINTLY HELD PROPERTY

If property is held by both parties jointly as legal co-owners, then the property cannot be sold or transferred without the consent of both parties. If the parties do not intend the property to be shared 50/50 on sale, then the parties should execute a declaration of trust. A declaration of trust is a document that states the shares in which each joint owner holds the property, e.g. 50/50 or some other proportion. Unfortunately, not everyone is advised about the importance of making such a declaration when purchasing a home.

Completion of the TR1 form in the conveyance of a house is crucial and parties buying a house should be fully advised on how the property is held and to properly execute the form and/or execute a declaration of trust to be held with the deeds. A problem can arise (with either married/civil partners or cohabitants) where the property is held jointly but a dispute arises concerning the shares the parties have on sale of the property.

The extent of the shares in jointly held property was considered by the House of Lords in *Stack v Dowden* [2007] UKHL 17. Baroness Hale (who gave the leading judgment) commented that it was the first time that the question had come before the House of Lords.

The facts of the case are worth noting. The parties, Mr Stack and Ms Dowden, met as teenagers and began to live together in their mid 20s in 1983. They had four children and separated in 2002. The house at the centre of the dispute (in Chatsworth Road) had been bought in joint names in 1993 and sold in November 2005 for £746,245. The conveyance contained no deed of trust. Prior to purchasing this house the parties had lived in a property (in Purves Road) in the sole name of Ms Dowden. She paid all the mortgage and bills. The house in Purves Road was held to be Ms Dowden's entirely.

The Chatsworth Rd property cost £190,000. £128,813 came from Ms Dowden's savings and a mortgage in joint names. By the time of the sale, Mr Stack had paid £27,000 towards reducing the mortgage and Ms Dowden had paid £38,345. Mr Stack paid the premiums of a joint endowment policy and Ms Dowden paid household bills. Both parties kept their finances absolutely separate.

At first instance the court held that property was held 50/50. Ms Dowden appealed. The Court of Appeal upheld Ms Dowden's appeal and held that the interests of the property were held 65% to Ms Dowden and 35% to Mr Stack. The House of Lords upheld the Court of Appeal's decision. Their Lordships found that the property was held in joint names but that the proceeds should be divided in the proportions decided by the Court of Appeal. Ms Dowden could demonstrate that the shares were not equal as a result of the unequal contributions to the property and the fact that the parties had not pooled their resources.

The assumption would be that beneficial interests would follow legal title unless the contrary is proved. Joint legal owners will be assumed to hold the property as beneficial joint tenants and sole legal owners will be assumed to hold the beneficial interest unless the contrary is proved. The contrary is established by the parties' express, implied, and imputed intentions. Baroness Hale gave the following guidance:

- each case will turn on its own facts;
- advice or discussions at the time of transfer that cast light on parties' intentions;
- the reasons why the home was acquired in joint names;
- the purpose for which the home was acquired and the nature of the parties' relationship and children;
- how the purchase was financed both initially and subsequently;
- how the parties arranged their finances.

The onus is on the person seeking to show that the beneficial ownership is different from the legal ownership.

In *Kernott v Jones* [2010] EWCA Civ 578, a cohabitants' property dispute was heard by the Court of Appeal. The principal issue at trial before the court was whether and, if so, to what extent the equal beneficial interests of the co-owners had been varied after their separation.

In May 1985 the parties, who had an infant child, purchased the property in joint names for £30,000. The woman, Jones, contributed £6,000 and the balance of the purchase price was raised by means of an endowment mortgage. In 1986 a further loan of £2,000 was taken out for an extension, built and paid for largely by Kernott, enhancing the value of the house from about £30,000 to £44,000. The parties' second child was born that year. Jones and Kernott shared household bills including mortgage payments. They separated in 1993, Jones and the children staying in the property. It was common ground at trial that at that time their beneficial interests were equal. Thereafter, Jones assumed sole responsibility for the outgoings on the property and the children's maintenance.

In May 1996 Kernott bought another property for £57,000. He raised the deposit, with Jones' agreement, by cashing in a separate life policy which they owned, whose proceeds they divided equally. The trial judge ruled that Jones' investment towards the purchase of the property, particularly since separation, meant that she was entitled to a greater share. In addition she received very little contribution from Kernott to the maintenance and support of the two children.

He found that at the outset the parties' intentions may well have been to provide a home for them and their children, but they had altered since separation to the extent that Kernott demonstrated that he had no intention until recently of availing himself of the beneficial ownership, having ignored it completely by way of any investment in it or attempt to maintain or repair it whilst he had his own property upon which he concentrated.

The judge turned to assess the altered shares on the basis of what was 'fair and just'. He fixed the beneficial interests at: Jones, 90%; Kernott, 10%.

The Court of Appeal dismissed Kernott's appeal. It was held that, so far as the intention of the parties cannot be inferred, the court is free to impute a common intention to them. The judge was quite right to infer or impute the parties' intention to change their beneficial interests. 'Fair and just' was the appropriate criterion to quantify the varied interests by imputation.

The Court of Appeal allowed Kernott's second appeal, by a 2–1 majority (Jacob LJ dissenting). The judge had identified no evidence from which could properly be inferred a common intention to vary the equal beneficial interests held on separation. The parties' beneficial interests were equal. The case was heard by the Supreme Court and the question to be resolved by their Lordships was 'whether a court can properly infer an agreement by an unmarried couple, who hold a property in equal shares at the date of their separation, to the effect that thereafter their respective beneficial interests should alter'.

In the Supreme Court, their Lordships restored the judgment made at first instance and awarded Mrs Jones 90% of the proceeds of the property. The presumption of equal beneficial ownership can be rebutted by the demonstration that the parties had different common

intention as to the quantum of their respective shares in a property, either at the time of acquisition or at a later date. These intentions as to shares can change over time and can be ambulatory in nature.

The method by which the court divines the parties' intention was considered by the court and their Lordship exhorted the need to use best efforts at this stage and not to shrink from making inferences from disputed evidence. Differences arose between their Lordships on the issue of whether it is possible to draw inferences as to a change over time in the parties' intention to the shares in the disputed property. The majority (with Lord Kerr and Lord Wilson dissenting) held that such a change can be inferred.

There arises a question about whether the court can *impute* such an intention if the court is unable to infer the parties' common intention from the evidence. This is done by looking at the whole course of dealing between the parties. Lord Kerr emphasized the dichotomy between inferring intention and imputing intention and Lord Kerr felt that there had to be strong demarcation between the two. Lord Kerr questioned the aptness of imputation but considered that it may not be practicable to discard it. Lord Collins was robust in that he held that the difference 'will hardly ever matter'.

The main conclusion to draw from this case is that their Lordships were able to find that the parties' interests in the property had changed over time and their Lordships were willing to embrace 'fair and just' as an appropriate measure of assessing those interests.

This decision may be problematic for practitioners as it does appear to give a great deal of discretion to district judges in such cases and makes the predicted outcomes of cases less certain. Online resources contain more information on this case.

23.4 PROPERTY OWNED BY ONE PARTY

The law in England and Wales has never developed a system of law to deal with family property. The law of property is applied to family property, often with harsh results. The reason for this is possibly that, until relatively recently, cohabitation was uncommon and divorce rates were low. Family property division following breakdown of a cohabiting relationship has come before the court increasingly since post-war societal changes.

The law is completely different to that of the MCA 1973 and the Civil Partnership Act 2004. There is no statutory guidance for the distribution of family property and there is no doctrine of community of property. As a result, the only way that a cohabitant can seek a beneficial interest in a property where the legal title is vested in another is to demonstrate that the legal owner holds the property in trust for the person claiming the interest. Orders for the benefit of children are available under Sch 1 CA 1989 (see **11.8**).

23.4.1 ESTABLISHING LEGAL TITLE

The conveyance of a property will indicate not only the legal owner of a property but also the beneficial interests of the property. The title deeds to the property should be carefully checked.

23.4.2 ESTABLISHING A BENEFICIAL INTEREST

The person claiming an interest is called a 'claimant' as proceedings will be in the civil courts, not family courts. In order to claim a share of the property the claimant will have to demonstrate that a legal owner holds the property in trust for the claimant. The establishment of such a trust depends upon the parties' intention. Establishing the common intention can be extremely problematic.

In *Gissing v Gissing* [1971] AC 886 Lord Diplock stated that a party's intention means that both words and conduct led the other to believe that he holds a beneficial interest in the property.

In *Midland Bank v Cooke* [1995] 4 All ER 562 the court held that even if both parties admit that neither had discussed nor intended any agreement as to the proportion of their interests, this did not preclude the court from inferring one.

S53(1)(b) Law of Property Act 1925 (LPA 1925) requires that a valid declaration of a trust of a beneficial interest in land must be in writing. If one partner buys the home out of their own money and has it conveyed into their sole name, any oral agreement between the parties for one to take a beneficial share will not (per se) give that person an entitlement. The agreement will amount to an imperfect gift, which equity will not perfect. However, s53(2) LPA 1925 does not require the creation or operation of resulting, implied, or constructive trusts to be evidenced in writing. In *Gissing v Gissing*, Lord Diplock stated that in the absence of writing, the claimant to a beneficial interest will need to establish an interest under a resulting, implied, or constructive trust. The classification of trusts can be problematic but it is important to do so as this may impact the quantum of interest available.

Whilst the creation of a trust requires the parties to have a common intention, the court will not find a trust when the intention does not exist. The court does not devise or invent a legal result, according to Lord Morris in *Pettitt v Pettitt* [1970] AC 777. An agreement may be inferred from conduct or words as they would be reasonably understood by the parties.

23.4.2.1 Resulting trusts

A resulting trust arises when property is bought by one party and put into the name of the other; the property is presumptively held on a resulting trust by the latter for the purchaser. If one person puts money into the property at the time of purchase (and it is not a gift), a trust is created to recognize this fact and is called a resulting trust. The person's beneficial interest will consist of the amount of money which they have paid into the property where their name is not on the deeds as a legal owner. Case-law suggests that resulting trusts arise only at the time of the purchase of the property. Resulting trusts are fairly easy to prove as there is a direct financial contribution to the purchase of the property.

Example

The facts of the case *Carleton v Goodman* [2002] EWCA Civ 545 are a good illustration of a resulting trust in real life.

Mr Goodman wished to buy a house but lacked sufficient income to finance a mortgage. He was in a relationship with Ms Carleton but did not live with her. Mr Goodman and Ms Carleton applied for a mortgage based on their joint income and the house was conveyed into their joint names. The deposit and mortgage payments were all met by Mr Goodman. Mr Goodman died without making a will and a dispute arose concerning whether Ms Carleton had a beneficial interest in the property.

It was held that the presumption that the joint owners held the property on trust absolutely for Mr Goodman, on the basis of his having made all the payments, was not rebutted. The court held that, on the facts, the parties had not intended to allow Ms Carleton a share.

The shares that the parties will receive from the property will depend upon their contributions.

Example

Hilary and Denny decide to live together and buy a house together jointly for £100,000. Hilary provides £79,000 from her savings. The remaining £21,000 is obtained from a joint repayment mortgage. Hilary is doing a degree as a mature student and has no income and so Denny makes all of the mortgage repayments until the mortgage is paid off in full. The relationship subsequently breaks down. Denny seeks clarification of how the property was held and the shares each party are entitled to on sale.

The property will be held as a resulting trust. Hilary will be treated as having contributed her cash contribution and Denny will be treated as having made a cash contribution and the house was owned in proportionate shares to the contribution made. Hilary will own 79% and Denny will own 21%.

23.4.2.2 Constructive trusts

Where there is no evidence of direct contributions made to the purchase price giving rise to the presumption of a resulting trust, there may be a constructive trust between the parties. This is a much 'looser' type of trust but is often difficult to establish. There are two hurdles for a client to establish:

1. there must be evidence of common intention between the parties to share in the ownership of a property, and
2. there must also be evidence of a detrimental reliance by the party on this common intention seeking to establish the trust.

This would establish a constructive trust.

There are two ways of demonstrating a constructive trust; first by evidence of agreement between the parties, and secondly, where there is no evidence of a common agreement, the court may infer common intention.

Where there is evidence of an agreement between the parties to share the property, this will establish the first limb of a constructive trust. The evidence may be that of a written deed (the author never found this in practice!) or evidence of an oral agreement or discussions about a common intention to share the property. This is also uncommon in practice and is often simply contradictory evidence. If there is no common agreement between the parties, then the court will look for evidence of inferred (or indirect) intention.

23.4.2.3 Evidence of common intention

In *Lloyds Bank plc v Rossett* [1991] 1 AC 107, Lord Bridge stated that the question that must be resolved is whether the parties at the time of acquisition of the property (or exceptionally at a later date) agreed, arranged, or came to an understanding that the property is to be shared beneficially.

There must be evidence of an express agreement between the parties based on discussion between the parties. This is clearly problematic as discussions may have been held some time ago and may have been vague or not felt to be serious at the time. The courts have generally looked for clear evidence. In *Hammond v Mitchell* [1992] 2 All ER 109, the man said to the woman shortly after completion, 'don't worry about the future because when we are married [the home] will be half yours and I'll always look after you'. This was held to be sufficiently clear to establish a constructive trust.

In *Springette v Defoe* [1992] 2 FLR 388, the court held that it was not sufficient to have a mutual but an uncommunicated intention to share the property. Steyn LJ commented that 'law does not allow property rights to be affected by telepathy'.

 **Example**

A communicated intention has been found by the courts in the following circumstances:

- a woman was assured her partner would put her name on the title deeds 'when he had time';
- a woman helping a man with his business when he was in prison was promised an (unclear) share of assets;
- a woman is assured that her assumption of a joint liability for a mortgage would be sufficient proof of her entitlement to a share of the property.

Two cases are very good examples of the court finding a trust through expressly declared intention.

In *Eves v Eves* [1975] 3 All ER 768 the couple were cohabitants. The man told the woman that as she was under 21, the house had to be in his sole name and that but for her age he would have put the house into joint names. The woman did a great deal of heavy manual work on the house including demolishing a shed, breaking up concrete, painting woodwork, and stripping wallpaper. All this work helped to renovate the property from an initially dilapidated state.

In *Grant v Edwards* [1986] Ch 638 the man told his cohabitant that she should not have her name on the deed as this would prejudice her ongoing matrimonial proceedings. The woman made no financial contribution to the purchase price but went out to work and looked after four children. The woman's wages allowed the mortgage to be paid whilst leaving sufficient for the family to live on.

Both cases demonstrate contributions made that amounted to conduct on which they could not reasonably have been expected to embark unless they were to have an interest in the house. This conduct was a detrimental reliance even where a share had been stated in advance. The conduct demonstrated more than simply living in the property and caring for the home and family. However, this conduct (although considered to be a detrimental reliance) was subject to a less rigorous test as there had been prior agreement to share. In order to establish a constructive trust, the client will have to show detrimental reliance as well as common intention.

Where there is no prior agreement to share the home, the test is more difficult to establish.

23.4.2.4 No evidence of common intention

Where there is no evidence for the court to find that the parties agreed or arranged or came to an understanding that the property was to be shared, the court must rely entirely on the conduct of the parties to see if an intention to share can be inferred from the evidence. If an intention to share can be inferred from the conduct of the parties, the court may find a constructive trust. As will be seen from the case-law, the courts have been very reluctant to infer an intention from anything less than a contribution to the purchase price of the house.

The leading case is *Lloyds Bank plc v Rossett* [1991] 1 All ER 1111, where neither the wife's extensive renovations of the house nor a common intention to share the family home was enough to indicate that both parties were to have an interest. The court held that her work was that which could be expected of a wife to do with no expectation of a beneficial interest.

This case was preceded by cases with similar decisions. In *Pettitt v Pettitt* [1970] AC 777 unusually the house was in the wife's name and the husband failed to establish an interest by reason of home improvements, e.g. internal decorating, laying a lawn, and building a wall in the garden. In *Gissing v Gissing* [1971] AC 886 Mrs Gissing's payments for household expenses and family clothing did not amount to a beneficial interest. Both parties would have been better off paying mortgage repayments.

Practical Considerations

The case of *Burns v Burns* [1984] Ch 317 is strongly reminiscent of cases the author has seen in practice. Mrs Burns lived with her partner for 19 years, although they never married. Mrs Burns gave up her job to take care of the family's two children and then contributed her wages on return to work to the household expenses, family clothing, and fixtures and fittings in the house. This was not a sufficient contribution for the court to find a beneficial interest. Even the indirect contributions to the mortgage contributions through paying household expenses to free up the partner's income for mortgage payments will not suffice if there is no express agreement to share the property.

Clients in Mrs Burns' position are often very distressed, firstly at the break-up of a relationship but then to find themselves in straitened financial circumstances as a result of having made no provision for housing during the life of their relationship. Clients who are coming to the end of their working life are particularly vulnerable. Advice is vital on welfare benefit and housing entitlement and any provision available for child support maintenance or orders for children under Sch 1 CA 1989 (see **11.8**).

The other problem that clients face is that these types of proceedings are taken in civil courts, not family courts, and are subject to the Civil Procedure Rules with associated risks on costs.

There is a glimmer of hope for clients in Mrs Burns' position in *Le Foe v Le Foe and Woolwich plc* [2001] 2 FLR 970. Following comments made in the case of *Bernard v Josephs* [1982] Ch 391, the trial judge found that an inference that the parties intended to share can be drawn from indirect contributions to the mortgage, thus enabling the family economy to function. This was a first instance decision only, however. In *Stack v Dowden* above, Baroness Hale stated that the law had moved on since *Pettitt* and *Gissing* in response to changing social and economic conditions. Lord Walker commented that the court should take into account a broad view of the contributions. He referred to the Court of Appeal's decision in *Oxley v Hiscock* [2005] Fam 211 with approval. In this case, it was held that the court should refer to the 'the whole course of dealing between them in relation to the property'. However, their Lordships failed to elaborate fully on the status of the inferred common intention constructive trust. It is hoped that their Lordships take the opportunity to do so in *Kernott v Jones* (see **23.3**).

For those advising clients in this position, a careful reading of case-law is essential. It is to be hoped that either the courts or Parliament will provide greater clarity in due course.

23.4.2.5 Quantification of the shares

In cases of an express trust, the shares will be as agreed by the parties. If the court finds or infers a common intention, it has a wide discretion when deciding the shares of the parties.

In *Oxley v Hiscock* (**23.4.2.4**, Practical Considerations), it was held that the parties are entitled to that share which the court considers fair having regard to the whole course of dealing between them in relation to the property. In that context, the whole course of dealing includes the arrangements that they make from time to time in order to meet the outgoings that have to be met (mortgage contributions, council tax and utilities, repairs, insurance, and housekeeping). The court will look at the evidence of any discussions between the parties regarding the amount of shares that each was to have.

This approach in *Oxley v Hiscock* to looking at the 'whole course of dealing' was approved in *Stack v Dowden*.

23.5 TRUSTS OF LAND AND APPOINTMENT OF TRUSTEES ACT 1996

The Trusts of Land and Appointment of Trustees Act 1996 (TOLATA 1996) has an impact on property held by cohabitants.

S12 TOLATA 1996 gives any beneficiary who is beneficially entitled to an interest in possession in land subject to a trust in land a right to occupy the land at any time (unless it is unavailable or unsuitable for occupation by him). Of course, the beneficial entitlement must be first established.

The more common use of TOLATA 1996 within family law is the power contained in s14 TOLATA 1996 for the court to hear an application for a trustee of the land relating to the exercise of their function or to declare the nature or extent of a person's interest in property. Commonly the function of cohabitant trustees concerns the sale of the property. A cohabitant with an interest in a property can apply under s14 TOLATA 1996 for an order to sell the property.

If an application is brought under s14 TOLATA 1996, the matters to which the court must have regard are found in s15 TOLATA 1996. These matters include:

- the intentions of the person or persons who created the trust;
- the purposes for which the property subject to the trust is held;
- the welfare of any minor who occupies or might reasonably be expected to occupy any land subject to the trust as his home; and
- the interest of any secured creditor of any beneficiary.

Example

Margaret and Peter bought a property jointly to live together and are tenants in common in equal shares in 2002. They have two children (aged 10 and 11). They separate in 2010 and Peter moves out. In 2013 Peter decides that he needs the money from his share of the house to buy his own property and applies for an order for sale under s14 TOLATA 1996 on the basis that the intention and purpose behind the purchase was for their cohabitation and that cohabitation is at an end. Margaret resists the application on the basis that the children require a home and that the trust was for the purpose of a family home including the children of the family.

SUMMARY POINTS

- Cohabiting couples do not have any intrinsic legal rights by simply cohabiting. The 'common law wife/husband' does not exist in law.
- Cohabitants must rely on a mixture of property and trust law to resolve property disputes.
- The Law Commission has reported on potential reforms to the law relating to cohabitants but there appears to be no move to legislate on the part of the Government.
- When property is held jointly, the court will presume that the beneficial interests reflect the legal ownership and the onus is on the party who wishes to prove otherwise unless there is a valid deed of trust.
- If a property is owned by one party solely, the other party may have to establish a beneficial interest through an express, resulting, or constructive trust.

- A resulting trust is established through contributions made directly to the purchase of a property.
- A constructive trust is established through either a directly expressed common intention to share the property or an inferred intention to share the property.
- The court can be asked for an order for sale under s14 TOLATA 1996.

SELF-TEST QUESTIONS

1. Ellie moved in with her girlfriend Lucy into Lucy's flat. Lucy is having difficulties paying her mortgage and asks Ellie to pay off her mortgage arrears of £7,000. Lucy says that banks discriminate against lesbians and so Ellie cannot put her name on the deeds. Lucy and Ellie live together for ten years with Ellie making more than half of the total mortgage payments. The house was bought by Lucy for £100,000 with Lucy paying £20,000 as a deposit and sells for £200,000 with Ellie contributing £30,000 to the repayments. Advise Ellie on whether she would be able to recover any of her money if she and Lucy separated.
2. Martin and Luke buy a house together. Luke contributes 25% of the deposit and pays only 25% of the mortgage payments as he is in a low paid job. A deed of trust was not executed and the property is held as joint tenants. Luke and Martin separate. Martin wishes to know if he can claim 75% of the sale proceeds of the house. Advise Martin.
3. Henrik meets Abri during a business trip. Henrik is a very wealthy businessman whose personal wealth runs into many millions of pounds. They meet up for drinks and have a brief relationship. Henrik thinks of their relationship as a 'fling' and does not plan to see Abri again. Four months later, Abri contacts Henrik to tell him that she is pregnant with his child and that she wants him to support her and the child. Advise Henrik on the claims, if any, that Abri can make on behalf of the child and for herself.
4. Describe the proposals made by the Law Commission to reform the law on cohabitation.

Answers to the questions above can be found on the Online Resource Centre: www.oxfordtextbooks.co.uk/orc/familyhandbook13/.

Part 5

CHILDREN

24 INTRODUCTION TO THE CHILDREN ACT 1989

24.1 INTRODUCTION

This chapter will:

- **examine the principles the court will follow in private children law proceedings;**
- **discuss the content of the 'welfare principle' and the 'welfare checklist' under the Children Act 1989;**
- **discuss the principles of 'no order' and 'no delay'.**

This part of the text deals with the law and practice relating to children. When family members cannot agree about the upbringing or arrangements concerning where a child shall live or with whom they shall have contact, this is described as 'private' children proceedings. When a child is subject to intervention by the local authority out of concern for the child's safety, development, or health, these proceedings are described as 'public' children proceedings. A family lawyer in practice will see both types of proceedings, although lawyers conducting public children proceedings are specialist lawyers who have many years of experience.

This part of the text will examine the law and practice for both types of proceedings. This chapter will look at the Children Act 1989 (CA 1989) and the main principles upon which Children Act proceedings are conducted.

A case study will continue to look at the ongoing proceedings of Helena and David Wilson in private Children Act proceedings.

24.1.1 FAMILY JUSTICE REVIEW

There has been a wide-ranging review into family law and the family law courts by the Ministry of Justice called the Family Justice Review. The final report was given in November 2011 and subsequently, Ryder J was appointed to make suggestions about its implementation. Ryder J's report into the modernization of Family Justice contains a series of proposals to improve the workings of family courts and covers most of family law but makes particular reference to cases involving children. His recommendations have been endorsed by the Lord Chief Justice and are intended to change the culture of the family courts for the children and families themselves, for judges, lawyers, social workers, CAFCASS, and social workers.

A principal area for the review and Ryder J has been private Children Act proceedings. Private law proceedings range from the most complex family breakdowns, involving intractable disputes and serious safeguarding issues, to relatively modest disagreements about contact arrangements. Most private law parties, ie parents, who seek to resolve their differences about the plans for their children will fall outside the scope of public funding in April 2013. Ryder J recommended that the judiciary must take steps to ensure that those who are entitled to family justice are provided with access to it, whether represented or not.

The courts will have to deal with a volume of previously represented parents who will not have had the benefit of legal advice to identify solutions or the merits or demerits of their proposals. Before their arrival at the court door they will not have had identified to them the issues the court can address. Many will have no idea what a conventional court process entails and some will have difficulty understanding its rules.

Ryder J recommended the publication of a private law pathway to describe what a court can and cannot do and how it does it. In a conventional case there may be restrictions on the right of one party to cross-examine another, relying on each party having their say, then the judge identifying further issues and asking questions him or herself.

24.2 CHILDREN ACT 1989

The CA 1989 was passed to reform the law relating to children and also to provide for local authority services for children in need and others, to amend the law with respect to children's homes, community homes, voluntary homes and voluntary organizations, and to make provision with respect to fostering, child minding, and day care for young children and adoption. The CA 1989 has been amended and these amendments will be dealt with in the text.

A child is defined in s105 CA 1989 as a person under the age of 18.

24.3 WELFARE PRINCIPLE

Section 1(1) of the CA 1989 states that:

> When a court determines any question with respect to—
>
> (a) the upbringing of a child; or
>
> (b) the administration of a child's property or the application of any income arising from it, the child's welfare shall be the court's paramount consideration.

This is described variously as the 'welfare' or 'paramountcy' principle. The effect of this section is to place the child's welfare before and above any other consideration when deciding whether to make an order.

Practical Considerations

When advising clients, it is essential to tell the client about the welfare principle and how the court will use this principle to place the children's interests ahead of their own. When a client is in the middle of stressful (and possibly antagonistic) proceedings, it may be difficult for them to place the children's interests first and they must be prepared to accept that the court will do this. Some clients feel that a court has not listened to their wishes sufficiently and may be dissatisfied with the court's decision and, possibly, their adviser's advice.

24.4 NO ORDER

S1(5) CA 1989 states that:

> where a court is considering whether or not to make one or more orders under this Act with respect to a child, it shall not make the order or any of the orders unless it considers that doing so would be better for the child than making no order at all.

This section does not create a presumption that the court should or should not make an order. The section requires the court to ask 'will it be better for the child to make the order than making no order at all?' (*Re G (Children)* [2006] 1 FLR 771). An example of the court's approach can be found in *Re K (Supervision Orders)* [1999] 2 FLR 303 where Wall J found that 'there must be something in the making or operation of an [order] which makes it better for the children for an order to be made'. In *Re X and Y (Leave to Remove from the Jurisdiction: No Order Principle)* [2001] 2 FLR 118, the court required that the party applying for the order has the burden of proof to make out a positive case on the balance of probabilities that it is in the interests of the child that the order be made.

 **Example**

Meera is the two-year-old child of Anil and Sarita. Anil and Sarita separate and Meera lives with Sarita. The pair initially cannot agree about how much time Meera spends with Anil and proceedings are commenced. During the proceedings, they agree the amount of contact. As they appear to have reached an agreement, there would not appear to be any need for the court to make this agreement into an order.

It is generally better for the parties to agree, as agreements are more likely to be adhered to than a court-imposed settlement. If the agreed arrangements fail, then the matter can return to the court and an order may have to be made. An order is sometimes necessary. If a child lives with someone who has no formal status as a parent or carer, it may be necessary to have an order for others, e.g. hospitals or schools, to recognize their status.

24.5 NO DELAY

S1(2) CA 1989 states that in any proceedings in which any question with respect to the upbringing of a child arises, the court shall have regard to the general principle that any delay in determining the question is likely to prejudice the welfare of the child.

The duty to avoid delay falls both upon the court and practitioners. The welfare principle states that the court's paramount consideration is the welfare of the child and it may be the case that the proper consideration of a case involves some delay, e.g. for experts to report or for further investigations.

Children progress quickly through development milestones and even a short delay can mean that a child who does not see a parent for a while will have undergone developmental changes. Avoiding delay will help to avoid disruption in a child's life. As will be seen in **Chapter 27**, a timetable is imposed by the court in CA 1989 proceedings to assist in minimizing delay.

24.6 WELFARE CHECKLIST

There is no definition of 'welfare' within the CA 1989. The CA 1989 provides a 'welfare' or 'statutory' checklist for the court to consider when the court is considering whether to make, vary, or discharge a section 8 order or whether to make, vary, or discharge an order under Part IV CA 1989. These orders will be explained in **Chapters 26 and 29.**

S1(3) of the CA 1989 states that:

> A court shall have regard in particular to:
>
> (a) the ascertainable wishes and feelings of the child concerned (considered in the light of his age and understanding);
>
> (b) his physical, emotional, and educational needs;
>
> (c) the likely effect on him of any change in his circumstances;
>
> (d) his age, sex, background, and any characteristics of his which the court considers relevant;
>
> (e) any harm which he has suffered or is at risk of suffering;
>
> (f) how capable each of his parents, and any other person in relation to whom the court considers the question to be relevant, is of meeting his needs;
>
> (g) the range of powers available to the court under this Act in the proceedings in question.

The checklist is not in any order of importance and the full circumstances of the case must be considered.

Practical Considerations

The checklist is at the heart of decisions made by the courts concerning children. It is extremely important that the checklist is applied fully to the client's case as the court will make decisions based on it and may expect a lawyer to address the court on the checklist.

24.6.1 WISHES AND FEELINGS OF THE CHILD (S1(3)(A) CA 1989)

When a child expresses their wishes and feelings, the court will try to give them their due weight. The court will be conscious that their wishes and feelings may be influenced deliberately or unconsciously by their parents, that the child's views may be influenced by the desire to please one parent or to avoid hurting another, or by saying what they believe the adults involved in proceedings wish to hear.

The court rarely seeks the child's opinions directly (see **Chapter 27**) and the views of the child can become known through the evidence of parents. The better way of seeking evidence is through the Child and Family Court Advisory and Support Service (CAFCASS) report (see **Chapter 27**). The CAFCASS officer will report what he has heard from the child during his investigations or, with older children, he may ask them directly. Rarely, the judge can hear evidence from the child directly.

Example

In the case of *Re P (A Minor) (Education: Child's Views)* [1992] 1 FLR 316, the court was asked to decide where a child should go to school. The child in question was 14 years old and mature. He expressed a wish to go to a local day school instead of an expensive boarding school and the court listened to his wishes.

24.6.2 CHILD'S PHYSICAL, EMOTIONAL, AND EDUCATIONAL NEEDS (S1(3)(B) CA 1989)

The level of material comfort offered by a parent has little influence over the court's decision—a fear often expressed by clients. The courts will strive to use their powers in proceedings for financial orders to provide both parents with suitable homes. Cohabitant parents may find that child support maintenance equalizes parties' positions. Clearly, unsatisfactory accommodation because of poorly maintained or damp conditions or being in a dangerous area will influence the court's decision and the information provided by the CAFCASS officer will contain information on parties' living situations.

If a move is proposed to a new place by either party, the court will take this into account. Even if the proposed accommodation is suitable, a move to a new area will involve the removal of the child from their school and friends, and the child will have to make friends again and form new relationships following a move. A parent contemplating such a move should make investigations concerning schools and affordable accommodation in the new area in good time for the court (and the other parent) to consider the move.

More importantly, the standard of day-to-day care offered by either parent in caring for a child's physical and emotional needs will be considered by the courts. Although no party's care can be beyond any criticism, minor issues or grumbles will not be entertained as a reason to deny a parent to care for a child.

 **Example**

Anil has criticized Sarita's care of Meera. He claims that Sarita allowed Meera to eat sweets (of which he disapproves), that she should be sent to bed at 7pm rather than 7.30pm, and that she should not be allowed to watch any television at all.

These criticisms are minor and a matter of personal choice. Meera will not suffer from Sarita's choices and the court will disregard these criticisms.

The child's emotional ties to parents and siblings will carry a great deal of weight with the court and courts are reluctant to split up siblings (*Re P (Custody of Children: Split Custody Order)* [1991] 1 FLR 337) as this can create lasting damage. But there have been cases where this has been ordered (*B v B (Residence Order: Restricting Applications)* [1997] 1 FLR 139).

Contrary to many clients' beliefs, the court does not favour the care of a mother over that of a father. In the online resources, you can find details of research done into contact applications.

A report found that the court did not favour parents with the children living with them (usually the mother) and the decisions of the courts reflect this (see particularly *Re S (A Minor)(Custody)* [1991] 2 FLR 394). In reality a mother will have a far greater chance of remaining as the principal carer of babies and very small children (e.g. *Re W (A Minor) (Residence Order)* [1992] 2 FLR 332). Where one parent is working and the other cares for the children, the caring parent has a greater advantage as they have the greater experience of day-to-day care. As children get older, they rely less and less on having a parent at home all day and so this perceived advantage diminishes.

Educational needs can also prove decisive when the court decides an order. Educational needs can encompass a wide variety of situations. If a parent proposes a move away from a particular school at a crucial time in a child's education, e.g. when they are taking GCSEs or A-levels, the parent offering the least disruption to schooling may have an advantage, although this is less important when a child is at an earlier stage in their education.

24.6.3 LIKELY EFFECT ON THE CHILD OF A CHANGE IN CIRCUMSTANCES (S1(3)(C) CA 1989)

The court will seek to avoid any major disruption within the child's life; this is known as keeping the 'status quo'. This is particularly important where the question is where the child shall live. In this situation, the parent with the child's current care has the greater advantage. The longer any situation continues, the greater the status quo of a situation becomes. This is only one factor in the checklist and other factors may outweigh this factor when the court is weighing its decision.

Example

Meera lives with Sarita and has done since Anil and Sarita's separation. She attends a local nursery and Sarita regularly attends a mother and toddler group. Anil proposes that Meera comes to live with him. The disruption caused to Meera would be considerable and she may suffer harm as a result. The status quo is for Meera to remain with Sarita.

24.6.4 THE CHILD'S AGE, SEX, BACKGROUND, AND ANY RELEVANT CHARACTERISTICS (S1(3)(D) CA 1989)

This can cover a multitude of factors within a child's life.

The age of a child can be crucial; if the child is very young, their needs may be best met by their mother. As a child becomes more mature, it matters less which parent cares for them and their views will become more important. The sex of the child can be important as a child may benefit from being with the parent of the same sex as they approach puberty and may benefit from a role model. The background of a child can cover many factors including religious upbringing, race, nationality, cultural background, disability, or illness.

Where a child grows up with a background of a mixed heritage, the court will look at the characteristics of both parents and will try to keep the child in touch with all aspects of their parents' different backgrounds.

24.6.5 ANY HARM WHICH THE CHILD HAS SUFFERED OR IS AT RISK OF SUFFERING (S1(3)(E) CA 1989)

Harm can cover physical, mental, or emotional harm. The Adoption and Children Act 2002 amended the CA 1989 to extend the definition of harm to include the impairment suffered from seeing or hearing the ill treatment of another. This will encompass the child who witnesses domestic abuse.

24.6.6 THE CAPABILITY OF THE PARENTS OF MEETING THE CHILD'S NEEDS (S1(3)(F) CA 1989)

When a parent applies to the court to have their child(ren) live with them or applies to have contact that involves their sole care of the child(ren) for any period, the court will consider whether the parent can care for the children properly.

The court may have to consider very serious questions of a parent's capability. A parent may have previously harmed the child and this will prejudice a claim for their child to live with them. A parent who fails to prevent their child from harm from another may similarly struggle to convince the court that they are a capable parent.

The religious views of a parent are not often considered under this factor but the court may be reluctant to allow a child to remain with a parent belonging to a sect or group with extreme views harmful to a child. A court can allay some fears by attaching conditions to orders.

Example

A child is living with a parent whose religious views do not permit inoculations against common diseases. A condition is attached to the order requiring the parent to take the child for inoculations.

Some parents may have mental or physical illnesses that are relevant to the care of the child. The court may require medical evidence to explain the impact of the illness on the parent's ability to care for the child. If there is evidence that the illness may place the child at risk of harm, where a parent may require regular in-patient treatment at hospital, or the child has an inappropriate level of responsibility for the care of the parent, the court may decide that the illness affects the capability of the parent to care for the child. The evidence may equally reveal that the illness does not affect the parent's capability.

This factor covers the capability of any other person in relation to whom the court considers the question to be relevant. This may include the new partner of one parent, the child's grandparents, extended family, nurseries, and child minders. Family solicitors are used to allegations that the other parent's new partner or friends are unsuitable for a number of reasons. These allegations should be investigated thoroughly.

24.6.7 RANGE OF POWERS AVAILABLE TO THE COURT (S1(3)(G) CA 1989)

The court has a wide range of powers under the CA 1989 and can make an order if they believe it is appropriate to the case, even if none of the parties have applied for that particular order. The court has a great deal of control over the proceedings and can grant orders where it is in the interests of the children.

 **Example**

Anil and Sarita make very serious allegations about each other's care of Meera. The court receives evidence that both parties' behaviour is having a very bad emotional impact on Meera and that she is at risk of psychological harm. Although Meera's grandparents are not parties to the court proceedings, the court hears evidence of their capability as carers for Meera. The court uses its power under the CA 1989 to order that Meera live with her grandparents.

The court also has the power under s91(14) CA 1989 to prevent a party making repeated applications, e.g. parental responsibility, without the permission of the court.

24.7 GOOD PRACTICE

It is particularly important that proceedings are conducted sensitively and within good practice guidelines. The Law Society's Family Law Protocol offers guidance on the correct approach to mediation and the need to be mindful of the need to attempt to reach an early resolution of any dispute.

SUMMARY POINTS

- The CA 1989 is the principal Act concerning the law on children.
- Private children proceedings involve disputes between individual members of a family.
- Public children proceedings involve the intervention by the local authority to safeguard a child.
- The child's welfare is the paramount consideration when the court is deciding whether to make an order.
- The court must also ensure that it is in the child's interest to make an order.
- The court and parties must seek to avoid delay in the proceedings.
- The court must also have regard to a 'welfare checklist' that lists a number of important considerations to a child's life including the child's wishes and feelings, their physical, emotional, and educational needs and any change of circumstances, the child's age, sex, background, and other characteristics, any harm that the child is at risk of suffering, and the parent's capability.

- It is important to remember that the child should be at the centre of a case and clients should be encouraged to make decisions accordingly.

SELF-TEST QUESTIONS

1. Imagine that you are advising a client on the CA 1989. Explain to them what the central principles of the CA 1989 are in language that a non-lawyer would understand.

Case Study Two

Following their divorce, Helena and David Wilson are having some further difficulties. Their child, Richard, has remained with Helena, and David has been having regular contact; for about the last nine months this system has worked very well.

However, Helena seeks your advice. David has moved in with a new partner, Anna. Anna already has two children. Richard gets on very well with Anna and Helena has been quite happy to allow David to have generous contact as she believes that it is in Richard's best interests for everyone to get along.

Last week, Richard came home from David's house and told Helena that his father had told him that it would be nicer if he could live with him and Anna as a 'proper family'. Helena was very upset by this and telephoned David. David told her that he felt he could offer Richard a better home with him and Anna and that he wanted Richard to come and live with him. Helena was so upset that she has told David that he cannot have contact with Richard.

Yesterday, Helena received a letter from David's solicitors stating that David wished Richard to come and live with him (see online for document CA 1). Helena is very upset and asks what the court will decide. Helena admits that David's decision has probably arisen as she has started a new relationship with Phillip and that David is simply being difficult. Phillip does not live with Helena and Richard.

The child is the paramount consideration of the court. When the court is deciding whether to make an order, they will consider the welfare checklist under s1(3) CA 1989. Your supervisor asks you to consider the information and the documents online and apply the checklist to the case.

Answers to the questions above can be found on the Online Resource Centre: www.oxfordtextbooks.co.uk/orc/familyhandbook13/.

25 PARENTAL RESPONSIBILITY

25.1 INTRODUCTION

This chapter will:

- **examine the concept of parental responsibility;**
- **discuss the circumstances in which a parent has parental responsibility and how parental responsibility can be gained by a parent.**

Parental responsibility (PR) is one of the most important concepts in the Children Act 1989 (CA 1989) and was introduced by the CA 1989. Clients must be advised about what PR is and its effects and whether or not they have PR for their children. The Law Society Family Law Protocol recommends that clients are always advised on who has PR for a particular child as part of the general advice given to a client. Whether or not a parent has PR can also affect the orders for which they are able to apply (see **Chapters 26 and 27**). PR is also an important consideration in public children law (see **Chapters 29–32**).

This chapter examines the nature and scope of PR and how it is acquired.

25.2 WHAT IS PARENTAL RESPONSIBILITY?

S3 CA 1989 defines PR as 'all the rights, duties, powers, responsibilities and authority that by law a parent of a child has in relation to the child and his property.'

Practical Considerations

Many clients do not understand the scope of PR when faced with the above definition and often clients focus on the rights and powers parts of the definition. It is important to be able to describe what PR is and how the law views the client's duties and responsibilities.

PR covers all the decisions and responsibilities that a parent may make on behalf of their child during their childhood and can include:

- access to the child's medical records;
- access to a child's school reports;
- consenting to medical treatment;
- deciding where a child is educated;
- teaching a child about the family's religion or culture;

- providing suitable food, clothing, and discipline;
- deciding where a child shall live.

Clearly, when a child is very young, PR will encompass most, if not all of the decisions made on behalf of a child. As the child gets older and more able to make decisions concerning their own lives, PR applies more to the larger decisions in a child's life. This reflects the approach of the court in *Gillick v West Norfolk and Wisbech Area Health Authority* [1985] 3 All ER 402. The case dealt with a mother who objected to her teenage daughter being prescribed the contraceptive pill without the mother's knowledge or consent. The House of Lords held that a child had sufficient competency to consent if the child had sufficient maturity and understanding of the issues involved. This is often referred to as 'Gillick' competency.

Under s2(5) CA 1989 more than one person may have PR for the same child at the same time and s2(6) CA 1989 states that a person who has PR for a child at any time shall not cease to have that responsibility solely because some other person subsequently acquires PR for the child.

Therefore two (or more) people may share PR for a child and they all have an equal say about the child's upbringing. **Chapter 26** gives details of orders that the court can make should parents disagree. The parent with day-to-day care of the child will make ordinary decisions concerning the child and should be allowed to do so without undue interference from those with PR who do not live with the child (see *D v S (Parental Responsibility)* [1995] 3 FLR 783). PR is delegable under s2(9) CA 1989 and one person can meet the responsibilities of PR for a child with the others with PR having delegated PR to them. This may occur when a child goes on holiday with one person with PR and the others with PR delegate PR during the period of the holiday.

There are some very important decisions that should not be made by one person with PR alone. Although s2(9) CA 1989 states that a person who has PR for a child may not surrender or transfer any part of that responsibility to another but may arrange for some or all of it to be met by one or more persons acting on his behalf, the Court of Appeal held in *Re J (Specific Issue Orders: Muslim Upbringing and Circumcision)* [2000] 1 FLR 571 that there are a small group of decisions made on behalf of a child which, in the absence of agreement of those with PR, ought not to be carried out by one person.

The CA 1989 also provides for someone who cares for a child and does not have PR for that child. S3(5) CA 1989 states that a person who does not have PR for a particular child but has care of the child may do what is reasonable in all the circumstances of the case for the purpose of safeguarding or promoting the child's welfare.

25.3 AUTOMATIC PARENTAL RESPONSIBILITY

S4 CA 1989 states that:

> (1) Where a child's father and mother were married to each other at the time of his birth, they shall each have parental responsibility for the child.
>
> (2) Where a child's father and mother were not married to each other at the time of his birth—
>
> (a) the mother shall have parental responsibility for the child;
>
> (b) the father shall not have parental responsibility for the child, unless he acquires it in accordance with the provisions of this Act.

A mother of a child will automatically have PR for the child irrespective of her marital status.

A father will automatically have PR if he was married to the mother at the time of the child's birth or subsequently marries the mother of his child as s2(3) CA 1989 imports ss1 and 10 Family Law Reform Act 1987, which deals with the legitimacy of children.

PR is lost when a child is adopted.

The following have automatic PR:

- the mother of the child;
- the natural father of the child if married to the mother of the child.

25.4 UNMARRIED FATHERS

As above, only mothers and married fathers have automatic PR. Unmarried fathers can acquire PR in a number of ways.

The Adoption and Children Act 2002, s111 amended s4 CA 1989 so that a father who was not married to the mother at the time of the child's birth has PR if his name is placed on the birth certificate at registration or re-registration of the birth under the Births and Deaths Registration Act 1953. In reality the father cannot register his name without the consent of the mother. Once an unmarried father gains PR by registration, it can only be removed by order of the court, on application by a person with PR for the child, or by the child (with leave of the court) if they have sufficient understanding. This amendment came into force on 1 December 2003 and so children born before that date will not be covered by this amendment.

S4(1) CA 1989 states that:

> where a child's father and mother were not married to each other at the time of his birth the court may, on the application of the father, order that he shall have parental responsibility for the child or the father and mother may by agreement ('a parental responsibility agreement') provide for the father to have parental responsibility for the child.

FIGURE 25.1 HOW A FATHER CAN OBTAIN PR

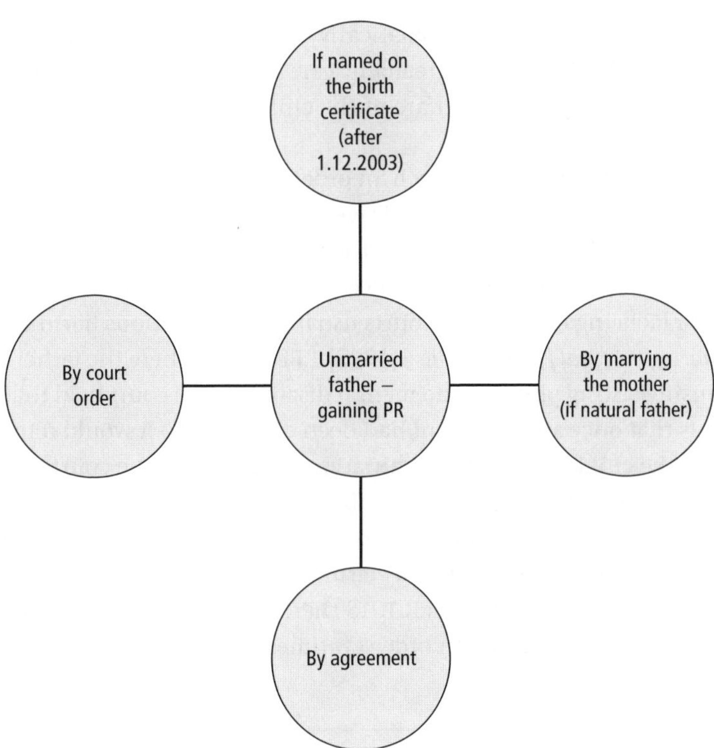

This means that there are a number of options for an unmarried father. Where the parents agree that the father should have PR, they can enter into a PR agreement. A PR agreement is a straightforward document that the parents can obtain from and complete at a family proceedings court.

If the mother of the child will not agree to the father having PR, he will have to apply for a PR order from the court. The procedure for obtaining orders under the CA 1989 can be found in **Chapter 27**.

As seen in **Chapter 24**, the welfare of the child is the paramount consideration of the court. The court must be satisfied that the applicant is the father of the child before granting him PR. S55A Family Law Act 1986 provides for a party to apply for a declaration of parentage to confirm whether or not the person making the application is the parent of the child named in the application.

The court will always consider the commitment of the applicant father to the child, the degree of attachment between father and child, and the father's reasons for applying for PR (see *Re P (A Minor)(Parental Responsibility Order)* [1994] 1 FLR 578). These factors are not exhaustive and the court must take into account all relevant circumstances including a lack of a responsible attitude towards the child or evidence that the grant of PR will be used to undermine the mother's care of the child. In these circumstances the court may refuse to make an order (see *Re H (Parental Responsibility)* [1998] 1 FLR 855 and *Re P (Parental Responsibility)* [1998] 2 FLR 96). The court will also consider the welfare checklist under s1(3) CA 1989 (see **Chapter 24**).

Practical Considerations

It is important to establish as early as possible in the case who has PR for a child. This is important as a father may need advice on how to obtain PR and those with PR may need advice on how it is shared and exercised with respect to a child. The ability to apply for orders under the CA 1989 is affected by whether a person has PR.

25.4.1 TERMINATION OF PR ORDERS AND AGREEMENTS

A PR order or agreement will end automatically upon the child reaching the age of 18 (s91(7) and (8) CA 1989). A PR order or agreement can be discharged by the court under s4(2A) and (3). The court will have the welfare of the child as the paramount consideration when considering making such an order.

Any person with PR can apply for such an order as can the child if they are of sufficient age and understanding and the court gives leave (s4(3)(b) and (4) CA 1989). The exception to this is where a person is granted PR during the currency of a residence order (see **Chapter 26**) and PR will continue as long as the residence order (s12(2) CA 1989).

Examples of PR being removed by courts usually involve serious harm to the child; e.g. in *Re P (Terminating Parental Responsibility)* [1995] 1 FLR 1048 where the father seriously injured the child causing lasting physical and mental disability. The court held that the normal presumption was that once an agreement had been entered into it would remain in force until the welfare of the child requires its termination. In this case, the court considered whether it would have made a PR order had one not been in force already and held that there was no aspect of PR that this father could have exercised in a way that would be beneficial to the child and the existing PR agreement was terminated.

In *Re F (Indirect Contact)* [2007] 1 FLR 1015 there was a history of domestic abuse with the father breaching a non-molestation order 68 times. The family moved ten times to escape the father and he served two terms of imprisonment. The court terminated the father's PR agreement on the basis that it did not benefit the child.

25.5 PARENTAL RESPONSIBILITY FOR NON-NATURAL PARENTS

Others can apply for PR for a child. Under the CA 1989, the following people can gain PR:

- guardians under s5(6) CA 1989;
- adopters who acquire PR on the passing of an adoption order;
- step-parents (see **25.5.1**);
- local authorities when a care order is made (see **Chapter 29**), although parents do not lose PR, it is shared;
- a person with a residence order, who will have PR for the duration of the order (see **Chapter 26**);
- a person with a special guardianship order (see **Chapter 26**).

25.5.1 STEP-PARENTS

If a step-parent becomes a guardian of the child or has a residence order granted in their favour or adopts a child, they will acquire PR in the same way as any other person. This is the same for a person who obtains a special guardianship order.

S4A CA 1989 allows a step-parent to acquire PR either with the agreement of those parents with PR for the child concerned or by order of the court. S4A CA 1989 requires that the step-parent be married to or in a civil partnership with the parent of the child concerned; being a cohabitant will not suffice. PR acquired in this way can be ended by a court order on the application of a person with PR or the child itself (with the leave of the court).

Step-parents without PR still have duties toward the child. As seen at **25.2**, s3(5) CA 1989 provides a duty for anyone without PR with the care of a child to do what is reasonable to safeguard and promote the child's welfare.

SUMMARY POINTS

- PR is a concept introduced by the CA 1989.
- PR encompasses the rights, duties, powers, responsibilities, and authority that by law a parent of a child has in relation to the child.
- PR covers all the decisions that are made concerning a child as well as the duty to care for the child.

SELF-TEST QUESTIONS

1. Feli and Abdul have two children, Miri (born 1 March 2003) and Kim (born 3 July 2007). Abdul is named as the children's father on their birth certificates. Feli and Abdul are not married and separate. Feli refuses to allow Abdul to see the children. Advise Abdul on whether he has PR for the children and, if not, how he may acquire it.

2. Advise Abdul on what the effect of having PR will be. Abdul wishes to receive school reports and to go to hospital appointments. How does having PR affect these wishes?

Case Study Two

Look at the documents contained in the Online Resource Centre. Who has PR for Richard?

David has now moved in with Anna and her children. Anna's ex-partner, William, is the children's natural father but they were not married and the children were born before 2003; William's name is not registered on their birth certificates. William does not approve of David and he has decided to apply for PR. Who has PR for Anna's children and how could William gain PR?

Answers to the questions above can be found on the Online Resource Centre: www.oxfordtextbooks.co.uk/orc/familyhandbook13/.

26 PRIVATE CHILDREN LAW

26.1 INTRODUCTION

This chapter will:

- **discuss the orders available under s8 of the Children Act 1989 to resolve disagreements between parents;**
- **discuss special guardianship orders.**

As explained in **Chapter 24**, private children law concerns disputes between family members about children; generally parents' disputes about children. Private children law concerns itself with whom a child shall live, with whom they should have contact, and what steps a parent can take in their exercise of parental responsibility. The Children Act 1989 (CA 1989) has orders that the court can make to help to resolve these disputes and the principles discussed in **Chapter 24** will be taken into account when the court is deciding which order to make or whether to make an order. This chapter will look at the orders available in private children proceedings, who can apply for them, and the individual considerations of each order.

Private children proceedings can be very emotionally charged as they are a continued reminder of the end of a relationship and unresolved disputes. There are often entrenched positions maintained by either party which can be difficult to resolve. The problems faced by some parents in terms of maintaining contact with children after separation are a topic of some controversy and the perceived faults of private children proceedings have also produced campaigning groups such as Fathers 4 Justice. More details can be found in the online resources that accompany this book. This chapter will consider the enforcement of orders for contact and residence.

It should be noted that all of the principles discussed in **Chapter 24** apply when the court is considering orders described in this chapter. Orders discussed in this chapter also have relevance in public children law proceedings as a court can make an order for residence or special guardianship in care proceedings (see **Chapters 29–32**).

The Family Justice Review has been considering how the courts deal with private family law cases, especially as many parents will not be eligible for public funding after April 2013. More details are available in the online resources.

26.2 RESIDENCE ORDERS

Under s8 CA 1989, a residence order is used to settle the arrangements to be made as to the person with whom a child is to live and so residence is the correct term when describing with whom a child shall live. It does not give the person the deciding word on the exercise of parental responsibility (PR); it settles where the child shall live.

A residence order does not affect the existing PR held by parents or others but under s12(1) CA 1989, if a court makes a residence order in favour of the father of the child, the father is granted PR if he did not already have it by the court making an order under s4 CA 1989 (see **Chapter 25**). S12(2) CA 1989 grants PR to any person who is not the parent or guardian of the child for the duration of the residence order. Once the residence order lapses, PR is lost.

Example

Mario and Honore separate. After some disagreement the couple both apply to the court to resolve where their children shall live. The court decides that the children shall live with Mario and make a residence order. If Mario did not have PR before the residence, he will have PR during the life of the order.

The importance of biological parentage was highlighted in the case of *Re G (Children)* [2006] 2 FLR 629. The House of Lords found that where an applicant is both the psychological and biological parent of a child, this is an important and significant factor in determining what would be best for the children in the long and short term. This case concerned children of a lesbian couple. The House of Lords awarded residence to the natural mother of the children.

Practical Considerations

'Custody' and 'access' are emotive words commonly used in the media or in soap operas to describe where a child lives or with whom they should have contact. It is important that you use the correct terminology with clients and doubly important that you use the correct terms in court or you will be sharply corrected!

26.2.1 SHARED RESIDENCE ORDERS

S11(4) CA 1989 allows the court to make a residence order in favour of more than one person. It also allows a court to specify the periods during which the child is to live in the different households concerned. This gives rise to the possibility of residence being shared between two parties.

Example

Libby and Pierre have three children aged between 10 and 14 years old. Following their separation, the couple live very closely to one another and the children spend equal amounts of time at their parents' houses. The children do not have fixed times for contact and the couple arrange the children's time on a relaxed, ad hoc basis.

In both *D V D (Shared Residence Order)* [2001] 1 FLR 495 and *Re F (Shared Residence Order)* [2003] 2 FLR 397, the court found that it is not necessary to show exceptional circumstances before a shared residence may be granted. The courts require a clear demonstration that the order is in the interests of the child in accordance with s3(1) CA 1989. In *Re P (Shared Residence Order)* [2006] 2 FLR 347, the children spent 55% of their time with their mother and 45% of their time with their father. The court held that this was plainly a case for a shared residence order as this would reflect the reality of the situation between the parents.

The court should not make a shared residence order simply to avoid resistance to a contact order (*Re W (Children)* [2003] EWCA Civ 116) but the existence of hostility between the parents is not necessarily a bar to a shared residence order where it is the right order in all other respects (*Re R (Residence: Shared Care: Children's Views)* [2006] 1 FLR 491).

A shared residence order can be granted to confer PR on a person who is not the child's biological father. In *Re A (Joint Residence: Parental Responsibility)* [2008] EWCA Civ 867, a child had been brought up on the assumption that a man was his father (he was present at the birth and lived with the child and mother for two years before the relationship had broken down). During an application for contact, residence, and PR, it emerged that the man was not the biological father. The court awarded shared residence in order for the man to obtain PR and the recorder stated in a separate order that the man was to be regarded as the child's father.

There is a move away from the term 'shared residence' in the Family Justice Review and the term 'cooperative parenting' is suggested as an alternative. It remains to be seen whether this will have legislative force.

26.2.2 CHANGE OF SURNAME

Under s13(1) CA 1989, where a residence order is in force with respect to a child, no person may cause the child to be known by a new surname. The House of Lords found in *Dawson v Wearmouth* [1997] 2 FLR 629 that the change of a child's surname has been viewed as a profound and not merely formal issue by the courts, whatever the age of the child. They ruled that any dispute should be referred to the courts for determination, whether or not there is a residence order in existence and whomsoever has or has not PR.

When a child is born, he or she must be registered in accordance with the Births and Deaths Registration Act 1953 (BDRA 1953). If the parents are married, the duty to register lies with both the mother and father. If the parents are not married, the duty is on the mother alone. The surname registered is to be the one by which the child is intended to be known. Once the surname has been registered, there is nothing in the BDRA 1953 to permit it to be changed and this point was extensively considered in the case of *Dawson v Wearmouth* (above). The court's powers are limited to those contained in s13(1) CA 1989 when the surname can be changed with the written consent of every person who has PR for the child or by the leave of the court.

A change of name is generally evidenced by a deed poll. Informal steps to change the child's name are prohibited.

 **Example**

Asha has separated from the father of her children. She wishes to change the children's surname to hers but knows that their father will not agree (he has PR). Instead of changing the children's surname formally by deed poll, Asha asks the children's school to call the children by her surname and registers the children in her surname at the GP and dentist. By these informal (and inadvisable) steps, the children are generally known by Asha's surname.

If the requirements of s1(5) CA 1989 mean that a residence order is not made, Practice Direction (1994) [1995] 1 FLR 458 is important. Any application for the registration of a deed poll to change the surname of a child under the age of 18 must be supported by the production of the consent in writing of every person having responsibility for the child or leave of the court (see also the Enrolment of Deeds (Change of Name) Regulations 1994 and *Re T (Change of Surname)* [1998] 2 FLR 620).

Practical Considerations

From case-law, it appears that the proper approach in all cases for seeking a change of name will be as follows:

- everyone with PR should be consulted, whether or not a residence order is in force (*Re PC (Change of Surname)* [1997] 2 FLR 730);
- if a father does not have PR, there is some uncertainty about the extent to which he is entitled to be consulted. S13 CA 1989 refers to those with PR giving consent and so one may infer that a father without PR has no right of consultation. However, case-law suggests that a father without PR can object to the proposed name change if he learns of it (*Dawson v Wearmouth*). In *Re C (Change of Surname)* [1998] 2 FLR 656, the court held that at the first sign of a dispute, the court should become involved. It is wise, therefore, to consult a father without PR before attempting to make a change in surname;
- if consent is obtained from all with PR, it is probably wise to gain such consent in writing;
- if the proposed change of name is disputed, the case should be referred to the courts under s13 CA 1989 if there is a residence order in force and under s8 CA 1989 if there is no residence order.

The welfare principle was demonstrated in *Re S (Change of Names: Cultural Factors)* [2001] 2 FLR 1005. A child's name was changed with the court's permission from a recognizably Sikh name to a recognizably Muslim name, in order to allow the mother and child to integrate fully into the Muslim community. However, the change of surname was to be used for school and registration with a GP but would not be completed by deed poll and so the change of name was essentially informal to prevent the child's Sikh identity being eliminated altogether.

In the case of *Re W; Re A; Re B (Change of Name)* [1999] 2 FLR 930, Butler-Sloss LJ gave guidelines for cases (although warned that these are not exhaustive). Each case should be decided on its own facts with the welfare of the child being the paramount consideration and all relevant factors weighed in the balance. The guidelines are as follows:

- if parents are married, they both have the power and duty to register their child's name;
- if not married, only the mother has the power and duty to do so;
- following registration of the child's name, if a residence order is granted any person wishing to change the child's surname must obtain the permission of the court or written consent of all with PR;
- if there is no residence order in existence, a person wishing to change a child's surname should obtain the written consent of those with PR or apply for a specific issue order to gain the permission of the court;
- when considering any application, the welfare of the child is paramount and the court must have regard to s1(3) CA 1989 factors;
- the court should have regard to the registered surname and the reasons for registration (e.g. the recognition of the biological link with the father). Registration is always important but not in itself decisive and the weight given to it by the court will depend upon the other relevant factors or valid countervailing reasons;
- the considerations include factors that may arise in the future;
- reasons given for changing or seeking to change a child's name based on the fact that the child's name is or is not the same as a parent making the application do not generally carry much weight;
- the reasons for a prior unilateral decision to change the child's name may be relevant;
- any change of circumstances of the child since original registration may be relevant;

- if a child's parents were married, the fact of the marriage is important and there would have to be strong reasons to change the name from the father's surname if that was the surname that was registered;
- if the child's parents were not married, the mother has the sole power to register the child's name. On an application to change the name of a child, the court will consider the commitment shown by the father to the child: quality of contact (if any) between father and child and the existence or absence of PR are all relevant factors to be taken into account.

26.2.3 REMOVAL FROM THE JURISDICTION

The right to remove the child from the jurisdiction is covered extensively in **Chapter 28**.

If one parent wishes to move permanently to another jurisdiction, then the court's permission should be sought unless the other parent or all those with PR consent to the removal.

26.2.4 ENFORCEMENT OF RESIDENCE ORDERS

Under s14 CA 1989, a residence order can be enforced through s63(3) Magistrates' Court Act 1980 as if it were an order requiring the other person to produce the child to him and the magistrates' court has the power to punish with a daily fine a parent who does not deliver the child.

For more details, see **28.4.2**.

26.2.5 REMOVING THE CHILD FROM THE JURISDICTION TO LIVE ELSEWHERE

Occasionally a parent may wish to move to a different country for work, to be nearer family, or for a better life. The court's permission will be required to remove the child from the jurisdiction (see **Chapter 28**).

The principle that the welfare of the child is the paramount consideration will apply. The general approach of the courts is to grant permission to the parent wishing to move unless the reasons for the move are unreasonable and there are compelling reasons to refuse. The court will look at the reasons for wishing to move and the plans for contact between the child and parent in the other jurisdiction to see if the child's welfare is safeguarded.

There are human rights implications concerning a decision to allow a child to be removed from the jurisdiction as this interferes with one parent's right to family life under Art. 8 of the European Convention on Human Rights (ECHR). In *Payne v Payne* [2001] 1 FLR 1052, the Court of Appeal ruled that all parties had rights under Art. 8 and when such rights conflicted, the rights of the parties had to be balanced against each other. The child's welfare is of crucial importance and if in conflict with a parent's rights would override the parent's rights. Article 8(2) ECHR allows a public authority to interfere with the right to family life where it is necessary to protect the rights and freedoms of others and where the need is proportionate to the need demonstrated. The court must consider the effect of the application on the applicant proposing the move and the respondent who opposes it. If this is properly done, then there will be no appeal. This case has been the focus of increasing criticism both judicially and academically.

This issue has recently been re-examined in *Re K (Children)* [2011] EWCA Civ 793. In this case, the parents of two children had a shared residence arrangement but the Canadian mother wished to relocate the children to Canada so she could live with her parents and maintained that she would have greater support there. The father opposed the application as he wished to avoid losing close contact with the children. This is an unremarkable case and reflects the position which occurs most commonly in practice.

At first instance, the judge followed the guidance given in *Payne v Payne*. At the Court of Appeal, their Lordships agreed that the only principle to come from *Payne* was that the welfare of the child is paramount. The rest is guidance to be applied or distinguished depending on the circumstances. The judge should apply the statutory checklist in s1(3) of the Children Act 1989 in order to exercise his discretion. Thorpe LJ confirmed that the guidance in *Payne* is only applicable where the applicant is the primary carer. Where parents share the burden of caring for the children in 'more or less equal proportions' the approach in *Payne* at para 40 should not be applied. The label 'shared residence' is not significant in itself. Their Lordships considered that future cases should not become embroiled in arguments as to whether the amount of time a child spends with each parent makes it 'a *Payne* case'. All the facts of the case must be considered.

There is currently a major research project on the issue of relocating families and it may bring about changes to the law.

26.3 CONTACT ORDERS

As with residence orders, contact between parents and children is often described as 'access'. S8 CA 1989 states that an order requiring the person with whom a child lives to allow the child to visit or stay with the person named in the order or for that person and the child otherwise to have contact with each other is a *contact* order. It is instructive to note that the law is drafted to state that the child is to have contact with the other person and contact is often stated as being the right of the child. Usually the court expects parents to resolve contact issues between themselves and to be flexible. However, when parents cannot agree about the level of contact and even whether contact should occur, the courts may become involved.

Contact orders concern parents and children and there is no presumption about the right contact between parents and adult children.

Contact can take the form of staying overnight, visiting, meeting for a meal or activity, telephone calls, emails, and birthday cards. Contact can be direct or indirect. Direct contact is where the child has contact with the person by visiting or staying with them, whereas 'indirect' contact is where the contact takes place via letters, telephone calls, or emails. Indirect contact is generally ordered when it is not suitable or appropriate for the child to see the person directly. Contact can be supervised if there is any risk to the child of unsuitable or inappropriate behaviour and indirect contact can be supervised as well as direct contact. The usual order for contact is 'reasonable contact', which is usually direct contact between the child and the person concerned with the arrangements and frequency agreed between the parties. If there are some difficulties concerning agreement or the arrangements being made, then a defined contact order may be made. This either sets out the actual times/places for contact to take place or it can resolve particular disputes, e.g. where a child should spend school holidays or Christmas Day.

Example

Bill and Melissa have three children. Neither party can agree when the children should have contact with Bill and, as a result of the dispute, Bill does not see the children for some time. The court makes an order that Bill telephones the children three times a week to reintroduce himself and then the contact progresses to the children meeting Bill for tea twice a week. After six months contact is going very well and so the children stay with Bill at the weekend.

26.3.1 CHILD CONTACT CENTRES

Where contact requires careful reintroduction or security for one party, child contact centres can be extremely useful. Most child contact centres do not offer supervised contact but do offer supported contact. The National Association of Child Contact Centres (NACCC) describes supported contact as taking place in a variety of neutral community venues where there are facilities that enable children to develop and maintain positive relationships with non-resident parents and other family members. Supported child contact centres are suitable for families when no significant risk to the child or those around the child has been identified.

Example

If Bill from the earlier example had lost touch with his children, a contact centre may have been a useful way of reintroducing their relationship in a neutral, safe place.

The basic elements of supported contact are:

- impartiality;
- staff and volunteers are available for assistance but there is no close observation;
- monitoring or evaluation of individual contacts/conversations;
- several families are usually together in one or a number of rooms;
- encouragement for families to develop mutual trust and consider more satisfactory family venues.

NACCC has issued a protocol, which can be found in the online resources, concerning the use of contact centres in terms of the categories of cases that are suitable for these centres and the practical steps to be taken to get in touch with an appropriate centre.

Practical Considerations

The following matters should be checked:

1. that the Child Contact Centre Co-ordinator has been contacted and has confirmed:
   - the referral appears to be suitable for that particular centre. Child contact centres can refuse to accept families if the circumstances appear inappropriate for the centre;
   - the intended day and times are available at the particular centre concerned;
   - a vacancy is available or a place on the waiting list has been allocated;
2. that it has been agreed who will have the responsibility for completing and returning the centre's referral form. Solicitors for both parties should agree the contents and it should be forwarded to the child contact centre within 24 hours of the court hearing;
3. if contact is to be observed at the child contact centre by a family court welfare officer (CAFCASS officer) or other third party that this is a facility offered by that centre and that the centre has agreed to this course of action (many do not permit such attendance);
4. that the parties understand whether the centre offers supported or supervised contact and appreciate the difference;
5. that it is agreed who is going to tell the children where and when they will see their non-resident parent.

26.3.2 CONTACT AND HUMAN RIGHTS

Unmarried fathers have used the Human Rights Act 1998 (HRA 1998) and the European Convention on Human Rights (ECHR) to complain that the refusal of a court to order contact with their children is a breach of Art. 8 ECHR, the right to family life.

The European Court of Human Rights upheld complaints by unmarried fathers in *Elsholz v Germany* [2000] 2 FLR 486. In *Hendriks v Netherlands* [1982] 5 D&R 225, it was stated:

> the Commission has consistently held that, in assessing the question of whether or not the refusal of the right of access to the non-custodial parent was in conformity with article 8 of the Convention, the interests of the child will predominate.

26.3.3 CONTACT AND DOMESTIC VIOLENCE

In many cases there are allegations of domestic abuse and practitioners will come across clients who allege that a contact application is a device by which a person can continue abuse. Equally, many clients will instruct you that allegations of domestic abuse are simply a device to prevent contact.

This issue was considered by the Court of Appeal in the case of *Re L (Contact: Domestic Violence); Re V (Contact: Domestic Violence); Re M (Contact: Domestic Violence); Re H (Contact: Domestic Violence)* [2000] 2 FLR 334.

The Court of Appeal requested that the Official Solicitor act as an amicus in each case and the Official Solicitor commissioned a report by Dr Sturge and Dr Glaser. This can be found at [2000] Fam Law 615 and it is suggested that all practitioners should read it carefully.

The President said:

> The family judges and magistrates need to have a heightened awareness of the existence of and consequences, (some long-term), on children of exposure to domestic violence between their parents or other partners. There has, perhaps, been a tendency in the past for courts not to tackle allegations of violence and to leave them in the background on the premise that they were matters affecting the adults and not relevant to issues regarding the children. The general principle that contact with the non-resident parent is in the interests of the child may sometimes have discouraged sufficient attention being paid to the adverse effects on children living in the household where violence has occurred. It may not necessarily be widely appreciated that violence to a partner involves a significant failure in parenting—failure to protect the child's carer and failure to protect the child emotionally.
>
> In both contact and other section 8 applications, where allegations of domestic violence are made which might have an effect on the outcome, those allegations must be adjudicated upon and found proved or not proved. It will be necessary to scrutinise such allegations which may not always be true or may be grossly exaggerated. If however there is a firm basis for finding that violence has occurred, the psychiatric advice becomes very important. There is not, however, nor should there be, any presumption that, on proof of domestic violence, the offending parent has to surmount a prima facie barrier of no contact. As a matter of principle, domestic violence of itself cannot constitute a bar to contact. It is one factor in the difficult and delicate balancing exercise of discretion. The court deals with the facts of a specific case in which the degree of violence and the seriousness of the impact on the child and on the resident parent have to be taken into account. In cases of proved domestic violence, as in cases of other proved harm or risk of harm to the child, the court has the task of weighing in the balance the seriousness of the domestic violence, the risks involved and the impact on the child against the positive factors, (if any), of contact between the parent found to have been violent and the child. In this context, the ability of the offending parent to recognize his past conduct, be aware of the need to change and make genuine efforts to do so, will be likely to be an important consideration.

The court must refer to the welfare principle and the checklist in s1(3) CA 1989. Since October 2005 a copy of every s8 CA 1989 application under the CA 1989 that is to be listed for a directions hearing will be sent to CAFCASS in order to screen the application for domestic abuse. Further information on the procedure to be adopted where one party makes allegations of domestic abuse can be found at **Chapter 27**.

26.3.4 CONTACT ACTIVITY DIRECTIONS AND CONDITIONS

There are sometimes difficulties in enforcing contact orders. The traditional method of enforcing orders made under the CA 1989, under the laws of contempt of court, is problematic for the courts. Contempt of court is not really effective in enforcing contact orders as the choice of the court to fine or imprison the parent with care of the child is most probably not in the best interests of that child. The courts give parents many opportunities to comply with the order, which is time consuming and very frustrating for a parent who is anxious to see their child.

The online resources contain links to organizations that have campaigned on this issue.

The CA 1989 has been amended by the Children and Adoption Act 2006 (CAA 2006) to introduce contact activity and directions in ss11A–H CA 1989. These contact activity directions and conditions as part of a strategy to encourage contact came into force on 8 December 2008.

26.3.4.1 Contact activity directions

Directions can be made when the court is considering whether to make (or to vary or discharge) a contact order.

S11A(3) CA 1989 states that a contact activity direction is a direction requiring an individual who is a party to the proceedings to take part in an activity that promotes contact with the child concerned. The direction is to specify the activity and the person providing the activity.

The activities under s11A CA 1989 that may be required include:

(a) programmes, classes, and counselling or guidance sessions of a kind that—

- (i) may assist a person as regards establishing, maintaining, or improving contact with a child;
- (ii) may, by addressing a person's violent behaviour, enable or facilitate contact with a child;

(f) sessions in which information or advice is given as regards making or operating arrangements for contact with a child, including making arrangements by means of mediation.

It is likely that a report will be required on whether there has been compliance with the direction and to assess the effectiveness of the directions in resolving contact difficulties before the court decides whether to make a contact order.

26.3.4.2 Contact activity conditions

A contact activity condition may only be attached to a final contact order and is enforceable in contempt proceedings in the event of a breach.

S11C(2) CA 1989 allows the imposition of a contact activity condition requiring an individual falling within sub-s (3) to take part in an activity that promotes contact with the child concerned.

A contact order may not impose a contact activity condition on an individual who is a child unless the individual is a parent of the child concerned.

The CAA 2006 does not develop any further the type of conditions that would promote contact, but presumably attendance at a contact centre or some form of parenting guidance may feature in contact activity conditions.

26.3.4.3 The imposition of contact activity directions and conditions

S11E(2) CA 1989 states that the first matter is that the activity proposed to be specified is appropriate in the circumstances of the case. In considering whether to make a contact activity *direction*, the welfare of the child concerned is to be the court's paramount consideration. However, there is no express provision for the child's welfare when making a contact activity *condition*.

A court may not make a contact activity direction in any proceedings unless there is a dispute as regards the provision about contact that the court is considering whether to make in the proceedings. For contact activity conditions, there appears to be no such requirement.

26.3.4.4 Monitoring contact and enforcing activities

Under s11H CA 1989, a CAFCASS officer can be asked to monitor contact and report on compliance with the order. A warning notice can be attached to an order warning of the consequences of a failure to comply. Under s11J CA 1989, if the court is satisfied beyond reasonable doubt that a person has failed to comply with the contact order, it may make an enforcement order imposing on the person an unpaid work requirement.

These provisions are very new and it is anticipated that it will be some time before there is a clear idea of the types of orders being made by the courts and an evaluation of their effectiveness.

26.4 SPECIFIC ISSUE ORDERS

A specific issue order can be made as a free-standing order or in concert with a contact or residence order. This order allows the court to make an order concerning an issue that has arisen in connection with the exercise of PR.

Example

Semaab and Sean separate and their daughter lives with Semaab. Sean wishes to bring the child up as a Catholic and Semaab wishes to raise the child as a Muslim. The couple cannot agree about this and apply to the court for a specific issue order. The court orders that the child is exposed to both religious cultures until such time as the child can make up their own mind.

The courts can become involved where those with PR simply cannot agree on a major aspect of a child's upbringing. The court will place a great deal of pressure on parties to agree such issues, as an imposed decision is often unsuccessful.

Local authorities can apply for a specific issue order for a decision involving a child in care. In **Chapter 29**, you will see that when a care order is made, a local authority gains PR for the child.

26.5 PROHIBITED STEPS ORDERS

A prohibited steps order allows a court to prevent a person taking a step that could be taken in meeting PR for a child. The step may only be taken with the permission of the court.

Example

Martin is worried that his ex-wife Soraya will take their children to live outside of the UK. He obtains a prohibited steps order to prevent her from removing the children from the UK.

The order will specify the action or steps that are prohibited by the court. The order can be made as a free-standing order or in concert with a contact or residence order.

Prohibited steps orders are discussed in connection with parental child abduction in **Chapter 28**.

26.5.1 RESTRICTIONS ON PROHIBITED STEPS AND SPECIFIC ISSUE ORDERS

Neither a prohibited steps or a specific issue order may be made in relation to a child over the age of 16 (ss9(7) and 12(5) CA 1989).

Importantly, neither of these orders can be used to achieve a contact or residence order by the 'back door' under s9(5)(a) CA 1989.

 **Example**

Mandy and Isobel have two children but decide to separate. Mandy decides to represent herself and applies for a specific issue order to settle where the children shall live. This is not the correct order. The correct order is a residence order.

26.5.2 DIRECTIONS

S11(7) CA 1989 allows the court to attach directions to a s8 order about how it is to be carried into effect and impose conditions that must be complied with by any person in whose favour the order is made or by a parent of the child or any person who has PR for the child.

26.6 SPECIAL GUARDIANSHIP ORDERS

Special guardianship orders (SGO) are private children law orders which give the special guardian PR for the child subject to the order. It is an order that allows a child to be cared for by someone other than their parents but avoids the need for care proceedings. The order is designed to give a child permanence and security where adoption is not appropriate but where it is not appropriate that they live with their natural parents. The legal links between the child and their parents is preserved. A special guardian cannot be a parent of the child.

SGOs were introduced by the Adoption and Children Act 2002 and the provisions are in s14A CA 1989. The same regime of eligibility for s8 CA 1989 also applies to an application for an SGO (s14A(5) CA 1989). An applicant must give three months' notice to the relevant local authority so that a report can be prepared about the applicant's suitability and the court will not make an SGO unless the report is made (s14A(11) CA 1989).

The effect of an SGO under s14C CA 1989 is that while it remains in force:

- the special guardian has PR for the child;
- the special guardian is entitled to exercise PR for the child to the exclusion of any other person with PR for the child.

While an SGO is in force, a child's surname cannot be changed and they cannot be removed from the UK without the written consent of all those with PR for the child.

S14F CA 1989 provides that the local authority must provide special guardianship support services including counselling, advice, and information.

SUMMARY POINTS

- S8 CA 1989 provides a set of orders to assist the courts in resolving disputes arising between parents and carers.
- All of the usual principles in the CA 1989 apply when considering s8 CA 1989 orders including the welfare principle, the no order principle, no delay, and the welfare checklist.
- A residence order decides where and with whom a child shall live.
- Whilst a residence order is in force a child should not have their surname changed and should not be removed from the jurisdiction (except in certain circumstances).

- A contact order decides with whom a child shall have contact.
- Contact comes in many forms: direct and indirect, by direct visits, letters, cards, and emails.
- The court can make an order for reasonable contact where the parties agree when contact will take place. Alternatively the court can make an order for defined contact where the court specifies when contact will take place.
- Where there are allegations of domestic violence then the court must first of all make a finding on the allegations and then consider the impact of the violence on the child and what the impact will be of continuing contact.
- The CA 1989 has been amended to include contact activity directions and conditions in order to promote and encourage contact. These provisions are very new and as yet untested.
- Specific issue orders resolve disputes between all those people who have PR for a child. The order resolves disputes over a step which can be taken in the exercise of PR.
- A prohibited steps order prevents someone from taking a step in the exercise of the PR and can be used to prevent a child being removed from the jurisdiction.
- A special guardianship order allows someone other than a parent of the child to gain and exercise PR for the child to the exclusion of anyone else with PR.

SELF-TEST QUESTIONS

1. Albert Morton has a residence order for his daughter, Maddie Phelps, and Maddie has contact with her mother every weekend. Albert wishes to take her on holiday to France for two weeks and to change her surname to Morton. Advise Albert on whether this is possible and the steps he should take.
2. Sarah is the daughter of a French mother and Italian father who have recently divorced. Both parents wish their daughter to come and live with them in their respective countries of origin. Advise which orders will be necessary should the parties be unable to agree and the factors that the court will consider when deciding.
3. Would your answer to question 2 above be any different if there were allegations of domestic violence?

Case Study Two

David has made an application to the court for an order (see the **Case Study to Chapter 27** for details of forms and procedure). He wishes Richard to live with him and states that he is willing to allow contact with Helena. Helena then issues an application for an order as she wishes Richard to continue living with her.

Which orders should (a) Helena and (b) David apply for?

See **Chapter 27** for a discussion of the procedural aspects of the case study.

online resource centre

Answers to the questions above can be found on the Online Resource Centre: www.oxfordtextbooks.co.uk/orc/familyhandbook13/.

27 PRIVATE CHILDREN LAW PROCEDURE

27.1 INTRODUCTION

This chapter will:

- **describe who is entitled to apply for an order under s8 Children Act 1989;**
- **explore public funding available for proceedings under the Children Act 1989;**
- **examine the procedure for obtaining an order under the Children Act 1989 in private law proceedings.**

Many trainee solicitors and paralegals advise upon and run private children law cases and gain experience of court advocacy and also negotiating contact and residence orders between clients. The procedure is not complex but it is worth understanding all the guidance from the courts and practice directions concerning aspects of procedure. Private children law cases often run during or after other proceedings, such as divorce or applications for domestic violence injunctions, and emotions often run very high. It is essential that clients are properly advised on the opportunities to enter into conciliation or mediation and that proceedings are conducted sensitively and within good practice guidelines within a system that is struggling with scarce resources. There is a link in the online resources to a speech made by Coleridge J on the state of the family law system and the speech sets out many of the issues very clearly.

As stated in **Chapter 2**, public funding will be withdrawn from private children proceedings except in cases of child abuse or domestic violence, which will mean that many parents may come to court unrepresented. This will present challenges to both courts and family lawyers. As stated by Ryder J, many parents will not have had the opportunity to learn about the approach of the courts to disputes and may need to take a greater amount of court time to engage fully in their case.

This chapter covers the basic procedure for a s8 CA 1989 order.

27.2 WHO IS ELIGIBLE TO APPLY FOR A S8 ORDER?

Chapter 26 outlined the orders available under s8 CA 1989 and **Chapter 25** discussed parental responsibility (PR) and its importance in private children work. As stated in **Chapter 25**, it is important to identify at the earliest opportunity which parents or carers have PR as this will affect who can apply for which orders and the procedure followed in the application for an order.

There are differences between the categories of people who can apply for s8 orders. Under s10(4) CA 1989, the following persons are entitled to apply to the court for any s8 order with respect to a child:

- any parent, guardian, or special guardian of the child;
- any person who by virtue of s4A CA 1989 has PR for the child;
- any person in whose favour a residence order is in force with respect to the child.

The following persons can apply for a contact or residence order with respect to a child under s10(5) CA 1989:

- any party to a marriage (whether or not subsisting) in relation to whom the child is a child of the family. A child is a child of the family in relation to the parties to a marriage, which means a child of both of those parties and any other child, except a foster child, who has been treated by both of those parties as a child of their family under s105 CA 1989;
- any person with whom the child has lived for a period of at least three years. The period of three years need not be continuous but must not have begun more than five years before, or ended more than three months before, the making of the application;
- local authority foster carers who have had the child living with them for one year prior to the application;
- any person who:
    - (i) in any case where a residence order is in force with respect to the child, has the consent of each of the persons in whose favour the order was made;
    - (ii) in any case where the child is in the care of a local authority, has the consent of that authority; or
    - (iii) in any other case, has the consent of each of those (if any) who have parental responsibility for the child.

In limited circumstances a local authority foster carer and a special guardian can apply for a residence order under the CA 1989 and further reference should be made to practitioner texts.

If a client does not fall into the above categories, they must apply to the court for leave to apply for an order under s10(2) CA 1989.

27.2.1 CHILDREN APPLYING FOR AN ORDER

A child can apply for leave to apply for a s8 CA 1989 order (see the **Glossary** for 'Leave'). Leave is the permission of the court. Where the person applying for leave to make an application for a s8 CA 1989 order is the child concerned, the court may only grant leave if it is satisfied that he has sufficient understanding to make the proposed application for the s8 CA 1989 order.

Even if the child has sufficient understanding, the granting of leave by the court remains a discretion only and the child's welfare is not paramount (*M v Warwickshire County Council* [2007] EWCA Civ 1084). Applications should be approached cautiously as the parents are in conflict and the child may be exposed to evidence of the parents that it would be better for them not to hear and may have to be cross-examined (*Re N (Contact: Minor Seeking Leave to Defend and Removal of Guardian)* [2003] 1 FLR 652). Whilst the s1(3) CA 1989 checklist does not specifically apply, the court may consider other matters as being relevant to deliberations about granting leave to a child. The leading case for the approach that the court should take is *Re H (Residence Order: Child's Application for Leave)* [2000] I FLR 780 where a 12-year-old boy applied for leave. The application was refused as the son wished to live with the father and the father could advance the son's wishes through his own application.

27.2.2 OTHER POTENTIAL APPLICANTS

Where a person does not fit into any of the categories listed above, an application for leave will have to be made.

Practical Considerations

Grandparents are a category of applicants who wish to apply for a s8 CA 1989 order and will have to apply for leave. When families separate, often grandparents lose contact as their son or daughter ceases to have contact with their child or relationships break down and contact becomes very difficult. Sometimes a grandparent will apply for a residence order should neither parent prove capable of caring for the child. Grandparents will have to apply for leave to apply for a contact or residence order but it is the author's experience that leave is rarely refused in such circumstances.

S10(9) CA 1989 states that where the person applying for leave to make an application for a s8 order is not the child concerned, the court shall, in deciding whether or not to grant leave, have particular regard to:

- the nature of the proposed application for the s8 order;
- the applicant's connection with the child;
- any risk there might be of that proposed application disrupting the child's life to such an extent that he would be harmed by it; and
- where the child is being looked after by a local authority:
  - the authority's plans for the child's future; and
  - the wishes and feelings of the child's parents.

Other factors may also be relevant but the child's welfare is not the paramount consideration as stated in *G v F (Contact and Shared Residence: Application for Leave)* [1998] 2 FLR 799 and the court must have regard to the merits of the proposed application (*M v Warwickshire County Council* [2007] EWCA Civ 1084). In considering the risk of disruption, it is not only the risk of disruption from the making of the substantive application that is relevant, but also the disruption that there may be to the child's life if the application succeeds (*Re M (Care: Contact: Grandmother's Application)* [1995] 2 FLR 86). However, in *Re H (Children)* [2003] EWCA Civ 369, the Court of Appeal stated that the test used should be that found in s10(9) CA 1989 and that the question for the court was whether the application was disruptive to the litigation process.

27.2.3 PROCEDURE FOR OBTAINING LEAVE

The party wishing to apply for leave should file:

- Form C2 requesting permission setting out the reasons for the application; and
- Form C100 stating the s8 order applied for (assuming leave is granted to proceed) (reproduced at the end of this chapter).

From the court granting leave, the procedure is as described at **27.5**.

27.2.4 EXISTING PROCEEDINGS

One of the aims of the CA 1989 was to avoid the duplication of proceedings concerning children and the CA 1989 tries to ensure that orders concerning children can be made within existing proceedings. The court can make a s8 CA 1989 order within the following existing proceedings under s8(3) and (4) CA 1989 in 'family proceedings'. Family proceedings are any proceedings:

- under the inherent jurisdiction (see **Glossary**) of the High Court in relation to children; and
- Parts I, II, and IV of the Children Act 1989;
- the Matrimonial Causes Act 1973;
- Schs 5 and 6 to the Civil Partnership Act 2004;
- the Adoption and Children Act 2002;
- the Domestic Proceedings and Magistrates' Courts Act 1978;
- Part III of the Matrimonial and Family Proceedings Act 1984;
- the Family Law Act 1996;
- ss11 and 12 of the Crime and Disorder Act 1998.

27.3 FUNDING AND ADR

As described in **Chapter 2**, public funding will only be available for private children law proceedings until April 2013. As stated above, a limited number of cases involving child abuse or domestic violence may attract some funding. Until April 2013, initial advice and assistance can be secured through Legal Help if the client is eligible. Should the case require funding for further negotiation, family help (lower) can fund further negotiation, subject to eligibility. If it is necessary to issue proceedings, family help (higher) will be required, again subject to eligibility. It is important to advise clients that application for family help (higher) will require attendance at a meeting with a mediator (unless the case is deemed unsuitable) before any application can be processed. Usually the funding is restricted to commencing proceedings in the family proceedings courts, as this is a cheaper option. If there are existing proceedings, these proceedings should be consolidated to be heard together.

Clients should also be encouraged to attempt to settle any dispute about children informally through mediation or collaborative law (see **Chapter 3**). As public funding is withdrawn, more parents may choose to use mediation to resolve disputes.

27.4 RULES AND COURTS

For applications under the CA 1989, the rules for applications are found in the Family Procedure Rules 2010 (FPR 2010). Prior to this set of rules, there were a number of complex sets of rules. The FPR 2010 aims to combine most types of proceedings concerning children into Part 12 (save for a few rare and unusual applications). Adoption is covered in Part 14 FPR 2010 (and is not covered by this text) and rules regarding the representation of children are found in Part 15 FPR.

The CA 1989 created a unified structure involving the High Court, county courts, and the family proceedings courts. How work is allocated between them is dealt with by the Allocation and Transfer of Proceedings Order 2008. Certain proceedings must be started in certain courts:

- High Court—if proceedings are complex, the outcome of the proceedings would be important to the public in general, or for other substantial reasons, proceedings may be commenced in the High Court;
- county courts, which are divided into the following categories:
  - divorce county court;
  - family hearing centre;
  - care centre.

The county court can be used for proceedings that are more complex than usual (but insufficiently complex for the High Court) or where proceedings are linked to already existing proceedings;

- family proceedings courts.

There are some proceedings that should be started in the family proceedings courts, e.g. an application for PR by the child's father, and the order is drafted to ensure that as many applications as possible are commenced in family proceedings courts. Family proceedings courts are staffed by specially trained magistrates.

27.5 PROCEDURE FOR A S8 CA 1989 ORDER

27.5.1 ISSUING THE APPLICATION

Where the application is for a free-standing order (see **Glossary**), the Form C100 is completed to commence proceedings for a s8 CA 1989 order. A Form C1 is used for all other applications (see **Chapter 31** for an example). Form C100 is straightforward to complete, although the following guidance is offered on the following paragraphs:

Section 5 asks whether the children named have suffered or are at risk of suffering harm from any of the following:

- any form of domestic abuse;
- violence within the household;
- child abduction;
- other conduct or behaviour;

by any person who is or has been involved in caring for the child(ren) or who lives with, or has contact with, the child(ren). Form C2 also asks the same question.

If the applicant answers 'yes', the Supplemental Information Form C1A must be completed.

The procedure to be adopted in cases of domestic abuse is dealt with at **27.6**.

Paragraph 3 of Form C100 must also be completed with care. The form asks for brief reasons for the application and to indicate the order sought from the court. Avoid the temptation to write a full statement in this part of the form. The information required should address the no order principle as stated in s1(5) CA 1989 but not give a huge amount of detail.

For applications made within divorce proceedings or for the dissolution of a civil partnership, an application is made on Form C100. The application will be heard within the divorce or dissolution proceedings by a district or circuit judge. If the parents do not agree about residence or contact, this can be indicated in the statement of arrangements (Form M4: see **Chapter 8**). This will not be sufficient to commence s8 CA 1989 proceedings and Form C100 must be issued. The respondent can apply in their own right on Form C2. The district judge or circuit judge will hear the proceedings and the judge will not have to consider the arrangements for children under s41 Matrimonial Causes Act 1973 (see **Chapter 8**).

27.5.2 RESPONDENTS

There are a number of people who must be made respondents to an application for a s8 CA 1989 order and these are found in Appendix 3 CA 1989:

- every person the applicant believes to have PR for the child;
- where the child is subject to a care order, every person the applicant believes to have PR immediately prior to the making of the care order;
- if the application is to vary, extend, or to discharge an order, the parties to the proceedings leading to the original order that the applicant wishes to vary, extend, or discharge.

27.5.3 JOINING IN OTHER PARTIES

If a person wishes to become a party or cease to be a party, this is done by filing a Form C2. If a person has PR, the court must grant their request (r12.3(2) FPR 2010). For a person without PR, the court can grant the order with a hearing or representations or have a hearing where parties can make representations.

Practical Considerations

If acting for an unmarried father without PR, an application for PR should in most cases be made should proceedings commence.

27.5.4 SERVICE

The application must be served on the respondent(s) together with Form C6. Form C6 sets out the time, date, and place of the hearing or directions appointment. These must be served on all respondents at least 14 days before the hearing or directions appointment. R12.8 FPR 2010 deals with service. The customary method of service is by first class post to the respondent(s) or their solicitor, if they are represented.

The applicant must complete and file Form C9, a statement of service. Form C9 confirms the date of service, method of service, documents served, and gives the details of the party who has been served.

27.5.5 WITHOUT NOTICE APPLICATIONS

An application may be made without notice in cases of emergency and the rules are found at r12.16 FPR 2010. In *Note: Re J (Children: Ex Parte Orders)* [1997] 1 FLR 606 Hale J made some observations regarding the care required when making without notice orders. Courts have a special responsibility to ensure that ex parte orders that can harm the interests of a child or an adult are not made without good reason. An order forcing a child to be handed over to a parent they do not know well should only be made in exceptional circumstances. Practitioners should take scrupulous care in relation to the application and the implementation of any order.

27.5.6 ACKNOWLEDGEMENT

Each respondent to the application is required to complete and file a Form C7 in acknowledgement within 14 days of being served with the application.

Form C7 requires the respondent to give details identifying him and whether he has a solicitor (and details of that solicitor) and an address to where correspondence may be sent. The respondent must state whether he has received the application, whether he opposes it, and whether he intends to apply for an order. Indicating such an intention is not sufficient to commence an application and proceedings for an order should be commenced in the usual way (see **27.5.1**).

If a Form C1A has been served, the C7 asks if this has been received and whether the respondent wishes to comment on any of the statements made by the applicant. This is done by completing a Form C1A. If the respondent believes that the child has suffered harm as described at **27.5.1**, the respondent should complete and file his own Form C1A.

27.5.7 CONCILIATION APPOINTMENT

The District Judge's Direction (Children: Conciliation) (12 March 2004) [2004] 1 FLR 974 requires that all s8 CA 1989 applications are listed in the conciliation list. The party with care of the child should bring all children over nine years old to the court to be seen by a CAFCASS officer. Regular conciliation lists are held at courts every week.

All parties and their legal advisers must attend. This is an opportunity for parents/parties to reach agreement with the assistance of the CAFCASS officer. If the parties reach agreement, the court can make orders if necessary to do so. If no agreement is forthcoming, the district judge will give directions.

Conciliation appointments are conducted slightly differently in different parts of the country.

27.5.8 DIRECTIONS

On 21 July 2004, the President of the Family Division announced the implementation of a new framework for private children law cases, the Private Law Programme; this can be found in the online resources. In November 2004, guidance was circulated to county courts and High Courts and extended to family proceedings courts in 2006. It now forms Practice Direction 12B FPR 2010. It has an overriding objective and this is to enable the court to deal with every (children) case:

(a) expeditiously and fairly;

(b) in ways that ensure, so far as is practicable, that the parties are on an equal footing;

(c) so far as is practicable, in ways which are proportionate:

- to the nature, importance and complexity of the issues; and
- to the nature and extent of the intervention proposed in the private and family life of the children and adults involved.

The first hearing dispute resolution appointments (FHDRA) will take place four to six weeks after the issue of the application and, as stated earlier, be attended by parents and children over nine years. The district judge will identify immediate safety issues, identify the aim of the proceedings, the timescale within which the aim can be achieved, the issues between the parties, the opportunities for the resolution of those issues by appropriate referrals for support and assistance, and any subsequent steps that may be permitted or required. Wherever possible, a CAFCASS practitioner shall be available to the court and to the family whose purpose and priority is to facilitate early dispute resolution rather than the provision of a formal report.

Save in exceptional circumstances (e.g. safety) or where immediate agreement is possible so that the principle of early dispute resolution can be facilitated, the district judge will direct that the family shall be referred for support and assistance.

Directions are made at preliminary hearings in order to prepare the case for a final hearing, and to produce the evidence required to hear all of the issues: the rule can be found at r12.12 FPR 2010. Directions can be made of the court's own motion having given the parties notice of its intention to do so, and an opportunity to attend and be heard or to make written representations, on the written request of a party specifying the direction that is sought, filed, and served on the other parties, or on the written request of a party specifying the direction that is sought, to which the other parties consent and which they or their representatives have signed.

In an urgent case directions can be made orally or without notice to the parties.

The court has a very wide discretion to grant directions. At r12.12(2) FPR 2010 are examples of the types of directions that can be given; it is not an exhaustive list. The list at r12.12(2) FPR 2010 comprises directions for:

(a) the timetable for the proceedings;

(b) varying the time within which or by which an act is required, by these rules or by other rules or court, to be done;

(c) the attendance of the child;

(d) the appointment of a guardian ad litem, whether under s41 or otherwise, or of a solicitor under s41(3);

(e) the service of documents;

(f) the submission of evidence including experts' reports;

(g) the preparation of welfare reports under s7.

The Practice Direction: Revised Private Law Programme [2010] came into force on 1 April 2010. It replaced the prior practice direction and has been revised to build on the successes of the initial programme and to take account of recent developments in the law and practice associated with private family law.

There has been growing recognition of the impact of domestic violence and abuse, drug and alcohol misuse, and mental illness, on the proper consideration of the issues in private family law; this includes the acceptance that court orders, even those made by consent, must be scrutinized to ensure that they are safe and take account of any risk factors. Coupled with this is the need to take account of the duty on CAFCASS, pursuant to s16A CA 1989, to undertake risk assessments where a child is at risk of harm.

Where an application is made to a court under the CA 1989, the child's welfare is the court's paramount concern. The court will apply the principle of the 'overriding objective' to enable it to deal with a case justly, having regard to the welfare principles involved. So far as practicable the court will:

- deal expeditiously and fairly with every case;
- deal with a case in ways which are proportionate to the nature, importance, and complexity of the issues;
- ensure that the parties are on an equal footing;
- save unnecessary expense;
- allot to each case an appropriate share of the court's resources, while taking account of the need to allot resources to other cases.

The court will give effect to the overriding objective when applying this programme and when exercising its powers to manage cases.

27.5.9 TIMETABLES

S1(2) CA 1989 states that the court should avoid delay as this is detrimental to the child and s11(1) CA 1989 requires the court to draw up a timetable and give directions to ensure that parties adhere to the timetable.

27.5.10 DOCUMENTARY EVIDENCE

Evidence can only be submitted in s8 CA 1989 proceedings with the permission of the court (r12.19(2) FPR 2010). This is to prevent a multiplicity of documents that may only increase the dispute and add to the time that the court must use to consider the proceedings. Where documentary evidence is required by the courts, it is clear that advance disclosure should be given. Evidence cannot be admitted or relied upon unless it has been disclosed to the other parties, unless the court gives permission.

Practical Considerations

When drafting a statement, the client's position should be made clear and the statement should be drafted with the principles of the CA 1989 in mind. Restraint should be practised if the client suggests that material should be included in the statement that attacks the other party gratuitously or seeks to inflame the situation further.

As well as statements, thought should be given to any other supporting evidence required by the client's case. Independent witnesses can offer evidence on a party's lifestyle or unsavoury associations. Care should be taken when a client suggests a number of witnesses claiming to support their case, as the client may be overly optimistic about the client's evidence or it may merely repeat evidence stated elsewhere.

27.5.11 CAFCASS

The Children and Family Court Advisory and Support Service (CAFCASS) was set up on 1 April 2001 under the provisions of the Criminal Justice and Court Services Act 2000, which brought together the family court services previously provided by the Family Court Welfare Service, the Guardian ad Litem Service, and the Children's Division of the Official Solicitor's Office. CAFCASS is independent of the courts, social services, education and health authorities, and all similar agencies.

Its role is to:

- safeguard and promote the welfare of children;
- give advice to the family courts;
- make provision for children to be represented;
- provide information, advice, and support to children and their families.

Its website is part of the online resources.

In s8 CA 1989 disputes, the court may under s7 CA 1989 order a report, commonly known as a welfare report, to be compiled by CAFCASS.

A CAFCASS officer will have access to all of the court files and documents and will be aware of the issues between the parties. The CAFCASS officer will visit both parents (and all other parties to the proceedings) in their homes, if possible. The CAFCASS officer will also expect to see the parties with the child(ren) and observe how they interact. If the children are old enough and have sufficient maturity, the CAFCASS officer may meet the children separately to gain their views. The CAFCASS officer may also make other enquiries that are necessary for the report, including of the children's teacher, GP, or social workers. The CAFCASS officer will use all of this information to compile her report and the report may make recommendations concerning the application before the court.

The gathering of this information will take some time and the wait for a CAFCASS report can be quite lengthy. The expected wait for a report can be between 12 and 18 weeks. Any report should be requested early in proceedings if the court does not order one of its own right. To ask for a CAFCASS report late in proceedings may run the risk that the court considers that the harm caused by the delay outweighs the benefit of the court having the report.

The CAFCASS report will inevitably contain some evidence that would normally be considered to be hearsay, e.g. 'Sarah's primary school teacher, Mrs Billings, told me that Sarah is very disruptive following contact with her father.' Courts will accept this evidence and attach the weight that they feel to be appropriate.

Once a CAFCASS report is received, it is essential to gain client's instructions on it and to gain their reaction to the comments and recommendations made by the CAFCASS officer. Clients should take a realistic view of their case if the CAFCASS officer makes a recommendation in favour of the other parent or party. The court greatly values the CAFCASS report as the CAFCASS officer has seen the parties, children, and others at first hand, unlike the court, and as a result the report carries great weight. A client needs to be given realistic advice if the recommendation in the report does not support their position. In *Re M (Residence)* [2005] 1 FLR 656, it was stated that the court should not depart from the recommendations of the CAFCASS officer without first giving them the opportunity to respond to any misgivings held by the court.

The CAFCASS officer can be cross-examined by either party if there are flaws in the reporting of evidence or recommendations that are unsound given the evidence of the case and this was confirmed in *Re I and H (Contact: Right to Give Evidence)* [1998] 1 FLR 876.

27.5.12 EXPERT EVIDENCE

Should either party wish to introduce medical or psychological evidence concerning a child, they will have to gain the permission of the court under r12.19(2) FPR 2010. The child may not be examined without the court's permission for the purposes of compiling expert evidence and any such evidence will not be admitted without the court's permission.

The Practice Direction (Experts in Family Proceedings Relating to Children) came into effect on 1 April 2008 and aims to assist the court to:

- identify, narrow, and, where possible, agree the issues between the parties;
- provide an opinion about a matter not within the expertise and skill of the court;
- encourage the early identification of questions that need to be answered by an expert;
- encourage disclosure of full and frank information between the parties, the court, and any expert instructed.

27.5.13 ATTENDANCE AT HEARINGS

All parties must attend the hearing of which they have had notice unless the court directs otherwise under r12.14 FPR 2010. If the child is a party, they should attend unless the court believes that the child should be absent having regard to the matters being discussed or evidence to be given at the hearing, or if the child is represented by a children's guardian or solicitor.

If a respondent is absent, the court may only proceed in their absence if it is proved that he had reasonable notice and the circumstances of the case justify proceeding. If the applicant does not appear, the case can proceed if the court has sufficient evidence or can refuse the application. If neither party appears, the court may refuse the application.

27.5.14 THE HEARING

Hearings, whether directions appointments or final hearings, are heard privately in chambers or hearing rooms under r12.21 FPR 2010.

The Ministry of Justice announced on 16 December 2008 that family courts at all levels will be opened up to media access. Under the proposed rule changes:

- accredited media will be allowed to attend family proceedings;
- the judge will be able to exclude the media from specific proceedings where the welfare of children or the safety of the parties requires it;
- there will be a pilot project, which started in spring 2009, involving publication of anonymized judgments from the lower courts;
- parties will be allowed to disclose information to advisers (such as MPs) during the course of proceedings.

Consideration will also be given to allowing access to adoption proceedings.

The court may decide the order of proceedings in a final hearing in terms of evidence and speeches and generally, according to r12.12(2) FPR 2010, the order is as follows:

- applicant;
- any party with PR for the child;
- other respondents;
- guardian ad litem (very rare in private law cases);
- the child, if a party.

A note of evidence will be kept by the court.

27.5.15 THE DECISION

The decision of the court should be made as soon as practicable after the final hearing of proceedings (r29.11). The order shall be recorded by an officer of the court in the proper form. The order shall be served as soon as practicable by the proper officer on the parties to the proceedings and on anyone with whom the child is living.

27.5.16 APPEALS

An appeal from the family proceedings courts is heard in the High Court (s91(4) CA 1989) and will be heard by a High Court judge of the Family Division who will generally sit in public.

An appeal from the county court or the High Court will be directly to the Court of Appeal. An appeal against the decision of a district judge will usually be made to the judge of the court in which the decision is made (r30 FPR 2010) but it is not a rehearing.

The time-limits for filing and serving a notice of appeal are:

- 14 days after the decision against which the appeal is brought; or
- as the court may direct.

27.5.17 INTERIM APPLICATIONS

In an emergency (see child abduction), an application can be completed asking for an early hearing before a judge in chambers. The hearing is likely to be brief as the application itself will be at an early stage. The court will make a decision, any directions requested or required, and, most probably, a welfare report from CAFCASS.

FIGURE 27.1 FLOWCHART OF PROCEDURE IN PRIVATE CHILDREN CASES

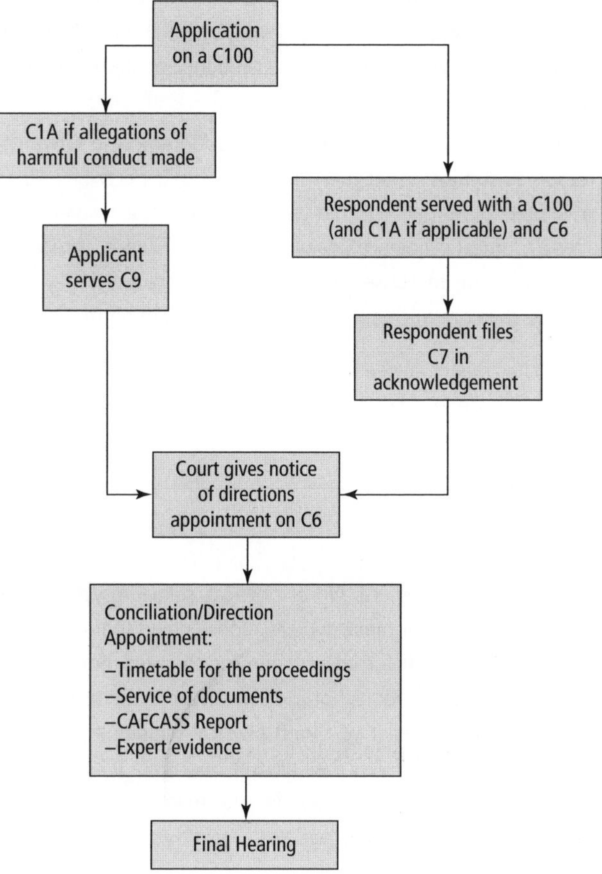

The funding for such an application will have to be secured before the hearing. This will be straightforward if the client is privately paying but less so if publicly funded. An application can be made to the Legal Services Commission for emergency funding (see **Chapter 2**) until April 2013; a decision can be made through devolved powers. If no funding is secured, the application will have to be made using the usual procedure.

27.6 ALLEGATIONS OF DOMESTIC ABUSE

In the Form C1A, the applicant is required to give the court details of any harm or violence referred to in Forms C100, C1, or C2. This highlights to the court at a very early stage the possibility that the child(ren) involved in the proceedings have suffered, or are at risk of suffering, specific forms of harm.

On 9 May 2008, the President of the Family Division issued a Practice Direction: Residence and Contact Orders: Domestic Violence and Harm [2008] 2 FLR 103 and can be found in Practice Direction 12J FPR 2010. This Practice Direction prescribes the procedure to be adopted when there are allegations or reasons to suppose that a child or party has experienced domestic abuse, violence, or other harm or there is a risk of this occurring. The Practice Direction is reproduced almost in its entirety here with some added explanation as it is extremely important in practice, although, as yet, there has been little guidance from the court. The Practice Direction issued on 9 May 2008 was reissued to reflect the decision of the House of Lords in *Re B (Children)* [2008] UKHL 35, in which Baroness Hale confirmed that a fact-finding hearing is part of the process of trying a case and is not a separate exercise, and that where the case is then adjourned for further hearing it remains part heard. Paragraphs 15 and 23 of the Practice Direction have been amended to reinforce this principle and are reproduced here.

Introduction

1. This Practice Direction applies to any family proceedings in the High Court, a county court or a magistrates' court in which an application is made for a residence order or a contact order in respect of a child under the Children Act 1989 ('the 1989 Act') or the Adoption and Children Act 2002 ('the 2002 Act') or in which any question arises about residence or about contact between a child and a parent or other family member.
2. The practice set out in this Direction is to be followed in any case in which it is alleged, or there is otherwise reason to suppose, that the subject child or a party has experienced domestic violence perpetrated by another party or that there is a risk of such violence. For the purpose of this Direction, the term 'domestic violence' includes physical violence, threatening or intimidating behaviour and any other form of abuse which, directly or indirectly, may have caused harm to the other party or to the child or which may give rise to the risk of harm.

('Harm' in relation to a child means ill-treatment or the impairment of health or development, including, for example, impairment suffered from seeing or hearing the ill-treatment of another: Children Act 1989, ss 31(9),105(1).)

Example

Domestic violence is defined by Women's Aid as physical, sexual, psychological, or financial violence that takes place within an intimate or family-type relationship and that forms a pattern of coercive and controlling behaviour. This can include forced marriage and so-called 'honour crimes'. Domestic violence may include a range of abusive behaviours, not all of which are in themselves inherently 'violent'.

A client may not necessarily present you with physical injuries and a client should be carefully screened to see if there is domestic violence within a relationship. A client may be suffering domestic violence if their partner financially controls them, isolates them from friends and family, suffers verbal or emotional abuse, and this can be categorized as domestic violence.

General principles

3. The court must, at all stages of the proceedings, consider whether domestic violence is raised as an issue, either by the parties or otherwise, and if so must:

   - identify at the earliest opportunity the factual and welfare issues involved;
   - consider the nature of any allegation or admission of domestic violence and the extent to which any domestic violence which is admitted, or which may be proved, would be relevant in deciding whether to make an order about residence or contact and, if so, in what terms;
   - give directions to enable the relevant factual and welfare issues to be determined expeditiously and fairly.

Practical Considerations

If a client instructs you that domestic violence is an issue, this should be raised within the court proceedings at the earliest opportunity in the interests of allowing a court to identify issues early in the proceedings. Should the client only divulge domestic violence as an issue late within the proceedings, this should be raised as soon as possible with the court.

4. In all cases it is for the court to decide whether an order for residence or contact accords with Section 1(1) of the 1989 Act or section 1(2) of the 2002 Act, as appropriate; any proposed residence or contact order, whether to be made by agreement between the parties or otherwise must be scrutinised by the court accordingly. The court shall not make a consent order for residence or contact or give permission for an application for a residence or contact order to be withdrawn, unless the parties are present in court, except where it is satisfied that there is no risk of harm to the child in so doing.
5. In considering, on an application for a consent order for residence or contact, whether there is any risk of harm to the child, the court shall consider all the evidence and information available. The court may direct a report under Section 7 of the 1989 Act either orally or in writing before it makes its determination; in such a case, the court may ask for information about any advice given by the officer preparing the report to the parties and whether they or the child have been referred to any other agency, including local authority children's services. If the report is not in writing, the court shall make a note of its substance on the court file.

Issue

6. Immediately on receipt of an application for a residence order or a contact order, or of the acknowledgement of the application, the court shall send a copy of it, together with any accompanying documents, to Cafcass or Cafcass Cymru, as appropriate, to enable Cafcass or Cafcass Cymru to undertake initial screening in accordance with their safeguarding policies.

Liaison

7. The Designated Family Judge, or in the magistrates' court the Justices' Clerk, shall take steps to ensure that arrangements are in place for:

   - the prompt delivery of documents to Cafcass or Cafcass Cymru in accordance with paragraph 6;
   - any information obtained by Cafcass or Cafcass Cymru as a result of initial screening or otherwise and any risk assessments prepared by Cafcass or Cafcass Cymru under section 16A of the 1989 Act to be placed before the appropriate court for consideration and directions;
   - a copy of any record of admissions or findings of fact made pursuant to paragraphs 12 & 21 below to be made available as soon as possible to any Officer of Cafcass or Welsh family proceedings officer or local authority officer preparing a report under section 7 of the 1989 Act.

Response of the court on receipt of information

8. Where any information provided to the court before the first hearing, whether as a result of initial screening by Cafcass or Cafcass Cymru or otherwise, indicates that there are issues of domestic

violence which may be relevant to the court's determination, the court may give directions about the conduct of the hearing and for written evidence to be filed by the parties before the hearing.

9. If at any stage the court is advised by Cafcass or Cafcass Cymru or otherwise that there is a need for special arrangements to secure the safety of any party or child attending any hearing, the court shall ensure that appropriate arrangements are made for the hearing and for all subsequent hearings in the case, unless it considers that these are no longer necessary.

First hearing

10. At the first hearing, the court shall inform the parties of the content of any screening report or other informations which has been provided by Cafcass or Cafcass Cymru, unless it considers that to do so would create a risk of harm to a party or the child.
11. The court must ascertain at the earliest opportunity whether domestic violence is raised as an issue and must consider the likely impact of that issue on the conduct and outcome of the proceedings. In particular, the court should consider whether the nature and effect of the domestic violence alleged is such that, if proved, the decision of the court is likely to be affected.

Admissions

12. Where at any hearing an admission of domestic violence to another person or the child is made by a party, the admission should be recorded in writing and retained on the court file.

Directions for a fact-finding hearing

13. The court should determine as soon as possible whether it is necessary to conduct a fact-finding hearing in relation to any disputed allegation of domestic violence before it can proceed to consider any final order(s) for residence or contact. Where the court determines that a finding of fact hearing is not necessary, the order shall record the reasons for that decision.
14. Where the court considers that a fact-finding hearing is necessary, it must give directions to ensure that the matters in issue are determined expeditiously and fairly and in particular it should consider:
    - directing the parties to file written statements giving particulars of the allegations made and of any response in such a way as to identify clearly the issues for determination;
    - whether material is required from third parties such as the police or health services and may give directions accordingly;
    - whether any other evidence is required to enable the court to make findings of fact in relation to the allegations and may give directions accordingly.

Practical Considerations

When advising a client, it is advisable to gather any evidence of domestic violence including medical evidence from the hospital or a GP, the police, or any witnesses. Should you be acting for someone accused of domestic violence, it is advisable to gather as much evidence as possible to support the client's case.

15. Where the court fixes a fact-finding hearing, it must at the same time fix a further hearing for determination of the application. The hearings should be arranged in such a way that they are conducted by the same judge or, in the magistrates' court, by at least the same chairperson of the justices.

Reports under s7

16. In any case where domestic violence is raised as an issue, the court should consider directing that a report on the question of contact, or any other matters relating to the welfare of the child, be prepared under section 7 of the 1989 Act by an Officer of Cafcass or a Welsh family proceedings officer (or local authority officer if appropriate), unless the court is satisfied that it is not necessary

to do so in order to safeguard the child's interests. If the court so directs, it should consider the extent of any enquiries which can properly be made at this stage and whether it is appropriate to seek information on the wishes and feelings of the child before findings of fact have been made.

Representation of the child

17. Subject to the seriousness of the allegations made and the difficulty of the case, the court shall consider whether it is appropriate for the child who is the subject of the application to be made a party to the proceedings and be separately represented. If the case is proceeding in the magistrates' court and the court considers that it may be appropriate for the child to be made a party to the proceedings, it may transfer the case to the relevant county court for determination of that issue and following such transfer the county court shall give such directions for the further conduct of the case as it considers appropriate.

Interim orders before determination of relevant facts

18. Where the court gives directions for a fact-finding hearing, the court should consider whether an interim order for residence or contact is in the interests of the child; and in particular whether the safety of the child and the residential parent can be secured before, during and after any contact.
19. In deciding any question of interim residence or contact pending a full hearing the court should:

    (a) take into account the matters set out in section 1(3) of the 1989 Act or section 1(4) of the 2002 Act ('the welfare check-list'), as appropriate;

    (b) give particular consideration to the likely effect on the child of any contact and any risk of harm, whether physical, emotional or psychological, which the child is likely to suffer as a consequence of making or declining to make an order.

20. Where the court is considering whether to make an order for interim contact, it should in addition consider:

    - the arrangements required to ensure, as far as possible, that any risk of harm to the child is minimised and that the safety of the child and the parties is secured; and in particular:
    - whether the contact should be supervised or supported, and if so, where and by whom; and
    - the availability of appropriate facilities for that purpose;
    - if direct contact is not appropriate, whether it is in the best interests of the child to make an order for indirect contact.

Practical Considerations

When there are allegations of domestic violence, the court's paramount consideration will be the welfare of the child and this encompasses their safety and emotional well-being. Although it may be frustrating for a parent who denies any allegations of domestic violence, the court may be cautious when considering an interim order as protecting the child is their priority.

The fact-finding hearing

21. At the fact-finding hearing, the court should, wherever practicable, make findings of fact as to the nature and degree of any domestic violence which is established and its effect on the child, the child's parents and any other relevant person. The court shall record its findings in writing, and shall serve a copy on the parties. A copy of any record of findings of fact or of admissions must be sent to any officer preparing a report under section 7 of the 1989 Act.
22. At the conclusion of any fact-finding hearing, the court shall consider, notwithstanding any earlier direction for a section 7 report, whether it is in the best interests of the child for the court to give further directions about the preparation or scope of any report under section 7; where necessary,

it may adjourn the proceedings for a brief period to enable the officer to make representations about the preparation or scope of any further enquiries.

The court should also consider whether it would be assisted by any social work, psychiatric, psychological or other assessment of any party or the child and if so (subject to any necessary consent) make directions for such assessment to be undertaken and for the filing of any consequent report.

23. Where the court has made findings of fact on disputed allegations, any subsequent hearing in the proceedings should be conducted by the same judge or, in the magistrates' court, by at least the same chairperson of the justices. Exceptions may be made only where observing this requirement would result in delay to the planned timetable and the judge or chairperson is satisfied, for reasons recorded in writing, that the detriment to the welfare of the child would outweigh the detriment to the fair trial of the proceedings.

In May 2010, Sir Nicholas Wall P issued his guidance in relation to split hearings, concerned that many had been taking place unnecessarily and those which were needed had nevertheless consumed disproportionate time and resources.

The main points of the President's guidance are:

- the fact that domestic abuse is put forward by the residential parent as a reason for denying contact is not automatically a reason for a split hearing;
- if the allegations are unlikely to have any impact on the court's order, there is no need for a separate fact-finding hearing;
- cases suitable for split hearings would be cases where there is a clear and stark issue, such as sexual or physical abuse;
- the attempt to avoid inefficient use of an expert's availability and cost is a good reason for a separate fact-finding hearing.

In all cases where domestic violence has occurred

24. The court should take steps to obtain (or direct the parties or an Officer of Cafcass or a Welsh family proceedings officer to obtain) information about the facilities available locally to assist any party or the child in cases where domestic violence has occurred.

25. Following any determination of the nature and extent of domestic violence, whether or not following a fact-finding hearing, the court should consider whether any party should seek advice or treatment as a precondition to an order for residence or contact being made or as a means of assisting the court in ascertaining the likely risk of harm to the child from that person, and may (with the consent of that party) give directions for such attendance and the filing of any consequent report.

Factors to be taken into account when determining whether to make residence or contact orders in all cases where domestic violence has occurred

26. When deciding the issue of residence or contact the court should, in the light of any findings of fact, apply the individual matters in the welfare checklist with reference to those findings; in particular, where relevant findings of domestic violence have been made, the court should in every case consider any harm which the child has suffered as a consequence of that violence and any harm which the child is at risk of suffering if an order for residence or contact is made and should only make an order for contact if it can be satisfied that the physical and emotional safety of the child and the parent with whom the child is living can, as far as possible, be secured before, during and after contact.

27. In every case where a finding of domestic violence is made, the court should consider the conduct of both parents towards each other and towards the child; in particular, the court should consider:

    (a) the effect of the domestic violence which has been established on the child and on the parent with whom the child is living;

(b) the extent to which the parent seeking residence or contact is motivated by a desire to promote the best interests of the child or may be doing so as a means of continuing a process of violence, intimidation or harassment against the other parent;

(c) the likely behaviour during contact of the parent seeking contact and its effect on the child;

(d) the capacity of the parent seeking residence or contact to appreciate the effect of past violence and the potential for future violence on the other parent and the child;

(e) the attitude of the parent seeking residence or contact to past violent conduct by that parent; and in particular whether that parent has the capacity to change and to behave appropriately.

Directions as to how contact is to proceed

28. Where the court has made findings of domestic violence but, having applied the welfare check-list, nonetheless considers that direct contact is in the best interests of the child, the court should consider what if any directions or conditions are required to enable the order to be carried into effect and in particular should consider:

(a) whether or not contact should be supervised, and if so, where and by whom;

(b) whether to impose any conditions to be complied with by the party in whose favour the order for contact has been made and if so, the nature of those conditions, for example by way of seeking advice or treatment (subject to any necessary consent);

(c) whether such contact should be for a specified period or should contain provisions which are to have effect for a specified period;

(d) whether or not the operation of the order needs to be reviewed; if so the court should set a date for the review and give directions to ensure that at the review the court has full information about the operation of the order.

29. Where the court does not consider direct contact to be appropriate, it shall consider whether it is in the best interests of the child to make an order for indirect contact.

The reasons of the court

30. In its judgment or reasons the court should always make clear how its findings on the issue of domestic violence have influenced its decision on the issue of residence or contact. In particular, where the court has found domestic violence proved but nonetheless makes an order, the court should always explain, whether by way of reference to the welfare check-list or otherwise, why it takes the view that the order which it has made is in the best interests of the child.

SUMMARY POINTS

- S10(4) CA 1989 outlines those people who can apply for any order and s10(5) CA 1989 those people who can apply for a contact or residence order. Those not covered by these provisions must apply for the leave of the court.
- The court will consider the nature of the application, the applicant's connection with the child, and the risk of disruption to the child's life when considering an application for leave.
- An application for a s8 order is made on a Form C100 and for all other applications the Form C1 is completed. A Form C1A should be completed in addition if there are allegations of domestic violence or other harm to the child.
- The respondent will acknowledge the application on Form C7 and the court will set a date for a conciliation/directions.
- The parties will be expected to negotiate or enter into some form of mediation, conciliation, or ADR.
- The court will make directions to allow the case to be fully explored including a timetable of the proceedings and a report form a CAFCASS officer.

- If there are allegations of domestic violence made during the proceedings, the court must follow the procedure set out in the Practice Direction: Residence and Contact Orders: Domestic Violence and Harm.

SELF-TEST QUESTIONS

1. Mary (born 3 June 2000) is the daughter of Simon and Katie, who are unmarried. Simon was arrested after assaulting Katie and was given community service. Katie is having difficulty coping on her own and asks her parents, Tim and Annie, to look after Mary.

   (a) Advise Tim and Annie whether they can apply for a residence order and the procedure that will be followed.

   (b) Advise Simon whether he can apply for a contact order and whether there are any other orders that he should apply for at the time of applying for a contact order.

   (c) Advise Katie how the court will deal with her allegations of domestic violence.

Case Study Two

David and Helena have both applied for a residence order (see Documents CA 2 and 3) at the local county court. Helena acknowledges David's application on a Form C7 (Document CA 4) and the court confirms the first hearing resolution dispute hearing (FHDRA) on Form C6 and David files a C9, a statement of service.

David's instructions to his solicitor are that Richard should be brought up with a father in order for him to have a male role model. He and Anna have created a loving home with two parents to care for Richard. David is concerned that Richard attends nursery for three mornings a week and that he should not be out of the home as much. David has moved away from Longtown, England to London and he acknowledges that Richard would have to move away from his nursery and his friends. David is convinced that Helena's new boyfriend is unsuitable company for Richard, but gives no reasons why.

Helena's instructions are that Richard is settled with her and has a routine that he enjoys. He attends an excellent nursery that he enjoys. Helena felt that Richard needed more stimulation as he is a bright child. Richard has made many friends and Helena believes that the disruption of a move would be very damaging, given that the divorce was fairly recent.

At the FHDRA, David and Helena both speak to the CAFCASS officer in an attempt to settle the case. Both parties are adamant that they wish Richard to live with them and that it would be in his best interests. Neither Helena nor David will attend mediation.

At the FHDRA, the court makes a set of directions including a report from CAFCASS (Document CA 6 gives the full set of directions) and, after 16 weeks, the report is filed at court (see Document CA 6). To find out what happens in the case, see the online case study materials!

Answers to the questions above can be found on the Online Resource Centre: www.oxfordtextbooks.co.uk/orc/familyhandbook13/.

C100

Application under the Children Act 1989 for a residence, contact, prohibited steps, specific issue section 8 order or to vary or discharge a section 8 order

To be completed by the court
Name of court
Date issued
Case number

Before completing this form please read the leaflet **'CB1 – Making an application – Children and the Family Courts'**. You can get a copy from your local court or at www.justice.gov.uk.

- Failure to complete every question or state if it does not apply, could delay the case, as the court will have to ask you to provide the additional information required.
- If there is not enough space please attach separate sheets, clearly showing the details of the children, parties, question and page number they refer to.
- Cafcass/CAFCASS CYMRU will carry out checks as it considers necessary. See Section J of leaflet CB1 for more information about Cafcass and CAFCASS CYMRU.

1. Summary of application

Some people need permission to apply - See Section C of the leaflet CB1 for details on who needs permission and how to get permission

Have you applied to the court for permission to make this application? ☐ Yes ☑ Permission not required

Your name (the applicant(s)): David Wilson

The respondent's name(s): Helena Wilson
See Sections G and H of the booklet CB1.

Please list the name(s) of the child(ren) and the type(s) of order you are applying for, starting with the oldest. To understand which order to apply for read the booklet CB1 Section D.

Child 1 - Full name of child	Date of birth	Gender	Order(s) applied for
Richard Wilson	23/02/2008	☑ Male ☐ Female	Residence Order
Relationship to applicant(s)		Relationship to respondent(s)	

Child 2 - Full name of child	Date of birth	Gender	Order(s) applied for
	__/__/____	☐ Male ☐ Female	
Relationship to applicant(s)		Relationship to respondent(s)	

Child 3 - Full name of child	Date of birth	Gender	Order(s) applied for
	__/__/____	☐ Male ☐ Female	
Relationship to applicant(s)		Relationship to respondent(s)	

C100 Application under the Children Act 1989 for a residence, contact, prohibited steps, specific issue section 8 order or to vary or discharge a section 8 order **(04.11)**

2. About you (the applicant(s))

	Applicant 1 (You)	**Applicant 2 (if applicable)**
Full names	David Wilson	
Previous names (if any)		
Gender	☑ Male ☐ Female	☐ Male ☐ Female
Date of birth (If under 18 read section R of leaflet CB1)	03/06/1971	/ /
Place of birth (town/county/country)	Longtown, England	

If you do not wish your address to be made known to the respondent, leave the details below blank and complete Confidential contact details Form C8.

Address	24 Hay Street Longtown Postcode LG2 7RD	Postcode
Home telephone number	0113789665	
Mobile telephone number	070331654	
Email address	d.wilson150@abl.com	
Have you lived at this address for more than 5 years?	☐ Yes ☑ No	☐ Yes ☐ No

If No, please provide details of all previous addresses you have lived at for the last 5 years.

If you do not wish your contact details to be made known to the Respondent, leave the details blank and complete Confidential contact details Form C8		

3. The respondents

Sections G and H of the the booklet **'CB1 - Making an application - Children and the Family Courts'** explain who a respondent is.

If there are more than 2 respondents please continue on a separate sheet.

	Respondent 1	**Respondent 2**
Full names	Helena Wilson	
Previous names (if known)		
Gender	☐ Male ☑ Female	☐ Male ☐ Female
Date of birth (If party under 18 read section R of leaflet CB1)	13/04/1971	/ /
Place of birth (town/county/country)	Longtown, England	
Address (to which documents relating to this application should be sent)	31 Rosebery Avenue Longtown Postcode LG1 8GH	Postcode
Home telephone number	0113789562	
Mobile telephone number	07033451236	
Email address	hel@skylife.com	
Have they lived at this address for more than 5 years?	☐ Yes ☑ No ☐ Don't know	☐ Yes ☐ No ☐ Don't know

If No, please provide details of all previous addresses for the last 5 years below (if known, including the dates and starting with the most recent)

Respondent 1	Respondent 2
24 Hay Street Longtown	

4. Others who should be given notice

There may be other people who should be notified of your application, for example, someone who cares for the child but is not a parent. Sections G and I of the the booklet **'CB1 - Making an application - Children and the Family Courts'** explain who others are.

	Person 1	**Person 2**
Full names		
Previous names (if known)		
Gender	☐ Male ☐ Female	☐ Male ☐ Female
Date of birth	☐☐/☐☐/☐☐☐☐	☐☐/☐☐/☐☐☐☐
Address	Postcode	Postcode
Please state their relationship to the children listed on page 1. If their relationship is not the same to each child please state their relationship to each child.		

5. Solicitors details

Do you have a solicitor acting for you?	✓ Yes ☐ No If No, see section R of leaflet CB1 for more information
	If Yes, please give the following details
Your solicitor's name	Hubert Black
Name of firm	Cooper Black
Address	67 High Street Longtown Postcode LG1 9HT
Telephone number	01333456891
Fax number	01337895412
DX number	49 Longtown
Solicitor's Reference	BB/12.12
Email address	hubert.black@cb.com

6. The child(ren)

Are any of the children known to the local authority children's services?	☐ Yes ☑ No ☐ Don't know
If Yes please state which child and the name of the Local Authority and Social worker (if known)	
Are any of the children the subject of a child protection plan	☐ Yes ☑ No ☐ Don't know
Do all the children share the same parents?	☑ Yes ☐ No
If Yes, what are the name of the parents?	David and Helena Wilson
If No, please give details of each parent and their children involved in this application	
Please state everyone who has parental responsibility for each child and how they have parental responsibility (e.g. 'child's mother', 'child's father and was married to the mother when the child was born' etc.) (See Section E of leaflet CB1 for more information)	Myself and Helena Wilson
Who do the children currently live with?	☐ Applicant(s) ☑ Respondent(s) ☐ Other
If other, please give the full address of the child, the names of any adults living with the children and their relationship to or involvement with the child. If you do not wish this information to be made known to the Respondent, leave the details blank and complete Confidential contact details Form C8	

7. Why are you making this application?

Please give brief details:	**Do not give a full statement, please provide a summary of any relevant grounds and reasons.** You may be asked to provide a full statement later.
• any previous agreements (formal or informal), and how they have broken down • your reasons for bringing this application to the court • what you want the court to do • reasons given by the respondent(s) for their actions in relation to this application.	I am concerned that my son is not properly cared for by his mother. I have a stable family life and Richard would have two people to care for him as I have a partner living with me. I wish to apply for a residence order so that Richard can come and live with me. I would offer generous contact with his mother.

8. Agreements about residence and/or contact

Have you received a copy of the 'Parenting Plan: Putting your children first: A guide for separating parents', booklet?	☑ Yes	☐ No	If No, you can get a copy free of charge from your local court or you can download a copy from the website www.tso.co.uk
Have you attended a mediation information/assessment meeting as suggested in the pre-action protocol and/or attached form FM1?	☑ Yes	☐ No	You can find your nearest family mediation service by visiting the government's website DirectGov (www.direct.gov.uk) and search using the words 'family mediation'. You will find a database of accredited family mediation services on the website.

Please give brief details about:	
• If you attended a mediation information/assessment meeting what was the outcome? • If you attended full mediation sessions what was the outcome? • If you did not use mediation please explain why	Helena refused to attend and did not come to the appointment.

9. Risk

Do you believe that the child(ren) named at Section 1 have experienced or are at risk of experiencing harm from any of the following by any person who has had contact with the child?

any form of domestic abuse/violence	☐ Yes	☑ No
child abduction	☐ Yes	☑ No
child abuse	☐ Yes	☑ No
drugs, alcohol or substance abuse	☐ Yes	☑ No
other safety or welfare concerns	☐ Yes	☑ No

If you answered Yes to any of the above, please complete form C1A (Supplemental information form).

10. Other court cases which concern the child(ren) listed on page 1

Are you aware of any other court cases now, or at any time in the past, which concern any of the child(ren) at Section 1?

☐ Yes — If Yes, please attach a copy of any relevant order, and completed the details of the Cafcass/CAFCASS CYMRU officer and child's solicitor below. If you do not have a copy of the order please complete all the additional details below.

☑ No — If No, please **go to Section 11**

Additional details

Name of child(ren)

Name of the court where proceedings heard

Case no.

Date/year (if known)

Name and office (if known) of Cafcass/CAFCASS CYMRU officer

Name and address of child's solicitor, if known

Postcode

If the above details are different for each child please provide details on additional sheets.

Please tick if additional sheets are attached. ☐

11. Attending the court

Section N of the booklet **'CB1 - Making an application - Children and the Family Courts'** provides information about attending court.

If you require an interpreter, you must tell the court now so that one can be arranged.

Do you or any of the parties need an interpreter at court? ☐ Yes ☑ No

If Yes, please specify the language and dialect:

If attending the court, do you or any of the parties involved have a disability for which you require special assistance or special facilities? ☐ Yes ☑ No

If Yes, please say what the needs are

Please say whether the court needs to make any special arrangements for you to attend court (e.g. providing you with a separate waiting room from the respondent or other security provisions).

Court staff may get in touch with you about the requirements

12. Statement of truth

*delete as appropriate

*[I believe] [The applicant/respondent believes] that the facts stated in this application are true.

*I am duly authorised by the applicant/respondent to sign this statement.

Print full name: David Wilson

Name of applicant solicitors firm: Cooper Black

Signed: [signature] Dated 01/06/2012

(Applicant) (Applicant's solicitor)

Position or office held (If signing on behalf of firm or company)

Proceedings for contempt of court may be brought against a person who makes or causes to be made, a false statement in a document verified by a statement of truth.

continued over the page

What to do now

- ☑ Check you have attached copies of any **relevant orders** (as per Section 10).
- ☑ Check you have completed and **signed** Section 12.
- ☑ You must provide a **copy** of the application and attached documents for each of the respondents and one for the Children and Family Court Advisory and Support Service (Cafcass or CAFCASS CYMRU).
- ☑ Check you have included dates of birth for all parties and children
- ☑ Is Form C1A attached (if applicable)?
- ☑ Are any additional sheets attached?
- ☑ If you have included additional sheets you must add the names of the parties and children at the top of the page and details of the questions and page number the additional sheets relate to.
- ☑ Check you have attached the correct fee. The leaflet 'EX50 County court fees' provides information about court fees you will have to pay.

Now take or send your application with the correct fee and correct number of copies to the court.

Court fees

You may be exempt from paying all or part of the fee. The combined booklet and application form 'EX160A Court Fees - Do you have to pay them' gives more information. You can get a copy from the court or download a copy from our website at www.justice.gov.uk

28 CHILD ABDUCTION

28.1 INTRODUCTION

This chapter will:

- **examine the phenomenon of parental child abduction;**
- **examine the national and international law assisting parents seeking the return of a child;**
- **examine the law and procedure relevant to preventing child abduction.**

'Child abduction' is an emotive term conjuring images of children being removed by strangers and disappearing and the involvement of police and the criminal law. In the context of family, child abduction refers to the removal of children by a parent to another country without the permission of the other parent or the permission of the court. This chapter covers the law and procedure of recovering a child removed from the jurisdiction as well as considering what steps can be taken to prevent a child being removed in the first place. This chapter covers a highly specialist area of law and does so as an introduction only. The Law Society's Family Law Protocol recommends that all lawyers should know the steps and procedures to be taken if a child is threatened with abduction or is actually abducted. However, this area of work is highly complex and should only be undertaken by specialist lawyers.

28.2 THE PROBLEM

In the online resources, you will find links to organizations dealing with child abduction and also the Ministry of Justice and the Foreign Office. There are three main categories of parental child abduction dealt with by the Foreign Office:

- wrongful removal abduction—the removal of a child from the jurisdiction without the other parent's consent;
- wrongful retention—where a child has been wrongfully retained during an overseas trip;
- threat of abduction—a risk that a child may be taken out of the jurisdiction.

Reunite, a charity specializing in advice and information on parental child abduction, reports a 158% increase in the number of abduction cases reported to it between 1995 and 2007. It reports that one child per day is abducted by a parent. Clearly the 'left behind' parent will wish to see the child and satisfy themselves that the child is safe and well. From a legal point of view, the parent has disobeyed the law and taken the child from the jurisdiction, irrespective of whether it is in the best interests of the child.

28.2.1 JURISDICTION

When a child is removed from 'the jurisdiction', this means from England and Wales. Removal of a child to Scotland and Northern Ireland will be considered a removal from the jurisdiction as much as a removal to the USA would be. Where the child has been removed to or wrongfully retained in has an impact on which rules will apply (see **28.5**).

28.2.2 IN WHICH CIRCUMSTANCES IS REMOVAL LAWFUL?

There are some circumstances when the removal of a child from the jurisdiction is lawful, e.g. if there are no Children Act 1989 (CA 1989) orders preventing the parent from removing the child from the jurisdiction (see **28.4**) and all parents and people with parental responsibility (PR) or guardians agree to the child being removed. This would be the case where the child goes on a foreign holiday with the consent of every parent and person with PR.

Where a residence order is in force (see **Chapter 26**) under s13(2) CA 1989, a child may be taken out of the jurisdiction for a period of less than one month by the person in whose favour the residence order is made.

28.2.3 CHILD ABDUCTION ACT 1984

S1(1) Child Abduction Act 1984 (CAA 1984) makes it a criminal offence for a person 'connected' with a child under 16 to take or send the child out of the UK without the appropriate consent. When advising a client about taking a child out of the jurisdiction, their attention should be drawn to this offence, as many clients are not aware of it.

A person is connected with a child if:

- he is a parent of the child; or
- in the case of a child whose parents were not married to each other at the time of his birth, there are reasonable grounds for believing that he is the father of the child; or
- he is a guardian of the child; or
- he is a person in whose favour a residence order is in force with respect to the child; or
- he has custody of the child.

'Appropriate consent', in relation to a child, means the consent of the child's mother or father (if he has PR), any guardian of the child, any person in whose favour a residence order is in force, any person who has custody of the child, or the leave of the court granted under or by virtue of any provision of Part II of the CA 1989.

As stated at **28.2.2**, a person with a residence order can remove the child for a period of less than one month.

The law does provide a limited defence to this offence. A person does not commit an offence under this section by doing anything without the consent of another person whose consent is required if he does it in the belief that the other person has consented; or would consent if he was aware of all the relevant circumstances; or he has taken all reasonable steps to communicate with the other person but has been unable to communicate with him; or the other person has unreasonably refused to consent.

As with all criminal offences, it is a deterrent to such actions but not a preventative measure in its own right. There are other measures that a parent fearing unlawful removal can take.

28.3 PREVENTATIVE MEASURES AND THE CRIMINAL LAW

There are some preventative measures that can be taken by a parent concerned by the risk of abduction by the other parent.

28.3.1 SELF-HELP

Practical Considerations

Reunite is a charity specializing in advice and support to parents involved in child abduction cases. Reunite produces an extremely useful guide to preventing abduction, which can be accessed by parents who wish to take any preventative measures they can.

Further details can be found in the online resources.

A parent can compile a file of documents relating to the child including photographs, birth certificate, any CA 1989 orders, and a set of fingerprints. For a potential abductor, a recent photograph should be kept and as much information as possible about them including details of any family abroad or possible contacts.

28.3.2 PASSPORTS

A passport is obtainable for the child by either parent unless an objection has been lodged at a passport office of the United Kingdom Identity and Passport Service. A father will require the consent of the mother if he does not have PR. An objector can ask the Passport Service not to issue a child with a passport if a UK court has made one of the following orders:

- a prohibited steps order under s8 CA 1989;
- a residence order if the objector has the residence order made in favour of the objector;
- an order that the removal of the child from the jurisdiction is against the court's wishes (e.g. s36 Family Law Act 1986);
- an order awarding the objector care and control or custody of the child;
- an order specifying that the objector's consent is necessary to the removal of the child;
- an order requiring surrender of the passport and forbidding the issue of a further passport.

A mother can lodge an objection where the father does not have PR. If the child has their own passport, it should be recovered, if necessary by court order.

28.3.3 PORT ALERT

If the client is fearful of their child being removed by the other parent within the next 48 hours, the police should be contacted and the system of 'port alert' commenced. Details of port alert can be found in Practice Direction [1986] 1 All ER 983. This system is operated by the police in conjunction with immigration officers who attempt to prevent the removal of the child.

In order to issue a port alert, the police must be satisfied that:

- there is a real and imminent danger of the child being removed. 'Imminent' means within the next 24–48 hours and 'real' means that the port alert is necessary and must not be used as an insurance measure;
- the child is under 16 or a ward or there is a residence order in force or an order of the court preventing removal.

The client or their solicitor should attend a police station and be prepared to give detailed information concerning the child, the potential abductor's flights or travel plans, and the person applying. If there is a court order in existence, this should be produced to the police or, if one is being applied for, the details should be telephoned or faxed to the police as soon as possible.

If the police are satisfied that there is a real and imminent danger of the child being abducted, the child's name and details are circulated on a 'stop list' to airports and ferry ports. The child's name remains on the stop list for four weeks and immigration officers will attempt to prevent the child from being removed. Realistically, a port alert has a much better chance of success if the travel details (e.g. flight numbers) can be given in as much detail as possible or the port from which the child may be taken is known.

28.4 COURT APPLICATIONS

Child abduction cases involve great urgency and great expertise in a complex area of national and international law. The Family Law Protocol cautions that international child abduction law is a rapidly developing, highly specialist area of law and that specialist advice is essential for parents.

The Solicitors Regulatory Code of Conduct also states that a solicitor should not act for a client where they have insufficient resources or lack the competence to deal with the matter.

Unless a solicitor has experience in dealing with international child abduction, the case must be passed urgently to a firm that has the necessary experience.

There are a variety of applications that can be taken before the courts and each will depend upon whether abduction is threatened and where the child has been removed to.

Practical Considerations

When a client walks through the door, an adviser should act urgently and do the following:

- take full details of the child—the parents, people with PR, their foreign connections, any recent travel or travel plans, the whereabouts of the child's passport (if they have one), and the current whereabouts of the child;
- take full details of the events leading up to the abduction or any threats of abductions;
- take full details of any existing CA 1989 orders or any proceedings already in existence in this jurisdiction or any other jurisdiction;
- consider involving the police for a port alert—find out as much as possible about the potential routes of travel;
- take the names and addresses of anyone who may have information concerning the child's whereabouts or may be hiding the child and abducting parent;
- if the child has been removed consider which law will apply—the European Convention or the Hague Convention.

As stated above, do not take on a case unless the firm has sufficient experience of acting in such cases. Reunite's website contains a list of firms that undertake this type of work should a referral be required. This can be found in the online resources.

28.4.1 DISCLOSURE OF CHILD'S WHEREABOUTS

Section 33 Family Law Act 1986 allows the court to order a person to disclose information concerning a child if the court has reason to believe they may have relevant information.

A person is not excused by reason that giving the information may incriminate them, although any admission or statement made in compliance with an order under s33 Family Law Act 1986 will not be admissible in evidence against them except in proceedings for any offence other than perjury.

An order can be ordered against a person who is not a party to the proceedings, e.g. a legal adviser, relatives, or friends. Where a mother has taken a child to a domestic violence refuge, the police should be directed not to disclose the address (*Chief Constable of West Yorkshire Police v S* [1998] 2 FLR 973).

Example

There are often people with information about a child's whereabouts, including family members, travel agents, or work colleagues. A solicitor should use their skills of deduction and interview skills in order to build up a picture of the abducting parent's life and who may have information concerning the child.

28.4.2 ENFORCING RESIDENCE ORDERS

As stated at **28.2.2**, under s13(2) CA 1989, when a residence order is in force a parent with a residence order in their favour can remove the child for a period of less than one month.

If there is no existing CA 1989 order, an interim residence order could be applied for in order to be able to enforce the order in a number of ways.

Under s14 CA 1989, a residence order can be enforced through s63(3) Magistrates' Court Act 1980 as if it were an order requiring the other person to produce the child to him and the magistrates' court has the power to punish with a daily fine a parent who does not deliver the child.

A residence order can also be enforced using s34 Family Law Act 1986, which allows a court to order that a child be delivered up to the care of the person in accordance with the residence order (it can also be used for contact orders). The court can make an order authorizing a police officer or an officer of the court to take charge of the child and deliver them to the person concerned.

For a consideration of seeking leave to remove a child, see **Chapter 26**.

28.4.3 PROHIBITED STEPS ORDER

The prohibited steps order is a useful tool for the prevention of removal of a child from the jurisdiction and further details of this order can be found in **Chapter 26**.

In the context of parental child abduction, the removal of a child from the jurisdiction is a step that can be taken in the exercise of PR. As such, a prohibited steps order can be obtained preventing the removal of the child from the jurisdiction.

28.4.4 REGISTRATION OF ORDERS IN OTHER PARTS OF THE UK

Sections 27–31 Family Law Act 1986, as amended by the CA 1989, establishes a procedure for a 'Part 1 order' (e.g. a s8 CA 1989 order) made in one part of the UK in relation to a child aged under 16 to be registered in another part of the UK and recognized as if it had been made in that part of the UK. Once registered, the order can be enforced as if it were one of the court's own orders. This is relevant for children living in England and Wales being removed to Scotland or Northern Ireland.

 **Example**

Hannah lives with her mother in the north east of England. There are great problems surrounding contact and domestic abuse between her mother, Elizabeth, and her father, Henry. A contact order is made in Newcastle county court. After further problems, Elizabeth moves, without telling Henry, to Glasgow and refuses to allow contact.

Henry uses the Family Law Act 1986 to register his contact order in Glasgow and enforce contact with Hannah through the Scottish courts.

A specialist practitioner text should be consulted for the procedure of such an application.

28.5 RECOVERING A CHILD REMOVED ABROAD

If a child has been removed abroad, the next step will be to secure their recovery. The law in this area is extremely complex and should not be undertaken by a non-specialist lawyer. This part of the chapter gives an overview of the law. For a more detailed consideration of the law, reference should be made to a specialist practitioner text.

28.5.1 APPLICABLE LAW

There are two main pieces of legislation:

- the Hague Convention on the Civil Aspects of International Child Abduction;
- Council Regulation (EC) No. 2201/2003 of 27 November 2003.

Both pieces of legislation are discussed here in outline.

28.5.1.1 The Hague Convention

The Hague Convention on the Civil Aspects of International Child Abduction ('the Hague Convention') is an international treaty with over 50 signatories, which was brought into being as a response to concern about the harm that parental child abduction causes children. The list of signatories can be found in the online resources as the list does change from time to time.

The principle at the heart of the Hague Convention is that disputes over children should be resolved in the country where the child is habitually resident.

Any person, institution, or other body claiming that a child has been removed or retained in breach of custody rights can invoke the Hague Convention. It applies to any child under 16 who is habitually resident in one contracting state but has been wrongfully removed or retained in another contracting state.

'Habitual residence' is where the child lives normally and is settled. Children normally take the habitual residence of their parents and, if parents separate, the child's habitual residence follows that of their primary carer. A wrongful removal does not change the child's habitual residence. To change a habitual residence requires an intention to settle in the new country.

28.5.1.2 'Right of custody'

A removal or retention is wrongful if the act is contrary to the rights of custody under the law of the contracting state in which the child is habitually resident. Clearly, if there were a court order or a general law against removal this would be wrongful but in *Re V-B (Abduction: Custody Rights)* [1999] 2 FLR 192 the Court of Appeal stated that a right to be consulted but not to veto the removal did not amount to a custody right.

Under the Hague Convention, if an application is brought within 12 months of the removal or retention, the court must order the return of the child unless one of the defences available under the Hague Convention applies.

The defences available in the Hague Convention are:

- if the person bringing the application consented or acquiesced in the removal or retention. The evidence of purported consent must be unequivocal but, once given, consent cannot be withdrawn. Acquiescence depends upon the state of mind of the person said to have acquiesced and whether or not the other parent believed them to have acquiesced. Delay can be evidence of acquiescence;
- a court may refuse to return a child if there is a grave risk that his or her return would expose the child to physical or psychological harm or otherwise place the child in an intolerable situation. Risk of violence to a mother may also fall within this defence. There must be clear and compelling evidence of grave and serious harm. This defence was considered fully by the Supreme Court in *Re E (Children)* [2011] UKSC 27 where the abducting mother made serious allegations of abuse against the children's father. The Supreme Court found that the exceptions to the obligation to return are by their nature restricted in scope and should be applied without extra interpretation or gloss. Violence and abuse between parents may constitute a grave risk to the children. But where there are disputed allegations which can neither be tried nor objectively verified, the focus of the inquiry is bound to be on the sufficiency of any protective measures which can be put in place to reduce the risk. The clearer the need for protection, the more effective the measures will have to be. In this case, the trial judge was satisfied that medical treatment would be available for the mother and that there were legal remedies to protect the children should they be needed;
- if the child objects to being returned and has attained an age and degree of maturity at which it is appropriate to take account of their views. The child's wishes will never finally determine the issue; the court takes into account the surrounding policies of the Hague Convention including the welfare of the child;
- if a child was in England and Wales, a court could refuse to return a child if it were contrary to respect for human rights and fundamental freedoms. This is rarely relied upon;
- the court also has a residual discretion to refuse to return a child.

28.5.1.3 The Council Regulation

Council Regulation (EC) No. 2201/2003 of 27 November 2003 ('the Council Regulation') is relevant as Art. 60(e) provides that in relations between member states of the European Union the Regulations take precedence over the Hague Convention. The regulation is commonly known as 'Brussels II Regulation' (BIIR) and revises an earlier regulation. BIIR binds all EU member states except for Denmark.

The impact on the Hague Convention is that BIIR preserves the pre-eminence of the Hague Convention for dealing with applications for the return of abducted children but gives direction as to how the Hague Convention should be applied between member states.

Article 11 BIIR regulates how the courts should operate return applications under the Hague Convention.

28.5.1.4 Children abducted to a non-Hague Convention country

If a child is wrongfully removed or retained in a country that is not a signatory to the Hague Convention or BIIR, the parent left behind will face grave difficulties in retrieving the child. There are only two alternatives: one is to take proceedings in the country where the child is (if they can be found); the other is to seek extradition of the removing parent for an offence under the CAA 1984. This is only an option if there is an extradition treaty in force between the UK and that country.

If the child has been removed to a non-Hague Convention country, the court can make use of wardship and the court's inherent jurisdiction. Wardship is where the court takes control of a child's person and property; it is not often used following the passing of the CA 1989. Once a child is a ward no important step can be taken without the court's consent and the court will make an assessment of what is in the child's best interests. There is a presumption that it is in the best interests of the child for the child's future to be decided by the courts of the country from which the child has been abducted. The inherent jurisdiction is the court's power to make orders concerning a child living or connected with the UK.

The UK has reached consensus with a limited number of countries regarding the approach that courts shall take where a child is abducted to a non-Hague Convention country, e.g. the Protocol (Child Abduction Cases Between the UK and Pakistan) [2003] Fam Law 199 or the Cairo Declaration (resulting from Anglo-Egyptian Meetings on Judicial Co-operation in International Child Abduction Matters between Egypt and the UK) 17 January 2005. These agreements do not have the force of an international agreement but are a useful starting point for the conduct of proceedings in these countries.

SUMMARY POINTS

- Parental child abduction is a significant problem.
- Abduction can refer to the removal of a child from the jurisdiction or the retention of a child following contact outside of the jurisdiction.
- The removal of a child without the appropriate permission is a criminal offence.
- If there is a real and imminent danger of removal, the police can institute a port alert in order to prevent a child being removed from the jurisdiction.
- Applications can be made under the CA 1989 for a prohibited steps order, under ss33 and 34 Family Law Act 1986 for an order for disclosure of the child's whereabouts and their recovery, or to enforce a residence order.
- The Family Law Act 1986 allows the registration of a CA 1989 order in the courts of other jurisdictions within the UK.
- If the child has been abducted to a country within the European Union (save for Denmark), the Council Regulation will apply to proceedings to recover the child. If the child is outside of the European Union, the Hague Convention will apply.
- The court will look at the habitual residence of the child before the abduction and will return the child to that country unless a defence applies.

SELF-TEST QUESTIONS

1. Your client, Ali, has two children with his ex-wife Samantha. The couple cannot agree where their children shall live. Ali receives a telephone call from Samantha threatening to take the children to live with her in Edinburgh. Advise Ali which court orders he can seek to prevent Samantha from taking the children.
2. Would your answer differ if Samantha had threatened to take the children to Spain?
3. Samantha manages to remove the children to Spain. Advise Ali on the steps that can be taken to recover the children.
4. Would your answer differ if Samantha had removed the children to India? (You may need to use your IT skills to look on the internet for signatories to the Hague Convention!)

Answers to the questions above can be found on the Online Resource Centre: www.oxfordtextbooks.co.uk/orc/familyhandbook13/.

29 CHILDREN IN LOCAL AUTHORITY CARE

29.1 INTRODUCTION

This chapter will:

- **discuss the nature of public children law proceedings;**
- **discuss the 'threshold criteria' under the Children Act 1989;**
- **discuss the role of the local authority in public children law;**
- **discuss the orders available under the Children Act 1989 in public children law proceedings.**

When children and their families need assistance or intervention from their local authority, this kind of law is referred to as public children law. This is an area of law that trainee solicitors may encounter during a family law seat but one in which they will have limited involvement. Most public law children work is done by specialist solicitors who are members of the specialist children law panel. However, trainee solicitors are often involved in assisting in such cases; trainees often attend hearings to assist advocates, prepare documents, and assist clients at case conferences.

Children at risk of harm and the protection offered by local authorities are often the subject of news headlines. In the online resources there are details of high profile cases, in 2008 of Baby P at the hands of his carers, following the death in the same local authority of Victoria Climbie in 2000. These cases brought publicity due to the reported failures of the local authorities to protect them. In 2003, Lord Laming reported, following a public inquiry into the death of Victoria Climbie, and his recommendations are still being implemented by local authorities and will influence practice in this area for some time to come. The online resources accompanying this book contain more background information.

Public children law can be an extremely emotive and challenging area of law. Clients are in the position of having their children removed from their care and are obviously upset and worried about proceedings. Many clients have mental health difficulties, drug and alcohol addictions, or a combination of many problems and this can make giving legal advice complicated; such clients require skilful handling.

This chapter will look at the role of local authorities in protecting the child from harm and the orders available under the Children Act 1989 (CA 1989) which are used in cases of alleged harm to children. The 'threshold criteria' is the standard which the court uses to decide whether an order should be made. This is an important concept and will be applied in many of the subsequent chapters dealing with public children law. The following chapters also describe how children are protected in emergency situations and the procedures followed for orders involving local authority care of children.

The Family Justice Review (discussed throughout this text) has taken particular interest in public children law proceedings. One of the central themes is to reduce the delay experienced with the proposal that all but exceptional cases should be resolved in less than 26 weeks. The other major change is a set of principles to encourage a greater inquisitorial approach to public cases. Further details are available in the online resources.

29.2 THRESHOLD CRITERIA

Making a care order or supervision order is a serious step and the CA 1989 has rigorous criteria under s31(2) CA 1989. This states that the court must be satisfied:

> (a) that the child concerned is suffering, or is likely to suffer, significant harm; and
>
> (b) that the harm, or likelihood of harm, is attributable to:
>
> (i) the care given to the child, or likely to be given to him if the order were not made, not being what it would be reasonable to expect a parent to give to him; or
>
> (ii) the child's being beyond parental control.

This is referred to as the 'threshold criteria' as these criteria must be met before the court can make a care, supervision, or emergency protection order. The grounds in s31(2)(a) and (b) are cumulative and both must be satisfied before the court can make a care or supervision order. In s31(2)(b) CA 1989, either part may be satisfied.

In addition to s31(2) CA 1989, the court must also take into account s1 CA 1989, including:

- the child's welfare is the paramount consideration under s1(1) CA 1989;
- the court must apply the welfare/statutory checklist under s1(3) CA 1989;
- the principle that any delay in proceedings is likely to prejudice the welfare of the child under s1(2) CA 1989;
- the principle that the court should not make an order unless it considers that making it would be better for the child than making no order at all under s1(5) CA 1989.

In s31(2) CA 1989, the following terms are defined:

- 'harm' means ill-treatment or the impairment of health or development;
- 'development' means physical, intellectual, emotional, social, or behavioural-development;
- 'health' means physical or mental health; and
- 'ill-treatment' includes sexual abuse and forms of ill-treatment that are not physical.

29.2.1 WHAT IS 'SIGNIFICANT'?

'Significant' is not defined in the CA 1989 but s31(10) CA 1989 states that where the question of whether harm suffered by a child is significant turns on the child's health or development, his health or development shall be compared with that which could reasonably be expected of a similar child. The term 'significant' turns on the health and development of an individual child and s31(10) CA 1989 allows the court to firstly take a subjective view of the individual child in question. The court then takes an objective view of whether the standard of her health and development is a standard that could reasonably be expected of a child with similar characteristics.

Practical Considerations

How the court interprets this objective standard is well illustrated by the case of *Re L (Care: Threshold Criteria)* [2007] 1 FLR 2050. In this case Hedley J held that it would not be wise for the courts to attempt an all-embracing definition of significant harm. The parents in this case had learning disabilities and were in many ways inadequate as parents, although not malicious. The judge found that society must be tolerant of the diverse standards of parenting that exist. Some children are disadvantaged from their experience of parenting while others will flourish and the state cannot protect children from all of the consequences of flawed parenting. It is important that the CA 1989 should operate in this context. It is not possible to have an all-embracing definition of significant harm. It is dependent on the facts of each case and needs to be sufficiently broad to encompass human fallibility. It must involve something more than commonplace human inadequacy.

'Care' is similarly not defined in the CA 1989 but encompasses mental and emotional care as well as providing for a child's physical needs.

29.2.2 STANDARD AND BURDEN OF PROOF

29.2.2.1 'Is suffering/is likely to suffer'

S31(2)(a) CA 1989 refers to the child 'suffering or likely to suffer' significant harm. The date at which this is measured is the date on which the local authority initiates procedures for protection of the child (*Re M (A Minor)(Care Order: Threshold Criteria)* [1994] 3 All ER 298).

Example

A local authority takes steps to protect a child on 1 March 2009. A care order is subsequently made nine months later. The court will look to see if on 1 March 2009 the child was suffering significant harm.

The Public Law Outline (see **Chapter 31**) 'frontloads' applications for orders by a local authority, and the local authority should have undertaken a core assessment and a number of investigatory steps before an application is made. The local authority's investigations do not have to be complete at the time of the initiation of protection and the local authority will continue to gather evidence; this evidence can be taken into account by the court. On the issue of 'likely harm', the court can hear evidence that has been gathered after the relevant date (*Re G (Care Proceedings: Threshold Conditions)* [2001] 2 FLR 1111). The court will have to evaluate on the balance of probabilities whether the events alleged occurred and whether harm is likely to occur in the future.

29.2.2.2 Cause of harm

S31(2) CA 1989 requires the court to attribute the harm and to find the cause of the harm:

(b) that the harm, or likelihood of harm, is attributable to:

- (i) the care given to the child, or likely to be given to him if the order were not made, not being what it would be reasonable to expect a parent to give to him; or
- (ii) the child's being beyond parental control.

'Attributable' implies a causal connection between the harm and the care given to the child or the child being beyond parental control. The causal connection can be direct, e.g. where a parent physically injures their child, or indirect, e.g. where a parent does not sufficiently check the credentials of a person and leaves the child in that person's care and the child is injured or abused in some way. The harm suffered by the child can be considered to be attributed to the inadequate care of the parent as well as the third party (*Lancashire County Council v B* [2000] 1 FLR 583).

There may be doubt about who has caused the harm where the care of the child is shared between the parents and other carers. In the case of *Lancashire County Council v B*, the child was looked after by a number of carers including a child minder. The child suffered a serious intentional assault, which caused significant harm. The local authority applied for a care order but it was difficult to pinpoint blame on one individual on the evidence available to the court. The House of Lords held that s31(2)(b) CA 1989 and 'care of the child' refers primarily to the care given to the child by the parent(s) or other primary carers. Where the care is shared and the court is unable to distinguish between the care given by the parent(s) or primary carers and the care given by other carers then the court will approach the matter differently. Where the care given by one or other of the carers is proved to have been inadequate with the child suffering harm as a consequence, but the court is unable to identify which one carer was responsible for the inadequate care, then the care given to the child embraces not just the care given by the parents or primary carer but any of the carers. This leads to the possibility of a parent losing their child even if they are wholly innocent; the court still has discretion to grant a supervision or care order.

29.2.2.3 Case-law on burden and standard of proof

The legal burden rests on the applicant to establish that the threshold criteria have been met. The standard of proof is the balance of probabilities, the usual civil standard of proof.

In the case of *Re H and R (Child Sexual Abuse)* [1996] 1 FLR 80, the House of Lords held that the burden of proof is upon the applicant to establish on the balance of probabilities that the alleged events occurred and in all cases the standard of proof is the ordinary civil standard. However (as per Lord Nicholls) stronger evidence is required for a court to be satisfied that an event that is inherently improbable actually occurred than where an event is more likely to have occurred. When the court is satisfied that the alleged event has occurred according to the requisite standard of proof, it may then (on the strength of that finding) decide that there is a real risk of significant harm occurring in the future. It is not necessary for the court to be satisfied that the future significant harm is more likely than not.

However, this test has been questioned in the case of *Re B* [2008] UKHL 35. Both Lord Hoffmann and Baroness Hale made clear there is only one standard of proof and that is proof that the fact in issue more probably occurred than it did not.

Baroness Hale made clear that the s31(2) CA 1989 threshold is there to protect both the children and their parents from unjustified intervention in their lives from local authorities and that it would provide no protection if the threshold could be established on the basis of unsubstantiated suspicions or allegations.

Lord Hoffmann held that the often quoted formula of Lord Nicholls in *Re H and R* (discussed earlier) is not a rule of law but rather an application of common sense to whatever is required by the particular case. It would be absurd that the tribunal must in all cases assume serious conduct is unlikely to have occurred. So if, for example, it is clear that a child was sexually assaulted, it would make no sense to start one's reasoning by saying sexually assaulting children is a serious matter and therefore neither of the carers is likely to have done it.

Baroness Hale went further by announcing 'loud and clear' that the standard of proof in care cases is the simple balance of probabilities, 'neither more nor less'. When determining the fact and considering the standard of proof, the court should ignore the seriousness of the allegations and the seriousness of the consequences. Baroness Hale gave the example of a parent causing multiple fractures as being unlikely, but once the evidence establishes that to have occurred, it ceases to be improbable. Someone looking after the child at the relevant time must have done it, however improbable the event is. Proof of likelihood depends on the facts and circumstances of a particular case.

There were some proceedings, though civil in form, whose nature was such that it was appropriate to apply a higher standard of proof. But care proceedings were not of that nature. They were not there to punish or deter anyone but were there to protect a child from harm. The consequences for the child of getting them wrong were equally serious either way.

29.3 LOCAL AUTHORITY DUTIES, CHILDREN IN NEED, AND VOLUNTARY ACCOMMODATION

A local authority is under an obligation (s17 CA 1989) to provide services for children in need, their families and others, and to:

- safeguard and promote the welfare of children within their area who are in need; and
- so far as is consistent with that duty, to promote the upbringing of such children by their families.

S17 CA 1989 requires the local authority to provide a range and level of services appropriate to that child's needs. The CA 1989 imposes a duty to *promote* a child's upbringing by their parents. The CA 1989 requires a local authority to assist parents to undertake this responsibility by providing services to parents. All local authorities have children's services and/or a social services department to provide services. A local authority may offer services to parents that try to improve parenting skills and abilities.

The duty of the local authority applies to children within their area, although the level of services varies enormously from authority to authority. A child, for these purposes, is a person under 18 years old. 'Within their area' refers to a physical presence within the area (*R v Wandsworth London Borough Council, Hammersmith & Fulham London Borough Council and Lambeth London Borough Council, ex p Stewart* [2002] EWHC 709 (Admin)). There may be more than one local authority involved with a child if the child of the family moves from one authority to another. In *R v London Borough of Barking & Dagenham, ex p Bilkisu Mohammed* [2002] EWHC 2663 (Admin), Crane J stated that as there are no formal guidelines to assist local authorities, it is vital that the needs of the children are considered primarily and that arguments about who considers and meets those needs do not hold up the provision of services to those children. These needs must be met first and redistribution of resources should take place afterwards.

A 'child in need' is defined by s17(10) CA 1989 if:

> (a) he is unlikely to achieve or maintain, or have the opportunity of achieving or maintaining, a reasonable standard of health or development without the provision for him of services by a local authority;
>
> (b) his health or development is likely to be significantly impaired, or further impaired, without the provision for him of such services; or
>
> (c) he is disabled.

'Development' means physical, intellectual, emotional, social, or behavioural development and health means both physical and mental health (s17(11) CA 1989).

Example

Simone is eight years old and has cerebral palsy. Simone's parents care for her very well but Simone requires a great deal of care. She requires special equipment in order for her to be bathed and adaptations for the family car are required. Simone can communicate using a special computer, which she can use with help from her school. Simone's local authority provides Simone's parents with some of the specialist equipment and a regular carer as she is a child in need.

29.3.1 VOLUNTARY ACCOMMODATION

Every local authority has a duty to provide accommodation under s20(1) CA 1989 for any child in need within their area who appears to them to require accommodation as a result of:

- there being no person who has parental responsibility (PR) for them;
- there being no special guardian of the child;
- his being lost or having been abandoned;
- the person who has been caring for them being prevented (whether or nor permanently and for whatever reason) from providing him with suitable accommodation or care.

When a child is accommodated by the local authority, they are described as being 'looked after'. If a child is accommodated by the local authority other than through a care order (see **29.6**), the child can be removed by the person with PR at any time (except where a person has a residence order or is a special guardian). If there is more than one person with PR, then everyone with PR must agree to the accommodation of the child, or if a child is 16 or older they can consent.

Only a care order can grant the local authority PR for the child (see **29.6** and **Chapter 30** for emergency protection).

S20(6) CA 1989 directs the local authority to, as far as is reasonably practicable and consistent with the child's welfare, ascertain the child's wishes and feelings regarding the provision of accommodation and give due consideration (having regard to his age and understanding) to such wishes and feelings of the child as they have been able to ascertain. When a child is over 16, the CA 1989 allows the child autonomy in that she can consent to being provided with local authority care even if those with PR object or if those with PR can provide the child with accommodation (s20(4) CA 1989).

Example

Andy cares for his children, Ben (aged two) and Molly (aged three), as their mother is in prison for drug offences. Andy uses Class A drugs regularly and the local authority has become involved with the family as they are concerned about Andy's drug use. The local authority was contacted by a concerned neighbour who had witnessed Andy's drug use. Andy is offered a place in a drug rehabilitation scheme to address his drug use. Andy agrees to the children being accommodated with the local authority on a voluntary basis whilst he is undergoing drug rehabilitation.

When a child is looked after by a local authority, s22(3) CA 1989 imposes some general duties on the local authority. The local authority has a duty to safeguard and promote the welfare of the child as well as making such use of services available for children cared for by their own parents as appears reasonable to the authority. S3A CA 1989 further imposes a particular duty to promote the child's educational achievement. Before a local authority can make a decision about a child, s22(4) CA 1989 requires the local authority to ascertain the wishes and feelings of:

- the child;
- the child's parents;
- any person with PR;
- any other person whose wishes and feelings the local authority believes to be relevant.

When actually making the decision, the local authority is required to give consideration to the wishes and feelings of those listed above and also to have regard to the child's religious persuasion, racial origin, and cultural and linguistic background.

29.3.2 ACCOMMODATION AND CONTACT

Under s23(1) and (2) CA 1989, when a local authority is looking after a child, it has a duty to provide him with accommodation and maintain him. The local authority must make arrangements for the child to live with a parent, a person who is not a parent but has PR, a person who had a residence order immediately before a care order was made, or a relative, friend, or person connected with him unless this would not be reasonably practicable or consistent with her welfare (s23(6) CA 1989).

When a child is being looked after by the local authority, it must, as far as practicable and consistent with a child's welfare, promote contact between the child and his parents, a person who is not a parent but has parental responsibility, and any other person connected with him.

29.3.3 REVIEWS OF CARE

When a child is being looked after or accommodated by the local authority, the local authority is under a duty to regularly review the progress of the child. This is required by the Review of Children's Cases Regulations 1991.

S118 Adoption and Children Act 2002 introduced the new role of an independent reviewing officer (IRO) to review the progress of children being accommodated. The IRO must review the care plan and undertake revision of it if necessary. The IRO can refer the case to CAFCASS if required and detailed provisions can be found in the Review of Children's Cases (Amendment) (England) Regulations 2004. CAFCASS Legal can require that the case is brought to court to seek an order against the local authority requiring it to correct any failing in its care plan (see **29.4**).

29.4 LOCAL AUTHORITY INVESTIGATIONS

When the local authority becomes aware of a child potentially requiring an intervention due to the care that the child is receiving, the local authority has a duty to investigate whether the child is likely to suffer harm or is suffering harm. These investigations will be undertaken by the social services department within the local authority. **Chapter 31** has details of the investigations that a local authority should undertake.

Practical Considerations

A common question from students concerns how a local authority becomes aware of a family requiring assistance or investigation. There are a number of ways in which a local authority can become aware:

- reports from professionals involved with the family, e.g. GP, health visitor, teacher, or probation officer;
- concerned neighbours or friends contacting the local authority anonymously or otherwise;
- the police if the parents are investigated for criminal offences;
- during court proceedings for private children matters.

This is not an exhaustive list.

29.4.1 LOCAL AUTHORITY'S DUTY TO INVESTIGATE

S47 CA 1989 places a duty on a local authority to investigate where it suspects that a child may be at risk of significant harm or is suffering significant harm. S47(1) CA 1989 states that where a local authority is informed that a child who lives, or is found, in their area:

- is the subject of an emergency protection order; or
- is in police protection; or

it has reasonable cause to suspect that a child who lives, or is found, in its area is suffering, or is likely to suffer, significant harm, the authority shall make, or cause to be made, such enquiries as it considers necessary to enable it to decide whether it should take any action to safeguard or promote the child's welfare. For a discussion of significant harm, see **29.2**.

Where a local authority has obtained an emergency protection order with respect to a child, it shall make, or cause to be made, such enquiries as it considers necessary to enable it to decide what action it should take to safeguard or promote the child's welfare (see **Chapter 30** for further details on emergency protection orders).

S47(3) CA 1989 states that the enquiries shall, in particular, be directed towards establishing whether the authority should make any application to the court, or exercise any of its other powers, with respect to the child.

 **Example**

Andy's children have been turning up to their nursery looking unwashed and smelly in dirty clothes and appear to be hungry, according to nursery staff. A visit from a social worker to Andy's home confirms that Andy is not looking after them properly. The local authority decides to investigate the children's home and care.

Where a local authority is undertaking investigations with respect to a particular child, the local authority shall (with a view to enabling it to determine what action, if any, to take with respect to him) take such steps as are reasonably practicable, to obtain access to him or to ensure that access to him is obtained, on its behalf, by a person authorized by it for the purpose, unless it is satisfied that it already has sufficient information with respect to him.

Where, in the course of enquiries made under this section, any officer of the local authority concerned or any person authorized by the authority to act on its behalf in connection with those enquiries is refused access to the child concerned or is denied information as to his whereabouts, the authority shall apply for either an emergency protection order, a child assessment order, a care order, or a supervision order with respect to the child unless it is satisfied that his welfare can be satisfactorily safeguarded without its doing so (s47(6) CA 1989).

The local authority may decide that it is not necessary to apply for an emergency protection order, a child assessment order, a care order, or a supervision order. If these orders are not necessary the local authority shall consider whether it would be appropriate to review the case at a later date and, if it decides that it would be, determine the date on which that review is to begin. If under s47(8) CA 1989 the local authority concludes that it should take action to safeguard or promote the child's welfare, it shall take that action (so far as it is both within its power and reasonably practicable for it to do so).

29.4.2 CHILD ASSESSMENT ORDER

If a local authority believes that a child is at risk but does not require emergency intervention (see **Chapter 30**) and the parents refuse to cooperate to make an assessment, then the court may make a child assessment order under s43 CA 1989.

A child assessment order allows the local authority to complete an assessment in order to decide whether or not to take any further action.

A local authority may apply for an order and the court may make the order if, but only if, it is satisfied that:

- the applicant has reasonable cause to suspect that the child is suffering, or is likely to suffer, significant harm;

- an assessment of the state of the child's health or development, or of the way in which he has been treated, is required to enable the applicant to determine whether or not the child is suffering, or is likely to suffer, significant harm; and
- it is unlikely that such an assessment will be made, or be satisfactory, in the absence of an order under this section.

For a discussion of significant harm, see **29.2.** Where the application is made, under s43(11) CA 1989 the applicant shall ensure that they take such steps as are reasonably practicable to ensure that notice of the application is given to:

- the child's parents;
- any person who is not a parent of the child but who has PR for him;
- any other person caring for the child;
- any person in whose favour a contact order is in force with respect to the child;
- any person who is allowed to have contact with the child by virtue of an order under s34; and
- the child;

before the hearing of the application. A court will not make a child assessment order if it is satisfied that there are grounds for making an emergency protection order with respect to the child and that it ought to make such an order rather than a child assessment order. Under s43(3) CA 1989 a court may treat an application as an application for an emergency protection order if the court believes that it is necessary.

If the court makes a child assessment order, the order will specify the date by which the assessment is to begin and have effect for such period, not exceeding seven days beginning with that date, as may be specified in the order. S43(6) CA 1989 makes it the duty of any person who is in a position to produce the child to produce him to such person as may be named in the order and to comply with such directions relating to the assessment of the child as the court thinks fit to specify in the order.

The effect of a child assessment order is to authorize any person carrying out the assessment, or any part of the assessment, to do so in accordance with the terms of the order (s43(7) CA 1989) although under s43(8) CA 1989, regardless of this, if the child is of sufficient understanding to make an informed decision he may refuse to submit to a medical or psychiatric examination or other assessment.

Example

Andy has not allowed any of the social workers or health professionals into the house and has not taken children to appointments arranged by the local authority. The children have stopped attending their nursery and their allocated social worker is concerned that the children's health and well-being may be suffering. The local authority applies for a child assessment order in order to ensure that Andy brings the children to the local health centre for a medical assessment.

A child may only be kept away from home when a child assessment order is in force in accordance with directions specified in the order, if it is necessary for the purposes of the assessment and for such period or periods as may be specified in the order (s43(9) CA 1989). Where the child is kept away from home the court may order directions for contact with their parents and other family members.

29.4.3 POWER OF THE COURT TO ORDER INVESTIGATIONS

S37 CA 1989 allows the court of its own motion to direct a local authority to investigate the circumstances of a child with a view to taking action with respect to the child in terms of making a care or supervision order or providing assistance for the child and her family.

S37(1) CA 1989 states that where, in any family proceedings in which a question arises with respect to the welfare of any child, it appears to the court that it may be appropriate for a care or supervision order to be made with respect to him, the court may direct the appropriate authority to undertake an investigation of the child's circumstances. The local authority concerned shall, when undertaking the investigation, consider whether they should:

- apply for a care order or for a supervision order with respect to the child;
- provide services or assistance for the child or his family; or
- take any other action with respect to the child.

Where a local authority undertakes an investigation under s37(1) CA 1989 and decides not to apply for a care order or supervision order with respect to the child concerned, it shall inform the court of its reasons for its decision and any service or assistance that it has provided, or intends to provide, for the child and his family and any other action that it has taken, or proposes to take, with respect to the child under s37(3) CA 1989. There is a requirement that this information shall be given to the court before the end of the period of eight weeks beginning with the date of the direction, unless the court otherwise directs.

29.5 INTERIM ORDERS

It is very unlikely that a court will have all the evidence that it requires to make a final order straightaway. Investigations will have to be carried out and time is needed for all parties to prepare their cases. The court can make an interim order where proceedings are adjourned on an application for a care or supervision order.

Interim orders can be granted by the court under s38 CA 1989, if the grounds in s38(2) CA 1989 are met. These are that a court shall not make an interim care order or interim supervision order under this section unless it is satisfied that there are reasonable grounds for believing that the circumstances with respect to the child are as mentioned in s31(2) CA 1989. This means that the court only has to have reasonable grounds for believing that the threshold criteria have been met. Further guidance was given in *Hampshire County Council v S* [1993] 1 FLR 559 where it was held that an interim order is no more than a holding position and an early hearing of substantive issues is essential.

An interim order can last no longer than eight weeks under s38(4) CA 1989 although the court can order an extension of four weeks under s38(5) CA 1989. As discussed in **Chapter 31**, the court must draw up a timetable in order to ensure the early resolution of the case.

The effect of an interim order is the same as a full order. Orders for contact can be given at the time of the interim order. An exclusion order can be made under s38A CA 1989 in the same terms as discussed in **Chapter 30**.

29.6 CARE ORDERS

Orders under the CA 1989 are the only way of a child being taken into the care or supervision of a local authority. A care order allows the local authority to gain PR for the child and allows the local authority to remove the child from their parents if this is necessary.

29.6.1 WHO CAN APPLY FOR AN ORDER?

A local authority or 'authorised person' can apply for a care or supervision order under s31(1) CA 1989. The only authorized person under the CA 1989 to date is the NSPCC (see the **Glossary**). The court cannot order or instigate proceedings and the most a court can order is an investigation under s37(1) CA 1989 (see **29.4.3**).

The respondents to an application are found at r4.7 FPR 1991 and r7 of the Family Proceedings Court (Children Act 1989) Rules 1991 and are as follows:

- every person whom the applicant believes to have parental responsibility for the child;
- where the child is the subject of a care order, every person whom the applicant believes to have parental responsibility immediately prior to the making of the care order;
- in the case of an application to extend, vary, or discharge an order, the parties to the proceedings leading to the order that it is sought to have extended, varied, or discharged;
- the child.

Anyone can make a written request to become a party to proceedings or to cease to be a party (r4.7(2) FPR 1991). If a person with PR seeks to become a party, the court must grant the request. If the natural father of the child does not have PR, he will generally be allowed to do so unless there are justifiable reasons for not doing so (*Re B (Care Proceedings: Notification of Father without Parental Responsibility)* [1999] 2 FLR 408). For persons seeking to be parties, the court can grant permission without a hearing, or the court can fix a date for a hearing to consider the request, or the existing parties can make written representations.

29.6.2 WHERE CAN AN ORDER BE MADE?

An application can be made to the High Court, county court, or a family proceedings court. Most care proceedings will commence in the family proceedings court.

29.6.3 EFFECT OF A CARE ORDER

Where a care order is made with respect to a child it shall be the duty of the local authority designated by the order to receive the child into its care and to keep him in its care while the order remains in force. S33(3) CA 1989 states that while a care order is in force with respect to a child, the local authority designated by the order shall:

- have parental responsibility for the child; and
- have the power to determine the extent to which a parent or guardian of the child may meet his parental responsibility for him.

However, under s33(4) CA 1989 the authority may not exercise its power and responsibilities attached to PR unless it is satisfied that it is necessary to do so in order to safeguard or promote the child's welfare.

Example

An interim care order is made in respect of Andy's children, Ben and Molly, as he continues to use Class A drugs and the children have been found to be hungry, dirty, and living in a house that is littered with used needles and frequented by drug users. The local authority decides that Andy is not looking after the children and has failed to deal with his drug habit. The children are taken to live with foster parents as the local authority believes this is necessary to safeguard the children's welfare.

There are some limits to the local authority's exercise of parental responsibility. S33(6) CA 1989 states that while a care order is in force with respect to a child, the local authority designated by the order shall not:

- cause the child to be brought up in any religious persuasion other than that in which he would have been brought up if the order had not been made; or
- have the right to consent or refuse to consent to the making of an application with respect to the child under s18 of the Adoption Act 1976;

- have the right to agree or refuse to agree to the making of an adoption order, or an order under s55 of the 1976 Act, with respect to the child; or
- appoint a guardian for the child.

Similarly under s33(7) CA 1989, while a care order is in force with respect to a child, no person may:

- cause the child to be known by a new surname; or
- remove him from the UK;

without either the written consent of every person who has PR for the child or the leave of the court. This does not, however, prevent the removal of such a child, for a period of less than one month, by the authority in whose care he is, nor does it apply to arrangements for such a child to live outside England and Wales. Under s22(4) and (5) CA 1989, the child could choose to practise a different religion if he was of sufficient age and understanding as the child is entitled to be consulted about such matters.

A care order has the effect of discharging all existing s8 CA 1989 orders.

29.6.4 CARE PLANS AND TWIN-TRACK PLANNING

S121 Adoption and Children Act 2002 (ACA 2002) amends the CA 1989 to introduce s31A CA 1989.

Where an application is made on which a care order might be made with respect to a child, the appropriate local authority must, within such time as the court may direct, prepare a plan ('a s31A plan') for the future care of the child. This plan outlines what steps the local authority intends to take if a care order is made.

While the application is pending, the authority must keep any care plan prepared by it under review and, if it is of the opinion some change is required, revise the plan, or make a new plan, accordingly. This does not apply if the local authority has an interim care order.

There is guidance on the form and content of the s31A plan in 'Care Plans and Care Proceedings under the Children Act 1989' (Local Authority Circular of 12 August 1999 (LAC (99)129)) and this requires:

- reasons for the placement or course of action proposed by the local authority;
- achievable timescales leading up to specific outcomes for overall implementation.

The local authority should keep parents properly involved in the planning process when care proceedings are initiated (*Re S (Minors)(Care Order: Implementation of Care Plan); Re W(Minors)(Care Order: Adequacy of Care Plan)* [2002] 1 FLR 815).

Practical Considerations

Problems can arise when the local authority recognizes that steps should be taken in order to try to rehabilitate the family and return the child to the care of the family if possible but also recognizes that, should this fail, it will be necessary to plan for the child to be adopted. If the plans for adoption are not considered until a late stage in the proceedings, the court can face difficulties when making a care order and trying to approve a care plan. If an adoption is not planned for early in the proceedings, there will be a considerable delay in placing the child with a suitable family.

In order to plan for both rehabilitation within the family (often within quite strict timetables) or adoption without incurring delay, which may be detrimental to the child, 'twin-track' planning can be employed by the local authority. Twin-track planning allows the local authority to plan for both options outlined above, although parents of the child should be informed as early as possible that both options are being considered. This will help to reduce delay at the end of the proceedings (see *Re D and K (Care Plan: Twin Track Planning)* [1999] 2 FLR 872).

Alternatively 'concurrent planning' allows a local authority to choose foster parents who are trained and willing to foster children with a view to working with the family and rehabilitation.

29.6.5 PARENTAL CONTACT WITH CHILDREN IN CARE

S34(1) CA 1989 states that where a child is in the care of a local authority, the authority shall (subject to the provisions of this section) allow the child reasonable contact with:

- his parents;
- any guardian of his;
- where there was a residence order in force with respect to the child immediately before the care order was made, the person in whose favour the order was made; and
- where, immediately before the care order was made, a person had care of the child by virtue of an order made in the exercise of the High Court's inherent jurisdiction with respect to children, that person.

When an application is made for contact, the court may make such order as it considers appropriate with respect to the contact that is to be allowed between the child and any named person. If a person not listed above wishes to make an application for contact, they must have permission of the court.

29.6.5.1 Refusal of contact

As well as making an order for contact between a child and another person, the court has the power under s34(4) CA 1989 to make an order authorizing the authority to refuse to allow contact between the child and any person who is named in the order.

S34(5) CA 1989 states that when making a care order with respect to a child, or in any family proceedings in connection with a child who is in the care of a local authority, the court may make an order under this section, even though no application for such an order has been made with respect to the child, if it considers that the order should be made. Alternatively under s34(6) CA 1989, a local authority may refuse to allow the contact that would otherwise be required by virtue of s34(1) CA 1989 under this section if it is satisfied that it is necessary to do so in order to safeguard or promote the child's welfare and the refusal is decided upon as a matter of urgency and does not last for more than seven days. The court may impose such conditions as the court considers appropriate in order to safeguard the children's welfare.

If the local authority wishes to refuse contact for more than the seven days in s34(6) CA 1989, it must obtain an order for the contact to be refused for a longer period. S34(4) CA 1989 allows the court a complete discretion to authorize the refusal of contact for as long as it considers it to be for the child's welfare (*West Glamorgan County Council v P (No. 1)* [1992] 2 FLR 369). This is not an order that should be made lightly. In *Re K* [2008] EWHC 540 (Fam), Munby J stated that the circumstances for granting such an order should be 'extraordinarily compelling'. He also pointed out that such an order

> only 'authorises' the local authority to refuse to allow contact. It does not forbid such contact and a local authority, even if clothed with authority under section 34(4), is, of course, under a continuing duty to keep matters under review and to allow contact to resume as soon as it is safe and appropriate to do so.

Example

Andy's children are still with foster carers. The children had not seen Andy for some time and so he (through his solicitors) applies for contact. The court is concerned that Andy is not under the influence of drugs when he attends for contact and so contact remains supervised by the foster carers with the condition that contact will be refused if Andy is suspected to have taken drugs.

The court must start with the presumption that contact between parents and the child should continue. When an application is made under s34(4) CA 1989, the court must weigh up the benefits of contact against the disadvantages of disrupting the local authority's long-term plans (should these be inconsistent with continuing contact). *In Re E (A Minor) (Care Order: Contact)* [1994] 1 FLR 146 the Court of Appeal found that even when the threshold criteria under s31 CA 1989 are met, the court must consider that the long-term welfare of the child may require contact. Contact may allow a child to avoid a damaging sense of loss and provide a sense of security. Even if the child is to be adopted, contact may help to allow a child a necessary sense of family and personal identity. However, there will be cases in which the cessation of contact is necessary (e.g. *Re S (Care: Parental Contact)* [2005] 1 FLR 469).

If an order is made ending contact, it is possible to apply for a discharge of such an order, but the court stated in *Re T (Termination of Contact: Discharge of Order)* [1997] 1 FLR 517 that there must have been a change in circumstances between the making of the order and the application to discharge it.

29.6.6 REQUIREMENT OF AN ORDER BEFORE REMOVAL OF A CHILD

There must be a care order in place before a child is removed from the family, although under s20 CA 1989, a child can be removed from a family with consent. The case of *R v Nottingham City Council* [2008] EWHC 152 (Admin) received a high level of media attention. The applicant mother (M) applied for an order that she should be reunited with her newborn baby (X). M had a history of substance abuse and had self-harmed and had been in the care of the respondent local authority. As such, she was entitled to look to the local authority for continuing support at the time of the birth. Prior to M giving birth, it was recommended that the local authority should apply for an interim care order following X's birth and organize a foster placement following a case conference. The birth plan given to the hospital stated that X was to be removed from M's care at birth but made no reference to obtaining an emergency protection order or interim care order. Approximately two hours after M gave birth, X was removed from her mother and placed in a different room in the hospital. M submitted that separating her from X was unlawful as it had been done without legal authority.

The court held that local authorities and social workers had no power to remove children from their parents unless they had first obtained judicial sanction for what they were proposing to do. Only a court could make a care order. Only if a court had authorized that step, whether by making a care order or an interim care order or in some other way, could a local authority or social worker remove a child from a parent.

29.6.7 DISCHARGE OF A CARE ORDER

Under s91(12) CA 1989, a care order will remain in force until a child reaches 18 years unless it is discharged in one of the following ways:

- the court makes a residence order in respect of the child, so the care order is automatically discharged (s91(1) CA 1989);
- the court makes an adoption order (s46(2) ACA 2002);
- a successful application is made under s39 CA 1989 for a discharge of the order by a person with PR, the child, or the relevant local authority.

During an application to discharge a care order, the court can consider whether to make a supervision order (s39(4) CA 1989).

29.7 SUPERVISION ORDERS

A supervision order differs from a care order in that the local authority does not acquire PR for the child and, under s35(1) CA 1989, a supervision order allows the person supervising the child:

(a) to advise, assist, and befriend the supervised child;

(b) to take such steps as are reasonably necessary to give effect to the order; and

(c) where—

(i) the order is not wholly complied with; or

(ii) the supervisor considers that the order may no longer be necessary, to consider whether or not to apply to the court for its variation or discharge.

A supervision order lasts for one year but this may be extended to up to three years in total from the date it was first made following an application by the local authority (Sch 3, para 6 CA 1989). If the local authority wishes to apply for another supervision order, it will have to be proved that the threshold criteria still exist.

Further detail can be found in Sch 3 to CA 1989 concerning the types of directions that the supervisor can give:

(a) to live at a place or places specified in the directions for a period or periods so specified;

(b) to present himself to a person or persons specified in the directions at a place or places and on a day or days so specified and to participate in activities specified in the directions.

A supervision order may include a requirement that he take all reasonable steps to ensure that the supervised child complies with any direction or requirement given by the supervisor and that he comply with any directions given by the supervisor requiring him to attend at a place specified in the directions for the purpose of taking part in activities so specified.

As well as undertaking particular activities, under para 4(1), Sch 3 CA 1989, a supervision order may require the supervised child to submit to:

(a) a medical or psychological examination; or

(b) any such examination from time to time as directed by the supervisor.

Should a psychological examination be required, the court must be satisfied, on the evidence of a registered medical practitioner, that the child may be suffering from a physical or mental condition that requires, and may be susceptible to, treatment and a period as a resident patient is necessary if the examination is to be carried out properly.

29.8 COMPARISON OF A CARE ORDER AND A SUPERVISION ORDER

TABLE 29.1 COMPARISON OF A CARE ORDER AND A SUPERVISION ORDER

Care order	Supervision order
Threshold criteria must be met.	Threshold criteria must be met.
Local authority gains PR and makes most of the decisions concerning the child.	Parents retain PR and the local authority does not obtain it.
S34 CA 1989 allows the local authority to control contact in connection with the child.	The local authority cannot control contact.
S22 CA 1989 imposes a duty for the local authority to safeguard the welfare of the child.	The parent with PR retains the duty to safeguard the welfare of the child.

TABLE 29.1 CONTINUED

Care order	Supervision order
A care order allows the local authority to intervene to enforce its requirements and can remove a child from its parents.	A supervision order allows the supervisor to advise and assist the supervised child, not the parent.
A care order gives a local authority a greater ability to enforce its requirements as the local authority can remove a child if it feels the child is no longer safe.	A supervision order can require that information and access to a child is given by the carer and this can be enforced by warrant.

SUMMARY POINTS

- Where children are at risk of suffering harm or are in need, the local authority has a duty to investigate such allegations and safeguard the welfare of the children in its area.
- A child can be voluntarily accommodated by the local authority at the request of the parents or if there is no one to care for the child. Contact should be facilitated by the local authority and the child's welfare should be safeguarded.
- The local authority has a duty to investigate any child that it has reasonable cause to believe is suffering or is likely to suffer significant harm and to make enquiries into the child's health and development and whether there is a need to apply for a care or supervision order.
- A child assessment order can be used if a local authority's investigations are being obstructed by the child's parents or carers.
- A court can also direct that a local authority undertakes an investigation if the court believes that an investigation is necessary to establish whether a care or supervision order should be applied for.
- A care order has the effect of giving the local authority PR for the child with the ability to make the decisions in a child's life including whether the child shall live with their family. A local authority cannot change a child's surname or the child's religion.
- During the proceedings, a local authority may have a twin-track plan where rehabilitation is attempted with the child's family and an adoptive placement. Alternatively, concurrent planning may be appropriate where a potential adoptive family works with the child and family to attempt rehabilitation and adopts the child if the rehabilitation does not work.
- A parent can apply for contact if their child is taken into care. The court starts with a presumption that contact will continue although contact can be stopped in limited circumstances.
- A supervision order does not grant PR to a local authority. A supervision order permits a supervisor to befriend and advise the child.
- A court may only grant a care or supervision order if the 'threshold criteria' under s31(2) CA 1989 have been met. The threshold criteria examines whether a child is suffering or is likely to suffer significant harm attributable to the care from their parents or the child being beyond parental control.
- Harm relates to physical and mental harm and a child shall be compared to a child with similar characteristics.
- The burden of proof is on the applicant and the standard of proof is on the balance of probabilities.
- Interim orders are available where the court finds there is reasonable cause to believe that the threshold criteria have been met.

SELF-TEST QUESTIONS

1. Explain the standard of proof that the court must apply in care and supervision order applications.
2. The court finds that a child has suffered very serious physical harm at the hands of her parents. Which order should the court make and what is the effect of that order? In this case, the court asks whether twin-track planning is appropriate. What is twin-track planning?
3. List three differences between a care order and a supervision order.

Case Study Two

Helena has allowed her new partner to move into the house with her and Richard. Helena's new partner is a 42-year-old bailiff called Sean, whom she met through an online dating website. Everything works very well for the first month or so, although David is not very happy that Richard has a stepfather.

Helena comes into the office unexpectedly. Your supervisor takes instructions and these can be found on the online case study. Your supervisor asks you to consider what advice to give Helena on:

(a) what investigations the local authority may undertake; and

(b) what order(s) the local authority may apply for.

The online resources contain a full attendance note for you to compare your advice.

Answers to the questions above can be found on the Online Resource Centre: www.oxfordtextbooks.co.uk/orc/familyhandbook13/.

30 EMERGENCY PROTECTION OF CHILDREN

30.1 INTRODUCTION

This chapter will:

- **discuss the use of emergency protection orders in public children law;**
- **examine the powers of the police to protect children.**

As we have seen in **Chapter 29**, local authorities can become involved in a child's life if there appear to be serious concerns about their health, development, or safety. This is not a decision that is taken lightly and without the supervision of the court. There can be circumstances when a local authority must take urgent steps to secure a child's safety and to prevent a situation becoming very dangerous for the child. Such emergency steps are draconian measures and there are strict guidelines for emergency protection of children. This chapter will look at the orders available to the court and the factors a court will consider when being asked to make an emergency order. This chapter will also look at the powers available to the police when faced with a child in need of protection. This order is used in urgent situations. If the situation involving the child does not warrant the use of an emergency protection order, the local authority will apply for a care order in the usual way.

30.2 EMERGENCY PROTECTION ORDERS

When a child is in imminent need of protection, the order used to protect the child is an emergency protection order (EPO) under s44 Children Act 1989 (CA 1989). At the time of passing the CA 1989, the guidance given for EPO was as follows:

> the purpose of the new order, as its name suggests, is to enable the child in a *genuine emergency* to be removed from where he is or be kept where he is, if and only if this is what is necessary to provide immediate short-term protection. (Emphasis added).

30.2.1 WHO CAN APPLY AND TO WHICH COURT?

Under s44(1) CA 1989, any person can apply, including a local authority or an authorized person such as the NSPCC or a designated police officer.

Applications are generally made in the family proceedings court unless there are pending proceedings or the application arises out of a s37 CA 1989 investigation by a local authority (see **Chapter 29**). In this case, an application is made to the court where the proceedings are pending or the court that required the investigation, subject to any transfer of proceedings.

The application can be free-standing or made within existing proceedings or on application for a child assessment order (see **29.4.2**).

30.2.2 GROUNDS FOR APPLICATION

Under s44(1) CA 1989 where any person applies to the court for an order to be made under this section with respect to a child, the court may make the order if, but only if, it is satisfied that there is reasonable cause to believe that the child is likely to suffer significant harm if:

- he is not removed to accommodation provided by or on behalf of the applicant; or
- he does not remain in the place in which he is then being accommodated.

In the case of an application made by a local authority, the court may make an order if enquiries are being made with respect to the child under s47(1)(b) CA 1989 and those enquiries are being frustrated by access to the child being unreasonably refused to a person authorized to seek access and the applicant has reasonable cause to believe that access to the child is required as a matter of urgency.

In the case of an application made by an authorized person, the court may make the order if:

- the applicant has reasonable cause to suspect that a child is suffering, or is likely to suffer, significant harm;
- the applicant is making enquiries with respect to the child's welfare; and
- those enquiries are being frustrated by access to the child being unreasonably refused to a person authorized to seek access and the applicant has reasonable cause to believe that access to the child is required as a matter of urgency.

For a discussion of 'significant harm', see **Chapter 29**.

Example

Erin is brought to the hospital by her mother, Anji. The medical staff are concerned that the explanations given for Erin's injuries are not consistent with the injuries. A check of Erin's medical records reveals that Erin has attended A&E 12 times within the past nine months for injuries that are similar to the injuries that are presented on this occasion. When the paediatrician tries to talk to Anji about the injuries, a nurse chats to Erin. Erin tells the nurse that mummy has been nasty to her and that she does not want to go home. Anji tells the paediatrician that she is taking Erin home. The paediatrician contacts the local authority as he is concerned that Erin will suffer continuing harm at home.

In *X Council v B (Emergency Protection Orders)* [2004] EWHC 2015 (Fam), Munby J undertook a review of the law and practice relating to EPOs and gave a set of key points that all courts should consider when deciding whether to make an EPO:

- An EPO, summarily removing a child from his parents, is a 'draconian' and 'extremely harsh' measure, requiring 'exceptional justification' and 'extraordinarily compelling reasons'. Such an order should not be made unless the family proceedings court (FPC) is satisfied that it is both necessary and proportionate and that no other less radical form of order will achieve the essential end of promoting the welfare of the child. Separation is only to be contemplated if immediate separation is essential to secure the child's safety: 'imminent danger' must be 'actually established'.
- Both the local authority that seeks an EPO and the FPC that makes an EPO assume a heavy burden of responsibility. It is important that both the local authority and the FPC approach every application for an EPO with an anxious awareness of the extreme gravity of the relief being sought and a scrupulous regard for the European Convention rights of both the child and the parents.
- Any order must provide for the least interventionist solution consistent with the preservation of the child's immediate safety.

- If the real purpose of the local authority's application is to enable it to have the child assessed, then consideration should be given to whether that objective cannot equally effectively, and more proportionately, be achieved by an application for, or by the making of, a child assessment order under s43 of the CA 1989.
- No EPO should be made for any longer than is absolutely necessary to protect the child. Where the EPO is made on a without notice application very careful consideration should be given to the need to ensure that the initial order is made for the shortest possible period commensurate with the preservation of the child's immediate safety.
- The evidence in support of the application for an EPO must be full, detailed, precise, and compelling. The sources of hearsay evidence must be identified. Expressions of opinion must be supported by detailed evidence and properly articulated reasoning.
- Save in wholly exceptional cases, parents must be given adequate prior notice of the date, time, and place of any application by a local authority for an EPO. They must also be given proper notice of the evidence the local authority is relying upon.
- Where the application for an EPO is made without notice the local authority must make out a compelling case for applying without first giving the parents notice. A without notice application will normally be appropriate only if the case is genuinely one of emergency or other great urgency—and even then it should normally be possible to give some kind of albeit informal notice to the parents—or if there are compelling reasons to believe that the child's welfare will be compromised if the parents are alerted in advance to what is going on.
- The evidential burden on the local authority is even heavier if the application is made ex parte. Those who seek relief ex parte are under a duty to make the fullest and most candid and frank disclosure of all the relevant circumstances known to them. This duty is not confined to the material facts: it extends to all relevant matters, whether of fact or of law.
- The FPC must 'keep a note of the substance of the oral evidence' and must also record in writing not merely its reasons but also any findings of fact. Parents against whom an EPO is made ex parte are entitled to be given, if they ask, proper information as to what happened at the hearing and to be told exactly what documents, bundles, or other evidential materials were lodged with the FPC either before or during the course of the hearing. The local authority's legal representatives should respond forthwith to any reasonable request from the parents or their legal representatives either for copies of the materials read by the FPC or for information about what took place at the hearing.
- The local authority's positive obligation under Art. 8 to take appropriate action to reunite parent and child imposes on the local authority a continuing duty to keep the case under review day by day so as to ensure that parent and child are separated for no longer than is necessary to secure the child's safety. In this, the local authority is under a duty to exercise exceptional diligence.
- S44(13) of the CA 1989 requires the local authority (subject to s46 CA 1989) to obey any direction given by the FPC under s44(6), to allow a child who is subject to an EPO 'reasonable contact' with his parents. Arrangements for contact must be driven by the needs of the family and not stunted by lack of resources.

In *Re X (Emergency Protection Orders)* [2006] EWHC 510 (Fam), McFarlane J added that the hearing ought to be tape recorded. Further, unless there is very good reason to the contrary, the parents should always be given a full account of the material submitted to the court, the evidence given at the hearing, the submissions made to support the application, and the judge's reasons for the decision, whether they ask for this information or not. McFarlane J also added that the key points made by Munby J in *X Council v B* above should be copied and made available to the justices hearing an EPO on each and every occasion such an application is made.

30.2.3 EFFECT OF AN EPO

While an EPO is in force, s44 CA 1989 operates as a direction to any person who is in a position to do so to comply with any request to produce the child to the applicant, authorizing:

- the removal of the child at any time to accommodation provided by or on behalf of the applicant and his being kept there; or
- the prevention of the child's removal from any hospital, or other place, in which he was being accommodated immediately before the making of the order.

It also gives the applicant PR for the child.

The effect of the EPO is to allow the applicant to bring the child to a safe place or to prevent their removal from a place, e.g. a hospital.

Under s44(5) CA 1989 where an EPO is in force with respect to a child, the applicant:

- shall only exercise the power given by virtue of sub-s (4)(b) in order to safeguard the welfare of the child;
- shall take, and shall only take, such action in meeting his parental responsibility for the child as is reasonably required to safeguard or promote the welfare of the child (having regard in particular to the duration of the order).

Where the court makes an EPO, it may give such directions (if any) as it considers appropriate under s44(6) CA 1989 with respect to:

- the contact which is, or is not, to be allowed between the child and any named person (see **30.2.5**);
- the medical or psychiatric examination or other assessment of the child. Where any direction is given under sub-s (6)(b), the child may, if he is of sufficient understanding to make an informed decision, refuse to submit to the examination or other assessment.

The ability to conduct a medical or psychiatric examination fits in with the idea that the child is at risk of harm in a genuine emergency and that it is necessary to find out the extent of the risk or harm that has occurred.

However, where an EPO is in force with respect to a child and the applicant has exercised the power to remove the child but it appears to him that it is safe for the child to be returned, or the applicant has exercised the power given to prevent a removal of a child but it appears to him that it is safe for the child to be allowed to be removed from the place in question, he shall return the child or (as the case may be) allow him to be removed under s44(10) CA 1989.

30.2.4 EXCLUSION REQUIREMENT IN EMERGENCY PROTECTION

The court may include an exclusion requirement in an EPO or an interim care order under s44A CA 1989 (as amended by the Family Law Act 1996).

This allows a perpetrator to be removed from the home instead of having to remove the child. The court must be satisfied that there is reasonable cause to believe that if the person is excluded from the home in which the child lives:

- the child will cease to suffer, or cease to be likely to suffer, significant harm; or
- that enquires will cease to be frustrated; and

- another person living in the home is able, and willing, to give the child the care that it would be reasonable to expect a parent to give; and
- that person consents to the exclusion requirement.

Example

A child may be at risk from a particular person living in their home and an exclusion order may be a short-term method of removing that person and allowing the child to return home. An exclusion order will allow the person to be removed if there is another carer willing to care for the child.

An exclusion requirement is one or more of the following:

- a provision requiring the relevant person to leave a dwelling house in which he is living with the child;
- a provision prohibiting the relevant person from entering a dwelling house in which the child lives;
- a provision excluding the relevant person from a defined area in which the child lives or is situated.

A power of arrest may be attached to the order under s44A(5) CA 1989. Both the exclusion order and power of arrest can be for a shorter period than the EPO, although the period of duration of the power of arrest can be varied.

S44B CA 1989 allows the court to accept undertakings in any case where the court has a power to make an exclusion requirement.

See **Chapter 36** for a discussion of an undertaking. An undertaking is a promise to the court to do or not to do something and in this case would be a promise not to return to a certain place. An undertaking is enforced using the court's powers of contempt of court. However, a power of arrest cannot be attached to an undertaking.

If an exclusion requirement or undertaking is made, either will be discharged by the applicant removing the child from the dwelling house from which the relevant person is excluded to other accommodation for a continuous period of more than 24 hours (ss44A(10) and 44B(3) CA 1989).

30.2.5 CONTACT WHEN AN EPO IS IN FORCE

As an EPO is a major upheaval for a child, the CA 1989 makes provision for contact. S44(13) CA 1989 allows that where an EPO has been made with respect to a child, the applicant shall, subject to any exclusion requirement, allow the child reasonable contact with:

- his parents;
- any person who is not a parent of his but who has PR for him;
- any person with whom he was living immediately before the making of the order;
- any person in whose favour a contact order is in force with respect to him;
- any person who is allowed to have contact with the child by virtue of an order under s34; and
- any person acting on behalf of any of those persons.

30.2.6 DURATION AND DISCHARGE OF AN EPO

S45(1) CA 1989 states that an EPO shall have effect for such period, not exceeding eight days, as may be specified in the order.

Where an EPO is made on an application under s46(7), the period of eight days mentioned in sub-s (1) shall begin with the first day on which the child was taken into police protection under s44(3) CA 1989. See **30.3** for a discussion of police protection of children.

An application for an EPO to be extended may be made by any person who has parental responsibility for a child as the result of an EPO and is entitled to apply for a care order with respect to the child under s44(4) CA 1989. The court may extend the period during which the order is to have effect by such period, not exceeding seven days, as it thinks fit, but may do so only if it has reasonable cause to believe that the child concerned is likely to suffer significant harm if the order is not extended (s44(5) CA 1989). An EPO may only be extended once.

If a party applies for an extension, a court hearing an application for, or with respect to, an EPO may take account of any statement contained in any report made to the court in the course of, or in connection with, the hearing, or any evidence given during the hearing which is, in the opinion of the court, relevant to the application.

Any of the following may apply to the court for an EPO to be discharged under s44(8) CA 1989:

- the child;
- a parent of his;
- any person who is not a parent of his but who has PR for him; or
- any person with whom he was living immediately before the making of the order.

However, under s44(9) CA 1989 no application for the discharge of an EPO shall be heard by the court before the expiry of the period of 72 hours beginning with the making of the order.

30.2.7 PROCEDURE FOR APPLICATION

An application for an EPO is made on a Form C110 and Supplement C11 with copies for each respondent. There is no fee payable in the family proceedings court but there is a fee in the county court and the High Court.

The respondents will be every person whom the applicant believes has PR (including the situation of the family prior to a care order, if one is in force). Notice of the application should additionally be given in Form C6A to a local authority if they are providing care to the child, persons caring for the child at the commencement of proceedings, and every person whom the applicant believes is a parent.

A copy of the application, together with a Form C6, is to be served on the respondents at least one day before the date of the hearing or directions appointment (Practice Direction 12C, 2.1 FPR 2010). The Form C6A is to be served on additional persons at the same time the other parties are served.

30.2.7.1 Without notice application

In the family proceedings court, the leave of the justice's clerk is required. An application can be made by telephone and a Form C110 and Supplement C11 must be filed within 24 hours of the application.

30.3 POLICE POWERS AND VULNERABLE CHILDREN

When the police find a child in need of protection the CA 1989 places a duty on the police to safeguard the child's welfare under s46 CA 1989. The police may find that a child needs protection as their parents have been arrested and taken into custody and the child has no one to care for them. Alternatively the child may be discovered to be in need of protection during unrelated police enquiries into their parents' activities.

S46 CA 1989 allows a constable who has reasonable cause to believe that a child would otherwise be likely to suffer significant harm to:

- remove the child to suitable accommodation and keep him there; or
- take such steps as are reasonable to ensure that the child's removal from any hospital, or other place, in which he is then being accommodated is prevented.

A child with respect to whom a constable has exercised his powers under this section is referred to as having been taken into police protection.

According to s46(3) CA 1989, as soon as is reasonably practicable after taking a child into police protection, the constable concerned shall inform the local authority within whose area the child was found of the steps that have been, and are proposed to be, taken with respect to the child under this section and the reasons for taking them, and inform the child (if she has sufficient understanding) about the steps already taken and those to be taken, and try to discover the wishes and feelings of the child. If the child has been removed to accommodation not provided by the local authority or a refuge, the police should move the child to accommodation provided by either the local authority or a refuge.

As soon as is reasonably practicable after taking a child into police protection, under s46(4) CA 1989 the constable concerned shall take such steps as are reasonably practicable to inform the child's parents, and every person who is not a parent of his but who has PR for him, and any other person with whom the child was living of the steps that he has taken under this section with respect to the child, the reasons for taking them, and the further steps that may be taken with respect to him under this section.

On completing any inquiry by an officer under s46(3) CA 1989, the officer conducting it shall release the child from police protection unless he considers that there is still reasonable cause for believing that the child would be likely to suffer significant harm if released.

No child may be kept in police protection for more than 72 hours. Under s44(7) CA 1989, while a child is being kept in police protection, the designated officer may apply on behalf of the appropriate authority for an EPO to be made under s44 with respect to the child.

While a child is being kept in police protection, under s44(9) CA 1989, the police do not assume PR for the child, but shall do what is reasonable in all the circumstances of the case for the purpose of safeguarding or promoting the child's welfare (having regard in particular to the length of the period during which the child will be so protected). Under s44(10) CA 1989, the police shall allow contact with the child with the same persons listed in s44(13) CA 1989 above, if it is reasonable or in the child's best interests.

SUMMARY POINTS

- If a child is in need of protection from harm in a genuine emergency, the court may grant an EPO.
- The ground for granting such an order is if the child is likely to suffer significant harm if they are not removed to accommodation or prevented from being removed from the place where they are being accommodated.
- An EPO is an extremely draconian order and the courts have given strict guidelines concerning when they should be granted and the information that should be given to parents regarding the application and hearing.
- An EPO permits the applicant to remove the child from their current accommodation or prevent their removal from current accommodation. An EPO also permits the medical or psychiatric examination of the child.
- In certain circumstances an exclusion order can be made, allowing an alleged perpetrator to be removed from the child's home and prevents them from returning to the home or a defined area.
- During the course of an EPO, provision is made for contact between the child and their parents.
- The police have a duty to protect children if they believe that they will suffer significant harm.

SELF-TEST QUESTIONS

1. You work as a solicitor at Longtown City Council and you have received a telephone message from a paediatrician working at Longtown Royal Hospital concerning a child with non-accidental injuries whose mother wishes to remove the child from the hospital. The injuries are quite serious and include a deep cut to the head and a broken arm. The paediatrician is concerned that the child is being seen with injuries on an increasingly regular basis with ever more serious injuries and the child is afraid of her mother and is showing disturbed behaviour.

   (a) Do you think that the grounds for an EPO are met?

   (b) If an EPO is applied for, what steps will be taken?

   (c) Do you think that you should apply for an EPO without notice? Justify your decision with reference to *X Council v B (Emergency Protection Orders)*.

Case Study Two

Look at the documents on the Online Resource Centre. Richard is in hospital. Helena wishes to take him home. Does the local authority have sufficient grounds to apply for an EPO?

Answers to the questions above can be found on the Online Resource Centre: **www.oxfordtextbooks.co.uk/orc/familyhandbook13/.**

31 PUBLIC CHILDREN PROCEDURE

31.1 INTRODUCTION

This chapter will:

- **discuss the procedure undertaken to obtain orders in public children proceedings;**
- **discuss how a child's voice is heard in public children law.**

As seen from the previous chapters discussing public children law, any proceedings involving children potentially being taken into the care of the local authority must be very carefully and sensitively handled. Proceedings must strike the balance between thoroughly and carefully examining all the relevant evidence and ensuring that a decision is reached without delay and which is in the child's best interests. A study in 2009 found that 70% of cases were completed in 40 weeks and 84% within 50 weeks; however, Barnardo's found that children in care cases often waited 65 weeks for a decision in their case. As stated earlier, the Family Justice Review considers this one of the primary areas for reform and changes will be made to public children law procedures to ensure all but the most complex cases are heard within 26 weeks. The online resources will contain further details.

This chapter will look at the procedural issues involved in public children law proceedings. The procedure is technical and complex and this chapter will give an overview of the procedural steps taken in public children law proceedings in order to allow a trainee new to practice to understand the procedure.

31.2 PUBLIC LAW OUTLINE

Major changes to procedure were made in 2003 when the Protocol for Judicial Case Management in Public Law Children Act Cases ('the Protocol') came into operation. The Protocol distilled existing practice and promoted a new approach of active case management. The Protocol was designed to reduce delay, which was a feature of the system prior to the Protocol.

However, the Protocol did not solve all the outstanding problems present in the system. Causes of delay were identified as insufficient pre-proceedings work being done before the issue of a case, and lack of judicial case management leading to the failure to identify the major issues early in a case and also to resolve those issues early. Parents were not sufficiently involved in both pre-proceeding work and in the case itself and children may have suffered as a result.

As a result of these continuing problems, the Practice Direction: Guide to Case Management in Public Law Proceedings [2008] came into effect and applies to all cases commenced after April 2008. It is generally known as the Public Law Outline (PLO). The PLO was revised in 2010 and a copy of the Practice Direction can be found in the online resources. The Family Procedure Rules 2010 (FPR 2010) has incorporated the PLO into Practice Direction 12A and the general rules can be found in Part 12 FPR 2010.

The PLO applies to care and supervision proceedings and, as far as practicable, to all other public law proceedings.

31.2.1 OVERRIDING OBJECTIVE

As seen with proceedings for financial orders in **Chapter 14**, the PLO has an overriding objective that applies to the courts and all parties in the case.

The PLO has the overriding objective of enabling the court to deal with cases justly, having regard to the welfare issues involved. Dealing with a case justly includes, so far as is practicable:

- ensuring that it is dealt with expeditiously and fairly;
- dealing with the case in ways that are proportionate to the nature, importance and complexity of the issues;
- ensuring that the parties are on an equal footing;
- saving expense; and
- allotting to it an appropriate share of the court's resources, while taking into account the need to allot resources to other cases.

The court must seek to give effect to the overriding objective when it:

- exercises the case management powers referred to in the Practice Direction; or
- interprets any provision of the Practice Direction.

The parties are required to help the court further the overriding objective.

31.2.2 ACTIVE CASE MANAGEMENT

The main principles underlying court case management in public law proceedings are:

- judicial continuity: each case will be allocated to one or not more than two case management judges (in the case of magistrates' courts, case managers), who will be responsible for every case management stage in the proceedings through to the final hearing and, in relation to the High Court or county court, one of whom may be—and where possible should be—the judge who will conduct the final hearing;
- main case management tools: each case will be managed by the court by using the appropriate main case management tools;
- active case management: each case will be actively case managed by the court with a view at all times to furthering the overriding objective;
- consistency: each case will, so far as compatible with the overriding objective, be managed in a consistent way and using the standardized steps provided for in the PLO.

31.2.2.1 Active case management tools

The court will set an appropriate timetable for the child who is the subject of the proceedings. The timetable for the child will be set by the court to take account of all significant steps in the child's life that are likely to take place during the proceedings. Those steps include not only legal steps but also social, care, health, and education steps.

Example

Examples of the dates the court will record and take into account when setting the timetable for the child are the dates of:

- any formal review by the local authority of the case of a 'looked after' child (under s22(1) CA 1989);
- the child taking up a place at a new school;
- any review by the local authority of any statement of the child's special educational needs;
- an assessment by a paediatrician or other specialist.

Active case management includes encouraging the parties to cooperate with each other in the conduct of the proceedings, identifying all facts and matters that are in issue at the earliest stage in the proceedings and at each hearing, deciding promptly which issues need full investigation and hearing and which do not, and considering whether the likely benefits of taking a particular step justify any delay that will result and the cost of taking it. The court should also direct discussion between advocates and litigants in person before the case management conference (CMC) and issues resolution hearing (IRH). There should be control of the use and cost of experts, the nature and extent of the documents that are to be disclosed to the parties and presented to the court, whether and, if so, in what manner the documents disclosed are to be presented to the court, and the progress of the case. The parties should be encouraged to reach agreement in relation to the whole or part of the case. The court should not waste court time and should deal with as many aspects of the case as it can on the same occasion and give directions to ensure that the case proceeds quickly and efficiently.

The parties can assist the court in good case management. The applicant should prepare the case before proceedings are issued. In care and supervision proceedings the local authority should use the pre-proceedings checklist and the parties must use the case management documentation. The parties and their representatives should cooperate with the court in case management, including the fixing of timetables to avoid unacceptable delay, and in the crystallization and resolution of the issues on which the case turns.

The parties or their legal representatives should also monitor compliance with the court's directions and tell the court or court officer about any failure to comply with a direction of the court or any other delay in the proceedings.

31.3 REPRESENTATION OF THE CHILD

The child is a party to the proceedings for a care or supervision order. S41(6) CA 1989 lists the proceedings in which a representative should be appointed for the child in order to safeguard their welfare. Only if the court is satisfied that it is not necessary to appoint a representative will one not be appointed. The proceedings covered by s41(6) CA 1989 include:

- an application for a care or supervision order;
- where the court has been given a discretion under s37(1) CA 1989 and has made or is considering whether to make an interim order.

Further details can be found in Part 16 FPR 2010 which now deals with the issue of representation of children in one single chapter of the FPR. A children's guardian (previously known as a 'guardian ad litem') provides the court with an independent view of the child's needs and wishes. A children's guardian (often simply referred to as a 'guardian') is an experienced social worker who has expertise in working with children and families. The children's guardian will review all of the files, visit the children, and will speak to all of the parties in order to write reports for the court giving their views and those of the child (if of sufficient age and understanding to give a view). The children's guardian will appoint a solicitor to represent the child. The solicitor appointed by the children's guardian will present the child's case to the court with the children's guardian giving the solicitor instructions on the child's case. If the child is old enough to give independent instructions, the solicitor will present the views of the child whilst telling the court how these views differ from those of the children's guardian.

31.4 STEPS TO BE TAKEN BEFORE PROCEEDINGS

There is a pre-proceedings checklist that parties should refer to before commencing proceedings. The PLO 'frontloads' proceedings so that the court has a wide range of documents with details of the investigations undertaken by the local authority.

The Checklist documents

The documents to be disclosed from the local authority's files are:

- any relevant assessment materials:
  - initial and core assessments;
  - s7 and s37 reports;
  - relatives' and friends' materials (e.g. a genogram);
- other relevant reports and records:
  - single, joint, or inter-agency materials (e.g. health and education/Home Office and Immigration documents);
  - records of discussions with the family;
  - key local authority minutes and records for the child (including strategy discussion record);
- pre-existing care plans (e.g. child in need plan, looked after child plan, and child protection plan);
- social work chronology;
- letters before proceedings.

Documents to be prepared for the proceedings

The documents to be prepared for the proceedings are:

- schedule of proposed findings;
- initial social work statement;
- care plan;
- allocation record and timetable for the child.

Practical Considerations

A core assessment is an in-depth study of the child and their family undertaken by social workers in order to understand the family better.

The applicant, which in care and supervision proceedings will ordinarily be the local authority, must apply on the Form C110 which replaces some forms used under the initial PLO.

The documents that the court will expect to see attached to the application form for a care or supervision order are set out in the pre-proceedings checklist in the PLO. The pre-proceedings checklist should be used at the earliest opportunity as a guide to what documents the court will expect to see at the start of the proceedings and should be filed with the application form. The pre-proceedings checklist will promote good case preparation.

Practical Considerations

It is recognized that in some cases the circumstances are such that the safety and welfare of the child may be jeopardized if the start of proceedings is delayed until all of the documents appropriate to the case and referred to in the pre-proceedings checklist are available. The court recognizes that the preparation may need to be varied to suit the circumstances of the case. The court is likely to make directions relating to the preparation of any missing documentation at the start of the proceedings and at the first appointment. The court also recognizes that some documents on the pre-proceedings checklist may not exist and may never exist, e.g. the s37 report, and that in urgent proceedings no letter before proceedings may have been sent.

31.5 ISSUE OF PROCEEDINGS

Day 1 is the date of issue of proceedings in the PLO. The objectives for the issue of proceedings stated in the PLO are: to ensure compliance with the pre-proceedings checklist; to allocate proceedings; to obtain the information necessary for initial case management at the first appointment (FA) (see **31.6**). The following box shows the steps that should be taken by the parties and the court.

ON DAY 1:

- The local authority files:
  - application Form C110;
  - checklist documents.
- Court officer issues application.
- Court nominates case manager(s).
- Court gives standard directions on issue including:
  - pre-proceedings checklist compliance;
  - allocate and/or transfer;
  - appoint children's guardian;
  - appoint solicitor for the child;
  - case analysis for FA;
  - invite Official Solicitor to act for protected persons (non-subject children and incapacitated adults);
  - list FA by Day 6;
  - make arrangements for contested hearing (if necessary).

BY DAY 3:

- Allocation of a children's guardian expected.
- Local authority serves the application form and the checklist documents on parties.

The court will consider allocation of the case and transfer those cases to the county court that are obviously suitable for immediate transfer. The court will consider giving directions appropriate to the case and in care and supervision proceedings, relating to the preparation and filing of documents on the pre-proceedings checklist that are not yet available. The court will appoint a children's guardian in specified proceedings (in relation to care and supervision proceedings the court will expect that CAFCASS will have received notice from the local authority that proceedings were going to be started) and appoint a solicitor for the child under s41(3) CA 1989 where appropriate and request the children's guardian to prepare a case analysis and recommendations for the first appointment and to make arrangements for a contested hearing, if necessary.

The court will set a date for the first appointment normally no later than six days from the date of issue of the proceedings and in any event in line with the draft timetable for the child.

31.6 FIRST APPOINTMENT

By Day 6 of the proceedings, the PLO's objectives are to confirm allocation and to give initial case management directions. The following box details the steps to be taken by the court.

- Parties notify local authority and court of need for a contested hearing.
- Court makes arrangements for a contested hearing.
- Initial case management by court including:
  —confirm timetable for the child;
  —confirm allocation or transfer;
  —identify additional parties and representation (including allocation of children's guardian);
  —identify 'early final hearing' cases;
  —scrutinize care plan.
- Court gives standard directions on FA including:
  —a timetable for the child;
  —case analysis and recommendations;
  —LA case summary;
  —other parties' case summaries;
  —parties' initial witness statements;
  —for the advocates' meeting;
  —list CMC or (if appropriate) an early final hearing.

The first appointment is the first hearing in the proceedings. The main objectives of the first appointment are to confirm allocation and to give initial case management directions having regard to the PLO.

The court will confirm the timetable for the child and make arrangements for any contested interim hearing such as an application for an interim care order. The court will confirm the allocation of the case and transfer the case, if necessary. The court will request the children's guardian and scrutinize the care plan. If necessary, the court will consider giving directions relating to those matters in the PLO that remain to be considered and the joining of a person who would not otherwise be a respondent under the Rules as a party to the proceedings.

31.6.1 EARLY FINAL HEARING CASES

Cases that are suitable for an early final hearing are likely to be those cases where the child has no parents, guardians, relatives who want to care for the child, or other carers. Examples are those cases where the child is an abandoned baby or where a child has been brought into this country and abandoned. The court will identify at the first appointment whether the case is one that is suitable for an early final hearing and set a date for that final hearing.

31.6.2 SETTING A DATE FOR THE CASE MANAGEMENT CONFERENCE

The court will set a date for the CMC normally no later than 45 days from the date of issue of the proceedings and in any event in line with the timetable for the child.

31.6.3 ADVOCATES' MEETING/DISCUSSION AND THE DRAFT CASE MANAGEMENT ORDER

The court will consider directing a discussion between the parties' advocates and any litigant in person and the preparation of a draft case management order as outlined below.

31.6.4 EXPERTS

An expert is a person who assists the court to understand issues through their knowledge of a particular subject.

Example

In public children law, experts commonly called to provide reports or evidence to the court include psychologists and paediatricians. The court's permission is required to instruct an expert.

A party who wishes to instruct an expert should comply with Practice Direction 25A FPR 2010 which incorporates and supersedes the Experts In Family Proceedings Relating to Children Practice Direction of 1 April 2008. The court should be provided with early information to decide whether an expert or expert evidence will assist the court to identify, narrow, and (where possible) to agree the issues between the parties, provide an opinion about a question that is not within the skill and experience of the court, as well as the identification of the questions that require assistance from an expert, and to encourage full and frank disclosure between the parties, court, and any expert instructed.

An expert's overriding duty is to the court, which takes precedence over any obligation to the person from whom the expert has received instructions or by whom the expert is paid.

PD 25A FPR 2010 gives full details of the process of instruction and should be consulted before instructing an expert. Where the parties are agreed on any matter relating to experts or expert evidence, the draft agreement must be submitted for the court's approval as early as possible in the proceedings.

At the advocates' meeting or discussion before the CMC, the advocates should also try to agree the questions to be put to any proposed expert (whether jointly instructed or not) if not previously agreed. Under the Practice Direction, the questions on which the proposed expert is to give an opinion are a crucial component of the expert directions that the court is required to consider at the CMC.

31.7 CASE MANAGEMENT CONFERENCE AND ADVOCATES' MEETING

No later than two days before the CMC and no later than Day 45, the advocates involved in the case should have a meeting in order to prepare the draft case management order, to identify experts and draft questions for them, and to identify issue(s). The box at **31.8** describes what the advocates should discuss at the advocates' meeting. Timing of the discussions is of the utmost importance. The need for discussions outside the 'court room door' of matters that could have been discussed at an earlier time is to be avoided. Discussions are to take place no later than two days before the CMC or the IRH whichever is appropriate. The discussions may take place more than two days before those hearings, e.g. up to seven days before them. Following discussion the advocates should prepare or adjust the draft case management order. In practice the intention is that the advocate for the applicant, which in care and supervision proceedings will ordinarily be the local authority, should take the lead in preparing and adjusting the draft case management order following discussion with the other advocates.

Where it is not possible for the advocates to agree the terms of the draft case management order, the advocates should specify on the draft case management order, or on a separate document if more practicable:

- those provisions on which they agree; and
- those provisions on which they disagree.

Unless the court directs otherwise, the draft case management order must be filed with the court no later than 11am on the day before the CMC or the IRH whichever may be appropriate.

Practical Considerations

When preparing for the CMC, a solicitor should:

- consider all the other parties' case summaries and case analysis and recommendations;
- identify proposed experts and draft questions in accordance with the Experts Practice Direction;
- draft the case management order;
- notify the court of need for a contested hearing;
- file the draft case management order with the case manager/case management judge by 11am one working day before the CMC.

The CMC is the main hearing at which the court manages the case. The main objectives of the conference are to identify key issues and give full case management directions, including:

- review and confirm the timetable for the child;
- confirm the allocation or the transfer of the case;
- scrutinize the care plan;
- identify the key issues;
- identify the remaining case management issues;
- resolve remaining case management issues by reference to the draft case management order;
- identify any special measures such as the need for access for the disabled or provision for vulnerable witnesses;
- scrutinize the case management record to check whether directions have been complied with and, if not, consider making further directions as appropriate;
- where expert evidence is required, check whether the parties have complied with the Experts Practice Direction.

The court will issue the approved case management order. Parties or their legal representatives will be expected to submit in electronic form the final approved draft case management order on the conclusion of, and the same day as, the CMC.

The court will set a date for the IRH normally at any time between 16 and 25 weeks from the date of issue of the proceedings and in any event in line with the timetable for the child and, if necessary, specify a period within which the final hearing of the application is to take place, unless a date has already been set. This is often referred to as a 'warned period'.

31.8 ISSUES RESOLUTION HEARING

The objectives of this IRH are to resolve and narrow issues and to identify key remaining issues requiring resolution by the court. The IRH is likely to be the hearing before the final hearing. Final case management directions and other preparations for the final hearing will be made at this hearing.

There should be another advocates' meeting at least two days before the IRH and the following box shows the matters that the advocates should discuss.

- Consider all other parties' case summaries and case analysis and recommendations.
- Draft case management order.
- Notify court of need for a contested hearing/time for oral evidence to be given.
- File draft case management order with the case manager/case management judge by 11am one working day before the IRH.

The following box indicates the steps a court will take during the IRH.

- Identification by the court of the key issue(s) (if any) to be determined.
- Final case management by the court:
  —scrutinize compliance with directions;
  —consider case management directions in the draft case management order;
  —scrutinize care plan;
  —give directions for hearing documents;
  —threshold agreement or facts/issues remaining to be determined;
  —final evidence and care plan;
  —case analysis and recommendations;
  —witness templates;
  —skeleton arguments;
  —judicial reading list/reading time/judgment writing time;
  —time estimate;
  —bundles practice direction compliance;
  —list or confirm hearing.
- Court issues case management order.

The purpose of an IRH is to identify key issues that are not agreed, examine if those key issues can be agreed, and where those issues cannot be agreed, examine the most proportionate method of resolving those issues. The expectation is that the method of resolving the key issues that cannot be agreed will be at a hearing (ordinarily the final hearing) where there is an opportunity for the relevant oral evidence to be heard and challenged.

An advocate who has conduct of the final hearing should ordinarily attend the CMC and the IRH. Where the attendance of this advocate is not possible, then an advocate who is familiar with the issues in the proceedings should attend.

The court may give directions without a hearing, including setting a date for the final hearing or a period within which the final hearing will take place. The steps, which the court will ordinarily take at the various stages of the proceedings provided for in the PLO, may be taken by the court at another stage in the proceedings if the circumstances of the case merit this approach.

31.9 THE FINAL HEARING

The final hearing is used to resolve any remaining issues, but will ultimately be concerned with the courts deciding whether the threshold criteria have been met and whether an order should be made. In preparation for the final hearing, all parties file and serve updated case management documents and bundles for the court's reading.

The court will hear evidence from the parents, experts, social workers, and anyone else necessary to resolve the case. These witnesses can be cross-examined. The judge will give a judgment with reasons and an order will be drafted.

SUMMARY

FIGURE 31.1 THE STAGES OF THE PLO

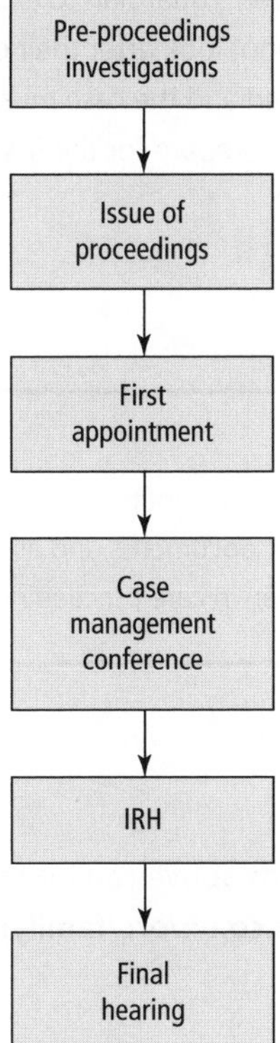

SUMMARY POINTS

- The Public Law Outline (PLO) applies to care and supervision proceedings and its overriding objective is to deal with cases expeditiously and fairly.
- The court has a duty of active case management, including setting a timetable, encouraging cooperation, identifying issues in the case, and controlling the use of experts.
- The child is a party to proceedings and is represented by a children's guardian.
- Before proceedings are issued, the courts will expect a number of investigations to be completed and a number of documents to be filed.
- Proceedings are issued on Day 1 using Forms C1 and PLO1.
- At the first appointment, the court gives initial case management decisions including a timetable of proceedings.
- An expert can be instructed with the permission of the court if expert opinion is required on an aspect of the case.
- At the CMC, the court will confirm the timetable, scrutinize the care plan, make any further directions, and set a date for an IRH.
- The IRH resolves and narrows issues and identifies any remaining issues between the parties, and makes directions in preparation for the final hearing.
- The final hearing addresses the threshold criteria and makes any orders that the court feels is necessary.

SELF-TEST QUESTIONS

1. Your firm has been asked by a children's guardian to act in care proceedings. The local authority believes that the child's parents cannot look after their child due to their heroin addiction. Proceedings have already been issued and the case must be prepared for the first appointment. Explain what steps must be taken to prepare for the first appointment and what duties the court has in relation to case management.
2. Explain the purpose of the CMC.

Case Study Two

Helena comes into the office and tells you that care proceedings have been issued with respect to Richard. Helena brings in a number of documents and asks you what will happen next. Write a short letter advising Helena what will happen in care proceedings.

Answers to the questions above can be found on the Online Resource Centre: www.oxfordtextbooks.co.uk/orc/familyhandbook13/.

C110

Application under the Children Act 1989 for a care or supervision order

To be completed by the court	
Name of court	
Date issued	
Case number	
Child(ren)'s name(s)	Child(ren)'s number(s)

Summary of application

Name of applicant

Name of respondent(s)

Child 1 - Name of child	Date of birth	Order(s) applied for (including interim orders)
	D D / M M / Y Y Y Y	
Name of mother	Name of father	Parental Responsibility
		Yes No

Child 2 - Name of child	Date of birth	Order(s) applied for (including interim orders)
	D D / M M / Y Y Y Y	
Name of mother	Name of father	Parental Responsibility
		Yes No

Child 3 - Name of child	Date of birth	Order(s) applied for (including interim orders)
	D D / M M / Y Y Y Y	
Name of mother	Name of father	Parental Responsibility
		Yes No

Child 4 - Name of child	Date of birth	Order(s) applied for (including interim orders)
	D D / M M / Y Y Y Y	
Name of mother	Name of father	Parental Responsibility
		Yes No

1. The applicant

Name of applicant
(local authority or authorised person)

Name of contact

Job title

Address

Postcode

Contact telephone number

Mobile telephone number

Fax number

Email

DX number

Solicitor's details

Solicitor's name

Address

Postcode

Telephone number

Mobile telephone number

Fax number

Email

DX number

Solicitor's Reference

2. The child(ren)

Please give details of the child(ren) and the order(s) you are applying for.
If there are more than 4 children please continue on a separate sheet.

Child 1

Child's first name

Middle name(s)

Surname

Date of birth D D / M M / Y Y Y Y Gender ☐ Male ☐ Female

Name of Social worker and telephone number

Is the child subject of a child protection plan? ☐ Yes ☐ No

Are there any health or disability issues relating to the child? ☐ Yes ☐ No

If Yes, please give details

Who does the child live with?

At which address does the child live?

Postcode

Please give the full names of any other adults living at the same address and their relationship to the child.

Are there any contact arrangements in place for this child? ☐ Yes ☐ No

If Yes, please give details

Name of person	Frequency of contact	Supervised contact
		☐ Yes ☐ No
		☐ Yes ☐ No
		☐ Yes ☐ No
		☐ Yes ☐ No

Child 2

Child's first name

Middle name(s)

Surname

Date of birth D D / M M / Y Y Y Y Gender Male Female

Name of Social worker and telephone number

Is the child subject of a child protection plan? Yes No

Are there any health or disability issues relating to the child? Yes No

If Yes, please give details

Who does the child live with?

At which address does the child live?

Postcode

Please give the full names of any other adults living at the same address and their relationship to the child.

Are there any contact arrangements in place for this child? Yes No

If Yes, please give details

Name of person	Frequency of contact	Supervised contact
		Yes No
		Yes No
		Yes No
		Yes No

Child 3

Child's first name

Middle name(s)

Surname

Date of birth D D / M M / Y Y Y Y Gender ☐ Male ☐ Female

Name of Social worker and telephone number

Is the child subject of a child protection plan? ☐ Yes ☐ No

Are there any health or disability issues relating to the child? ☐ Yes ☐ No

If Yes, please give details

Who does the child live with?

At which address does the child live?

Postcode

Please give the full names of any other adults living at the same address and their relationship to the child.

Are there any contact arrangements in place for this child? ☐ Yes ☐ No

If Yes, please give details

Name of person	Frequency of contact	Supervised contact
		☐ Yes ☐ No
		☐ Yes ☐ No
		☐ Yes ☐ No
		☐ Yes ☐ No

Child 4

Child's first name

Middle name(s)

Surname

Date of birth D D / M M / Y Y Y Y   Gender ☐ Male ☐ Female

Name of Social worker and telephone number

Is the child subject of a child protection plan? ☐ Yes ☐ No

Are there any health or disability issues relating to the child? ☐ Yes ☐ No

If Yes, please give details

Who does the child live with?

At which address does the child live?

Postcode

Please give the full names of any other adults living at the same address and their relationship to the child.

Are there any contact arrangements in place for this child? ☐ Yes ☐ No

If Yes, please give details

Name of person	Frequency of contact	Supervised contact
		☐ Yes ☐ No
		☐ Yes ☐ No
		☐ Yes ☐ No
		☐ Yes ☐ No

3. The respondents

If there are more than 2 respondents please continue on a separate sheet.

Respondent 1

Respondent's first name

Middle name(s)

Surname

Date of birth D D / M M / Y Y Y Y   Gender ☐ Male ☐ Female

Place of birth (town/county/country, if known)

Current address

Postcode

Telephone number

Are you aware of any relevant family court proceedings involving the respondent? ☐ Yes ☐ No

If Yes, give details (include type of order, date, name of court and case no.)

Relationship to the child(ren)

Name of child(ren)	Relationship	Parental Responsibility
		☐ Yes ☐ No
		☐ Yes ☐ No
		☐ Yes ☐ No
		☐ Yes ☐ No

Respondent 2

Respondent's first name

Middle name(s)

Surname

Date of birth D D / M M / Y Y Y Y Gender ☐ Male ☐ Female

Place of birth (town/county/country, if known)

Current address

Postcode

Telephone number

Are you aware of any relevant family court proceedings involving the respondent? ☐ Yes ☐ No

If Yes, give details (include type of order, date, name of court and case no.)

Relationship to the child(ren)

Name of child(ren)	Relationship	Parental Responsibility
		☐ Yes ☐ No
		☐ Yes ☐ No
		☐ Yes ☐ No
		☐ Yes ☐ No

4. Grounds for the application

The grounds for the application are that the child(ren) is suffering or is likely to suffer, significant harm and the harm or likelihood of harm is because the child is:

- ☐ not receiving care that would be reasonably expected from a parent
- ☐ beyond parental control

5. Why are you making this application?

Please give a brief summary of why you are making this application. You should include:

- the background circumstances
- the precipitating circumstances

In this summary it is not sufficient just to refer to existing or future documents.

6. Factors affecting ability to participate in proceedings

Do you have any reason to believe that any respondent or other person to be given notice of the application may lack capacity to conduct proceedings?

☐ Yes ☐ No

If Yes, please give details

Provide details of any referral to or assessment by the Adult Learning Disability team, together with the outcome

Are you aware of any other factors which may affect the ability of the person concerned to take part in the proceedings?

7. Plans for the child(ren)

Please give a brief summary of the plans for the child(ren).

- **for supervision orders only**, any requirements which you will invite the court to impose under Part 1 of Schedule 3 Children Act 1989

In this summary it is not sufficient just to refer to or repeat the Care Plan.

8. Timetable for the child(ren)

The timetable for the child will be set by the court to take account of dates of the significant steps in the child's life that are likely to take place during the proceedings. Those steps include not only legal steps but also social, care, health and education steps.

Please give any relevant dates/events in relation to the child(ren)
- it may be necessary to give different dates for each child.

Are you aware of any significant event in the timetable, before which the case should be concluded?

☐ Yes ☐ No

If Yes, please give a date

D D / M M / Y Y Y Y

and give your reasons

9. Your allocation proposal

You need to provide the court with your proposal for allocation of this case.

Please select from the following:

☐ magistrates' court

☐ county court (Care Centre)

☐ High Court

and give your reasons

10. Other court cases which concern the child(ren)

Are you aware of any other court cases, including cases concerning the children, which are relevant to this application?

☐ Yes

☐ No If No, **go to section 11**

If Yes, give details (include type of order, date, name of court and case no.) and in cases where the child was represented the name of any guardian and solicitor for the child.

11. Others who should be given notice

Person 1

Person's first name

Middle name(s)

Surname

Date of birth D D / M M / Y Y Y Y Gender ☐ Male ☐ Female

Address

Postcode

Relationship to the child(ren)

Name of child	Relationship	Parental Responsibility
		☐ Yes ☐ No
		☐ Yes ☐ No
		☐ Yes ☐ No
		☐ Yes ☐ No

Relationship to the respondents

Name of respondent	Relationship

Person 2

Person's first name

Middle name(s)

Surname

Date of birth D D / M M / Y Y Y Y   Gender ☐ Male ☐ Female

Address

Postcode

Relationship to the child(ren)

Name of child	Relationship	Parental Responsibility	
		☐ Yes	☐ No
		☐ Yes	☐ No
		☐ Yes	☐ No
		☐ Yes	☐ No

Relationship to the respondents

Name of respondent	Relationship

12. Signature

Print full name

Your role/position held

Signed

Applicant

Date D D / M M / Y Y Y Y

13. Attending the court

If an interpreter will be required, you must tell the court now so that one can be arranged.

Are you aware of whether an interpreter will be required?

☐ Yes ☐ No

If Yes, please specify the language and dialect:

If attending the court, do any of the parties involved have a disability for which special assistance or special facilities would be required?

☐ Yes ☐ No

If Yes, please specifiy what the needs are:

Please state whether the court needs to make any special arrangements for the parties attending court (e.g. providing a separate waiting room or other security requirements).

Court staff may get in contact with you about the requirements

continued over the page

Annex

This annex must be completed by the applicant with any application for a care order or supervision order.
The documents specified in this annex must be filed with the application if available.
If any relevant document is not filed with the application, the reason and any expected date of filing must be stated.
All documents filed with the application must be clearly marked with their title and numbered consecutively.

1. Social Work Chronology ☐ attached ☐ to follow

(A succinct summary)

If **to follow** please give reasons why not included and the date when the document will be sent to the court.

2. Initial Social Work Statement ☐ attached ☐ to follow

If **to follow** please give reasons why not included and the date when the document will be sent to the court.

3. Initial and Core Assessments ☐ attached ☐ to follow

If **to follow** please give reasons why not included and the date when the document will be sent to the court.

4. Letters Before Proceedings ☐ attached ☐ to follow

If **to follow** please give reasons why not included and the date when the document will be sent to the court.

5. Schedule of Proposed Findings ☐ attached ☐ to follow

If **to follow** please give reasons why not included and the date when the document will be sent to the court.

6. Care Plan ☐ attached ☐ to follow

If **to follow** please give reasons why not included and the date when the document will be sent to the court.

What to do once you have completed this form

Ensure that you have:

- ☐ attached copies of any **relevant** documents.
- ☐ **signed** the form at Section 12.
- ☐ provided a **copy** of the application and attached documents for each of the respondents, and for Cafcass or CAFCASS CYMRU.
- ☐ given details of the additional children if there are more than 4 in Section 2.
- ☐ given details of the additional respondents if there are more than 2 in Section 3.
- ☐ the correct fee.

It is good practice to inform Cafcass or CAFCASS CYMRU that you are making this application. The court will expect the local authority to have informed Cafcass or CAFCASS CYMRU that proceedings are being issued.

Have you notified Cafcass - Children and Family Court Advisory and Support Service (for England)

or

CAFCASS CYMRU - Children and Family Court Advisory and Support Service Wales.

☐ Yes ☐ No

If Yes, please give the date of notification

D D / M M / Y Y Y Y

Now take or send your application with the correct fee and correct number of copies to the court.

32 CASE CONFERENCES

32.1 INTRODUCTION

This chapter will:

- **discuss the role of a case conference in public children law;**
- **discuss the role of the solicitor in a case conference.**

As part of a local authority's investigation into a child's health and development under s47 Children Act 1989 (CA 1989), a case conference will be held so that information about the child can be shared by those who are involved with the child and family. The case conference is key to all agencies involved with the child communicating and sharing information with each other. Following an inquiry into the death of Victoria Climbie (see online resources), Lord Laming's report identified themes that led to the child being left at risk, including poor coordination and a failure to share information. Clients frequently ask their solicitors to attend case conferences and it is a job frequently undertaken by trainees. This chapter is a brief introduction to the function of a case conference and the role of a solicitor in the case conference.

32.2 WHAT IS A CHILD PROTECTION CONFERENCE?

The child protection conference is a key part of the arrangements for inter-agency cooperation for the protection of children. The child protection conference brings together the child (if appropriate), the family, and the professionals involved with the child and family following enquiries under s47 CA 1989. According to the document, 'Working Together to Safeguard Children', its purpose is to:

- bring together and analyse the information that has been obtained about the child's development and needs and the parent or carer's capacity to meet those needs to ensure the child's safety and to promote the child's health and development. The information will be shared between different agencies (see **32.3**);
- consider the evidence presented to the conference, make judgements about the likelihood of a child suffering significant harm in the future, and decide whether the child is at continued risk of significant harm;
- decide what future action is required to safeguard and promote the welfare of the child and how that action will be taken forward and with what intended outcomes.

32.3 WHO ATTENDS THE CASE CONFERENCE?

The initial child protection conference encompasses the child, the parents, and all the professionals most closely involved with the child and family following s47 CA 1989 enquiries (see **Chapter 29**).

Professionals and others involved with children include:

- GPs, practice nurses, and other community-based health professionals;
- midwives;
- health visitors;
- hospital doctors and nurses;
- school or nursery teachers and the school nurse;
- youth workers or services;
- social workers;
- police;
- foster carers;
- NSPCC or other voluntary organizations;
- housing associations or council housing departments;
- drugs and alcohol counsellors.

Those attending a case conference should be able to make a significant contribution, either through their knowledge of the child and/or their professional expertise. There should be sufficient expertise if information is required in a specialist area, e.g. a medical professional who can present and explain medical evidence. The conference should have sufficient information and expertise to make decisions, but the conference should not be too full and intimidate the child and family members.

As well as the professionals listed earlier, the child (or their representative) and family members may attend. The child would attend if they are of a sufficient age and understanding, and the operation of the case conference will be explained to the child. If a child does not attend the conference, the social care professional working most closely with the child should ascertain their wishes and feelings and make these known to the conference. Family members should normally be invited to attend and helped to participate. There may be times when it is not appropriate for a family member to be present.

 **Example**

A child may allege violence or sexual abuse on the part of their parent, step-parent, or carer. It may not be appropriate for the alleged perpetrator to be party to some of the discussions regarding the child.

32.4 WHEN WILL A CASE CONFERENCE BE HELD?

The initial case conference will be held within 15 working days of the strategy discussion. The urgency of the case and the length of time that is required to gather relevant information may affect this timing. In order for a conference to reach a well-informed decision, it is essential for the conference to have an adequate assessment of the child's needs and circumstances.

32.4.1 THE CHILD PROTECTION REVIEW CONFERENCE

The first child protection review conference should be held within three months of the initial child protection conference, and further reviews should be held at intervals of not more than six months for as long as the child remains the subject of a child protection plan.

This is to ensure that momentum is maintained in the process of safeguarding and promoting the welfare of the child. Where necessary, reviews should be brought forward to address changes in the child's circumstances. Attendees should include those most involved with the child and family in the same way as at an initial child protection conference.

Practical Considerations

A parent or carer of a child may be shocked at the involvement of social services or equally they could be hostile, distressed, or uncooperative. If you are attending a case conference with a client, you must ensure that they understand what will happen at the case conference, how much they will be allowed to say, and the decisions that will be made. It is also important for the client to understand the effect that an angry outburst or inappropriate behaviour will have on their case.

32.5 PURPOSE OF A CASE CONFERENCE

The purposes of the child protection review are to:

- review the safety, health, and development of the child against planned outcomes set out in the child protection plan;
- ensure that the child continues to be safeguarded from harm; and
- consider whether the child protection plan should continue in place or should be changed.

The reviewing of the child's progress and the effectiveness of interventions are critical to achieving the best possible outcomes for the child. The child's wishes and feelings should be sought and taken into account during the reviewing process.

32.5.1 CHILD PROTECTION PLAN

The case conference should decide whether the child has suffered ill-treatment or impairment of health or development and is at risk of further ill-treatment or impairment and if so should be the subject of a child protection plan. This will require inter-agency help and cooperation and the case conference will formulate the plan to protect the child. The plan will identify what services the child requires and what agencies need to be involved with the family and the child.

32.6 ROLE OF A LEGAL ADVISER AT A CASE CONFERENCE

The Law Society's Family Law Committee issued guidance for solicitors attending child protection conferences and a link to this can be found in the online resources.

The CA 1989 places strong emphasis on the need for all to work in partnership in all stages of planning and decision making affecting children. Solicitors are involved in the decision making process, either working for local authorities, representing the parents or the child, or other parties. The chair of the child protection conference should clarify the role of the solicitor within the conference and local practice may vary.

Representatives of the parents should not make legal representations but should assist their client to express their views. Ideally, permission should be sought from the chair to speak. Anyone attending a case conference with a parent should be knowledgeable in child protection law and procedures and fully informed of the circumstances of the case. Parents should be encouraged to attend and advised on what may happen during the conference. Consideration should be given to advising the parents on what information they give to the conference, especially if court proceedings may follow with the cross-examination of the client.

The chair should outline as part of the introduction to the conference whether or not the parent's solicitor can ask questions or raise points on their client's behalf.

32.7 CONFIDENTIALITY AND THE CASE CONFERENCE

Parents can be excluded from the conference if this is considered necessary and a point may arise about the confidentiality of information given in the absence of parents and their advisers. In *Re X (Emergency Protection Orders)* [2006] EWHC 510 (Fam), the court gave some guidance on confidential information and held that, in line with the guidance, and in accordance with fairness, good practice, and, if proceedings take place, the need for the court to have an accurate record of what is said in all parts of a case conference, the following are basic requirements:

- if the circumstances are sufficient to justify the exclusion of the parents from part of a case conference (such circumstances are described in the paragraphs of guidance referred to above), or the parents are otherwise absent, a full minute should nevertheless be taken of everything that is said during the conference;
- if it is considered necessary to treat part of what is minuted as confidential from the parents, that part of the minutes should be disclosed for approval to the professionals who attended the conference, but that part of the draft/approved minutes should be maintained separately from the body of the minutes that are sent to the parents;
- the non-confidential section of the minutes should expressly record at the appropriate stage that confidential information was disclosed or discussed;
- the need for continued confidentiality with respect to confidential sections of the minutes should be kept under review by the conference chair, with confidentiality only being maintained if it continues to be necessary.

SUMMARY POINTS

- Case conferences are a meeting of professionals and agencies involved with the child and family and are an opportunity for information to be shared.
- Decisions about the child and future plans to safeguard the child's welfare will be made at the case conference.
- Parents can attend the case conference and often take their legal representatives to the conference.
- The role of the legal adviser at the case conference varies according to local practice but the legal adviser should assist their client in taking their part in the conference.
- Whether or not the legal representative can speak or raise points on behalf of their client depends upon the discretion of the chair of the conference.
- If a client is excluded from part of the conference, any confidential minutes should be kept separately from the non-confidential minutes and the need for confidentiality should be kept under review.

SELF-TEST QUESTIONS

1. Your client has been asked to come to a case conference regarding their child. Explain the purpose of a case conference, who will be there, and when it will be held.
2. Your client wishes you to question members of the conference. Is this your role?

Answers to the questions above can be found on the Online Resource Centre: www.oxfordtextbooks.co.uk/orc/familyhandbook13/.

Part 6

DOMESTIC ABUSE

33 PROTECTION UNDER THE FAMILY LAW ACT 1996: NON-MOLESTATION ORDERS

33.1 INTRODUCTION

This chapter will:

- **discuss the law regarding domestic abuse;**
- **consider practical issues arising from acting for clients facing domestic abuse;**
- **consider the availability of remedies under the Family Law Act 1996;**
- **consider funding for orders under the Family Law Act 1996;**
- **consider the concept of 'associated persons';**
- **consider non-molestation orders under the Family Law Act 1996;**
- **consider remedies for clients escaping a forced marriage.**

Clients seeking advice because of domestic violence will form a part of all family lawyers' case-loads. Most commonly referred to as domestic *violence,* the Law Society's Family Law Protocol chooses the term domestic *abuse* as it covers a wider set of behaviour than domestic violence suggests. This text will use the term domestic violence as it is most commonly used in practice.

There are many definitions of domestic violence. The Inter-Ministerial Group on Domestic Violence signed up to the following definition in 2004, which is used by the police, the Crown Prosecution Service (CPS), and local authorities:

> Any incident of threatening behaviour, violence or abuse (psychological, physical, sexual, financial or emotional) between adults who are or have been intimate partners or family members, regardless of gender or sexuality.

Practical Considerations

Domestic violence can include but is not limited to:

- physical abuse (pushing, slapping, punching, or intimidation);
- sexual abuse (including female genital mutilation);
- psychological abuse (harassment, pestering, shouting) and controlling behaviour (financial control and social isolation);
- forced marriage;
- causing a child to witness abuse.

Domestic violence may be a series of acts forming a pattern of behaviour or a single act.

Clients need clear advice on protection available from the courts but will also require practical advice too. Clients will need advice on:

- housing;
- welfare benefits;
- help from the police and social services;
- debt and financial problems;
- immigration status;
- support services, e.g. local refuges.

The following chapters cover the orders available under Part IV of the Family Law Act 1996 (FLA 1996). Part IV of the FLA 1996 came into force on 1 October 1997, with the exception of s60. The orders available are non-molestation orders and occupation orders. This chapter (see **33.5**) and **Chapter 34** will explore the essential characteristics of each order as well as considering if the parties are associated persons. Choosing the correct occupation order is essential and this will be explored in depth later in this chapter. Whether to apply with or without notice will be considered in **Chapter 35**, as will court procedure and the enforcement of orders, which is essential to ensuring that the client is protected. The Domestic Violence, Crime and Victims Act 2004 (DVCVA 2004) made important changes to the FLA 1996 and will be considered fully.

33.2 PRACTICAL ISSUES

The suggested reading online will assist you to understand the main issues in domestic violence. Your clients may not fall into the expected categories and you must be careful not to fall into stereotyping.

Practical Considerations

The clients seen by solicitors seeking advice about domestic violence tend to be women in a heterosexual relationship, although this is not always the case.

Many other categories of people suffer domestic violence including:

- gay men and women;
- men;
- parents, suffering violence from adult children;
- adult children being forced into marriage;
- separated or divorced spouses;
- parents of the same child.

Not all clients seeking protection from domestic violence will take court proceedings. There are many reasons for this: some clients do not wish to involve others in what they regard as a private matter, some clients are too afraid to bring court proceedings, and some clients return many times to see their solicitor before having the courage to leave the abuser.

The criminal law provides a remedy for those who have suffered physical assault or harassment. The DVCVA 2004 makes the offence of common assault an arrestable one and so the police can remove an abuser from the scene of a potential crime more easily than in the past. Police forces have specialist domestic violence teams that deal specifically with this work and officers are highly experienced. Some clients will have involved the police but some will not due to fear of what the abusive person will do should the police become involved.

If a person is charged with an offence, bail conditions may be imposed that prevent an offender from contacting or visiting the victim of crime. Bail conditions can be problematic as the victim of crime is rarely at court and is often unaware of a change in bail conditions. These bail conditions end either at conviction or if the criminal charge is dropped, even though the domestic violence may continue. Criminal charges may be dropped as the victim of crime is too afraid to give evidence or does not wish to criminalize the perpetrator; however, the CPS can continue the case against the wishes of the victim of crime.

Practitioners should be aware of all agencies and organizations in their area working in domestic violence. There may be refuges (see the **Glossary**) that provide a secure place for those fleeing domestic violence, but they can be overcrowded. There will often be a domestic violence forum in your local area. This is an umbrella body for agencies working with those affected by domestic violence including local authority social services departments, education, police, voluntary agencies, and local courts. These forums are a useful source of contacts and solicitors are frequently involved with them. Some clients may also require specialist advice, e.g. regarding immigration or housing in cases of homelessness, and so you should be aware of where a client can seek advice.

Clearly, clients seeking advice on domestic violence issues may also require advice on many other aspects of family law. For example, failure to protect a child from domestic violence or witnessing domestic violence may amount to significant harm and involvement by the local authority social services department.

Practical Considerations

A client seeks advice on domestic violence. What other family law issues could flow from this? What other legal issues could arise?

- a client may seek a divorce or dissolution of civil partnership;
- a client may require assistance with a residence or contact order if there has been a separation;
- social services may be investigating the welfare of the child under s47 CA 1989 to see if the child has suffered significant harm.

In domestic abuse proceedings, the party applying for the order is an applicant and the person against whom the order is sought is the respondent.

33.3 FUNDING

The funding types appropriate to domestic violence cases are legal help for initial advice and then legal representation for the court hearing. A certificate may be restricted to a certain limit of costs or a step in proceedings (e.g. directions for trial). Although public funding is being cut severely in April 2013, this area of work will continue to be within the scope of funding. More details are available in the online resources.

The statutory charge may also apply. Mediation is a requirement of applying for legal representation but an exemption may apply because of the domestic violence alleged by the client.

The Community Legal Service requires that consideration is given to sending a warning letter to the alleged perpetrator and/or reporting the matter to police before applying for public funding. As discussed above, there are reasons why the police are not called. A warning letter must also be very carefully considered and it is very important that a client's safety is not put at risk by the sending of a warning letter. Warning letters can be successful in some cases.

33.4 THE FAMILY LAW ACT 1996

Part IV of the FLA 1996 provides remedies for domestic violence. Prior to the FLA 1996, there was a patchwork of statutes offering protection to a limited category of people. The FLA 1996 has brought a much wider range of applicants into the courts and offers a coherent set of orders.

33.4.1 JURISDICTION

The FLA 1996 unifies the jurisdiction between the High Court, county courts, and family proceedings courts for all orders; in practice, most applications are commenced in the county court. The High Court will hear applications by children. This will be considered in further detail in **Chapter 36**.

33.4.2 WHO CAN APPLY?

Before the FLA 1996, only a limited number of people could apply to the court for protection. The FLA 1996 introduced the concept of associated persons, defined in s62. It is a long list that encompasses most family situations that a practitioner will encounter. It is essential that the status of the parties as associated persons is established as a first step when considering whether to apply for an order.

Persons are 'associated' under ss62–63 FLA 1996 if:

(a) they are or have been married to each other;

(aa) they are or have been civil partners;

(b) they are cohabitants or former cohabitants;

(c) they live in the same household other than by reason of one of them being the other's employee, tenant, lodger or boarder;

(d) they are relatives;

(e) they have agreed to marry one another (whether or not that agreement has been terminated);

(eza) they have entered into a civil partnership agreement (as defined by section 73 of the Civil Partnership Act 2004) (whether or not that agreement has been terminated);

(ea) they have or have had an intimate personal relationship with each other which is or was of significant duration;

(f) in relation to a child, they are a parent of that child or has or had parental responsibility for the child;

(g) they are parties to the same family proceedings.

Some categories require greater scrutiny.

33.4.2.1 Cohabitants

S62(1)(a) of the FLA 1996 defines cohabitants as two persons who are neither married to each other nor civil partners of each other but are living together as man and wife or, if of the same sex, an equivalent relationship. *G v F (Non-molestation Order; Jurisdiction)* (2000) 2 FCR 638 stated that the concept of cohabitation should be generously interpreted in order not to exclude borderline cases.

33.4.2.2 Relative

Relatives are defined by s63 FLA 1996 to include the following:

- father; mother; stepfather; stepmother; son; daughter; stepson; stepdaughter; grandmother; grandfather; grandson; granddaughter of a person, or of that person's spouse or former spouse or civil partner or former civil partner; or

- brother; sister; uncle; aunt; niece; nephew; first cousin (whether of the first blood or of the half blood or by affinity) of a person, or of that person's spouse or former spouse, civil partner or former civil partner.

The above applies also to people who are cohabiting or were cohabiting and will include same-sex couples. Clearly, the definition of a relative is extremely wide.

 **Example**

Vera asks for advice. She is a 55-year-old woman living in a two-bedroom house in your local area. She is married to Eric and works in a local hospital as a medical secretary. Eric works as a caretaker in a local sports centre. She is not eligible for CLS funding.

Vera has been suffering intimidation and physical assault by Jimmy. Jimmy lives with Vera and Eric as he is a drug addict and his own mother finds him difficult to cope with. Jimmy is 22 and unemployed. He does not have a criminal record but Vera suspects that he is involved in petty crime. Jimmy regularly steals from Vera and becomes enraged when Vera refuses to give him money. Jimmy is Eric's sister's son.

Vera and Jimmy will be associated persons as they are relatives as Jimmy is a nephew of Eric who in turn is Vera's spouse.

Vera would be able to apply for orders under the FLA 1996.

33.4.2.3 Relevant child

S62(2) FLA 1996 defines a relevant child as:

- any child who is living with either party to the proceedings;
- any child who might reasonably be expected to live with either party to the proceedings;
- any child in relation to whom an order under the Adoption Act 1967 or Adoption and Children Act 2002 is in question in the proceedings;
- any child in relation to whom an order under the Children Act 1989 is in question in the proceedings;
- any other child whose interests the court considers relevant.

This is a wide-ranging definition that will cover children relevant to most families.

33.4.2.4 Agreement to marry/enter a civil partnership

This is the only category of associated persons where a time limit applies. S44 FLA 1996 defines an agreement to marry as one that is evidenced in writing or by a gift of a ring in contemplation of marriage/civil partnership or by a ceremony entered into by the parties in the presence of one or more witnesses assembled for the purposes of marriage/civil partnership. The agreement itself need not be in writing but there should be some form of written evidence, e.g. a press announcement or wedding/party invitations.

33.4.2.5 Intimate personal relationships

This category was added by the DVCVA 2004 and came into force on 1 July 2007. It addresses a category of people who have 'dated' for a period of time but have not lived together. Before this amendment, people in this category had to use the Protection from Harassment Act 1997 (see **Chapter 37**) as they were not associated persons. The terms 'intimate personal relationship' and 'significant duration' are untested by the courts.

33.4.2.6 Body corporate

Corporate bodies are exempt. The most practical application of this rule would be a local authority which acquires parental responsibility for a child when a care order is granted.

33.4.3 FAMILY PROCEEDINGS

These are defined in s63 of the FLA 1996 as any proceedings under:

(a) the inherent jurisdiction of the High Court in relation to children;

(b) Part IV of the FLA 1996;

(c) the Matrimonial Causes Act 1973;

(d) the Adoption Act 1976;

(e) the Domestic Proceedings and Magistrates' Courts Act 1978;

(f) Part III of the Matrimonial and Proceedings Act 1984;

(g) Parts I, II, and III of the Children Act 1989;

(h) s30 of the Human Fertilisation and Embryology Act 1990;

(i) the Adoption and Children Act 2002;

(j) Schs 5 to 7 Civil Partnership Act 2004.

33.5 NON-MOLESTATION ORDER

The applicant and respondent must be associated persons or the child to be protected a relevant child.

Non-molestation order means an order containing either or both of the following provisions:

(a) a provision prohibiting the respondent from molesting another person who is associated with the respondent;

(b) a provision prohibiting the respondent from molesting a relevant child (s42(1)).

33.5.1 MOLESTATION

'Molestation' is not defined in the Act and so case-law has produced guidelines. Molestation embraces a wide range of behaviour, from violence and threats of violence to nuisance phone calls. The courts describe a situation where someone is at least pestering another (*Vaughan v Vaughan* [1973] 3 All ER 449). There must be a degree of harassment involved sufficient to justify intervention by the court (*Horner v Horner* (1982) Fam 90). Subject to the former, the behaviour covered is as wide as the ability of people to annoy, pester, and molest each other.

C v C (Non-Molestation Order: Jurisdiction) [1998] 1 FLR 554 indicates clearly that a non-molestation order should be made only if there was some deliberate conduct by the respondent that harassed the applicant and this affected the applicant to the extent that the intervention of the court was required. Non-molestation orders were not appropriate in a dispute about family property, which should be resolved by the civil courts; or in a case where the privacy of an applicant was at risk from publication of details of a marriage between the applicant and his former wife.

33.5.2 TEST FOR A NON-MOLESTATION ORDER

S42(5) FLA 1996 sets out the test for a non-molestation order:

> In deciding whether to exercise its powers under this section and, if so, in what manner, the court shall have regard to all the circumstances including the need to secure the health, safety and well-being—
>
> (a) of the applicant or, in a case falling within subsection (2)(b), the person for whose benefit the order would be made; and
>
> (b) of any relevant child.

'Health' as defined in s63 FLA 1996 includes both physical and mental health. This clearly encompasses a greater scope of behaviour than violence. As stated earlier, there is no definition of molestation and courts are guided by decided case-law and common sense. There is a very wide range of behaviour that this will cover and one should be careful of thinking too narrowly:

- pestering at home or place of work;
- persistent and/or abusive text messages or telephone calls;
- shouting or verbal abuse during contact visits;
- threatening language or physical intimidation;
- damaging property in the home, e.g. punching walls or doors;
- violence including pushing, shoving, slapping, punching, or kicking;

will all be covered by s42(5) FLA 1996.

In *Davies v Johnson* [1979] AC 264 Viscount Dilhorne stated:

> Violence is a form of molestation, but molestation may take many forms without a threat or use of violence and still be serious and inimical to mental or physical health.

Example

Vera is distressed and wants advice on protection from Jimmy.

Vera tells you that Jimmy sends her abusive texts, up to 50 a day, asking for money. These texts contain foul language and threats of violence. Almost every evening, he returns to the house clearly under the influence of drink or drugs and shouts abusive comments at Vera and Eric until they seek refuge in their bedroom. Vera says that she has asked Jimmy to leave, but he says that if she makes him leave or calls the police, he will send his friends to the house 'to sort Eric out'.

Last night Eric was out. After an argument, Jimmy held Vera by the throat until she agreed to give him money. Vera suffered bruising to her throat and is now fearful of being in the house on her own. She cannot stop crying during the client interview. You advise her that a non-molestation order would offer her protection from further molestation from Jimmy.

Would she be successful? Applying s42(5) FLA 1996 to her situation, Vera would probably be successful as she has suffered physical injury and her health (both physical and mental), safety, and well-being are at risk from Jimmy's behaviour.

33.5.3 EVIDENCE

In order to support an application for a non-molestation order, evidence must be produced to the court. This will be discussed further when considering procedure in **Chapter 36**.

33.5.4 APPLICATIONS BY CHILDREN

Children under 16, if of sufficient understanding, can apply for a non-molestation order with leave: s43(1) FLA 1996. The application is made to the High Court with a litigation friend and is highly unusual in practice.

33.6 DURATION OF ORDER

The order may be for a specified period or until further order (which gives the court a great deal of flexibility). This was confirmed by the Court of Appeal in *Re B-J (A Child) (Non-molestation Order: Power of Arrest)* (2000) 1 FLR 107.

33.7 FORCED MARRIAGE

The Forced Marriage (Civil Protection) Act 2007 amends the FLA 1996 to introduce a new order, the forced marriage protection order under s63A FLA 1996.
This order protects:

- a person from being forced into a marriage or from any attempt to be forced into a marriage; or
- a person who has been forced into a marriage.

In deciding whether to grant an order, the court must have regard to all the circumstances, including the need to secure the health, safety, and well-being of the person to be protected. In ascertaining that person's well-being, the court must, in particular, have such regard to the person's wishes and feelings (so far as they are reasonably ascertainable) as the court considers appropriate in the light of the person's age and understanding. It is not uncommon for those being forced into marriage to be teenagers or young adults and for others to take proceedings on their behalf. 'Force' includes coercion by threats or other psychological means.

Under s63B FLA 1996, the terms of any order may, in particular, relate to conduct outside England and Wales as well as (or instead of) conduct within England and Wales. The online resources contain details of an order made concerning behaviour abroad. The forced marriage protection order can be made against respondents who force or attempt to force, or may force or attempt to force, a person to enter into a marriage and other persons who are, or may become, involved in other respects as well as respondents of any kind. This encompasses a wide variety of people, some of whom may not be family members. The online resources contain more information concerning forced marriage.

SUMMARY POINTS

- Domestic abuse describes a wide variety of behaviour including threats, violence, harassment, and sexual and psychological abuse.
- Clients frequently come for advice on domestic abuse and require advice on the law as well as practical matters.
- There are two main orders under the FLA 1996. These are non-molestation orders and occupation orders.
- The DVCVA 2004 has introduced amendments to the FLA 1996.
- Non-molestation orders offer protection from many forms of behaviour constituting domestic violence.
- To apply for an order, an applicant must be an associated person, as defined in ss62–63 of the FLA 1996.
- The definition of associated person is wide-ranging and encompasses a huge variety of possible relationships.
- There is no definition of 'molestation' in the FLA 1996 and the test for a non-molestation order considers the 'health, safety and well-being' of an applicant under s42(5) of the Act.
- A forced marriage protection order can assist those being forced into marriage or those trying to escape a forced marriage.

SELF-TEST QUESTIONS

1. Alice and Julie are a same-sex couple who are not in a civil partnership. They have been going out for a year, regularly spend the night at each other's houses, but do not cohabit. Alice has become abusive to Julie. Will Julie be able to apply for a non-molestation order?
2. Your client was engaged to an alleged abuser two years ago. Can she apply for a non-molestation order? What evidence could you produce to the court?
3. Fela is applying for parental responsibility for his child and has suffered constant threats from the child's mother. Is he an associated person?
4. Explain the test that a court must consider when deciding whether to grant a non-molestation order.

Case Study Two

Helena comes into the office at the same time as the care proceedings are ongoing concerning Richard. She tells you that Sean, her new partner, has been violent towards her and Richard. Your supervisor takes instructions and asks you to write a letter to advise Helena. Compare your letter to the case study on the online resources.

Answers to the questions above can be found on the Online Resource Centre: www.oxfordtextbooks.co.uk/orc/familyhandbook13/.

34 PROTECTION UNDER THE FAMILY LAW ACT 1996: OCCUPATION ORDERS

34.1 INTRODUCTION

This chapter will:

- **examine the availability of occupation orders under the Family Law Act 1996;**
- **consider any ancillary orders under the Family Law Act 1996 when applying for occupation orders.**

As we have seen in **Chapter 33**, the Family Law Act 1996 (FLA 1996) offers orders to protect those suffering domestic abuse. A non-molestation order offers protection against pestering, harassment, and molestation, but does not deal with the issue of people who share a home and the exclusion of one party from the home. In addition to non-molestation orders, the FLA 1996 also allows a court to make occupation orders to regulate the occupation of the family home. These orders are extremely serious as they can exclude someone from the home in which they are entitled to live. For this reason, the FLA 1996 has strict tests for the different orders available. This chapter will discuss the effect of occupation orders, the tests for each order, and which order to choose for the client.

34.2 THE EFFECT OF AN OCCUPATION ORDER

Although the level of protection offered varies according to the order made by the court, the general aim of an occupation order is to regulate the occupation of the family home. The common perception is that an occupation order simply excludes someone from the family home. However, an occupation order can also:

- enforce the applicant's entitlement to remain in occupation as against the other person;
- require the respondent to permit the applicant to enter and remain in the dwelling house or part of the dwelling house;
- regulate the occupation of the dwelling house by either or both parties;
- prohibit, suspend, or restrict the exercise by him of his right to occupy the dwelling house;
- require the respondent to leave the dwelling house or part of the dwelling house;
- exclude the respondent from a defined area in which the dwelling house is included.

Practical Considerations

When applying for an occupation order it is important to consider what the occupation order should achieve. If the applicant has fled the home, the order should be drafted to allow the applicant to enter the property, for the respondent to leave and not to return. Alternatively, the respondent can be required to leave the home and not to return, to allow the applicant to remain there without the respondent.

It is possible for a court to make an order that restricts a respondent from entering distinct parts of the house, e.g. a bedroom. This brings with it some practical difficulties but could be a solution where the parties live in a large house and a part of the house could be used by one person.

Alternatively, a person can be excluded from the property and an area around the property. This can be by reference to an area around the property defined by distance, e.g. 500 metres around the home. This could be problematic if this inadvertently includes a major road, bus route, or the respondent's work or close family. This may have a disproportionately disruptive effect beyond what was intended by the order. Using a map and highlighting the excluded area is more effective and proportionate.

The exact availability of all of the above will be looked at with individual orders below.

34.3 OCCUPATION ORDERS

Ss33–41 FLA 1996 deal with occupation orders. There are five different sections of the FLA 1996 and the sections differ according to the property rights of the applicant. The different sections, each with different, self-contained tests for eligibility, apply to different situations and so the correct section must be chosen.

34.3.1 OCCUPATION ORDER WHERE THE APPLICANT HAS AN ESTATE OR INTEREST OR HAS HOME RIGHTS

S33 FLA 1996 applies to those applicants who have a legal or contractual right to occupy the dwelling house, and is much wider in scope than the other sections applying to occupation orders. There are three requirements that must be met before an applicant can apply under s33 FLA 1996. The first is that they have a legal or contractual benefit in the property or a right to occupy the property.

S33(1) FLA 1996 states that if the applicant is entitled to occupy a dwelling house by virtue of a beneficial estate or interest or contract or by virtue of any enactment giving him the right to remain in occupation, or has matrimonial home rights in relation to a dwelling house, the applicant qualifies to apply.

Example

The applicant can qualify to apply under s33 FLA 1996 in a number of ways:

- being a legal owner (solely or jointly);
- establishing a beneficial interest in the property
- being a legal tenant (solely or jointly);
- having home rights.

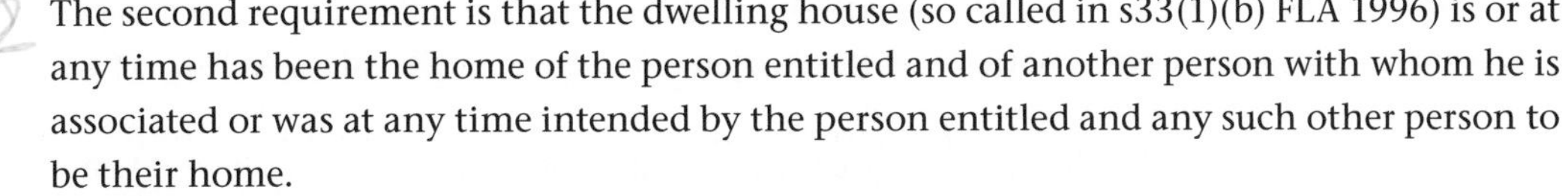

The second requirement is that the dwelling house (so called in s33(1)(b) FLA 1996) is or at any time has been the home of the person entitled and of another person with whom he is associated or was at any time intended by the person entitled and any such other person to be their home.

Practical Considerations

This requirement has three separate possibilities for the client:

- the dwelling house *is* the home of the applicant and of another person with whom s/he is associated;

- the dwelling house *has been* the home of the applicant and of another person with whom s/he is associated;
- the dwelling house was at any time *intended* to be the home of the applicant and of another person with whom s/he is associated.

This means that a second or holiday home will probably not qualify for an order under this section, nor a property bought by one of the parties with no intention of the parties living in it.

The third requirement is that the parties must be associated as s33(1)(b)(i) FLA 1996 refers to 'another person with whom he is associated'. For a discussion of associated persons, see **Chapter 33**.

Example

Martin and Andrea become engaged and discuss whether to move in together. Eventually they decide to rent a flat jointly for a while rather than move into Martin's flat, as both wish to start a new home together. Things go very well for the first six months, but Martin starts to question Andrea about where she has been and becomes possessively jealous. Andrea hopes that this will change but becomes alarmed when Martin begins to push her around and shouts and screams in extremely abusive terms when she comes home a little late. Martin starts to drink heavily and one night attacks Andrea, causing her to be hospitalized.

Andrea can apply under s33 FLA 1996. She has a contractual right to occupy the property as she is a joint tenant of the property. The dwelling house is their home, whereas Martin's flat would not be as they have never intended to live there. Martin and Andrea are associated as they have agreed to marry.

S33(4) FLA 1996 allows a county court to declare that the applicant is entitled to occupy the dwelling house by declaring a beneficial estate or interest in a contract or has matrimonial home rights.

34.3.2 THE TEST FOR AN ORDER UNDER S33 FLA 1996

34.3.2.1 The 'balance of harm' test

S33(7) FLA 1996 above is often described as the 'balance of harm' test. This is because the court balances up the harm suffered by the applicant or relevant child and whether or not they are likely to suffer significant harm if the order is not made. This is weighed against the harm suffered by the respondent or relevant child and whether that harm is significant if the order is made. If the applicant will suffer significant harm if the order is not made, the court must make an order unless the harm suffered by the respondent or any relevant child is as great as or greater than that of the applicant if the order is made. The wording of s33(7) FLA 1996 makes the order mandatory if the balance of harm test is made out.

Example

Andrea suffered serious injuries when Martin attacked her. She has nowhere to live if she cannot return to the house. She does not have a highly paid job and so may struggle to find housing. She is at risk of serious injury if she returns to the flat.

Martin has a flat in which he can go to live and has enough money to live on if he is ordered to leave the home. He is at no risk of injury from Andrea.

Andrea is likely to suffer significant harm if an order is not made and the potential harm to be suffered by Martin if an order is made does not outweigh this. The court may make an occupation order as the court finds that the balance of harm is made out.

Even if both parties establish that they will suffer significant harm but neither will suffer a greater degree of harm, the court retains the discretion to make an order but is not obliged to do so. The court will refer to s33(6) FLA 1996 (see **34.3.2.2**) and look at the parties' housing needs and resources, financial resources, the likely effect of an order on the health, safety, and well-being of the parties, and the conduct of the parties.

'Harm' is defined in s63 FLA 1996 as ill-treatment or impairment of health (or health and development if a relevant child under 18). Ill-treatment can include treatment that is not purely physical and health includes physical and mental health.

The courts have been active in elaborating on the balance of harm test. In *Chalmers v Johns* [1999] 1 FLR 392 there was a history of domestic abuse between both husband and wife. The court ordered an occupation order in favour of the wife, who had left the property with her daughter. This order was set aside by the Court of Appeal who found that a court should first apply s33(7) FLA 1996 to consider that if an order were not made, the applicant would suffer significant harm greater than the respondent if an order were made. If the answer was no, then the court still had a discretion to make an occupation order under s33(6) FLA 1996. The court found in this case that no significant harm would occur to the respondent husband if the order were not made and so the case was one for the exercise of the court's discretion.

In *G v G (Occupation Order: Conduct)* [2000] 2 FLR 36 the court emphasized that an occupation order that overrides proprietary rights should only be made in exceptional circumstances. In this case, the court re-emphasized the need to consider s33(7) FLA 1996 to see if an order must be made and then to move on to s33(6) FLA 1996 to see if the court should exercise its discretion to make an order.

Further, under s33(7) FLA 1996, significant harm must be attributable to the respondent's conduct but it does not have to be intentional conduct. The court held that each part of s33(6) FLA 1996 must be considered in turn. Thorpe LJ also reiterated that occupation orders are draconian and only to be made in exceptional circumstances.

34.3.2.2 S33(6) Test

S33(6) FLA 1996 provides that in deciding whether to exercise its powers under s33(3) the court shall have regard to all the circumstances including:

(a) the housing needs and housing resources of each of the parties and of any relevant child;
(b) the financial resources of each of the parties;
(c) the likely effect of any order, or of any decision by the court not to exercise its powers under subsection (3), on the health, safety, or well-being of the parties and of any relevant child; and
(d) the conduct of the parties in relation to each other and otherwise.

Following this, under s33(7) FLA 1996 if it appears to the court that the applicant or any relevant child is likely to suffer significant harm attributable to conduct of the respondent if an order under this section containing one or more of the provisions mentioned in s33(3) is not made, the court shall make the order unless it appears to it that:

(a) the respondent or any relevant child is likely to suffer significant harm if the order is made; and
(b) the harm likely to be suffered by the respondent or child in that event is as great as, or greater than, the harm attributable to conduct of the respondent which is likely to be suffered by the applicant or child if the order is not made.

In *Grubb v Grubb* [2009] EWCA Civ 976 a husband's application for permission to appeal an occupation order that he should vacate the matrimonial home was refused.

The case arose from defended divorce proceedings where the husband did not accept that the marriage had broken down irretrievably nor that the wife could not reasonably be expected to live with him. The husband and wife lived on an estate where the husband's family had lived for over a century although there were other homes on the estate. There were five children of the family and two children still lived at home when not at boarding school and so it was accepted that the wife should remain in the family home. The husband ran businesses from the family home and was perceived to be fearful of the situation after financial proceedings, although the wife did not wish to remain in the family home after the final settlement.

As the marriage broke down, the husband, among other acts, refused the wife keys to the house and threatened to lock her out if she did not return home in time from an evening out. The wife made the application for the occupation order under s33(6) FLA 1996 so that there was no requirement to establish the prospect of significant harm (in contrast to an application under s33(7) FLA 1996). At first instance the wife succeeded with her application for an occupation order.

The husband appealed on the basis that the trial judge had failed to recognize the seriousness of the order and that the likely duration of the order given the existing divorce proceedings, may be too long. The Court of Appeal rejected these arguments as the seriousness of the order was 'greatest' when there was no alternative accommodation available and the issue of the length of time was 'wholly unreal' as it was a matter entirely within the husband's control.

The Court of Appeal held that an occupation order was always serious, and no doubt could sometimes be particularly serious when it related to a spouse's removal from (in this particular case) his 'ancestral home'. But the occupation order was likely to carry its greatest level of seriousness when it was made against a spouse to whom alternative accommodation was not readily available. The Court of Appeal held that in this case the husband had access to alternative accommodation and in light of the husband's refusal to make proposals for alternative accommodation for the wife, it was the only way to achieve a necessary outcome of separate accommodation for the wife. The husband had plentiful resources with which to fund comfortable accommodation elsewhere.

The Court of Appeal was critical of the drafting of the order in terms of restraining the husband from threatening or using violence when (on the facts before the court) no violence had been alleged or proved.

The Court of Appeal approved the use of s33(6) FLA 1996 and that the wife did not seek the occupation order by reference to s33(7) FLA 1996 and did not argue that the wife or any of the children were likely to suffer 'significant harm' attributable to the husband's conduct were an occupation order not made. The Court accepted that the case was founded on s33(6) FLA 1996; and agreed that the facility to make an occupation order by reference to s33(6) FLA 1996, as an alternative to s33(7) FLA 1996, indicated that Parliament did not require the establishment of likely 'significant harm' before such an order could be made.

34.3.3 DURATION OF THE ORDER

Orders made under s33 FLA 1996 can be made for a specified period, until the occurrence of a specific event or until further order (s33(10) FLA 1996). In practice, orders tend to be for fairly short periods as a way of allowing the parties to find new housing arrangements.

34.3.4 WHAT THE COURT CAN ORDER UNDER S33 FLA 1996

Under s33(3) FLA 1996 an order may:

> (a) enforce the applicant's entitlement to remain in occupation as against the other person;
>
> (b) require the respondent to permit the applicant to enter and remain in the dwelling-house or part of the dwelling-house;
>
> (c) regulate the occupation of the dwelling-house by either or both parties;
>
> (d) if the respondent is entitled to occupy prohibit, suspend, or restrict the exercise by him of his right to occupy the dwelling-house;
>
> (e) if the respondent has matrimonial home rights in relation to the dwelling-house and the applicant is the other spouse, restrict or terminate those rights;

(f) require the respondent to leave the dwelling-house or part of the dwelling-house; or

(g) exclude the respondent from a defined area in which the dwelling-house is included.

34.3.5 SECTION 35 ORDERS

S35 FLA 1996 applies where one former spouse or former civil partner is entitled to occupy a dwelling house by virtue of a beneficial estate or interest or contract, or by virtue of any enactment giving him the right to remain in occupation where the other former spouse is not so entitled. The former spouse not so entitled may apply to the court for an order under this section against the other former spouse. This is not a commonly used provision in practice.

The dwelling house must have been their matrimonial home or was at any time intended by them to be their matrimonial home or in the case of former civil partners, their partnership home.

Under s35(3) FLA 1996, if the applicant is in occupation, an order under this section must contain provisions giving the applicant the right not to be evicted or excluded from the dwelling house or any part of it by the respondent for the period specified in the order and prohibiting the respondent from evicting or excluding the applicant during that period. If the applicant is not in occupation, an order under this section must contain provisions giving the applicant the right to enter into and occupy the dwelling house for the period specified in the order and requiring the respondent to permit the exercise of that right.

34.3.5.1 The test for an order under S35 FLA 1996

Under s35(6) FLA 1996, in deciding whether to make an order under this section, the court shall have regard to all the circumstances including:

(a) the housing needs and housing resources of each of the parties and of any relevant child;

(b) the financial resources of each of the parties;

(c) the likely effect of any order, or of any decision by the court not to exercise its powers under subsection (3) or (4), on the health, safety, or well-being of the parties and of any relevant child;

(d) the conduct of the parties in relation to each other and otherwise;

(e) the length of time that has elapsed since the parties ceased to live together;

(f) the length of time that has elapsed since the marriage was dissolved or annulled; and

(g) the existence of any pending proceedings between the parties—

 (i) for an order under sections 23A or 24 of the Matrimonial Causes Act 1973 (property adjustment orders in connection with divorce proceedings);

 (ia) for a property adjustment order under Part 2 of Schedule 5 to the Civil Partnership Act 2004;

 (ii) for an order under paragraph 1(2)(d) or (e) of Schedule 1 to the Children Act 1989 (orders for financial relief against parents); or

 (iii) relating to the legal or beneficial ownership of the dwelling-house.

This is similar to the test in s33(6) FLA 1996, although it can be seen that the court will look at the past history of the parties, including any prior legal proceedings and whether they have lived together recently. As well as this provision, under s35(8) FLA 1996 if the court decides to make an order under this section and it appears to it that, if the order does not include a s35(5) FLA 1996 provision, the applicant or any relevant child is likely to suffer significant harm attributable to conduct of the respondent, the court shall include the s35(5) FLA 1996 provision in the order unless it appears to the court that:

(a) the respondent or any relevant child is likely to suffer significant harm if the provision is included in the order; and

(b) the harm likely to be suffered by the respondent or child in that event is as great as or greater than the harm attributable to conduct of the respondent which is likely to be suffered by the applicant or child if the provision is not included.

This is a similar test to the 'balance of harm' test but only applies when the court is considering whether to make an order under s35(5) FLA 1996. The provisions of s35(5) FLA 1996 are that an order under this section may:

(a) regulate the occupation of the dwelling-house by either or both of the parties;

(b) prohibit, suspend, or restrict the exercise by the respondent of his right to occupy the dwelling-house;

(c) require the respondent to leave the dwelling-house or part of the dwelling-house; or

(d) exclude the respondent from a defined area in which the dwelling-house is included.

34.3.5.2 Duration of an order

Orders under s35 FLA 1996 can only be for a specified period not exceeding six months but can be extended on one or more occasions for a maximum of six months each (s35(10) FLA 1996).

34.3.6 SECTION 36 ORDERS

Orders made under s36 FLA 1996 are much more common in practice than under s34 FLA 1996 (or, indeed, ss37 and 38 FLA 1996). S36(1) FLA 1996 applies where one cohabitant or former cohabitant with no existing right to occupy applies against a cohabitant or former cohabitant with a right to occupy the property or dwelling house. There is the customary requirement that the dwelling house is the home in which they live together or a home in which they at any time cohabited or intended so to cohabit.

34.3.6.1 Test for a S36 FLA 1996 order

Under s33(6) FLA 1996 in deciding whether to make an order under this section, the court shall have regard to all the circumstances including—

(a) the housing needs and housing resources of each of the parties and of any relevant child;

(b) the financial resources of each of the parties;

(c) the likely effect of any order, or of any decision by the court not to exercise its powers on the health, safety, or well-being of the parties and of any relevant child;

(d) the conduct of the parties in relation to each other and otherwise;

(e) the nature of the parties' relationship and in particular the level of commitment involved in it;

(f) the length of time during which they have cohabited;

(g) whether there are or have been any children who are children of both parties or for whom both parties have or have had parental responsibility;

(h) the length of time that has elapsed since the parties ceased to live together; and

(i) the existence of any pending proceedings between the parties—

   (i) for an order under paragraph 1(2)(d) or (e) of Schedule 1 to the Children Act 1989 (orders for financial relief against parents); or

   (ii) relating to the legal or beneficial ownership of the dwelling-house.

There is a 'balance of harm' test similar to s33(7) FLA 1996 but the questions that it asks the court to consider do not impose a duty on the court. The court must simply consider the questions:

- whether the applicant or any relevant child is likely to suffer significant harm attributable to conduct of the respondent if the sub-s (5) provision is not included in the order; and
- whether the harm likely to be suffered by the respondent or child if the provision is included is as great as or greater than the harm attributable to conduct of the respondent that is likely to be suffered by the applicant or child if the provision is not included.

Therefore under s36 FLA 1996, the court has discretion whether to make an order and is under no duty to do so.

34.3.6.2 Protection offered by a S36 FLA 1996 order

Under s36(3) FLA 1996 if the applicant is in occupation, an order under this section must contain provision giving the applicant the right not to be evicted or excluded from the dwelling house or any part of it by the respondent for the period specified in the order; and prohibiting the respondent from evicting or excluding the applicant during that period. Similarly, s36(4) FLA 1996 states that if the applicant is not in occupation, an order under this section must contain provision giving the applicant the right to enter into and occupy the dwelling house for the period specified in the order and requiring the respondent to permit the exercise of that right.

S36(5) FLA 1996 further allows an order under this section to:

(a) regulate the occupation of the dwelling-house by either or both of the parties;

(b) prohibit, suspend, or restrict the exercise by the respondent of his right to occupy the dwelling-house;

(c) require the respondent to leave the dwelling-house or part of the dwelling-house; or

(d) exclude the respondent from a defined area in which the dwelling-house is included.

34.3.6.3 Duration of an order

Orders under s36 FLA 1996 can only be for a specified period not exceeding six months but can be extended on one occasion for a maximum of six months (s36(10) FLA 1996).

34.3.7 SECTION 37 ORDERS

Orders under s37 FLA 1996 are very rare in practice and will be considered here in outline only. This section applies where neither spouse nor civil partner or former spouse or civil partner is entitled to occupy a dwelling house that is or was the matrimonial or partnership home. The court is obliged to apply the 'balance of harm' test found at s33(7) FLA 1996 (s37(4) FLA 1996) in order to decide whether to make an order.

Either of the parties may apply to the court for an order against the other under this section.

An order under s37 FLA 1996 may:

- require the respondent to permit the applicant to enter and remain in the dwelling house or part of the dwelling house;
- regulate the occupation of the dwelling house by either or both of the spouses;
- require the respondent to leave the dwelling house or part of the dwelling house; or
- exclude the respondent from a defined area in which the dwelling house is included.

34.3.7.1 Duration of an order

S37(5) FLA 1996 states that an order under this section must be limited so as to have effect for a specified period not exceeding six months, but may be extended on one or more occasions for a further specified period not exceeding six months.

34.3.8 SECTION 38 ORDERS

S38 orders are also extremely rare (the author has never used this section in practice) and so this section is explained only in outline. S38 FLA 1996 applies where neither cohabitant nor former cohabitant are entitled to occupy a dwelling house that they cohabit or cohabited. Either of the parties may apply to the court for an order against the other under this section.

34.3.8.1 test for an order under S38 FLA 1996

Under s38(4) FLA 1996 in deciding whether to exercise its powers, the court shall have regard to all the circumstances including:

FIGURE 34.1 FLOWCHART ILLUSTRATING OCCUPATION ORDERS

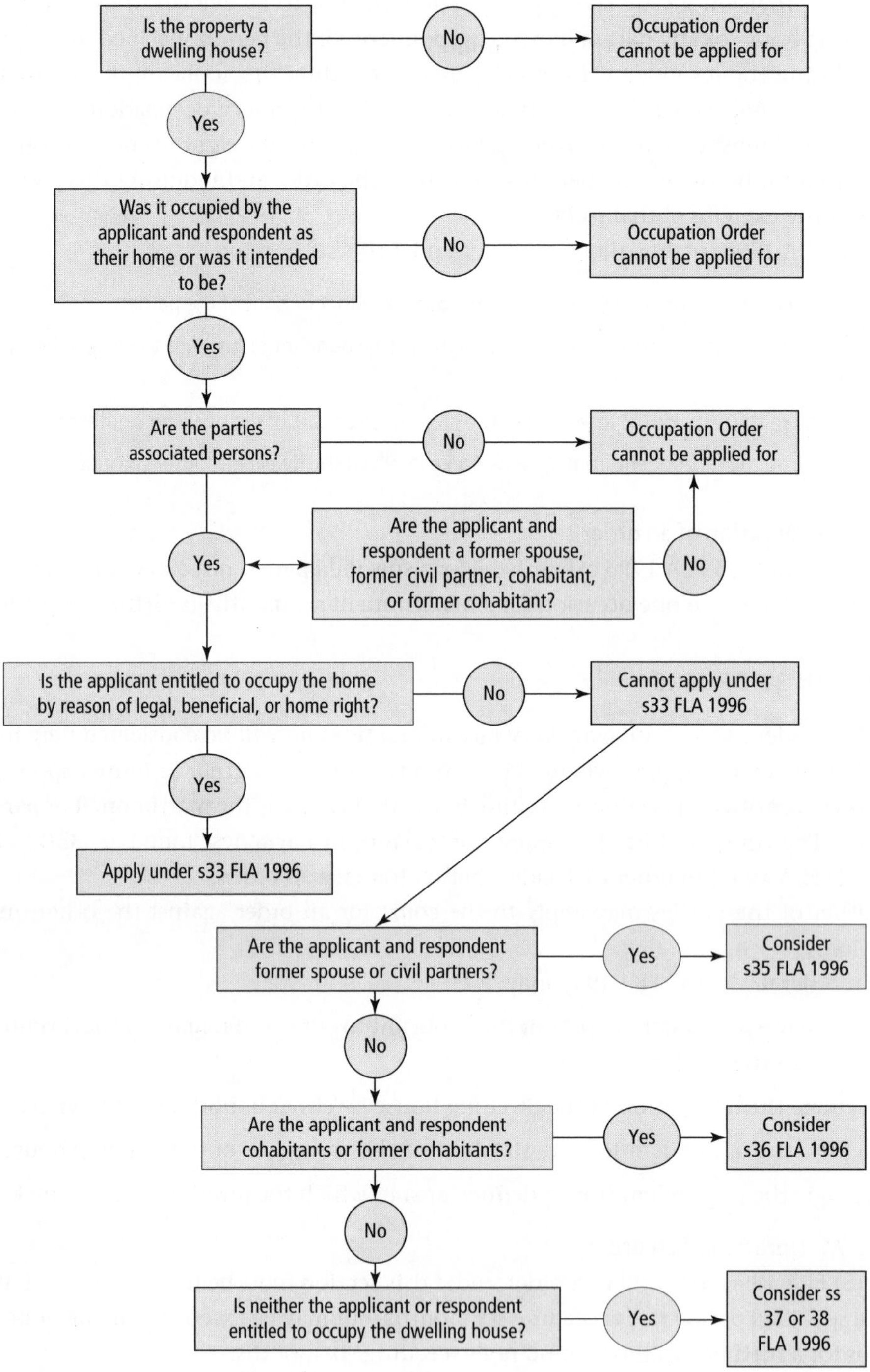

Is the property a dwelling house?
No → Occupation Order cannot be applied for
Yes ↓
Was it occupied by the applicant and respondent as their home or was it intended to be?
No → Occupation Order cannot be applied for
Yes ↓
Are the parties associated persons?
No → Occupation Order cannot be applied for
Yes ↔ Are the applicant and respondent a former spouse, former civil partner, cohabitant, or former cohabitant?
No → Occupation Order cannot be applied for
Yes ↓
Is the applicant entitled to occupy the home by reason of legal, beneficial, or home right?
No → Cannot apply under s33 FLA 1996
Yes ↓
Apply under s33 FLA 1996

Cannot apply under s33 FLA 1996 ↓
Are the applicant and respondent former spouse or civil partners?
Yes → Consider s35 FLA 1996
No ↓
Are the applicant and respondent cohabitants or former cohabitants?
Yes → Consider s36 FLA 1996
No ↓
Is neither the applicant or respondent entitled to occupy the dwelling house?
Yes → Consider ss 37 or 38 FLA 1996

(a) the housing needs and housing resources of each of the parties and of any relevant child;

(b) the financial resources of each of the parties;

(c) the likely effect of any order, or of any decision by the court not to exercise its powers under subsection (3), on the health, safety, or well-being of the parties and of any relevant child;

(d) the conduct of the parties in relation to each other and otherwise; and

(e) the questions mentioned in s38(5) FLA 1996.

The questions are:

(a) whether the applicant or any relevant child is likely to suffer significant harm attributable to conduct of the respondent if the subsection (3) provision is not included in the order; and

(b) whether the harm likely to be suffered by the respondent or child if the provision is included is as great as or greater than the harm attributable to conduct of the respondent which is likely to be suffered by the applicant or child if the provision is not included.

S38(3) FLA 1996 states that an order under this section may:

(a) require the respondent to permit the applicant to enter and remain in the dwelling-house or part of the dwelling-house;

(b) regulate the occupation of the dwelling-house by either or both of the parties;

(c) require the respondent to leave the dwelling-house or part of the dwelling-house; or

(d) exclude the respondent from a defined area in which the dwelling-house is included.

34.3.8.2 Duration of the order

Under s38(6) FLA 1996 an order under this section shall be limited so as to have effect for a specified period not exceeding six months, but may be extended on one occasion for a further specified period not exceeding six months.

34.4 ANCILLARY ORDERS

If the court makes an occupation order, s40(1) FLA 1996 allows the court to impose additional orders to the occupation order including:

(a) impose on either party obligations as to:

  (i) the repair and maintenance of the dwelling-house; or

  (ii) the discharge of rent, mortgage payments, or other outgoings affecting the dwelling-house;

(b) order a party occupying the dwelling-house or any part of it (including a party who is entitled to do so by virtue of a beneficial estate or interest or contract or by virtue of any enactment giving him the right to remain in occupation) to make periodical payments to the other party in respect of the accommodation, if the other party would (but for the order) be entitled to occupy the dwelling-house by virtue of a beneficial estate or interest or contract or by virtue of any such enactment;

(c) grant either party possession or use of furniture or other contents of the dwelling-house;

(d) order either party to take reasonable care of any furniture or other contents of the dwelling-house;

(e) order either party to take reasonable steps to keep the dwelling-house and any furniture or other contents secure.

In deciding whether and, if so, how to exercise its powers under this section, under s40(2) FLA 1996, the court shall have regard to all the circumstances of the case including:

(a) the financial needs and financial resources of the parties; and

(b) the financial obligations that they have, or are likely to have in the foreseeable future, including financial obligations to each other and to any relevant child.

An order under this section ceases to have effect when the occupation order to which it relates ceases to have effect.

Unfortunately, s40 FLA 1996 has been held to be unenforceable. In *Nwogbe v Nwogbe* [2000] 2 FLR 744, Butler-Sloss P held that:

> it was clear that order under s40 . . . were unenforceable and of no value to the spouse or cohabitee remaining in occupation. That was a serious omission which required urgent alteration.

The order may have some value if the respondent is likely to comply without the need for compliance proceedings.

34.4.1 TRANSFER OF TENANCIES

Sch 7 FLA 1996 allows the court to transfer a range of tenancies (including statutory tenancies) held by one or both spouses, civil partners, former spouses or civil partners, or cohabitants. The court has to consider the parties' suitability as tenants and whether to award compensation payable by the transferee. These orders are beyond the scope of this text and a specialist practitioner text should be consulted.

SUMMARY POINTS

- Occupation orders under the FLA 1996 regulate the occupation of the home, including ordering someone to leave a property or allowing a person to return.
- The parties must be associated persons, the home must be or intended to be the home of the applicant and respondent, and must be a dwelling house.
- There are a number of different sections of the FLA 1996 under which an application can be made. Choosing the correct section is essential.
- S33 FLA 1996 should be used where the applicant has a legal, beneficial right to remain in the home or has 'home' rights.
- When deciding whether to make an order under s33 FLA 1996, the court considers the 'balance of harm' test as well as a series of factors under s33(6) FLA 1996 including housing and financial resources, the likely effect of not making an order on the health, safety, and well-being of the parties, and the conduct of the parties.
- The balance of harm test is found in s33(7) FLA 1996 and asks the court to balance the risk of significant harm to the applicant if the order is not made with the risk of significant harm to the respondent if the order is made.
- If the applicant has no right to occupy the home but is a former spouse or cohabitant of the respondent who is entitled to occupy the home, s35 FLA 1996 will apply.
- If the applicant and respondent are cohabitants or former cohabitants and the respondent is entitled to occupy the home, s36 FLA 1996 may apply.
- If neither party is entitled to occupy the property, then s37 or 38 FLA 1996 may apply.
- Ss35, 36, 37, and 38 FLA 1996 have varying qualifying tests for entitlement and reference should be made to the individual section for the criteria.
- The duration of an occupation order depends on the section under which the order is granted.
- The court can make ancillary orders concerning the care and upkeep of the home, although there are some doubts about their enforceability.

SELF-TEST QUESTIONS

1. Louise and Imran are married and live at 25 Acacia Avenue with Amy, Louise's daughter from her first marriage. Louise has a very poorly paid part-time job and is Amy's full-time mum. Imran works as a highly paid accountant and owns a number of rental properties. It is a very large house and Louise and Imran own it jointly. In order to help to pay the mortgage, they take in lodgers and Martin moves into one room. Martin invites his girlfriend, Susi, to live with him but Louise and Imran do not realize this and think that she just comes to see Martin a great deal.

   Imran and Louise begin to experience difficulties in their marriage and Imran assaults Louise seriously on a number of occasions and also threatens to assault Amy.

(a) Louise wishes to apply for an occupation order. Advise Louise which section she should use to apply and whether she is likely to be successful.

(b) If Louise is successful, how long can any order last?

(c) Would your answer be any different if Louise and Imran were not married?

(d) If Imran owned the property in his sole name and Louise and Amy had moved in with him six months ago, would your advice be any different?

(e) Susi is also experiencing violence and threats from Martin. Would she be entitled to apply for an occupation order?

Case Study Two

Helena owns her own home. Sean is refusing to leave the home and your supervisor has asked you to advise on:

(a) under which section of the FLA 1996 should Helena apply for an occupation order?

(b) Will Helena be successful? Apply s33(6) and (7) FLA 1996 to the case.

online resource centre

Answers to the questions above can be found on the Online Resource Centre: www.oxfordtextbooks.co.uk/orc/familyhandbook13.

35 PROTECTION UNDER THE FAMILY LAW ACT 1996: EMERGENCY PROTECTION AND ENFORCEMENT

35.1 INTRODUCTION

This chapter will:

- **examine in which circumstances an order under the Family Law Act 1996 will be made without notice to the other party to proceedings;**
- **determine the availability and methods of enforcement of orders made under the Family Law Act 1996.**

Clients come to see a solicitor if they have suffered domestic abuse from a violent partner and require urgent protection and, as a result, a solicitor must be prepared to re-arrange their day and to take urgent steps. Once an order has been obtained, it must be properly enforced if the respondent does not obey the terms of the order. An order is essentially only a piece of paper from a court. It is really important to explain to a client that the order must be enforced properly and it is the responsibility of the client to contact their solicitor or the police to enforce the order.

This chapter covers the law on applications made without notice and the enforcement of orders.

35.2 ORDERS MADE WITHOUT NOTICE

An order may be made without notice to the respondent. The old terminology for a without notice hearing was 'ex parte' and sometimes it is still referred to in that way. If a client is at risk of serious harm, giving the respondent notice can exacerbate an already dangerous situation for the client. A without notice application is used when a client cannot move away to a refuge or another safe place whilst the respondent has notice of the hearing. This occurs fairly often in practice and often is very disruptive to a solicitor's day. However, if a client is in need of urgent protection, then a without notice application should be made.

The grounds for making an application are listed in s45 of the Family Law Act 1996 (FLA 1996) and the court may, in any case where it considers that it is *just and convenient* to do so, make an occupation order or a non-molestation order even though the respondent has not been given such notice of the proceedings as would otherwise be required by rules of court.

In determining whether to exercise its powers under s45(1) FLA 1996, the court shall have regard to all the circumstances including the factors listed in s45(2) FLA 1996:

(a) any risk of significant harm to the applicant or a relevant child, attributable to conduct of the respondent, if the order is not made immediately;

(b) whether it is likely that the applicant will be deterred or prevented from pursuing the application if an order is not made immediately; and

(c) whether there is reason to believe that the respondent is aware of the proceedings but is deliberately evading service and that the applicant or a relevant child will be seriously prejudiced by the delay involved

(i) where the court is a magistrates' court, in effecting service of proceedings; or

(ii) in any other case, in effecting substituted service.

 **Example**

Nosizwe lives with Josh. Josh has always been controlling of Nosizwe and has restricted her contact with friends and family since they moved in together. Josh has been increasingly abusive over the past few months and in the last couple of weeks has started to push, slap, and punch Nosizwe when he has had a few drinks. The assaults have grown increasingly serious over the last couple of weeks and Nosizwe has become increasingly afraid. Last night Nosizwe packed a bag and tried to leave. Unfortunately, Josh came home just as Nosizwe was on the point of leaving. Josh assaulted Nosizwe very seriously causing her bruising, a split lip, black eyes, and (she suspects) fractured ribs. Nosizwe managed to leave the house when Josh went to work and has come for advice. Josh has sent her text messages saying that she has to come home or he will come and find her at her family and friends and that he will not stop looking for her.

Nosizwe is terrified that Josh will find her and assault her more seriously. She says that there is nowhere that is safe for her to go. She states that if she cannot get an order straightaway she will not make an application as she will be worse off.

Nosizwe should apply for an order without notice as she is at risk of significant harm and will be deterred if an application is not made immediately.

If the court makes an order by virtue of s45(1) FLA 1996, under s45(3) FLA 1996 it must afford the respondent an opportunity to make representations relating to the order as soon as just and convenient at a full hearing, called a 'return date'.

 **Example**

Nosizwe obtains a non-molestation order without notice. The judge orders that a hearing is held in three days' time with Josh present. This is the 'return date'.

The court may accept that if an applicant has suffered violence they require the protection of a non-molestation order and may order a respondent to refrain from acts that are not lawful in any event. However, an occupation order deprives a respondent of their home and proprietary rights. Case-law prior to the FLA 1996 suggests that occupation orders should seldom be granted without notice and will apply to exceptional cases only (*G v G (Ouster: Ex parte application)* [1990] 1 FLR 395 and *Masich v Masich* [1977] Fam Law 245).

35.3 ENFORCING AN ORDER

The system of enforcing orders under the FLA 1996 differs for non-molestation orders and occupation orders. The Domestic Violence, Crime and Victims Act 2004 (DVCVA 2004) introduced a criminal sanction for the breach of a non-molestation order. This came into force in July 2007.

35.3.1 NON-MOLESTATION ORDERS

The DVCVA 2004 amended s42 FLA 1996 to make the breach of a non-molestation order a criminal offence. S42A(1) FLA 1996 states that a person who without reasonable excuse does anything that he is prohibited from doing by a non-molestation order is guilty of an offence. However, s42A(2) FLA 1996 ensures that a person cannot be convicted if they are unaware of the existence of the order. This makes it extremely important to serve an order promptly and to have good evidence of service (see **Chapter 8**). A person guilty of an offence under this section is liable on conviction on indictment to imprisonment for a term not exceeding five years, or a fine, or both and on summary conviction to imprisonment for a term not exceeding 12 months, or a fine not exceeding the statutory maximum, or both. For further details of the criminal charge, please refer to a specialist criminal law text.

Example

At the return date, the court makes a non-molestation order and Josh is served with the order the following day. A week later, Nosizwe starts to receive abusive text messages from Josh. Later the same day, Josh comes to where Nosizwe works and shouts abusive comments at her as she leaves work. Nosizwe calls the police and they arrest Josh and charge him with the criminal offence of breaching a non-molestation order.

The police can arrest someone they suspect of committing this offence and the prosecution will be dealt with by the CPS. This has the advantage of removing the responsibility for enforcement from the applicant. The potential disadvantages of this system are that the applicant may not wish to criminalize their partner and an applicant may be left unprotected if bail conditions are changed without notice to them. In the online resources there are details of an initial appraisal of these provisions.

It is possible for an applicant to enforce a non-molestation order by applying for a warrant of arrest under s47(8) FLA 1996 for the respondent to be brought to the court. The court will hear the allegations of the breach and decide whether the order has been breached. The punishment for breach is contempt of court and this is dealt with further at **35.3.3**. It is unlikely that a client will gain public funding to pursue a warrant.

The FLA 1996 avoids the potential pitfall of 'double jeopardy' of the respondent being convicted of a criminal offence and then being brought to a civil court in contempt proceedings. S42A(3) and (4) FLA 1996 provide that where a person is convicted of an offence under this section in respect of any conduct, that conduct is not punishable as a contempt of court. Similarly, a person cannot be convicted of an offence under this section in respect of any conduct that has been punished as a contempt of court.

35.3.2 OCCUPATION ORDERS

S47(2) FLA 1996 states that if:

(a) the court makes an occupation order; and

(b) it appears to the court that the respondent has used or threatened violence against the applicant or a relevant child,

it shall attach a power of arrest to one or more provisions of the order unless satisfied that in all the circumstances of the case the applicant or child will be adequately protected without such a power of arrest.

A power of arrest is a warning to the respondent that if the terms of the order are breached then s/he can be arrested and taken back to the court where the order was made. As discussed in **Chapter 36**, an order with a power of arrest must be delivered to a local police station. Should such an order be breached by the respondent, the police will arrest the respondent and then bring the respondent to the court that made the order.

Where an order is made without notice, the court may attach a power of arrest to one or more provisions of the order if it appears to it that:

(a) the respondent has used or threatened violence against the applicant or a relevant child; and

(b) there is a risk of significant harm to the applicant or child, attributable to conduct of the respondent, if the power of arrest is not attached to those provisions immediately under s47(3) FLA 1996.

Under s47(4) FLA 1996 if the court attaches a power of arrest to any provisions of a relevant order, it may provide that the power of arrest is to have effect for a shorter period than the other provisions of the order.

If a power of arrest is attached to certain provisions of an order, a constable may arrest without warrant a person whom he has reasonable cause for suspecting to be in breach of any such provision. He must be brought before the relevant judicial authority within the period of 24 hours beginning at the time of his arrest and if the matter is not then disposed of forthwith, the relevant judicial authority before whom he is brought may remand him. In reckoning for the purposes of this provision any period of 24 hours, no account is to be taken of Christmas Day, Good Friday, or any Sunday.

For the procedure for enforcement, see **Chapter 36**.

35.3.3 POWERS OF THE COURT TO ENFORCE AN OCCUPATION ORDER

When a breach of an order is proved, the court must consider the punishment of the respondent. The sentencing powers of the court arise as any breach of an order is contempt of court and the court can order a fine or up to two years' imprisonment. The Court of Appeal in *Neil v Ryan* [1998] EWCA Civ 1277 held that a serious breach of an order would indicate an immediate custodial sentence. In *Hale v Tanner* [2000] 2 FLR 879 the Court of Appeal established some guidelines on sentencing, although this was in the context of the law concerning a breach of a non-molestation order prior to the amendment to s42 FLA 1996 by the DVCVA 2004. The guidance was given in the judgment by Hale LJ. She stated that she would not wish to suggest that there should be any general principle that the statutory provisions related to sentencing in ordinary criminal cases should be applied to sentencing for contempt. The circumstances surrounding contempt cases are much more various and the objectives underlying the court's actions are also much more various. The guidance included:

- the full range of criminal sentencing options is not available;
- custody is not automatic;
- there is a power to fine, and a power to suspend a custodial sentence, which should nevertheless not affect the length of the sentence; i.e. you do not make the sentence longer because you are going to suspend it;
- the length of the sentence depends on the court's objectives, which will always include marking the court's disapproval of the disobedience of its order and securing compliance with it in the future;
- the length of the committal has to bear some relationship to the maximum statutory sentence of two years;
- the court has to bear in mind the context, which may be aggravating or mitigating in terms of the seriousness of the breach.

Hale LJ also said that it was rare to find reported cases of sentences of six months' imprisonment in the context of much more serious breaches than took place in the case then before the court, which mainly concerned serious, persistent, and threatening telephone calls.

Practical Considerations

In terms of sentencing, it is the experience of the author that the courts tend to balance the need to punish the breach with ensuring compliance with the order. The use of a suspended sentence is common. A suspended sentence is one where the court imposes a custodial sentence but suspends its implementation for a set period of time, e.g. three months. The respondent will not go to prison immediately but if there are any further breaches of the order, the custodial sentence will be implemented plus any further sentence for the further breach.

SUMMARY POINTS

- A client often requires protection urgently and this is dealt with by applying for an order without notice.
- 'Without notice' means that the respondent will not be given notice of the hearing for an order under the FLA 1996 and the court will not hear any evidence from the respondent.
- The court can only make an order without notice if there is risk of significant harm to the applicant or the applicant will be deterred from pursuing the application or the respondent is avoiding service.
- After the hearing of a without notice application, the court must order a hearing for all parties to attend, which is called a return date.
- A non-molestation order is enforced through the criminal law; breach of a non-molestation order is a criminal offence. Alternatively, the client may rely upon a warrant of arrest to enforce a non-molestation order.
- Occupation orders can still have a power of arrest attached to them allowing the police to arrest for a breach of the order. The enforcement proceedings are heard in the civil court in which the original order was made.
- A breach of an occupation order is a contempt of court that is punishable by a fine or imprisonment.

SELF-TEST QUESTIONS

1. See the example involving Nosizwe and Josh (starting at **35.2**). On the return date the court makes both an occupation order and a non-molestation order in favour of Nosizwe. The court attaches a power of arrest to the occupation order. Explain the effect of a power of arrest to Josh.
2. The terms of the occupation order are for Josh not to enter the family home. Nosizwe comes home on Friday evening after a night out to find Josh in the house. He calmly states that he is collecting some clothes and leaves immediately. Advise Josh on what enforcement action Nosizwe can take and the procedural steps required.

Case Study Two

Helena is extremely afraid of Sean. Helena is reluctant to admit that she and Richard have been suffering violence but states that if she does not get some form of protection they will both continue to suffer violence. What would you advise Helena to do?

Helena is granted a non-molestation order. She receives abusive texts from Sean and last night, at about 2am, Helena is woken up by a stone breaking her window. Her neighbours (who are returning from a night out) tell her that they saw Sean running away from the house. What would you advise Helena to do?

online resource centre

Answers to the questions above can be found on the Online Resource Centre: www.oxfordtextbooks.co.uk/orc/familyhandbook13/.

36 PROTECTION UNDER THE FAMILY LAW ACT 1996: PROCEDURE

36.1 INTRODUCTION

This chapter will:

- **examine the procedure for obtaining and enforcing orders under the Family Law Act 1996.**

The procedure to obtain an order under the Family Law Act 1996 (FLA 1996) is reasonably straightforward but often has to be undertaken in a hurry if a client instructs you at the last minute or requires an order without notice. This chapter will outline the procedure involved in applying for orders under the FLA 1996 without notice, on notice, and when enforcing orders.

36.2 COURTS AND RULES

An application for an order under the FLA 1996 can be made in either the county court or the family proceedings court. In practice, the vast majority of orders are brought in the county court.

36.2.1 RULES

In all courts, the relevant rules are the Family Procedure Rules 2010 (FPR 2010).

This chapter will describe the procedure in the county court as this is where the majority of applications are heard but will also highlight any differences in procedure between the courts. In practice, applications for orders are made mainly to the county court.

36.2.2 WHICH COURT?

The choice of court is guided by the Family Law Act 1996 (Part IV) (Allocation of Proceedings) Order 1997, S.I. 1997 No. 1896. An application can be made to any county court (whether a designated divorce county court, a family hearing centre, or a care centre) or a family proceedings court. There are some cases that have particular considerations:

- any case requiring the court to resolve a disputed question concerning any party's entitlement to occupy a property cannot be heard in a family proceedings court unless it is unnecessary to resolve the question in order to hear the application or make the order;
- the family proceedings court cannot hear applications for the transfer of tenancies on divorce or separation of cohabitants;

- applications from an applicant aged under 18 and applications under s43 FLA 1996 where the applicant requires permission to proceed as they are aged under 16 years and proceedings under this section must be commenced in the High Court.

36.3 FUNDING

Until April 2013, clients can fund proceedings privately or through Community Legal Service (CLS) funding, if eligible. As discussed in **Chapters 1 and 2**, a privately paying client will have to have the costs of the case discussed clearly and be given regular updates.

36.3.1 CLS FUNDING

Chapter 2 contains details of the types of funding available in domestic abuse proceedings until April 2013. After April 2013, cases involving applications under the FLA 1996 are still within the scope of public funding. It is envisaged that some changes will be made to the delivery of public funding in April 2013 and reference should be made to the online resources. The rest of this section deals with the position up until April 2013; updates will be available on the online resources. Currently, there are some particular considerations for clients seeking funding for domestic abuse orders. For an application for legal representation, the usual requirement is that the parties attend a mediation appointment. This, for obvious reasons, may be totally unsuitable for a client at risk of further violence and will be sufficient for a client not to attend such an appointment. Emergency funding may be necessary (see **Chapter 2**).

The Funding Code deals with several aspects of domestic abuse cases and funding and can be found on the CLS's website (and in the online resources).

Funding is not limited just to persons who have suffered actual physical violence.

Note that emergency cover should only be granted to take injunction proceedings where the applicant or relevant child is in imminent danger of significant harm. Significant harm is imminent if there is a real risk that it will occur before a substantive application can be processed and the matter brought before the court.

Legal representation will be refused if the prospects of obtaining the order sought in the proceedings are poor. Funding can therefore only be granted where the prospects of success are at least borderline or above. In relation to non-molestation orders the issue is whether the court is likely to be satisfied that the respondent has molested the other party or a relevant child and that an order is considered necessary by the court for the protection of that party or child having regard to all the circumstances, including the need to secure the health, safety, and well-being of the applicant, or of another party to the proceedings or of any relevant child.

Practical Considerations

As an example, the prospects of obtaining an order are likely to be poor if:

- the incidents complained of are of a trivial nature. However, where there has been a history of incidents, the cumulative effect of those incidents may be taken into account; or
- the conduct complained of is not likely to be repeated. If the conduct complained of took place more than three weeks prior to the application it will be necessary to set out in the application why it is considered that repetition is likely, e.g. if there has been a history of violent conduct.

The Funding Code states that an application may be refused to cover court proceedings if no warning letter has first been sent to the respondent. However, this is not an absolute rule. Practitioners should demonstrate that consideration has been given to whether a warning letter might endanger the client. A warning letter may be inappropriate, e.g. if the applicant and respondent are still living under the same roof or if the threat to the applicant is serious and imminent or if receipt of a warning letter by the respondent may trigger further violence to the applicant or any relevant child before a protective order can be obtained. However, in most other cases a warning letter, which can be issued under the legal help scheme, will be the appropriate first step.

The CLS may also require an explanation if the applicant has not involved the police. The CLS Funding Code states that where the incidents complained of constitute an assault or other crime against the applicant the police should normally be notified and given an opportunity to deal with the respondent. The CLS recognizes that there may be good reason not to pursue criminal proceedings, e.g. where this might jeopardize the long-term financial or other interests of the family. If so, or if there is reason to believe that the police will not be able to assist or if they are contacted but have failed to respond or to provide adequate assistance to protect the applicant and any relevant children, then a grant of legal representation may be appropriate.

For occupation orders, legal representation will only be granted where there are at least borderline prospects of obtaining an order. This involves considering whether the parties and property qualify to be covered by an order and whether an order is likely to be considered necessary by the court having regard to all the circumstances of the case including the 'balance of harm' test. Legal representation is most likely to be granted where the applicant is in a refuge or other temporary accommodation, having recently been excluded from a property, or where there is otherwise a significant likelihood of risk in remaining in or returning to the property without the protection of an order. Legal representation is likely to be refused if the respondent has already left voluntarily and does not appear likely to return.

Respondents are likely to be granted funding when defending committal proceedings as there is the potential for the respondent to be imprisoned and so the interests of justice will usually require that the respondent is represented.

36.4 PROCEDURE IN THE COUNTY COURT AND FAMILY PROCEEDINGS COURT

36.4.1 THE APPLICATION FORM

An application for a non-molestation or occupation order in a free-standing application is made on a Form FL401 (which is reproduced at the end of this chapter). If a client wishes to keep their address confidential they must complete Confidential Address Form C8. A witness statement must be attached as well as a draft of the order (r10.2 FPR 2010). The witness statement will contain a statement of truth.

A fee of £60 is payable unless the client gains a fee exemption.

Practical Considerations

The witness statement to accompany the Form FL401 must contain a statement of truth. The drafting of the statement must be carefully considered and the following points should be considered:

- the statement should start with an indication of what the statement concerns;
- the statement should be clear that the court has jurisdiction to hear the application and the statement should be clear about how the parties are associated or how the party is entitled to live in the property;
- there should be a chronology of the parties' lives together, including dates of marriage/civil partnership/cohabitation, dates of birth of any children, and any other important dates;
- the statement should set out the incidents relied upon in chronological order and give full details of the incident including any injuries, whether the police were called, and whether medical help was sought;

- the statement should address the statutory tests for the order sought under the FLA 1996, e.g. for a non-molestation order, and should cover how the health, safety, and well-being of the applicant or relevant child is affected;
- the statement should refer to all parts of the FLA 1996 that apply to the applicant's case; e.g. if applying without notice for an order, ensure the court understands that the client has the requisite grounds or state why a power of arrest should be attached to the order;
- if drafting a statement for a respondent who is replying to allegations made by the applicant, avoid the situation of flat denials or further attacks on the applicant. Give a full account of the respondent's actions, including an expression of remorse where appropriate;
- if drafting a statement for a respondent illustrate (in an application for an occupation order) the impact of an order and whether they will suffer significant harm;
- ask the court to make the orders applied for.

If an application is made to vary, extend, or discharge an order, a Form FL403 should be used. For the procedure to be adopted for an application by a child under 18, reference should be made to a practitioner text.

36.4.1.1 Application without notice

A Form FL401 is completed for a without notice application and the witness statement should address the reasons for applying without notice.

36.4.2 SERVICE

36.4.2.1 Respondent

The respondent should be served with the Form FL401 and the witness statement in support together with notice of proceedings on FL402 (r10.3(1) FPR 2010). Service must be personal service not less than two days before the application is to be heard. It is usual for a process server to be engaged to effect service. A process server is someone who, amongst other things, specializes in serving court proceedings and has a great deal of experience in finding recalcitrant respondents and serving individuals who can be volatile. To assist the process server, full details of the respondent, including a photograph, should be given and as much detail as possible about their home, work, and where and when is a suitable time for service.

Service will not be required if the application is made without notice. Once service has been completed, the applicant should file a statement in Form FL415 as proof of service (r.10.3(4) FPR 2010).

36.4.2.2 Third parties

Where the applicant makes an application for an occupation order under s33, 35, or 36 FLA 1996 a copy of the application must be served by first class post on the mortgage lender or the landlord of a rented house in Form FL 416. This form informs them of the right to make representations in writing or at any hearing (r10.3(3) FPR 2010).

36.4.3 THE HEARING

The rules in r10.5 FPR 2010 give little direction on the form of the hearing except that the application is dealt with in chambers unless the court otherwise directs. The application is heard by a deputy district judge, a district judge, or a circuit judge. The court must make a note of the hearing in Form FL405.

When the hearing is in a without notice case, the court will consider the witness statement and may ask the applicant some questions. The applicant should be told about the layout of the court, the personnel they are likely to encounter and the possibility of having to answer questions. The court must set a date for the matter to be heard with both parties present; this is referred to as the 'return date'. This is generally set to be fairly close to the initial hearing, as a potentially Draconian order may be made without giving the respondent an opportunity to put their case.

When the hearing is on notice or the return date, the court may either make the order or make a date for a further hearing. If a final hearing is necessary the court can make directions for statements from the respondent, any witnesses, or any medical or other expert evidence. At a final hearing, the court will hear oral evidence from any witnesses relevant to the case.

Practical Considerations

It is tempting to use the suggested guidelines in the FL401 as a basis for drafting and to produce generic orders. As the breach of a non-molestation order is a criminal offence (s42A FLA 1996), it may be worth considering a more specific form of drafting and to consider the ongoing contact between the parties if there are children in common.

For example, if a particular feature of a case is the persistent use of text messages to harass and threaten the applicant, an order could be drafted specifically to prevent the respondent texting the applicant. Any breach of the non-molestation order by sending a text would be far easier to prove in criminal proceedings.

36.4.4 SERVING THE ORDER

Any order made after a hearing must be served on the respondent personally (r10.6(1) FPR 2010). In an application for an occupation order under s33, 35, or 36 FLA 1996 a copy of the order must be served by first class post on the mortgage lender or the landlord of a rented house (r10.6(3) FPR 2010). Please note that a respondent cannot be prosecuted under s42A FLA 1996 unless the respondent has notice of the order. An order cannot be served on the respondent within the precincts of the court.

36.4.4.1 Notification of the police

If the court makes an occupation order with a power of arrest or a non-molestation order, (r10.10(2) FPR 2010), the following documents must be delivered to the officer in charge of the police station local to the applicant's address (or other station as the court orders):

- a copy of the Form FL404a and/or Form FL404; and
- a statement showing the respondent has been served with the order or informed of its terms (whether by being present when the order was made or by telephone or otherwise).

The applicant must deliver these documents unless the court is responsible for service (if the applicant is acting in person). If any order or part of the order is discharged or varied, the court must inform the officer and deliver a copy of the order to that officer (r10.10(6) FPR 2010).

36.4.5 DIFFERENCES IN PROCEDURE AT THE FAMILY PROCEEDINGS COURT

The FPR 2010 have largely unified the procedures in all courts. The main exception is the position where a person is arrested pursuant either to a power of arrest or a warrant of arrest. The procedure in this situation (highly unusually) is found in s144 Magistrates' Courts Act 1980. This is beyond the scope of this text and a practitioner's text should be consulted.

36.5 ENFORCEMENT PROCEDURE

36.5.1 ENFORCEMENT IN THE COUNTY COURT

The rules are found in r10.11 FPR 2010. Each order made by the court contains a 'penal notice' warning the respondent of the consequences of a breach of an order and the wording of the non-molestation order encompasses the breach as a criminal offence.

If a non-molestation order is breached, the client should contact the police using 999 (if an urgent situation) or the local police contact number.

36.5.2 OCCUPATION ORDER WITH A POWER OF ARREST

The provisions of an occupation order that have a power of arrest attached should be recorded on Form FL 406. If the order is breached, the applicant should telephone the police in order to report it. S47(7) FLA 1996 allows the police to arrest the respondent if there appear to be sufficient grounds for arrest. The arrested person should be brought before a judge, district judge, or magistrates' court within 24 hours beginning at the time of arrest.

The President's Practice Direction of 9 December 1999: Family Law Act 1996—Attendance of Arresting Officer [2000] 1 FLR 270 states that when an arrested person is brought before the relevant judicial authority, the attendance of the arresting officer is not necessary unless the arrest itself is in issue. The officer may have to attend if they were a witness to the events leading up to the arrest or the breach of the order.

Once the respondent has been arrested, the court may:

- conduct a full hearing in open court to determine whether the facts, and the circumstances which led to the arrest, amounted to disobedience of the order;
- adjourn the proceedings and, where such an order is made, the arrested person may be released.

The proceedings must be listed for hearing within 14 days of the date upon which the respondent was arrested, and the respondent should be given two business days' notice of the adjourned hearing. An application for bail can be made and applies where the respondent is kept in custody following arrest. For further details, a practitioner text should be consulted.

36.5.3 WARRANT OF ARREST

Where an occupation order contains no power of arrest or the applicant does not wish to use criminal proceedings to enforce a non-molestation order, a warrant of arrest can be used. S47(8) FLA 1996 can be used in order to apply to the court for a warrant of arrest to arrest the respondent. The application is made on Form FL407 and the warrant issued on Form FL 408. The applicant must give evidence on oath to satisfy the court that a breach of the order has occurred. The warrant authorizes the court bailiff or police to arrest the respondent. Once arrested, the procedure is as described at **36.5.2**.

36.5.4 COMMITTAL PROCEEDINGS

Committal proceedings are used where there has been a breach of an undertaking, breach of a term of an occupation order where there is no power of arrest, or a non-molestation order where there are no criminal proceedings. The application for the issue of a committal order, which is a notice to show good reason, is on Form N78 and must:

- specify the provisions of the order or undertaking that has been disobeyed;
- set out the ways in which it is alleged that the order has been disobeyed or broken;
- be supported by an affidavit (see the **Glossary**) by the applicant setting out the grounds for the application. These documents must be served personally on the respondent.

A fee of £60 is payable. Committal proceedings try the allegation that the respondent has committed a contempt of court and if the court finds that there is contempt, it has the power to imprison the respondent. The President's Direction of 16 March (Committal Applications and Procedure in which a Committal Order can be made) [2000] 1 FLR 949 gives guidance on the procedure to be followed.

36.5.5 ENFORCEMENT OF A NON-MOLESTATION ORDER UNDER S42A FLA 1996

When a respondent breaches a non-molestation order, the police may arrest the respondent as breach is a criminal offence. As a result, the usual criminal procedure will apply and the Crown Prosecution Service will be responsible for the conduct of the case.

SUMMARY POINTS

- Proceedings are commenced using a Form FL401 and a statement in support.
- Proceedings can be commenced in either the county court or family proceedings court (or occasionally in the High Court).
- Funding is available for those eligible for CLS funding. Consideration must be given to sending a warning letter or contacting the police before applying for funding.
- A statement in support of the application should be carefully drafted to ensure that the court has all the necessary information, including information required by the FLA 1996.
- The respondent should be personally served with the FL401 and the statement in support unless the application is to be made without notice.
- The application will be heard by the court and either an order will be made, directions given for a further hearing, or the application will be withdrawn.
- If an order is made, it is extremely important that the order is served. If applicable, the police should be notified of the order.
- If a non-molestation order is breached, the police should be contacted. Alternatively, the applicant may apply for a warrant of arrest, although it is unlikely that funding will be granted.
- If an occupation order has a power of arrest attached to it, the police should be contacted. If there is no power of arrest, a warrant of arrest should be sought.
- Committal proceedings can be used where there is an alleged breach of an undertaking or an order under FLA 1996 where there is no power of arrest.

SELF-TEST QUESTIONS

1. You represent Pamina who has been severely assaulted by her husband. She is extremely concerned that if her husband has notice of the proceedings, she will be assaulted again. You advise that she has the grounds to apply for a non-molestation and occupation order without notice. Describe the procedure required to obtain an order without notice.

Case Study Two

Your supervisor asks you to look at the statement in support of Helena's application. This can be found on the Online Resource Centre. Suggest which, if any, change you would make.

Answers to the questions above can be found on the Online Resource Centre: www.oxfordtextbooks.co.uk/orc/familyhandbook13/.

Application for:
a non-molestation order
an occupation order

Family Law Act 1996 (Part IV)

The court

To be completed by the court

Date issued

Case number

Please read the accompanying notes as you complete this form.

1 About you (the applicant)

State your title (Mr, Mrs etc), full name, address, telephone number and date of birth (if under 18):

Helena Wilson
31 Roseberry Avenue
Longtown
LG3 8GH

State your solicitor's name, address, reference, telephone, FAX and DX numbers:

Burrell, Young and Hepple
23 High Street
Longtown
LG1 9HN
Tel: 01336722777

2 About the respondent

State the respondent's name, address and date of birth (if known):

Sean Brown
31 Roseberry Avenue
Longtown
LG3 8GH

3 The Order(s) for which you are applying

This application is for:

☑ a non-molestation order

☑ an occupation order

☑ Tick this box if you wish the court to hear your application without notice being given to the respondent. The reasons relied on for an application being heard without notice must be stated in the statement in support.

4 Your relationship to the respondent (the person to be served with this application)

Your relationship to the respondent is:

(Please tick only one of the following)

1 ☐ Married

2 ☐ Civil Partners

3 ☐ Were married

4 ☐ Former civil partners

5 ☑ Cohabiting

6 ☐ Were cohabiting

7 ☐ Both of you live or have lived in the same household

8 ☐ Relative
State how related:

9 ☐ Agreed to marry.
Give the date the agreement was made.
If the agreement has ended, state when.

10 ☐ Agreed to form a civil partnership.
Give the date the agreement was made.
If the agreement has ended, state when.

11 ☐ Both of you are parents of, or have parental responsibility for, a child

12 ☐ One of you is a parent of a child and the other has parental responsibility for that child

13 ☐ One of you is the natural parent or grandparent of a child adopted, placed or freed for adoption, and the other is:

(i) the adoptive parent

or (ii) a person who has applied for an adoption order for the child

or (iii) a person with whom the child has been placed for adoption

or (iv) the child who has been adopted, placed or freed for adoption.

State whether (i), (ii), (iii) or (iv):

14 ☐ Both of you are the parties to the same family proceedings (see also Section 11 below).

5 Application for a non-molestation order

If you wish to apply for a non-molestation order, state briefly in this section the order you want.

That Sean Brown do not harass, pester, threaten or molest Helena Wilson

Give full details in support of your application in your supporting evidence.

6 Application for an occupation order

If you do not wish to apply for an occupation order, please go to section 9 of this form.

(A) State the address of the dwelling-house to which your application relates:

31 Roseberry Avenue
Longtown
LG3 8GH

(B) State whether it is occupied by you or the respondent now or in the past, or whether it was intended to be occupied by you or the respondent:

I occupy the property with the respondent

(C) State whether you are entitled to occupy the dwelling-house: ☑ Yes ☐ No

If yes, explain why:

(D) State whether the respondent is entitled to occupy the dwelling-house: ☑ Yes ☐ No

If yes, explain why:

On the basis of your answers to (C) and (D) above, tick one of the boxes 1 to 6 below to show the category into which you fit

1 ☑ a spouse or civil partner who has home rights in the dwelling-house, or a person who is entitled to occupy it by virtue of a beneficial estate or interest or contract or by virtue of any enactment giving him or her the right to remain in occupation.

If you tick box 1, state whether there is a dispute or pending proceedings between you and the respondent about your right to occupy the dwelling-house.

2 ☐ a former spouse or former civil partner with no existing right to occupy, where the respondent spouse or civil partner is so entitled.

3 ☐ a cohabitant or former cohabitant with no existing right to occupy, where the respondent cohabitant or former cohabitant is so entitled.

4 ☐ a spouse or former spouse who is not entitled to occupy, where the respondent spouse or former spouse is also not entitled.

5 ☐ a civil partner or former civil partner who is not entitled to occupy, where the respondent civil partner or former civil partner is also not entitled.

6 ☐ a cohabitant or former cohabitant who is not entitled to occupy, where the respondent cohabitant or former cohabitant is also not entitled.

Home Rights

If you do have home rights please:	Registered
State whether the title to the land is registered or unregistered (if known):	
If registered, state the Land Registry title number (if known):	48372621
If you wish to apply for an occupation order, state briefly here the order you want. Give full details in support of your application in your supporting evidence:	That Sean Brown leave the property and not return and not come within 100 metres of the property

7 Application for additional order(s) about the dwelling-house

If you want to apply for any of the orders listed in the notes to this section, state what order you would like the court to make:

8 Mortgage and rent

Is the dwelling-house subject to a mortgage?

☑ Yes ☐ No

If yes, please provide the name and address of the mortgagee:	Haliwide Building Society 33 High Street Longtown LG1 8TF

Is the dwelling-house rented?

☐ Yes ☑ No

If yes, please provide the name and address of the landlord:

9 At the court

Will you need an interpreter at court?

☐ Yes ☑ No

If yes, specify the language:

If you require an interpreter, you must notify the court immediately so that one can be arranged.

If you have a disability for which you require special assistance or special facilities, please state what your needs are. The court staff will get in touch with you about your requirements.

10 Other information

State the name and date of birth of any child living with or staying with, or likely to live with or stay with, you or the respondent:

Richard Wilson
DOB: 23.2.2008

State the name of any other person living in the same household as you and the respondent, and say why they live there:

11 Other Proceedings and Orders

If there are any other current family proceedings or orders in force involving you and the respondent, state the type of proceedings or orders, the court and the case number. This includes any application for an occupation order or non-molestation order against you by the respondent.

There are care proceedings issued in Longtown County Court, case number 4/CA1989

This application is to be served upon the respondent

Signed: Date:

Application for non-molestation order or occupation order
Notes for guidance

Section 1

If you do not wish your address to be made known to the respondent, leave the space on the form blank and complete Confidential Address Form C8. The court can give you this form.

If you are under 18, someone over 18 must help you make this application. That person, who might be one of your parents, is called a 'next friend'.

If you are under 16, you need permission to make this application. You must apply to the High Court for permission, using this form. If the High Court gives you permission to make this application, it will then either hear the application itself or transfer it to a county court.

Section 3

An urgent order made by the court before the notice of the application is served on the respondent is called an ex-parte order. In deciding whether to make an ex-parte order the court will consider all the circumstances of the case, including:

- any risk of significant harm to the applicant or a relevant child, attributable to conduct of the respondent, if the order is not made immediately
- whether it is likely that the applicant will be deterred or prevented from pursuing the application if an order is not made immediately
- whether there is reason to believe that the respondent is aware of the proceedings but is deliberately evading service and that the applicant or a relevant child will be seriously prejudiced by the delay involved.

If the court makes an ex-parte order, it must give the respondent an opportunity to make representations about the order as soon as just and convenient at a full hearing.

'Harm' in relation to a person who has reached the age of 18 means ill-treatment or the impairment of health, and in relation to a child means ill-treatment or the impairment of health and development.

'Ill-treatment' includes forms of ill-treatment which are not physical and, in relation to a child, includes sexual abuse. The court will require evidence of any harm which you allege in support of your application.

Section 4

For you to be able to apply for an order you must be related to the respondent in one of the ways listed in this section of the form. If you are not related in one of these ways you should seek legal advice.

Cohabitants are two persons who, although not married to each other, nor civil partners of each other, are living together as husband and wife or civil partners. People who have cohabited, but have then married or formed a civil partnership will not fall within this category but will fall within the category of married people or people who are civil partners of each other.

Those who live or have lived in the same household do not include people who share the same household because one of them is the other's employee, tenant, lodger or boarder.

You will only be able to apply as a relative of the respondent if you are:
(A) the father, mother, stepfather, stepmother, son, daughter, stepson, stepdaughter, grandmother, grandfather, grandson, granddaughter of the respondent or of the respondent's spouse, former spouse, civil partner or former civil partner.

(B) the brother, sister, uncle, aunt, niece, nephew or first cousin (whether of the full blood or of the half blood or by marriage or by civil partnership) of the respondent or of the respondent's spouse, former spouse, civil partner or former civil partner.

This includes, in relation to a person who is living or has lived with another person as husband and wife or as civil partners, any person who would fall within (A) or (B) if the parties were married to, or civil partners of, each other (for example, your cohabitee's father or brother).

Agreements to marry: You will fall within this category only if you make this application within three years of the termination of the agreement. The court will require the following evidence of the agreement:

evidence in writing

or the gift of an engagement ring in contemplation of marriage

or evidence that a ceremony has been entered into in the presence of one or more other persons assembled for the purpose of witnessing it.

Agreements to form a civil partnership: You will fall within this category only if you make this application within three years of the termination of the agreement. The court will require the following evidence of the agreement:

evidence in writing

or a gift from one party to the agreement to the other as a token of the agreement

or evidence that a ceremony has been entered into in the presence of one or more other persons assembled for the purpose of witnessing it.

Parents and parental responsibility:
You will fall within this category if

both you and the respondent are either the parents of the child or have parental responsibility for that child

or if one of you is the parent and the other has parental responsibility.

Section 4 continued

Under the Children Act 1989, parental responsibility is held automatically by a child's mother, and by the child's father if he and the mother were married to each other at the time of the child's birth or have married subsequently. Where a child's father and mother are not married to each other at the time of the child's birth, the father may also acquire parental responsibility for that child, if he registers the birth after 1st December 2003, in accordance with section 4(1)(a) of the Children Act 1989. Where neither of these circumstances apply, the father, in accordance with the provisions of the Children Act 1989, can acquire parental responsibility.

From 30 December 2005, where a person who is not the child's parent ("the step-parent") is married to, or a civil partner of, a parent who has parental responsibility for that child, he or she may also acquire parental responsibility for the child in accordance with the provisions of the Children Act 1989.

From 1st September 2009, specific provision has been made in relation to parental responsibility in certain cases involving assisted reproduction. Parental responsibility is held automatically by a woman if—

- she and the child's mother were in a civil partnership with each other at the time of treatment unless that woman did not consent to the treatment; or
- she is a parent of the child by virtue of section 43 of the Human Fertilisation and Embryology Act 2008 and subsequently enters into a civil partnership with the mother.

A woman who is a parent of the child by virtue of section 43 of the 2008 Act but who does not subsequently enter into a civil partnership with the mother may acquire parental responsibility in accordance with the provisions of section 4ZA of the Children Act 1989.

Section 5

A non-molestation order can forbid the respondent from molesting you or a relevant child. Molestation can include, for example, violence, threats, pestering and other forms of harassment. The court can forbid particular acts of the respondent, molestation in general, or both.

Section 6

If you wish to apply for an occupation order but you are uncertain about your answer to any question in this part of the application form, you should seek legal advice.

(A) A dwelling-house includes any building or part of a building which is occupied as a dwelling; any caravan, houseboat or structure which is occupied as a dwelling; and any yard, garden, garage or outhouse belonging to it and occupied with it.

(C) & (D) The following questions give examples to help you to decide if you or the respondent, or both of you, are entitled to occupy the dwelling-house:

(a) Are you the sole legal owner of the dwelling-house?

(b) Are you and the respondent joint legal owners of the dwelling-house?

(c) Is the respondent the sole legal owner of the dwelling-house?

(d) Do you rent the dwelling-house as a sole tenant?

(e) Do you and the respondent rent the dwelling-house as joint tenants?

(f) Does the respondent rent the dwelling-house as a sole tenant?

If you answer

- **Yes** to (a), (b), (d) or (e) you are likely to be entitled to occupy the dwelling-house
- **Yes** to (c) or (f) you may not be entitled (unless, for example, you are a spouse or civil partner and have home rights – see notes under 'Home Rights' below)
- **Yes** to (b), (c), (e) or (f), the respondent is likely to be entitled to occupy the dwelling-house
- **Yes** to (a) or (d) the respondent may not be entitled (unless, for example, he or she is a spouse or civil partner and has home rights).

Box 1 For example, if you are sole owner, joint owner or if you rent the property. If you are not a spouse, former spouse, civil partner, former civil partner, cohabitant or former cohabitant of the respondent, you will only be able to apply for an occupation order if you fall within this category.

If you answer yes to this question, it will not be possible for a magistrates' court to deal with the application, unless the court decides that it is unnecessary for it to decide this question in order to deal with the application or make the order. If the court decides that it cannot deal with the application, it will transfer the application to a county court.

Box 2 For example, if the respondent is or was married to you, or if you and the respondent are or were civil partners, and he or she is sole owner or rents the property.

Box 3 For example, if the respondent is or was cohabiting with you and is sole owner or rents the property.

Home Rights

Where one spouse or civil partner "**(A)**" is entitled to occupy the dwelling-house by virtue of a beneficial estate or interest or contract or by virtue of any enactment giving him or her the right to remain in occupation, and the other spouse or civil partner "**(B)**" is not so entitled, then **B** (who is not entitled) has home rights.

The rights are

(a) if **B** is in occupation, not to be evicted or excluded from the dwelling-house except with the leave of the court; and

(b) if **B** is not in occupation, the right, with the leave of the court, to enter into and occupy the dwelling-house.

Section 6 (continued)

Note: Home Rights do not exist if the dwelling-house has never been, and was never intended to be, the matrimonial or civil partnership home of the two spouses or civil partners. If the marriage or civil partnership has come to an end, home rights will also have ceased, unless a court order has been made during the marriage or civil partnership for the rights to continue after the end of that relationship.

Occupation Orders
The possible orders are:

If you have ticked box 1 above, an order under section 33 of the Act may:

- enforce the applicant's entitlement to remain in occupation as against the respondent
- require the respondent to permit the applicant to enter and remain in the dwelling-house or part of it
- regulate the occupation of the dwelling-house by either or both parties
- if the respondent is also entitled to occupy, the order may prohibit, suspend or restrict the exercise by him, of that right
- restrict or terminate any home rights of the respondent
- require the respondent to leave the dwelling-house or part of it
- exclude the respondent from a defined area around the dwelling-house
- declare that the applicant is entitled to occupy the dwelling-house or has home rights in it
- provide that the home rights of the applicant are not brought to an end by the death of the other spouse or civil partner or termination of the marriage or civil partnership.

If you have ticked box 2 or box 3 above, an order under section 35 or 36 of the Act may:

- give the applicant the right not to be evicted or excluded from the dwelling-house or any part of it by the respondent for a specified period
- prohibit the respondent from evicting or excluding the applicant during that period
- give the applicant the right to enter and occupy the dwelling-house for a specified period
- require the respondent to permit the exercise of that right
- regulate the occupation of the dwelling-house by either or both of the parties
- prohibit, suspend or restrict the exercise by the respondent of his right to occupy
- require the respondent to leave the dwelling-house or part of it
- exclude the respondent from a defined area around the dwelling-house.

If you have ticked box 4 or box 5 above, an order under section 37 or 38 of the Act may:

- require the respondent to permit the applicant to enter and remain in the dwelling-house or part of it
- regulate the occupation of the dwelling-house by either or both of the parties
- require the respondent to leave the dwelling-house or part of it
- exclude the respondent from a defined area around the dwelling-house.

You should provide any evidence which you have on the following matters in your evidence in support of this application. If necessary, further statements may be submitted after the application has been issued.

If you have ticked box 1, box 4 or box 5 above, the court will need any available evidence of the following:

- the housing needs and resources of you, the respondent and any relevant child
- the financial needs of you and the respondent
- the likely effect of any order, or any decision not to make an order, on the health, safety and well-being of you, the respondent and any relevant child
- the conduct of you and the respondent in relation to each other and otherwise.

If you have ticked box 2 above, the court will need any available evidence of:

- the housing needs and resources of you, the respondent and any relevant child
- the financial resources of you and the respondent
- the likely effect of any order, or of any decision not to make an order on the health, safety and well-being of you, the respondent and any relevant child
- the conduct of you and the respondent in relation to each other and otherwise
- the length of time that has elapsed since you and the respondent ceased to live together
- where you and the respondent were married, the length of time that has elapsed since the marriage was dissolved or annulled
- where you and the respondent were civil partners, the length of time that has elapsed since the dissolution or annulment of the civil partnership

Section 6 (continued)

- the existence of any pending proceedings between you and the respondent:

  under section 23A of the Matrimonial Causes Act 1973 (property adjustment orders in connection with divorce proceedings etc.)

  or under Part 2 of Schedule 5 to the Civil Partnership Act 2004 (property adjustment on or after dissolution, nullity or separation)

  or under Schedule 1 para 1(2)(d) or (e) of the Children Act 1989 (orders for financial relief against parents)

  or relating to the legal or beneficial ownership of the dwelling-house.

If you have ticked box 3 above, the court will need any available evidence of:

- the housing needs and resources of you, the respondent and any relevant child
- the financial resources of you and the respondent
- the likely effect of any order, or of any decision not to make an order, on the health, safety and well-being of you, the respondent and any relevant child
- the conduct of you and the respondent in relation to each other and otherwise
- the nature of your and the respondent's relationship
- the length of time during which you have lived together as husband and wife or civil partners
- whether you and the respondent have had any children, or have both had parental responsibility for any children
- the length of time that has elapsed since you and the respondent ceased to live together
- the existence of any pending proceedings between you and the respondent under Schedule 1 para 1(2)(d) or (e) of the Children Act 1989 or relating to the legal or beneficial ownership of the dwelling-house.

Section 7

Under section 40 of the Act the court may make the following additional orders when making an occupation order:

- impose on either party obligations as to the repair and maintenance of the dwelling-house
- impose on either party obligations as to the payment of rent, mortgage or other outgoings affecting it
- order a party occupying the dwelling-house to make periodical payments to the other party in respect of the accommodation, if the other party would (but for the order) be entitled to occupy it
- grant either party possession or use of furniture or other contents
- order either party to take reasonable care of any furniture or other contents
- order either party to take reasonable steps to keep the dwelling-house and any furniture or other contents secure.

Section 8

If the dwelling-house is rented or subject to a mortgage, the landlord or mortgagee must be served with notice of the proceedings in Form FL416. He or she will then be able to make representations to the court regarding the rent or mortgage.

Section 10

A person living in the same household may, for example, be a member of the family or a tenant or employee of you or the respondent.

37 PROTECTION FROM HARASSMENT

37.1 INTRODUCTION

This chapter will:

- **examine the law on harassment;**
- **examine the remedies available to clients not protected by the Family Law Act 1996.**

In **Chapter 34** the protection offered by the Family Law Act 1996 (FLA 1996) was discussed, including the group of associated persons who can apply for non-molestation or occupation orders. However, there will be those who are not protected as an associated person. Family lawyers may be consulted by those who are being harassed or stalked by someone who is not an associated person. Until the passage of the Protection from Harassment Act 1997 (PfHA 1997), a victim of stalking or harassment had few remedies. This chapter will look at both the civil and criminal remedies available to a client.

37.2 RELEVANCE TO FAMILY LAW

The definition of 'associated persons' under s62(1)(b) FLA 1996 is very wide and will encompass most family relationships, especially in light of the amendment made to encompass people who have had an intimate relationship which is or was of significant duration (s62(3)(ea) FLA 1996). However, this provision is not yet tested by the courts and may not cover a situation where the parties have 'dated' just once or twice. The FLA 1996 does not protect those who are work colleagues, neighbours, or those who have met socially but have not dated or had any form of relationship. In the case of *Tuppen v Microsoft Corporation Ltd* (2000) *Times*, 15 November it was held, after referring to Hansard, that the PfHA 1997 was directed at the prevention of stalking, anti-social behaviour by neighbours, and racial harassment.

Example

Emir works as an IT manager at a large department store. He works across the shop floor and the administration offices and looks after IT for the company. He is married to Anji and has two children. He often chats casually to shop assistants when repairing computers. He often chats to Katrina, a shop assistant working in the ladies clothing department. He notices that she has her lunch hour at the same time as his and they often chat in the shop canteen.

Emir begins to get up to 50 emails a day from Katrina, which he finds intrusive. He asks her to stop and makes a point of avoiding her. Katrina finds out his mobile phone number and sends him hundreds of texts, which are often sexually explicit. Katrina starts to follow Emir home and hangs around at his gate. He finds that he cannot leave the house without Katrina being there. Katrina tells everyone at work they are engaged and asks him to buy her a ring. Emir becomes very angry at this point and tells Katrina to leave him alone. Emir is then horrified to find that Katrina has rung his wife and his parents and told them that Katrina is having an affair with Emir. He finds that Katrina has been hanging around at his children's school telling the parents collecting the children that she is pregnant with Emir's child. The last straw for Emir is when Katrina breaks into the house and steals some of Emir's clothing. Katrina leaves a note for Emir's wife stating that Katrina is Emir's real wife.

Emir uses the PfHA 1997 in order to obtain an injunction to prevent Katrina from any further harassment.

Of course, if a person is assaulted by another, the criminal law can be used.

37.3 PROHIBITION OF HARASSMENT

S1(1) PfHA 1997 states that a person must not pursue a course of conduct:

(a) which amounts to harassment of another, and

(b) which he knows or ought to know amounts to harassment of the other.

S2 PfHA 1997 explains that the person whose course of conduct is in question ought to know that it amounts to harassment of another if a reasonable person in possession of the same information would think the course of conduct amounted to harassment of the other.

There are some circumstances where the PfHA 1997 will not apply to a course of conduct, e.g. if a person can show that:

- it was pursued for the purpose of preventing or detecting crime;
- it was pursued under any enactment or rule of law or to comply with any condition or requirement imposed by any person under any enactment; or
- in the particular circumstances the pursuit of the course of conduct was reasonable.

Conduct includes speech (s7(4) PfHA 1997). 'Harassment' includes, but is not restricted to, 'alarming the person' and 'causing the person distress' under s7(2) PfHA 1997. According to Lord Donaldson in *Johnson v Walton* [1990] 1 FLR 350, 'harassment...includes within it an element of intent, intent to cause distress or harm'.

 **Example**

Katrina's actions in telling Emir's wife and parents lies about their relationship and breaking into the house clearly demonstrate intent to cause alarm or distress.

Alternatively, s1A PfHA 1997 states that a person must not pursue a course of conduct which involves the harassment of two or more persons and which he knows or ought to know involves harassment to those persons and by which he intends to persuade any person (whether or not one of those mentioned above) not to do something that he is entitled or required to do or to do something that he is not under any obligation to do. The person whose course of conduct is in question ought to know that it amounts to harassment of another if a reasonable person in possession of the same information would think the course of conduct amounted to harassment of the other.

37.4 CIVIL REMEDY FOR HARASSMENT

Under s3 PfHA 1997, an actual or apprehended breach of s1 PfHA 1997 may be the subject of a claim in civil proceedings by the person who is or may be the victim of the course of conduct in question. If such a claim is successful damages can be awarded for (amongst other things) anxiety caused by the harassment and any financial loss resulting from the harassment. Of more practical use is the ability of the court to grant an injunction in free-standing proceedings in the county court or High Court and the terms of this injunction can be enforced by a warrant for the arrest of the defendant under s3(3) PfHA 1997.

Where the court has granted an injunction and without reasonable excuse the defendant does anything that he is prohibited from doing by the injunction, he is guilty of an offence under s3(6) PfHA 1997. Such an offence is punished by contempt of court or by criminal proceedings but not both. A person found guilty of such an offence is liable for a fine or up to six months' imprisonment.

37.5 CRIMINAL LIABILITY FOR HARASSMENT

If a person pursues a course of conduct in breach of s1(1) or 1A PfHA 1997 he is guilty of an offence under s2 PfHA 1997. It is a summary offence, which means that it can only be tried in the magistrates' court. If convicted the defendant would be liable for a fine or up to six months' imprisonment.

37.5.1 RESTRAINING ORDERS

S5 PfHA 1997 allows a court sentencing or otherwise dealing with a defendant convicted of an offence, as well as sentencing him or dealing with him in any other way, to make an order under this section.

The order may be made for the purpose of protecting the victim of the offence, or any other person mentioned in the order, from further conduct that:

- amounts to harassment; or
- will cause a fear of violence,

or to prohibit the defendant from doing anything described in the order.

The order may have effect for a specified period or until further order. In 2006, there were 194 restraining orders issued.

S5A PfHA 1997 (introduced into the PfHA 1997 by the Domestic Violence, Crime and Victims Act 2004) allows a court to make a restraining order even if the defendant is acquitted of an offence, if it considers it necessary to do so to protect a person from harassment by the defendant.

37.6 PROTECTION FROM HARASSMENT ACT 1997 AND FAMILY PRACTICE

The PfHA 1997 offers protection for those clients who are not within the scope of associated persons under the FLA 1996. Those advising clients in such a situation must weigh up whether the client should seek protection from the criminal law, which has the advantage for the client of not requiring funding of any kind, and for which the court has wide-ranging powers. There may be occasions where a client does not wish to involve the criminal law and will use the civil courts to pursue an injunction.

SUMMARY POINTS

- The PfHA 1997 was enacted to assist those who were suffering harassment through stalking, anti-social behaviour, or racial harassment.
- The provisions of the PfHA 1997 are useful protection for those clients who are not associated persons under the FLA 1996.
- The PfHA 1997 prohibits a course of conduct that amounts to the harassment of a person and conduct includes speech.
- 'Harassment' is where a person is alarmed or distressed.
- A client may pursue a civil remedy of damages or an injunction to prevent further harassment.
- Alternatively, a client can involve the criminal law, as harassment is a criminal offence and the courts have extensive powers, e.g. the grant of a restraining order, even when the defendant is acquitted.

SELF-TEST QUESTIONS

1. Can you think of any categories of people who may suffer harassment but not be an associated person under the FLA 1996?
2. Bill drinks regularly at a pub in his town. He gets to know Shellie, who works as a barmaid. They have one date and she tells him that she doesn't want to see him anymore. Bill continues to text, telephone, and email Shellie. Shellie finds that Bill has begun to follow her and sits outside her house in his car. Shellie finds that Bill turns up to any social event that she is at and threatens any man who tries to talk to her. Advise Shellie.

online
resource
centre

Answers to the questions above can be found on the Online Resource Centre: **www.oxfordtextbooks.co.uk/orc/familyhandbook13/.**

INDEX

D

E

F

G

H

I

J

R

S